THE BLACK BOX

Lady Bessie Borden's Family, 1863–1956

In a remarkable tale of tragedy, war, family conflict, and imperial diplomacy, *The Black Box* presents a collective biography of four generations of women in an elite Nova Scotia family during the late nineteenth to mid-twentieth century. These intelligent, educated, artistic women were pragmatic and autonomous persons who contributed to the development, maintenance, defence, and management of the Borden family's material resources.

Illustrating the changing nature of the time, the book explores the adventurous and curious lives of women who moved at the highest levels of society. It examines how the synergies of their private and public lives redefined their place in society during an era when the state and religion became more active and private lives more public. It also demonstrates the role and importance of the material components of social power, such as dress, residence, clubs, and travel.

Drawing on archival material retained by the family, the book reveals how the Borden family defined, secured, and sustained its status in society. *The Black Box* is a unique record of an elite family's response to the changing political economy of imperial Canada.

CARMAN MILLER is an emeritus professor in the Department of History at McGill University.

CARMAN MILLER

The Black Box

Lady Bessie Borden's Family, 1863–1956

UNIVERSITY OF TORONTO PRESS
Toronto Buffalo London

Toronto Buffalo London
utppublishing.com
Printed in Canada

ISBN 978-1-4875-5194-0 (cloth) ISBN 978-1-4875-5199-5 (EPUB)
ISBN 978-1-4875-5196-4 (paper) ISBN 978-1-4875-5197-1 (PDF)

Library and Archives Canada Cataloguing in Publication

Title: The black box : Lady Bessie Borden's family, 1863–1956 / Carman Miller.
Other titles: Lady Bessie Borden's family, 1863–1956
Names: Miller, Carman, 1940– author
Description: Includes bibliographical references and index.
Identifiers: Canadiana (print) 20250310295 | Canadiana (ebook) 20250310368 | ISBN 9781487551940 hardback | ISBN 9781487551964 paperback | ISBN 9781487551971 (PDF) | ISBN 9781487551995 (EPUB)
Subjects: LCSH: Borden family. | LCSH: Upper class women – Nova Scotia – Biography. | LCSH: Upper class families – Nova Scotia – Biography. | LCSH: Elite (Social sciences) – Nova Scotia. | LCSH: Nova Scotia – Biography. | LCSH: Nova Scotia – History. | LCSH: Nova Scotia – Genealogy.
Classification: LCC FC2305 .M55 2025 | DDC 929.209716–dc23 | 971.6/0099–dc23

Cover design: Val Cooke
Cover image: (top) vectortatu/Shutterstock.com; (bottom) Frank Hector Tompkins, "Lady Borden, Maude and Rosamond," c. 1910. Courtesy Julia Green MacKay.

Ornament: Shutterstock ID: 2200445235 LadadikArt

The manufacturer's authorised representative in the EU for product safety is Mare Nostrum Group B.V., Mauritskade 21D, 1091 GC Amsterdam, The Netherlands. Email: gpsr@mare-nostrum.co.uk.

We wish to acknowledge the land on which the University of Toronto Press operates. This land is the traditional territory of the Wendat, the Anishnaabeg, the Haudenosaunee, the Métis, and the Mississaugas of the Credit First Nation.

This book has been published with the help of a grant from the Federation for the Humanities and Social Sciences, through the Awards to Scholarly Publications Program, using funds provided by the Social Sciences and Humanities Research Council of Canada.

University of Toronto Press acknowledges the financial support of the Government of Canada, the Canada Council for the Arts, and the Ontario Arts Council, an agency of the Government of Ontario, for its publishing activities.

Canada Council for the Arts / Conseil des Arts du Canada

ONTARIO ARTS COUNCIL
CONSEIL DES ARTS DE L'ONTARIO
an Ontario government agency
un organisme du gouvernement de l'Ontario

Funded by the Government of Canada / Financé par le gouvernement du Canada

MIX
Paper | Supporting responsible forestry
FSC® C016245

Contents

Preface: The Black Box

"There will only ever be one Lady Borden," wrote Sir Frederick Borden to his wife in May 1914, upon learning that his cousin, Robert Laird Borden, was being knighted. Not only had Lady Elizabeth Blanche (Clarke) Borden (1863–1956) held her title since 1902 but she outlived Sir Robert's wife, Lady Laura (Bond) Borden (1861–1940), by sixteen years. Although neither lady saw the other as a rival, they provide a study in contrasts, as do their husbands. Lady Bessie Borden was an autonomous, sociable, educated, political companion, adept at social diplomacy and committed to culture and politics, whereas Lady Laura Borden was diffident, "austere," decorous, and dutiful, and "did not especially enjoy her role as a public figure"; nor did Sir Robert "discuss matters with her."[1]

I never intended to write a biographical study of Lady Elizabeth Bessie Borden and her family. But in the summer of 2011 Julia Green MacKay, Sir Frederick Borden's only great grandchild, arrived in Nova Scotia from British Columbia with a large black metal box of family papers that she entrusted to my care. In subsequent years she returned with additional records. For me, an aged historian who had written a biography of Lady Borden's husband, the "Black Box" held a trove of tantalizing information that had escaped my previous research on her husband, leaving Lady Borden's story a subject of "unfinished business."

During my research and writing of *A Knight in Politics: A Biography of Sir Frederick Borden*, Sir Frederick's second wife remained frustratingly elusive. A sophisticated witness of, and participant in, her husband's career, Lady Borden appeared only occasionally in the accessible public records, before vanishing into a presumed domestic obscurity, a casualty of past historians and archivists' definition of what constituted history, which largely excluded the private sphere and marginalized women, recognized only in their connection to men.[2]

When the Public Archives of Nova Scotia received its first three instalments of Sir Frederick Borden Papers, the first in 1950, the second in 1956, and a third in 1970,[3] its staff compiled a comprehensive inventory of what it considered appropriate for public scrutiny. Estate papers, genealogical records, land deeds, business transactions, court proceedings, personal diary fragments, photographs, social invitations, intimate and private letters were left in the discreet custody of the family.[4] Excluded from public scrutiny, these records contained a rich repository of information on the family, and the lives of its elite women.

Fortunately, much of the excluded private material (identified as "Private Borden Papers") remained in the Black Box and subsequent instalments. Not all the family's personal records survived, however, since well before the Nova Scotia Archives acquired its Borden Papers, Lady Borden culled the fond. How thorough her purge was and why it was undertaken is unclear. I and others have speculated that she intended to erase references to her husband's private life. In 1989 Mrs. Lewis Clarke, Lady Borden's relative by marriage and a neighbour, informed me that she had visited Lady Borden shortly after Sir Frederick's death in 1917, and remembered Lady Borden seated by her fireplace weeping and burning letters. Mrs. Clarke was uncertain if Lady Borden's grief was over her husband's death or the letters' contents.

Mrs. Lewis Clarke was not the only witness to Lady Borden's purges. Twice, Sir Frederick's elder daughter, Elizabeth, Lady Borden's stepdaughter (and niece), who intended to write a family biography, dissuaded Lady Borden from "tearing up" and burning family papers.[5] In 1926 Elizabeth watched with alarm as her stepmother sorted one file of Sir Frederick's papers each morning, discarding items until Elizabeth intervened to save the papers' "social and political history" for future generations.[6] In May 1944 Elizabeth again disrupted Lady Borden's purge of "two large" and "two small" trunks "packed full" of letters that had been stored in Borden Place's attic. Lady Borden had placed "thousands" of these letters in large baskets and had them carried to her second-floor bedsitting room, where for four days she engaged in "the hardest work" she had ever done, intending to burn "thousands of them" when Elizabeth "besought" her to desist as Elizabeth planned "to write a book of our lives."[7]

Lady Borden never doubted Elizabeth's desire and ability to write a family history, though the daunting quantity of archival material and Elizabeth's declining health made Lady Borden sceptical of Elizabeth's ability to complete her project. Lady Borden acceded to Elizabeth's intervention, however, and had the papers placed "in a room upstairs," though not before she "had burned a few." What Lady Borden burned in 1944 and why is unclear. All we know is that correspondence between Sir Frederick and Lady Borden remains sparse, even in the Black Box's Private Borden Papers and subsequent instalments.

Lady Borden was no vandal, indifferent to the claims of history, even if she may have wished to shape the record. After all, it was she who collected and preserved the bulk of the family's surviving personal papers, largely incoming correspondence from absent family members. Among the Black Box's papers none is more valuable than the records of the family's acrimonious, six-year legal battle over Sir Frederick's estate. A verbatim typescript of the probate court's hearings and supporting documentation reveal the nature, extent, and fragility of Sir Frederick's estate and its chaotic management, offering a fuller portrait of his business career than that which I provided in my earlier biographical study. Among the surviving records, two sets of correspondence stand out, the first generated during Lady Borden's daughter Maude's and granddaughter Rosamond's lengthy residence in France (1923–8), and another during Rosamond's family's sojourn in Stockholm (1948–52).

Although limited, fragmented, and sometimes ephemeral, the Private Borden Papers contain valuable miscellaneous materials on other family members. These include the diary of Sir Frederick's son, Harold Borden' (1898–9); Sir Frederick Borden's sketchy diary / agenda for 1902; Elizabeth's (Borden) Hewitt's "Chronicle" for 1926; Lady Borden and Elizabeth's occasional "Travel Diary"; Lady Borden's "Notebook and Travelogue"; Rosamond's (Green's), brief record of her father's early life; and a collection of family photographs and social invitations. While great gaps remain in the family's records, (especially Lady Borden's outgoing correspondence), thanks to Lady Borden's preservation of the Black Box's Private Borden Papers we can now write her and her family back into its story.

The shape and analysis of that story depend upon extracting meaning from its records. The Borden family's passion for travel, for example, generated a disproportionate quantity of travel records, a genre of historical writing that has recently attracted considerable scholarship.[8] London, Paris, Rome, Florence, and Venice were popular contemporary tourist sites. Britain, the Côte d'Azur, the Swiss and French Alps, Sicily, and the Amalfi Coast were fashionable, elite destinations. Tourists sought historic, genealogical, literary, and religious venues, galleries, museums, spectacles, and concerts. Redolent of class and character, Lady Borden's and Elizabeth's travel diaries suggest their values, perceptions, and aspirations and help compensate for the scarcity of their personal correspondence.

This book is "a story and a study"[9] of the ascent and decline of an affluent, late-nineteenth-/early twentieth-century Nova Scotia family (Canning's own *Budenbrooks*!).[10] It is a story of the complicity of politics and social mobility, of the translation of local power into national and imperial influence. Important as wealth was to to elite status and social mobility, the Borden family never occupied the ranks of the very rich. While public service undoubtedly enhanced access to economic power, wealth was not the Borden family's single goal. As Adam Smith observed, "it is not wealth that men desire, but the consideration and good opinion that wait upon riches."[11] For the Borden family social capital was both an objective and an asset, and one that outlasted their material and political base.

Although Sir Frederick may have considered Lady Borden unique, she was also a product of race, class, gender, family, and religion. In nineteenth- and early twentieth-century British North America/Canada, a European woman settler's most formative influence was probably her family.[12] Nineteenth-century and early twentieth-century families have often been characterized as male constructs, maintained in a patriarchal relationship grounded on property, law, religion, and notions of domesticity that cast women as dependent, subordinate, and submissive, relegated to childbearing and childrearing, cooking, household economy, and piety, and as consumers rather than producers, a characterization that leaves little space for agency, contingency, and the "affective."

More recent scholarship has suggested that by the late nineteenth/early twentieth century "sexual feudalism" had become "an empty shell."[13] In practice, family, class, and gender were less monolithic, hermetic, and utilitarian than an essentialist construction might suggest,[14] a myopic perspective that ignores the "polyphonic" nature of Canadian women's lives and voices, their kaleidoscopic ambiguities, continuities, and discontinuities, a world best understood "by looking at the lives of actual women" and in this study a family of elite women.[15]

This study confirms the chameleon nature of a European settler's family, class, and gender, and the synergies of private and public lives. It is the story of elite women redefining public space. It suggests the importance of character and contingency, how genetics, war, and disease cast a family of women in a leading, and in the last thirty-nine-years a dominant, role in managing their lives. It is bounded by Lady Borden's lifespan (1863–1956), who for three generations constituted its centrum. For, notwithstanding abiding legal, social, and political restraints, elite, late-nineteenth and early twentieth-century Atlantic Canadian women engaged in an increasingly diverse range of private and public activities, a period during which religion became more social, the state more active, and the private more public.[16]

Acknowledgments

This book is the result of Julia Green MacKay's initiative and assistance, preserving her family's private papers, transporting them from British Columbia to Nova Scotia, leaving them in my unrestricted possession, responding to questions, and granting permission to publish family photographs and a family portrait.

I wish also to acknowledge and thank other persons who have contributed to the book's content, presentation, and completion:

Jim Marlon-Lambert's interest, encouragement, and support have been more valuable than he may realize.

The late Gregory Donaghy, then head of the Historical Section of Global Affairs Canada, facilitated my access to Leslie Green's military records held by Library and Archives Canada (LAC), which Christopher Cook searched with his legendary skills, historical imagination, and commitment.

Two colleagues, Professors Elsbeth Heaman (McGill) and Donald Wright (UNB), took time from their charged agendas to read and comment on an earlier draft of this manuscript. Their comments and suggestions enabled me to revise and improve the manuscript.

The manuscript benefited, as well, from the very helpful assessment and advice of the two University of Toronto Press's anonymous readers.

Barry Roxburgh, Michael Rickley-Lancaster, Vicky Weil, and Alex Hughes responded to questions regarding their Cotton and Hughes families.

Ali Shan Khawaja, at Dalhousie University's help desk, provided invaluable technical assistance with the manuscript; and Alicia J. Kutchaw kindly facilitated reproduction of the cover's "family" portrait.

The University of Toronto Press's acquisitions editor Len Husband supervised the manuscript's acquisition and funding.

The University of Toronto Press's copy editor Anne Laughlin edited the manuscript with meticulous care and suggestions.

The University of Toronto Press's editorial director Suzanne Rancourt responded to my several questions and requests.

And, the University of Toronto Press's associate managing editor Barbara Porter supervised the manuscript's final production.

A very personal thanks to Pamela, Danielle, Marc, Andrew, Elin, Carly, Marius, Lukas, Eva, Thea, Alexandra, and Magnus.

THE BLACK BOX

Chapter One

Bessie

In late nineteenth- and early twentieth-century Canada class and gender defined private and public space. They moulded women's lives and delineated their access to power and influence. Class and gender permeated religion and education, the twin pillars of nineteenth- and early twentieth-century social "regeneration,"[1] that reformational zeal that reconfigured public spaces that women came to occupy in increasing numbers, however restricted in their scope. Charged with the physical, social, and moral health of their family and society, many middle-class women possessed the time, material means, and influence to implement their religion's social gospel and extend their gendered private roles into public space, working closely with schools, universities, and organizations devoted to social reform.

Elizabeth Blanche Clarke was born on 5 March 1863 to an affluent merchant family in Canning, Nova Scotia, a tidal port that drained the fertile Cornwallis Valley and opened into the Fundy's wider world. Canning was a small, dynamic village of some 600 people, a commercial and shipbuilding port, at the height of the region's "Golden Age." Male merchants, shipbuilders, and farmers dominated the community's economy and public life, aided increasingly by teachers, doctors, and lawyers. Together they managed its material and social services. Deeply embedded in the community's economic and social fabric, these men negotiated the community's interests within an Atlantic world whose borders were traced by geography, history, and opportunity. Within this public sphere women were active and essential, though often circumspect and invisible.

Although class was not impermeable or necessarily ostentatious, it evinced itself in wealth, public office, residence, education, dress, speech, and travel; it was acknowledged and rewarded by the community's respect, deference, and occasional resentment. Canning's small size, its inhabitants' consanguinity, physical proximity, and social familiarity gave inequity a human face, a moral economy of reciprocal, though unequal, self-interest, and obligation, encouraged and sanctified by religious belief and practice. While more muted in small, rural communities than in anonymous urban centres where work and home had become separate, class remained pervasive and determinative.

John Hopson Clarke (1810–1888) was fifty-three when his third and youngest child was born. Her parents named her Elizabeth but called her "Bessie" to distinguish her within a family dynasty of Elizabeths. John Clarke was one of Canning's most prominent and prosperous merchants and shipowners. In a region marked by occupational plurality, Clarke began his career as a farmer familiar with the coastal trade, exporting and importing goods in vessels that he owned partially or outright, and marketing his goods in wholesale / retail stores in Canning and Blomidon.

Clarke's large wooden residence, built shortly after his marriage in 1853, commanded a site on the corner of Canning's two principal intersecting streets: Main Street, which ran parallel to the Habitant River, and North Street, which ran perpendicular to Main through a fertile intervale toward the North Mountain. Clarke's well-appointed home, a testimony to his success, offered its occupants a convenient location, across the street from their Main Street store, backing onto the Habitant River, the community's waterway to the Fundy, the Atlantic Seaboard, and the world.

Successful Canning merchants required curiosity, knowledge, diligence, and vision to coordinate and exploit the community's rich land and sea resources. In the absence of an active state, merchants ordered the community's governance and promoted and financed its infrastructure, and its educational and cultural amenities, from which their families were the chief benefactors. To advance their personal interests and promote, mediate, and manage their communities' mercantile imperatives, merchants needed a shrewd understanding of the wider world's political economy.

Intelligent, restless, and ambitious, Clarke maximized his, and his community's human and physical resources during their Age of Sail, by navigating a world of opportunities, dreams, and schemes. As a young man Clarke had sailed the Fundy–Atlantic seaboard, gaining familiarity with its ports, people, and markets. John Clarke was also an engaged community leader, a devoted Methodist, a justice of the peace, a surveyor of highways, and a strong advocate for education. In short, he was a man of standing as well as substance, well placed to secure his community's trust and confidence. Sixteen years before his death in 1888 Clarke had amassed an estate estimated to be worth between $75,000 and $100,000 (roughly $2,000,000 in today's purchasing power).

Bessie was born at the height of the Fundy's "Golden Age," just before its slow, graceful transition to a land-based economy of capital-intensive commercial agriculture, railways, and steam power, its economy increasingly dependent upon a profitable English apple market. The new economy's demand for large acreages fortuitously coincided with a massive exodus (1871–1911) of "economic refugees" from the region's declining sea-orientated economy: persons in search of profitable employment along the prosperous, familiar Atlantic Seaboard from which their ancestors had migrated. The exodus created a mobile, cross-border social network of family, friends, and expatriots that generated opportunities and rivalries that transcended its fluid national borders, a world that "His Majesty's Yankees"[2] shrewdly managed to their advantage.

In Canning family mattered. It provided sustenance, protection, and identity, and entailed obligations and expectations. Mrs. Clarke's ancestors were Planters as were most of Canning's population, descendants of those mid-eighteenth-century Yankee land-grabbing religious dissenters who claimed the fertile lands from which the Acadians had been driven.[3] And however levelling and democratic this New England "priesthood of believers" may have been in doctrine and order, they readily accommodated themselves to the inequities created by wealth, public life, family, luck, and learning, tempered by a self-interested "civic humanism" that espoused duty and social obligation.[4]

Bessie's mother, Elizabeth Mary (Tupper) Clarke (1829–1919), traced her North American Tupper ancestry back to 1631. Of more contemporary importance, Mrs. Clarke's family occupied a prominent place in the province's public life. Her father, Augustus Tupper (1792–1850), a farmer in the western district of Cornwallis Township, was a brother of the Reverend Charles Tupper (1794–1881), the father of Sir Charles Tupper. The Reverend Charles Tupper had been a renowned Baptist minister, educator, editor, author, and "formidable scholar." An advocate of maritime Baptist union[5] and an educated clergy, the Reverend Charles Tupper twice served as interim principal of the maritime Baptists' coeducational seminary in Fredericton.[6]

Mrs. Clarke's father also had a penchant for public service and politics. A "descendant of a respected Cornwallis grantee," Augustus had been a zealous political reformer. In 1836 he had contested the Cornwallis Township constituency as the workingman's representative and promised to defend honest men of the soil from gentry who wished "to trample the common people."[7] Undeterred by his defeat, he recon-tested Cornwallis Township in 1840 but was defeated by a wide margin. A man of courage and conviction, Augustus stood once more in 1843–4, this time against the Tory / Baptist alliance's defence of public grants to the Baptists' Acadia College.[8] That he failed in Kings County was scarcely surprising given the Baptists' numerical strength and their sense of entitlement, comparable to a "state religion."[9]

Mrs. Clarke's first cousin, Sir Charles Tupper (1821–1915), had been more successful than his Uncle Augustus. Educated at the Baptists' Horton Academy, Charles Tupper had taught briefly in New Brunswick before studying medicine at the University of Edinburgh. Subsequently, he served as leader of the Nova Scotia Conservative Party, premier of the province (1864–7), a Father of Confederation, Canadian high commissioner to the United Kingdom (1884–96), and prime minister of Canada (1896). Few Tuppers seeking identity could ignore their family's legacy of religion, education, and public service.

In mid and late nineteenth-century British North America, Christian churches abounded. They bonded and branded their members, provided friendship, respectability, entertainment, and public engagement. They enjoined commitment and obligation. Biblical allusions shaped their language and imagination. Organized into several competing denominations, delineated by doctrine, governance, liturgy, and ethnic identification, churches moulded and reflected their communities. They exercised a moral governance that shaped, monitored, and enforced social conformity, and served as "reactionary organs of sectarian rivalry" and "progressive agencies of public service."[10]

Both of Bessie's parents were devout Wesleyan Methodists, a denomination constitutionally and financially dependent upon the British Wesleyan Missionary Society. In 1874 their Eastern British North American Wesleyan Methodist Conference united with its co-religionists in the rest of British North America / Canada to form the Wesleyan Church in Canada. A comparable pragmatism governed its clergy and laity's navigation of the North American border to educate their children and staff their pulpits.

According to Peter Waite, Methodism promoted a bourgeois gospel of wealth, work, thrift, social duty, and tolerance,[11] a convenient agenda for a competitive, mobile merchant class, and / or middling people on the make.[12] Methodists preached a self-regulated piety and accountability, a personal, introspective, experiential faith and sanctification laden by a heavy burden of individual responsibility, accountability, and autonomy. Without abandoning its pragmatic, mercantile appeal, late nineteenth-century Methodism preached a social gospel grounded on Christianity's ethical and social imperatives, a blend of idealism and social activism. To meet its ambitious home and foreign missions, and its devotional and social commitments, Methodism depended increasingly on lay leadership, particularly of middle-class women. As Methodist women assumed a greater place in delivering their church's teaching, exhorting, and caring mission, their denomination's lay leadership became "feminized,"[13] a mission that required access to public space and higher education, and one in which late nineteenth-century Maritime Methodists played a leading role.[14]

Methodists' late nineteenth- and early twentieth-century social gospel soon evolved into a "national gospel."[15] Their social mission's increasing need for personnel and material resources argued for interdenominational cooperation, a de-emphasis on doctrinal differences, and church union. Methodism soon became a uniting church with a messianic, civic mission, promoted by its geographically mobile clergy. After Confederation Canada's diverse Methodist expressions united to become Canada's largest Protestant denomination,[16] and later joined Congregationalists and Presbyterians to become the United Church of Canada. To build the Lord's Dominion in Canada Methodists often blended the sacred and secular, their nationalist mission an obvious and ambitious project for an emerging post-Confederation national class.[17]

Bessie grew up in a small, comfortable family, living within her mercantile parents' religious world, observing their rituals and obligations, and absorbing their ideas and values. As the youngest child of mature parents, Bessie enjoyed their full attention. At the time of her birth, her brother, Augustus [Gus] Tupper Clarke, seemed grown up. Fifteen years her senior, Gus was enrolled in the recently founded Acacia Villa boarding school at Horton Landing. Bessie's sister, Julia Maude, thirteen years her senior, was soon to leave home for the Wesleyan Methodist Women's Academy (1869–72) in Sackville, New Brunswick. After Gus completed his Acacia Villa studies, he attended King's College in Windsor, Nova Scotia, in preparation for medical studies at Harvard Medical School.

Bessie's family's values were deeply grounded in religion. For John and Elizabeth Clarke, Sunday worship was a moral imperative, a ritual that entailed morning and evening services, an orderly liturgy characterized by fervent moralistic preaching and spirited congregational singing. Bessie's Methodism entailed private devotion, daily Bible reading, prayer and moral accounting, in which she pondered her "lack of consistency in pursuing moral objectives."[18] It was a Protestantism that she described as requiring "retrospect, introspect[ion] & outlook,"[19] which sought no human mediation or clerical absolution,[20] but provided meaning and consolation during difficult moments. Bessie discussed religion with her friends. She spoke of God's love, of Christ's redemptive death on the cross and their meeting him in "a cloud ... in the air." Her religion was also a questioning faith, and her friends felt comfortable talking to her about their unorthodox beliefs, confident she would not "scold them" as "others" might.[21] Charity, public service, and her church's governance were no less important.

Bessie benefited, too, from her family`s commitment to private and public education, which they regarded as an extension of religious faith and practice and a means of material, commercial, and social advancement. In their view education was the basis of an ordered, responsible, respectful society, a means of ruling by schooling and pooling its costs.[22] They supported the establishment of Acacia Villa school in 1852, the Methodists' private school for boys,[23] and welcomed Charles Tupper's Free School Act (1864) that offered students province-wide public education. They were no less committed to female education. And, when Canning's seminary for boys became a ladies' seminary, following Tupper's Free School Act, they enrolled Bessie in its program of art, painting, and drawing, subjects that nourished Bessie's artistic interests and her parents' gendered class aspirations.[24]

Bessie's education began at home, well before she attended Canning's ladies' seminary, surrounded by books and inspired by her parents' example. Reading was a family passion. Early photographs of Mrs. Clarke show her reading to herself, her children, or grandchildren. Some years later Bessie's stepdaughter, Elizabeth, described Bessie's obsessive reading: "She cooks, reads, sews, reads, irons, reads, dusts, reads."[25] Bessie regarded reading "a real feast ... a chance to think," convinced that "a half hour so spent is beyond all value."[26] Her reading included history, biography, classical and contemporary literature, art, botany, and religion. Later, she belonged to reading clubs, funded libraries, and discussed books with family and friends. In later life, a cardinal rule for her caregivers was that she never be without books and magazines.

Books extended Bessie's horizons. They fed her curiosity, fired her aspirations, refined and affirmed her values. They freed her from the constraints of time, space, and convention. She hated to be unprepared or uninformed: knowledge instilled confidence and reassurance. Books cast her in different worlds, roles, and situations, in a theatre of imaginative self-expression and intellectual tourism that expanded her cultural, spiritual, and political borders. Books introduced her to the people, languages, culture, and customs of her empire and her church's missions and deepened her historical, literary, and cultural heritage.

Among her family's possessions was a well-worn atlas, useful to a missionary, seafaring community.

In his *Types of Canadian Women* (1903), Henry James Morgan denounced a society that relegated its women to a life of "ignorance" and "frivolity," or to service merely as "stewards," "cooks," and "slaves," conditions that could only be remedied by education.[27] To the Clarkes, Morgan was preaching to the converted. Three decades before Morgan's book appeared John and Elizabeth Clarke had resolved to send their daughters, Julia and Bessie, to the Wesleyan Methodists' Mount Allison College, a pioneer in higher education for women, as an investment in their children's religious, material, and social lives.

Chapter Two

Julia

Religion, class, and opportunity made Mount Allison College the Clarkes' choice for Julia's education. Neither the "Methodist" Acacia Villa in Horton's Landing or the Church of England's King's College in Windsor had a ladies' academy; and the Baptists Women's Seminary (1862) at Grande Pre and their Horton Academy's female department were precariously provisional. But, thanks to the resources and vision of Charles Frederick Allison, a Cornwallis Township–born Sackville businessman, in 1843 the Methodists had founded the Wesleyan Academy for boys in Sackville, New Brunswick, to which they added a "female division" in 1854.

From its beginning, a social ambiguity stalked the Methodist academy's female division, an ambiguity underscored by its 1859 redesignation, the "Ladies Academy." Notwithstanding its founders' insistence that the academy's female division be accessible to all social classes and its administrators' diligent search for private funds and government subsidies, the $135 per annum fee for room and board (in addition to tuition and miscellaneous expenses) limited its access to affluent families.[1] Its avowed mission to form teachers, missionaries, wives, sisters, mothers and community volunteers underscored its gendered class character, a mission to complement its boys' academy's formation of leaders in the church, state, industry, and commerce. John and Elizabeth Clarke had no quarrel with the ladies' academy's costs, class, or projected career paths.

The academy's location in Sackville, at the head of the Fundy, made it accessible to Canning, a shipbuilding port like Sackville. At nineteen, Julia was marginally older than the academy's average first-year student. About half of her seventy-eight classmates were boarders.[2] The rest were day students from Sackville and the adjacent counties of Westmorland and Cumberland.[3] Julia lived in a "commodious" steam-heated room in the three-storey ladies' academy, with access to its library, gymnasium, and scientific museum. The academy's dynamic preceptress (effectively its principal) and its seven vigilant teachers ordered its academic routine, while a chaplain supervised its religious life, conducted obligatory Sunday worship and daily chapel service. Among Julia's classmates were Mary Howe, Joseph Howe's granddaughter, and Grace Annie Lockhart, the British Empire's first female recipient of a bachelor's degree.

A decade after the ladies' academy's founding, a trade recession, rising costs, and falling enrolments threatened its existence. The 1869 appointment of David Allison as Mount Allison College's president, and Joseph Robert Inch as the ladies' academy's principal, however, combined with its alumni association and better times to re-establish the ladies' academy and reorient its curriculum. Inch appointed professors in music, painting, drawing, mathematics, and natural science. None of his appointments was more important than Mary Mellish (Archibald), the professor of mathematics and natural science, the academy's visionary future preceptress.[4] Equally significant was Inch's 1872 board of governors' motion to open college degrees to women, a resolution whose easy passage made it appear he was leaning on an open door.[5] Inch's reforms became so popular and ithe ladies academy's finances so solvent that the ladies' academy threatened to overshadow the male academy and college.

In 1875 Grace Annie Lockhart became the first woman in the British Empire to receive a bachelor of science degree (in science and literature). Few other academy students, however, followed her example. Most enrolled but failed to complete its three- to four-year mistress of arts diploma, with its "ornamental" offerings in literature, music, fine arts, and "polite" languages. Although the academy's "ornamental" offerings were designed to cultivate "social graces, refined taste and lady-like manners,"[6] its primary, intermediate, and college-level curriculum provided courses in classics, logic, mathematics, chemistry, and natural history, the latter tailored "to demonstrate Christianity's validity and utility" to female students.[7] Furthermore, anxious parents were assured that the sexes would remain strictly separated for teaching, and that gender-mixed private and public gatherings would be permitted only "in the presence of some officer of the institution."[8] Neither the academy's courses in science and mathematics nor its offerings in language and literature were lost on Julia and Bessie. Clearly, the ladies' academy offered a safe, ordered formation for the daughters of the region's elite.

Things were changing, however, and Julia was well placed in Sackville to witness her college, church, and country's transformation. Her church's Eastern British North American Wesleyan Methodist Conference, having outgrown its dependence upon the British Wesleyan Methodist Missionary Society, was negotiating a union with the Wesleyan Methodist Church in Canada, creating an east-west religious community of resources, personnel, and missions. Its realignment mirrored her country's recently redrawn geopolitical borders, a union tied together by the steel tracks that passed visibly and audibly through Sackville, facilitating its trade, travel, and communications.

Not all change was welcome. In 1872, an ominous, unidentified illness prevented Julia's return to Sackville for her fourth year of studies. She had contracted tuberculosis, a pervasive, debilitating disease, with recurring bouts of illness, which eventually claimed her life on 2 April 1880. More happily, Julia's withdrawal from the academy facilitated her relationship (the record is silent on its origins) with Canning's recently resident young physician, Dr. Frederick Borden, Gus's friend and classmate from Acacia Villa, King's College, and Harvard Medical School.

Only three years Julia's senior, Fred, had been born in 1847 at Upper Canard, eight kilometres from Canning, the only son of Dr. Jonathan Borden and Marie Frances Brown. Dr. Jonathan Borden was a university-educated physician, and Marie Frances Brown's large family were prosperous farmers, educated physicians, and Reform politicians from the Wolfville-Horton area. Fred began his Canning medical practice the same year Julia entered the ladies' academy; and as a friend and classmate of Gus, he was no stranger to Julia's family.

Although Julia and Fred's marriage on 1 October 1873 precluded her return to the ladies' academy, only four months after their marriage it failed to retard the launch of Fred's political career. Fred had not planned to seek public office, but the confusion of post-Confederation Nova Scotia politics had drawn him into the vacuum created by the Reform/Liberal Party leadership's repudiation of Leverett De Veber Chipman, the constituency's "renegade" member of Parliament.[9] The party's request that Canning's Liberal/Reform merchants nominate a "real friend" of the government was more easily made than met. Canning's Liberal/Reform merchants had tried but failed to unseat Chipman in 1872, having polled only 28 per cent of the county's popular vote.[10] Less than two weeks before the 5 February 1874 federal election, however, Dr. Fred Borden agreed to become their sacrificial lamb.

Fred's task was formidable. Not only was Chipman the incumbent MP, but he was the scion of the county's "'family compact," the 69th Militia battalion's commanding officer (a unit to which Fred, his father, and his

Uncle Andrew belonged), and the brother of Fred's Harvard classmate, Dr. Henry Chipman. Moreover, Fred was a twenty-six-year-old physician and political neophyte, with only ten days to persuade the electorate in the Kings constituency to defeat Chipman. To add to Fred's disadvantages, it was the dead of winter, and he was on crutches, having slipped on an icy doorstep and injured his knee shortly after his nomination. His opponents attributed his injury to drunkenness, a charge designed to sour his reputation among his constituents' temperance advocates.[11] In fact, Fred was still a member in good standing of the local temperance society!

Despite Fred's handicaps, when the returns were tallied from the snow-blocked outlying districts, he learned that he had won Kings by 98 votes. The Pacific Scandal,[12] Fred's access to federal and provincial patronage, his father-in-law's Canning influence, his father's popularity in Canard, and his maternal Brown relatives' professional and political standing in the Wolfville/Horton area[13] were enough to overcome Chipman's strong Kentville showing and give Fred a slender victory.

Slender and tenuous as was Fred's majority, his election fired his political aspirations. It also increased his dependence upon his Clarke in-laws, for only two days after their first wedding anniversary, Fred and Julia became parents. They named their daughter Elizabeth, after her maternal grandmother Clarke and her eleven-year-old Aunt Bessie – a worthy successor to the family's dynasty of redoubtable women. Given Fred's six-to-eight-week annual parliamentary sojourn in Ottawa, his competitive medical practice, and Julia's debilitating illness, the Clarkes became the Borden household's principal backstop.

Apart from accompanying Fred to Ottawa for Parliament's ceremonial and social activities, Julia remained in Canning, coping with her illness and managing her family and household. The birth of their second child, Harold Lothrop,[14] on 23 May 1876, obliged Fred and Julia to hire a housekeeper, Mrs. Saphronia Cox, a fifty-four-year-old widow, to lighten the household routine and child care.[15] By the time their third child was born, on 23 March 1879, Julia's health had become alarming. Named Julia Maude after her dying mother, Julia Maude was only a year and ten days old when her mother died of tuberculosis on 2 April 1880 (the disease that had killed Fred's mother in 1862 when he was fifteen), and Fred became even more dependent upon Mrs. Clarke's assistance.

Only ten years old at the time of Julia and Fred's marriage, Bessie had grown up inspired by her sister's example. Familiar with Julia's school days, marriage, children, Ottawa ventures, and deteriorating health, she had been spared witnessing the last painful months of her sister's life. For, in August 1877, three years before Julia's death, Bessie's parents had enrolled her in Mount Allison Ladies Academy. She was only fourteen years old at the time, among the youngest of the Academy's eighty-seven girls. Just eleven girls were fifteen years or younger.[16] Bessie's early enrolment may have been her parents attempt to shield her from her sister's tragic end.

Bessie had been well primed for the academy by Julia. She was familiar with the Academy's program, professors, and some of its students. Sixty-two of her classmates were boarders, drawn largely from Halifax and communities bordering the Fundy. Boarders lived in close quarters and were typically more engrossed in the academy's life than day students, and subject to more monitoring by the academy's vigilant staff. Their routine included morning chapel, compulsory Sunday service, and optional weekly Bible study.[17] Card-playing and dancing were forbidden. Bessie later learned to dance but never enjoyed cards.[18]

Much had changed since Julia's attendance at the ladies' academy. The recently completed Inter-Colonial Railway brought Bessie to a well-funded academy with a larger enrolment and an expanded program, thanks to Inch's reforms.[19] Students from privileged families had become the academy's principal clientele, attracted by its facilities and "ornamental" program. So popular had the academy become that egalitarian Methodist parents and supporters began to complain that it had become little more than a finishing school and preserve of the rich, and called for more academic and vocational options, and more modest attire.[20]

Defenders of the academy's less-than-rigorous academic program countered their criticism. They lauded the academy's development of character, spirituality, and moral control, essential to wives and mothers and the "cult of motherhood." They praised its cultivation of drawing-room decorum, "polite femininity," and refinement, and its contribution to the beautification of "the life of the Maritime provinces."[21] They reminded critics that the academy's "topics debates" introduced students to "issues of the day'" essential to building their church's New Jerusalem. Nor had the academy's ornamental subjects prevented Harriet Starr Stewart from completing her BA in July 1880, the first woman in Canada to do so. Apart from personal development and social betterment, the academy's ornamental program provided few career opportunities, however, since "finished" ladies were not expected to work for material profit.[22] Ladies who did so were largely single women; many of whom became teachers and nurses, but rarely occupied administrative or leadership positions.[23]

Bessie was interested in public issues. She enjoyed informed, lively conversation and debate. She profited from the academy's emphasis on languages, especially French, which became an asset to her in her later life and travels. Its library fed her reading addiction. Its gymnasium, its Almo Guards (who performed marching drills for special events, and its ponds and rinks for ice-skating (a sport Bessie enjoyed, despite her chronic dislike of the cold) provided outlets for her energy.[24]

Even more important, Bessie came to and left the academy with a mind of her own. A spirited, determined person, she resisted Methodism's strictures on women's attire and ungodly ostentation.e. To Bessie dress was more than an aesthetic choice; it signified character and status, and it facilitated leadership and social mobility. And Bessie had no intention of relinquishing her passion for fashion, public service, and social mobility. She returned to Canning in June 1881 without the mistress of liberal Arts diploma, as did most of her classmates, but she returned a sophisticated young woman, with new friends, interests, and aspirations.

Chapter Three

Mrs. Borden

Bessie's return to Canning brought timely relief to her mother, preoccupied by her elderly husband's failing health. At home, Lizzie, Harold, and Maude – six, five, and two years old respectively – were sad reminders of Julia's absence. Bessie's return was no less welcome to the children's father, still disoriented by Julia's death, and anxious about his children's care, his busy medical practice, and nascent entrepreneurial initiatives. He was also facing a difficult re-election. A survivor of the Liberal Party's general defeat in 1878, Fred had spent his last four years in the Opposition, with no access to federal or provincial patronage, politically vulnerable and very much on his own. Preoccupied by Julia's illness and death, his conspicuous absence during Parliament's last two sessions made him a vulnerable target for Douglas Benjamin Woodworth (1841–1900), Fred's seasoned electoral opponent.

Educated, well-connected, and treacherous, Douglas Benjamin Woodworth knew how to exploit Fred's vulnerabilities. A fellow resident of Canning, six years Fred's senior, Woodworth had graduated from the provincial Normal School in Truro and Harvard University in Boston, where he had received a LLB degree. He was also the son-in-law of the wealthy Conservative senator Ezra Churchill (1806–1874), and the half-brother of the editor of the *Canning Gazette*. With these assets Woodworth had been elected to the provincial legislative assembly in 1871, where he had attained notoriety in 1874 by accusing the provincial secretary of falsifying a record. Unable to substantiate and refusing to withdraw his charge, Woodworth had been expelled forcibly from the assembly for misconduct and contempt, a disciplinary action that the indomitable member contested successfully before the courts.[1] Fresh from his legal victory, in 1878 Woodworth had challenged Fred for the federal riding of Kings and lost. That contest began a relentless political duel between the two men that ended only with Woodworth's death in 1900.

The 1882 federal rematch was a particularly rude contest, and for Fred a rear-guard battle, marked by duplicity and betrayal, to which Bessie was an observant, sympathetic spectator. Fred's cousin, Robert Laird Borden, a Kentville lawyer and future leader of the Liberal-Conservative Party, came to Fred's assistance and spoke publicly and forcefully in Fred's support, denouncing Macdonald's National Policy. Although Fred was untypically bitter over his defeat, he had no intention of abandoning public life.

Fred's more pressing priority following his defeat was his personal life and his family's welfare. Above all, Fred sought a congenial companion and mother for his children while he re-established his political career. A convivial thirty-three-year-old widower with a marked interest in women, Fred was unlikely to remain single for long. Mrs. Gerald Kitson, the wife of the Royal Military College's commandant (1896–1900) , once observed that Fred had a fatal attraction to strong, attractive, "clever" women, who could then "do anything with" him.[2]

Fred did not have to look far for a qualified candidate. An Ottawa reporter described Bessie as a woman with "brown eyes, a fresh complexion ... and a sweet womanly expression" that "painters give their Madonas."[3] Contemporary photographs portray Bessie as well-dressed, poised, self-assured, and sophisticated. Her family and friends found her sympathetic, caring, generous, articulate, forthright, and public spirited.[4] Although Bessie was only nineteen in 1882, and sixteen years Fred's junior, she could stand her own, much as her mother had done despite being nineteen years younger than her husband. A more formidable impediment to Bessie and Fred's marriage was the Criminal Code's prohibition's of a man's marriage to the sister of his deceased wife. In 1880, Desire Girouard, the Conservative Member of Parliament, introduced a bill to strike that prohibition from the Canadian Criminal Code. The bill, however, failed to pass Parliament owing to imperfections in the proposed legislation and opposition from the Roman Catholic Church and the Church of England in Canada.[5] Even though Parliament approved Girouard's revised bill two years later, it failed to convince old believers, notably Canada's Church of England clergy.[6] (The latter agreed to marry formerly prescribed persons only after the British Parliament ended its blockage in 1907.) Risking old believers' and gossipmongers' criticisms, Bessie and Fred decided to ignore "what the world might think."[7] And on 12 June 1884 Canning's Methodist minister, the Reverend Robert A. Daniels, married Fred and

Bessie, in the presence of Bessie's parents, Fred's widowed stepmother and their witnesses, R.L. Borden, A.J. Chase, and Dr. Gus Tupper.[8]

Bessie and Fred's private lives, like those of Jose Harris's Victorian Britons, remain shrouded in "a culture of privacy and reticence."[9] Bessie and Fred's marriage, however, was more than a practical resolution to Fred's personal and professional needs.[10] The Borden Papers scarce extant correspondence suggest an affectionate, respectful, intimate relationship of shared private and personal space, interests, and activities, though later tested by Fred's alleged infidelity.[11]

Bessie and Fred enjoyed music, art, theatre, and travel and had a passion for books. They belonged to reading clubs in Canning and Ottawa, and amassed a personal library of some 3,000 volumes, including rare editions.[12] They loved vocal, choral, and chamber music, symphony, opera, and theatre. Fred sang, played the piano, flute, and violin. They patronized concerts sponsored by Ottawa's various musical societies. Fred was an associate member (1896–7), then a vice patron of the Ottawa Amateur Orchestral Society (1898–1911), a vice president of the Ottawa Choral Society, and a generous donor to the Ottawa Symphony Orchestra's Guarantee Fund (1910); and Bessie subscribed to the Canadian Conservatory of Music's Grand Symphony Concerts (1909). Their Canning and Ottawa "at homes" welcomed singers, pianists, and violinists; they shared their interest in music with their neighbours Zoe and Wilfrid Laurier. (Zoe had studied music at the Sacred Heart Convent in Saint-Vincent-de-Paul, Quebec, and gave private piano lessons in Ottawa.)

Bessie and Fred embraced Christianity's social imperatives. They donated generously to all religious denominations, even those that disapproved of their politics and private lives. Bessie's approach to religion was personal, introspective, fatalistic, and ecumenical. Wheras Fred seemed to see religion as a Sunday recreation, a consumer product, and a social service – ascetic, pragmatic, and occasional. He respected Bessie's insistence on regular family worship and reported his church attendance even when he travelled alone, commenting on the quality of the architecture, the minister's sermon, and the music, as he did after a service at St. Paul's in London in December 1897, where he heard "such music as I shall never forget."[13]

Bessie and Fred came from highly mobile families that navigated within a flourishing Atlantic world. Their relatives, friends, and former neighbours populated the Canadian West and the United States from New England to California, most of them "economic refugees" from Kings County's great exodus (1871–1911). Fred had at least six maternal Brown first cousins living in the Boston area, and Bessie's brother, Gus, moved from Nova Scotia to New Brunswick to Maine, finally settling in Colorado. A restless entrepreneurial medical practitioner, Gus invested in real estate and mining ventures, sometimes in association with Fred. Altogether, the region's migrant network became a fertile field for friendships, profits, feuds, and frauds.

In the early years of their marriage Bessie and Fred travelled to Boston and New York, accessible by ship from Yarmouth. In 1893 they attended the Chicago World's Fair, and in 1895 they visited London. After 1896 they travelled constantly. When their children were very young, Bessie and Fred left them in Mrs. Clarke's care. When the children were older, Mrs. Clarke travelled with the family. A form of "productive leisure,"[14] their travel combined public and private business with historical and cultural activities. Fascinated by industry and innovation, they visited trade fairs and exhibitions. Fred's passion for history and genealogy drew him to public record offices, bookstores, cemeteries, and historical sites. Bessie preferred theatre, galleries, and opera.

Bessie and Fred dressed in fashionable cosmopolitan attire. As Elizabeth later recalled, "Mother took shopping seriously, preferring good shops anywhere any day to museums and picture galleries."[15] While Boston and New York offered a broad choice of merchandise, Bessie and Fred looked to Paris and London for contemporary fashion. Apart from emphasizing certain social and aesthetic values, modes of dress signified identity, class, age, gender, and aspirations. And in their theatre of power costume mattered. As Julia Parker Drummond, one of Montreal's most prominent women explained: "beautiful dressing and fine living give you at once a peculiar power to lead."[16] During the nineteenth century dress codes among the elite became very elaborate, attuned to season, hour, occasion, and fashion,[17] a protocol promoted by catalogues and magazines that defined gentility, and to which Bessie subscribed.[18]

Staging was no less important, and during their travels Bessie and Fred shopped for props to refurbish their homes: furniture, silver, glass, and art, as well as books, stamps, and historical artifacts, instruments of self-promotion and memorialization. According to their great-granddaughter, Bessie and Fred were "notorious for buying cheap or getting a bargain [and though] many things looked impressive [they] were of little value."[19] Fred took a speculative approach toward money. He liked to dream and dare. Bessie was inclined to be more prudent, conscious that "saving was a form of making money."[20]

Bessie and Fred usually travelled together. But when they travelled separately, they corresponded regularly in affectionate exchanges, sprinkled with literary allusions, expressions of longing, and humour. Fred addressed Bessie as "my dear girl," teasing her about their age difference.[21] Although confident of her managerial abilities, Fred worried about Bessie's health and household burdens. He urged her to hire servant girls, to visit Halifax "and have a good time," and "not let any idea of economy prevent you" as "we are not so very hard up now."[22] He fretted if Bessie's letters were delayed; he scrutinized postmarks, and telephoned or telegraphed Bessie to determine the cause of the delay. Sometimes he was so "awfully lonesome" he felt he would "never again leave home without [her]."[23] He shopped for her during his absences.[24] He pressed her to meet him at his port of disembarkation.[25] When he travelled alone for any length of time, as he did for three weeks in December 1897 and early January 1898, they corresponded biweekly. He complained of his chilly room in London's Hotel Victoria on Northumberland Avenue, explaining that he was "terribly lonesome," and suffering from "diarrhea over-eating & under-heating"! Bessie liked to eat and loathed the cold.[26]

Bessie embraced their public life as a joint project. She protected Fred from public and private intrusion. She worried about his health, sent him pills, and nursed him during illness. She managed his social agenda and substituted or covered for his absences. She responded assiduously and correctly to Ottawa society's invitations, and "at homes," lunched with politicians' wives, penned gracious letters of thanks, and maintained a formidable social correspondence. She presided over Canning's social life as well, importing forms of vice-regal entertainment, such as celebrating the town's new ice rink with a fancy costume skating party that drew people by train from Wolfville and Kentville.[27] Bessie could also be imperious, and, for all her grace and charm, she had her sticking points. Those who offended walked warily until peace had been restored, something that Fred and the family understood and respected.[28]

In September 1911 Fred wrote Bessie a retrospective letter following his traumatic electoral defeat, a letter that captured a rare private moment. "I lay awake a while last night," he wrote, "trying to remember some of our many talks about the sort of life we would really prefer. I think we always agreed that our first desire would be to lead our own life, to speak regardless of what the world or society might think. I think we agreed that the *summum bonum* is to do some good to humanity, to help the other fellow without being so foolish, of course, as to hurt ourselves in doing it; and that to add to our store of knowledge is more important and more likely to bring happiness than to add to our store of wealth."[29] That was the ideal.

In the years that preceded Fred's nostalgic 1911 letter, however, that ideal had been tarnished by public allegations of Fred's infidelities.[30]

Nevertheless, what united them always seemed stronger than what tested their relationship,.[31] And though Bessie may have tried to "sanitize" the family archives to disguise a troubled marital relationship, the surviving records suggest a marriage founded on respect, affection, and mutual interests, a functional, fluid relationship rather than one circumscribed by conventional constraints. On the other hand, the absence of evidence of estrangement or acrimony may suggest either the success of Bessie's purge, her state of denial, or her acceptance of a prevailing "patrician double standard."[32]

Chapter Four

Business Partner

Had Fred been content to remain a village physician whose home was his workplace, Bessie might have led a quiet, conventional life, confined to a "separate sphere" of housework and childbearing, a "homemaker" rather than a "money-maker," excluded from Fred's life of business and politics. While separate spheres offered an "appropriate" contemporary "gender option" for some couples,[1] neither Bessie nor Fred was interested in confining themselves to separate spheres, not least because Fred depended upon Bessie's financial, political, and personal support. As a father of three young, active children, a popular physician, an ambitious entrepreneur, and a public figure, Fred profited from Bessie's commitment to his business and political career.

Well before their marriage, Fred had begun to mobilize his community's material resources, mixing private interests with public initiatives, a strategy that enhanced his income and extended his political influence. Even before his 1882 electoral defeat, he began investing his surplus income in shipping, land, and local utilities such as rail, telephone, and electricity lines, working in conjunction with relatives, friends, and local merchants.[2] Free from parliamentary duties he now had the time, incentive, and opportunity to expand and develop those initiatives.

Land became the central instrument of Fred's wealth accumulation, a project favoured by location and timing.[3] His location in the Annapolis Valley – a strip of deep, rich soil, four to fourteen kilometres wide, stretching from the Cornwallis River to the Annapolis Basin, sheltered by the south and north "mountains," and irrigated by five rivers emptying into the Fundy – provided fruit, potatoes, hay, and livestock access to lucrative external markets. Fortuitiously, his requisite land acquisitions occurred during a period when the region's declining wind, wood, and water economy created an exodus of its small- and medium-sized landowners, whose property was available at favourable prices to ambitious entrepreneurs who might purchase, consolidate, and use it for commercial agriculture.

As one of those entrepreneurs, Fred purchased, inherited, and secured a large quantity of land through various means: marriage, mortgages, insurance, and credit arrangements. By 1903 he owned about 4,893 acres of land, which he farmed and which served as capital for his investments in small industries and public utilities and funded his social and political life.[4] Among his assets were four, 100-acre or more, apple orchards, said to be among the largest in the Annapolis-Kings fruit belt,[5] a 150-acre livestock and dairy farm, reputed to be the largest in the province, and extensive grain fields and vegetable gardens. About half of his properties were woodlots that he harvested and had sawn into lumber at his Blomidon hydro-powered sawmill, and sold or crafted into doors, window sashes, boxes, barrels, and rafts at his Kingsport woodworking factory. He rented, sold, and mortgaged excess land to cover capital cost and operating shortfalls. His integrated land project generated income, employment, and political obligations.[6]

Shortly after his 1882 electoral defeat, Fred became Canning's first Bank of Nova Scotia agent, a post that provided an annual stipend of $1,000 plus commission on its business. He hired a series of clerks, invariably young male relatives, to manage the bank's daily business, reserving loans and important business for himself, and paid a supplement of $50 to the clerk's meagre $100 annual salary.[7] The region's emerging commercial agriculture created a lively market for capital and credit. Orchard farmers needed long-term loans to purchase properties and fund capital investments while awaiting the seven-year delay between planting and peak production. Others required short-term credit to withstand the perils of weather and markets, and to bridge the delay between "seedtime and harvest." Shippers and merchants sought cash, credit, and endorsements. Their business provided bank agents with information and opportunities to turn knowledge to personal advantage, and to accommodate privately what bank policy might prohibit.[8]

Banking introduced Fred to a bewitching array of mortgages and fire and and life insurance policies promoted by local agents of American insurance companies that dotted the region's migratory trajectory. Mortgages facilitated land acquisitions from land-rich, cash-poor out-migrants, elderly farmers, widows, and widowers, transactions facilitated by Fred's knowledge of their health and credit. On one occasion two timely fire insurance settlements forestalled Fred's own potential financial embarrassment. On another occasion, a life insurance scandal involving an ill, elderly woman, threatened to compromise his political career.[9]

Fred's greatest asset, however, was his marriage. Scarcely two months after Bessie and Fred's marriage, John Clarke made his will. Describing himself in contemporary legalese as "weak and infirm of body, but of sound and disposing mind and memory," Clarke named his wife and son his executors. During Mr. Clarke's last difficult years, Mrs. Clarke had monitored the family's business with a shrewd eye for opportunity, and indifference to gendered private and public space. Mr. Clarke's will bequeathed $6,000 (roughly $150,000 in today's purchasing power) to Bessie, his only living daughter. To each of his grandchildren, Elizabeth, Harold, and Maude, the children of his deceased daughter, he bequeathed $2,000, to be paid to them on their twenty-first year or day of marriage. His will entrusted the children's bequests to their father[10] to be "put out to interest on real estate" and the income employed for the children's maintenance and education, a provision that aligned well with Fred and Bessie's entrepreneurial plans and family objectives.[11] That bequest's administration became Bessie's responsibility.[12]

Upon Mr. Clarke's death in 1888, Mrs. Clarke moved into the Borden household, and Fred became her financial manager. He invested her $6,000 bequest from Mr. Clarke in mortgages and securities earning 6 per cent interest.[13] What other resources Mrs. Clarke possessed are unknown, but at the time of her death in 1919 Mrs. Clarke's estate was evaluated at $22,470, after taxes (about $500,000 in today's purchasing power) and included $9,483 in mortgages and $12,861 in bonds and stocks, invested largely in the family's Supply Company and in Montreal Tram, to which Fred had become deeply committed.[14]

Although Mr. Clarke bequested the "rest and residue" of his "real and personal estate" to his "affectionate" only son, Dr. Augustus Clarke, Fred soon acquired Gus's inherited real estate, including Mr. Clarke's two wholesale/retail stores in Canning and Blomidon. Five years before Mr. Clarke's death, Gus had left his Parrsboro medical practice to aid his ailing father and manage the family business. His experience, however, had killed his desire to continue his father's business. Upon Mr. Clarke's death Fred agreed to manage, then purchase, the stores from Gus, including two 50-acre woodlots in New Ross, and 3,000 acres of timberland. The stores served a wide local market with lumber, farm produce, groceries, dry goods, hardware, glassware, boots, shoes, furniture, stoves, harnesses, farm machinery, and wagons, merchandized by commission salesmen to farms and villages within Fred's constituency. The stores enhanced Fred's commercial and political power, casting him as buyer, seller, creditor, and employer.

Bessie was more than the landlord's daughter and faithful handmaiden, dependent on her husband's charity. Her inheritance gave her an independent income that she used or invested as she saw fit. Although the exact amount of Bessie's personal assets is unknown, her wealth grew over time, augmented by a $7,000 (roughly $94,000 in today's purchasing power) bequest from her mother in 1919.[15] Whatever the total sum of her assets, they enabled her to live comfortably for six years after Fred's death in 1917, while she awaited the settlement of his contested estate. Nor was she a passive, indifferent heir and investor, ignorant of finance and management. She maintained her own bank account. Each month Fred wrote her a cheque to cover household and personal expenses. He discussed and consulted her on the management of her assets and their family investments.[16] She monitored markets during his absences, discussed business with him in their private correspondence, relayed investment advice to his brokers, and on one occasion joked about making a million during his absence.[17] She applauded Fred's commercial dreams and schemes, including his attempts to develop the Annapolis Valley's tourist potential, capitalizing on the Valley's French heritage, popularized in Longfellow's *Evangeline*, by the creation of a national park and a rail line to Cap Blomidon.[18]

Although generous with her family and friends, Bessie remained ever the merchant's daughter, who sought value for money and accountability from her dependents and employees. Appreciative of her farm's economic, social, and political value, she contributed to its domestic economy.[19] Like many contemporary middle-class women, Bessie sewed, knitted, crocheted, and tended to the gardens and poultry. During her early marriage she worked in their Canning and Blomidon stores (as had her mother), clerking and taking stock. In Fred's absence she supervised outdoor staff, and in the absence of indoor or outdoor staff she stoked their home's ravenous coal furnace and wood-burning fireplaces and worked in the gardens.[20]

Bessie appreciated the ascetic, social, and spiritual qualities of their family's lands. Often the preserve of women, vegetable and flower gardens were prized for their decorative, medicinal, nutritional, didactic, and spiritual qualities,[21] and were esteemed as a class marker in Canada's replicative British world.[22] A student of botany and literature, Bessie was fascinated by plants' physiognomy and aesthetics, and their cultivation and management. When she painted (largely in watercolours) she depicted peaceful rivers and domesticated landscapes, with a meticulous eye for detail.[23] She read and reread John Ruskin's writings on nature, art, architecture, religion, social justice, and community, and saw springtime as proof of the resurrection of "a God who can perform this wonderful miracle of bringing dead nature to life."[24]

Bessie was no less a capable manager. A year before their marriage, Fred purchased a ten-acre property from H.R.D. Harris for $2,100. Located between Canning's Main Street and the Habitant River, a short walk from Bessie's parent's home, the property included a large Victorian house, known affectionally as the "Old Place," which Harris had purchased recently for $4,000. Although Harris had spent $1,000 on house repairs, the Old Place still required interior and exterior work, which Fred entrusted to Bessie's supervision, a project that enabled her to put her mark on their residence and demonstrate her managerial abilities and social aspirations.

While I found no evidence that Bessie subscribed to or read the popular American journal *Godey's Lady's Book and Magazine*, published in Philadelphia (1830–96), the journal's content mirrored Bessie's Anglo-American domestic interests, tastes, and social aspirations, qualities promoted by its illustrations and tinted fashion plates. It provided advice on domestic architecture, health, children's clothing, patterns, and crafts. Its piano sheet music, short stories, and poetry (including poetry by Oliver Wendell Holmes Sr., Fred's medical professor at Harvard), and its fascination with British royalty, offered entertainment and fired aspirations. Bessie believed that houses, grounds, furnishings, and presentation mattered, not least because Fred intended to return to federal politics. More important still, she believed that family mattered, and she had become mother to three very special children.

Chapter Five

Dearest Mother

Lizzie was nine, Harold eight, and Maude five years old when their Aunt Bessie became their mother. Julia Maude was too young to remember her birth mother, who had been dead for four years. Bessie had cared for Fred and Julia's children ever since she returned from Mount Allison, assisted less and less by Mrs. Clarke, who had become increasingly preoccupied with Mr. Clarke's declining health. Bessie was only twenty-one at the time of her marriage and intended to have children of her own. Subsequently, she had one child, and possibly more who died at birth, a loss that enhanced her commitment to Fred and Julia's children's care and upbringing.[1]

Bessie based her parenting on contemporary literature on childhood available to an educated, avid reader. From 1870 a flood of advice books, directed toward middle-class families, redefined and revaluated childhood, a preoccupation reflected in Canadian artists' focus on children.[2] Faced with smaller families and perceptions of extended childhood, advice books recommended more relaxed, child-centred parental relations. They advocated persuasion rather than coercion and religious intimidations. They suggested games, toys, reading for pleasure, and creative activities, and insisted on health, nutrition, and more informal, less constrained clothing.[3] Although Fred was far from absent from his children's upbringing, advice books focused primarily on mothers, charged with children's religious and moral development, what scholars have characterized as the professionalization or "cult of motherhood'." Even if Bessie read none of these books, their advice was difficult to escape, diffused as it was in periodicals, pulpits, and conversation. Whatever the source, Bessie's children enjoyed a modern, progressive upbringing, one that contrasted with that of Fred's childhood.[4]

Bessie's children lived in a small community, surrounded by caring family, friends, and neighbours, who moved freely between the

Old Place and their watchful grandparents' home. The children's extended family cushioned their maternal loss, and cemented family cohesion, so evident in extant letters and photographs. Outdoors they enjoyed making snowmen, skating, tobogganing, fishing, playing games, and gardening, surrounded by farm animals – ducks, hens, turkeys, cows, sheep, and rabbits. Indoors they read, drew, sang, and played the flute, piano, and violin, and cared for their dogs and cats, amused by their community's characters and committed to their father's political career.

Bessie monitored her children's physical, social, and spiritual welfare. She paid special attention to their health, dress, and manners, their cultural and religious formation. She insisted on nutritious food, recommended by "scientific" cookbooks, food readily available from their fruit orchards and vegetable gardens. Bessie liked food, could cook, and appreciated its relationship to health,[5] though she and Maude developed a sweet tooth during their later years. In fulfilling her nursing role, she used clinical language and contemporary professional remedies, appropriate to a wife and a sister of university-educated physicians, and with a verbal frankness that betrayed little trace of "Victorian" prudery.

Forthright and transparent with her children, Bessie cited her own faults as warnings, such as her self-described lack of consistency in pursuing moral objectives.[6] Above all, she advised her children to "be very faithful in the small things" since "they are the things we stumble on oftenest."[7] Small things included speech, dress, and manners, the hallmarks of character, class, and family. No less influential was Bessie's example. Her pragmatic approach to "gendered" work and household management became a model for her daughters, who later worked and supervised labour with little regard to gendered constraints.[8]

Music and reading occupied a privileged place in the children's education.[9] Lizzie had an aptitude for piano, as did Maude. All three children enjoyed choral singing, especially Harold. And all were chronic readers. Charles Dickens was among their favourite authors. His stories stirred their Methodist conscience, shaped their social topology, and confirmed their sense of civic responsibility.[10] Physical exercise was no less part of their formation, including swimming, skating, and skiing, activities encouraged by their health-conscious father and their physically active mother.

Bessie circulated correspondence among absent family members. They remembered birthdays and Christmas with gifts and greetings.[11] The children's correspondence with their "dearest mother" was open, attentive, and affectionate, tailored to their material needs and personal relationship. Lizzie was decisive, forthright, and didactic, all recognizable Clarke characteristics. She was organized and impatient with people who "dilly-dallied," ever the older sister. Only eleven years younger than her stepmother, Lizzie's relationship to Bessie resembled that of a younger sister, dependent but not always easy. Lizzie adored her father whose life, example, and civic commitment she idealized, emulated, and defended. Like him, she was a romantic, committed to family, community, and history. She was his "Girly": her childhood signature in her correspondence with her father.[12]

Bessie's affection for Harold was mutual, protective, vulnerable, and significantly different from her relationship with Lizzie or Maude. Bessie assumed maternal responsibility for raising her son, in a gendered hereditary role, as responsible, dutiful, and spiritual, a paragon of muscular Christianity. Harold possessed his family's energy, restlessness, and commitment to civic duty, his mother's religious sensibility, and his parents' passion for books and music. He was attentive to dress and deportment and sensitive to his parents' expectations. Harold's relationship to his mother complemented his affection for his father, an affectionate, fearless, bond that his father characterized as typical of the Clarke side of the family.[13]

Although Maude grew up in a family of strong personalities, she negotiated her own distinct path. As a child she played by herself for long periods of time. Quietly autonomous and determined, she was non-confrontational, non-judgmental, and able to manage difficult situations, much like her father. She, like he, spoke in quiet, measured tones and had a broad circle of friends, and was less attached to organized religion than her mother and siblings. Generous and sympathetic, she was convivial and had a lively sense of humour. She shared her family's fascination with design, fashion, and handicraft, and enjoyed theatre, art, and travel. Practical, adaptable, and resourceful, Maude was a survivor who often lived outside the family's parameters, a quality severely tested in the years ahead.

Until her death in 1919, Grandma Clarke commanded a dignified authority in her family, church, and community, serving as an anchor in her grandchildren's early lives. A widow at fifty-nine, after her husband's death, she occupied the large second floor, southwest bedroom in the Old Place. Lizzie's husband once described Mrs. Clarke as a "spacious" old lady, especially when dressed in her "numerous petticoats and things which increased her girth to a greater degree than that of an ordinary person."[14] She walked with a slight, inexplicable limp. She also inherited the Tupper family's legendary stamina and longevity and outlived her husband by thirty-one years.[15] Intelligent, humorous, and didactic, she loved reading and encouraged her grandchildren's knowledge of gardens, birds, and animals.[16]

Bessie and Fred agreed that knowledge should always trump wealth.[17] But in their world knowledge and wealth were reciprocal, a means to power and social mobility.[18] Harold loved literature, language, and music (especially Beethoven), but contemporary gender assumptions directed young middle-class men toward subjects "appropriate" to a professional and public career, and young middle-class women toward language, literature, art, and music.

Mount Allison's Ladies' College (its academy had been redesignated a college in 1886) seemed tailored to Elizabeth's interests and her family's aspirations. Its broad-based curriculum, the college boasted, was "unexcelled anywhere in Canada."[19] Besides, by 1890 Mount Allison had become a Borden family institution, counting among its graduates the Reverend Doctor Byron Crane Borden, Fred's cousin, and the Ladies' College's president (and later university's president in 1911), and other distinguished family members.[20] In August 1890, when Lizzie joined the college's department of literature and conservatory of music, its alumnae-financed conservatory was still under construction. By the next June the conservatory offered thirty-five teaching rooms for piano, violin, and voice, a music library, orchestra, and a pipe organ.[21] In 1893, Lizzie's last year, the college welcomed John Owens's collection of three hundred paintings, together with John A. Hammond (1843–1939),[22] the artist who had built the wealthy Saint John shipowner's art collection, and for which Mount Allison constructed Canada's first university art gallery in 1895.

The college's teaching staff matched its facilities. Six of its fifteen instructors taught music, piano, violin, and voice to its 174 students. Five others taught art, including its resident artist. So successful had the college's arts program become that austere Methodists complained that its fixation on "ladylike" pursuits had displaced its intellectual and professional mission.[23] The college responded by adding shorthand and typing to its program, giving "ornamental subjects" theoretical rigour,[24] and adding political science, history and English literature to its program, subjects that fed Lizzie's interest in contemporary literature and society.

Electric lights and other amenities made student life more congenial than during Lizzie's mother's residence, despite periodic infestations of mice.[25] Although attendance at evangelical crusades remained mandatory and students were closely monitored, college life was less cloistered in the 1890s than in Bessie's time. Its focus on social action, progress, trade unionism, women's rights, and temperance, topics revisited in "sensible drawing room talk,"[26] appealed to Elizabeth's desire to convert faith to action.

Lizzie left the Ladies' College in 1894 without the mistress of liberal arts diploma, as did most of her classmates. Lizzie, however, had not completed her formal education. She planned to study music in Boston. Her intention remains unclear. Did she consider a career in teaching or performance? Or was her interest solely personal? Nor is it clear who advised her where to study and with whom. All we know is that Lizzie left Yarmouth for Boston in November 1894 to study piano for six months under the supervision of Carl Baermann (1839–1913), a German-born pianist, teacher, and composer.[27] Carl Baermann's father and grandfather had been renowned German musicians, and Carl a student of Franz Liszt's (1811–86). After Carl's father's death in 1881, Carl settled in Boston, where he enjoyed a wide contemporary reputation.

Bessie and Fred accompanied Lizzie to Boston, to see their daughter safely settled, boarding with a distant cousin and former Canning residents, William and Fanny North, and their son Howard and daughter Grace.[28] A Harvard graduate, Fred knew and liked Boston, and returned frequently for business and pleasure. He was also a protective father who visited Lizzie at least four times during her year's studies, mixing parental responsibilities with business, and concerts whenever possible. And, on one occasion Fred brought Harold, Lizzie's "laughing, singing and teasing brother."[29]

For years, Lizzie recalled her happy year in Boston, lining up "week after week" for rush seats in the gallery of Symphony Hall in the old Mechanics Building to enjoy "blissful" opera, theatre, concerts, and rehearsals. One of her special memories was hearing Felix Mendelssohn's *St. Paul Oratorio* with her father.[30] Equally memorable was seeing Henry Irving (1838–1905) and Ellen Terry (1847–1928) in performances of *Twelfth Night, Olivia,* and *The Bells*.[31] Upon Baermann's recommendation, and with Bessie's consent, Lizzie extended her studies three more months.[32]

Harold had planned to join Lizzie at Mount Allison in August 1892 for Lizzie's last two years. But during Harold's final year at King's College School, he had developed chest pains that alarmed the school's physician and stoked his parents' fears of tuberculosis. Fred and Bessie's decision to keep Harold home for a year under a doctor's care and Bessie's watch, exercising in the fresh air and enduring mustard leaf plasters and cod liver oil, delayed his registration at Mount Allison until August 1893, Lizzie's final year.[33]

Mount Allison was not an obvious choice for Harold. Harold had followed his father and maternal uncles' educational trajectory, first at

Holmsworth School, then Acacia Villa, where he developed an interest in French and Latin, especially Phaedrus's Latinized, moral *Fables*.[34] He then enrolled at King's College School and matriculated in June 1892.[35] While he intended to follow his father, grandfather, and maternal uncles' medical careers, he did not follow them to Harvard. Although he had fully recovered from his chest pains, his apprehensive parents decided to keep him closer to home and under Lizzie's vigilant care.

Harold, however, needed little sibling supervision. Tall (six foot three), dark, handsome, polite, gregarious, and athletic,[36] he adapted readily to college life. Over-solicitous matrons, such as Mrs. Elizabeth (Powell) Allison, the university president's wife, fussed over his health; he resisted their interventions "with as much politeness as possible," protesting to his sister that he was "as well as anyone and don't [didn't] wish to be fussed over."[37] A year later, his gossipy letters to Lizzie in Boston, on Mount Allison's student life, shared friends, and romantic attachments, attest to his easy adjustment.[38]

One of sixty-two students enrolled in Mount Allison's four-year arts program, Harold lived in a comfortable new four-storey brick residence with stone facings, designed for 100 students. The growth of intercollegiate sports, team colours, and college rituals and yells nourished his disciplined, competitive nature. When skating and hockey competed with his conscience and studies, conscience usually triumphed. His classmates remembered him as unassuming, clear-minded, and quick to receive and retain information. He attended church and prayer meetings, sang in the church choir, practised acts of "kindness and charity done in quiet,"[39] committed to a muscular Christianity and fired by a passion to right the world's wrongs. He joined the Athletic Association, the YMCA, the Glee Club,[40] and the Debating Society, all useful preparation for a public career.

In August 1895 Maude joined Harold at Mount Allison. She came well briefed by Lizzie and Harold on her teachers. They knew her parents and siblings and invited her to their homes. A few of her classmates even came from Canning. Registered in the Ladies' College's Conservatory of Music, Maude studied violin, piano, and Latin. Her social life consisted of church, teas, "at homes," "topics nights," skating, and discussion of the boys' sports teams.[41] After attending Mount Allison for one year, Maude's academic life became a casualty of her family's plans following her father's appointment to Wilfrid Laurier's cabinet.

Bessie was her children's banker, counsellor, and overseer. She paid their room, board, and tuition. She distributed their allowances and scrutinized their regular, itemized expense accounts. She made curtains and cushions for their rooms, sent them apples and cakes, and plied them with news and advice.[42] The children informed her of their material and social needs, the holes in their stockings, trousers, and tunics, and their need for a seasonal rink pass.[43] They wrote of their studies, friends, old boys' suppers, and their contribution to the university's Sixties Jubilee Fund. Their letters enclosed messages for their busy father to whom they wrote less often, especially as he became more deeply embroiled in his Liberal Party's effort to topple the faltering Conservative government.

Chapter Six

Political Spouse

Civic life in late nineteenth-century Nova Scotia extended well beyond voting.[1] Bessie and Fred came from public-spirited families – farmers, merchants, and professionals who served in the militia, judiciary, legislature, church, and school. They identified with their community, were concerned with its welfare, and understood the importance of family, reciprocity, and mutual assistance. They appreciated the synergies of private interest and public service, and the opportunities for material and personal profit from a government increasingly committed to subsidizing infrastructure and economic development, regulating health, and providing social services, projects that enhanced the state's importance, and the role of politics and politicians.

Traditionally, Canning's merchant elite promoted public projects that served their personal and community interests.[2] As an emerging member of that elite Fred initiated civic projects alone or in cooperation with the community's leaders, projects that advanced his interests, amplified his public profile, and extended his political reach. Apart from his bank agency and mercantile business with their networks of financial and personal obligations, Fred invested in local telephone, power, and rail lines – collective, local initiatives that sought public charters, contracts, and subsidies, and that generated commerce, employment, civic pride, and personal profit.

For example, in 1887 Fred and a group of Canning's Liberal merchants chartered the Cornwallis Valley Railway, designed to integrate the region's land and sea economies and channel its agricultural produce through Kingsport, the county's chief Fundy port. Once completed, this twenty-two-kilometre track ran six daily trains between Kentville, Canning, and Kingsport, skirting Fred's property and the warehouses of his and thirty other apple producers, a service from which Fred profited as an investor, merchant, farmer, and politician.[3] Thanks to his political intervention, the railway enjoyed construction subsidies and mail contracts, assets best secured by a seat in the House of Commons.

Smaller private and public initiatives facilitated Fred's return to and retention of a Commons seat. His establishment of a small community library (a project dear to Bessie's heart), and his donation of his coach house to the Church of England for a chapel, cast Fred in the role of a community benefactor. His promotion of collective health and sanitary measures, wooden sidewalks, sewers, organized garbage collection, and the delivery of potable spring water from the "North Mountain" marked him as a progressive, scientific man, familiar with contemporary health hazards and municipal causes. His 1893 appointment to the province's newly formed board of health[4] cast him as a well-placed political broker with provincial influence. By 1887 he had even rejoined Canning's Order of Good Templars.[5]

Useful as were Fred and Bessie's family, business connections, local initiatives, and progressive agenda in garnering political support, the disgrace of D. B. Woodworth, Fred's Conservative, scandal-plagued political rival, virtually assured his reclamation of Kings in 1887.[6] During that electoral contest Fred regaled his constituents with the sordid details of Woodworth's implication in a land scandal in Manitoba. Nova Scotia's ailing economy and Fred's business experience made him a more than credible replacement of his disgraced opponent. And a friendly provincial government helped compensate for his lack of federal patronage.

More important was Fred's conspicuous silence on the "repeal" issue, a legacy of the previous year's provincial election, when the province's premier, W.S. Fielding, won an election to take the province out of Confederation. Fred had participated in that contest and denounced the National Policy's "unjust and iniquitous" constraints on his province's economy, contrasting it with the "prosperity of Newfoundland" and calling upon the electorate to "vote for repeal to get better terms."[7] But when Fred's erstwhile political supporter, W.E. Roscoe, tried to rekindle the repeal issue in Kings during the 1887 federal election, Fred remained silent, a strategy that infuriated his diehard secessionist friends, who correctly interpreted it as his decision to choose Canada. If Fred's silence irritated the premier and future federal colleague, it was not evident. The two men were never close friends – being so different in background, personality, and style – but worked in harmony, Fielding an ever-helpful assistant in Fred's "Baptist" constituency.[8]

Fred's constituency, however, was no sinecure, even after he reclaimed it it in 1887. His constituents made that clear during the 1891 general election, and the subsequent 1892 by-election necessitated by

Conservative charges of irregularities, which reduced Fred's margin from 161 to 131 votes. Nonetheless, the Conservatives' failure to drive one of their chief tormenters from public life demonstrated Fred's political commitment, resilience, and increasing prominence within Laurier's Liberal Party.[9]

During Fred's disastrous 1882 electoral performance, he had excused his party's unpopular regional policies by pleading his lack of influence. He was, he explained, merely a "humble follower," a verbal slip Woodworth never let him forget. A reformed, assiduous Fred returned to Ottawa in 1887, determined to be a visible, vigilant, and vocal regional leader. He was now a successful entrepreneur, popular physician, and public benefactor, free from family worries, with an able spouse committed to his public life.

Bessie, however, was no more a silent partner in politics than she was in Fred's entrepreneurial endeavours. She was the wife of a member of Parliament with responsibilities, expectations, and opportunities. Although only twenty-four years old in 1887 and married scarcely three years, Bessie knew how to win friends and influence people. An attentive, shrewd analyst of character and circumstances, often more perceptive than her husband, she relished the theatre of power and politics, and was able to sift the substance from the rhetoric and staging.

Far from the stereotypical polite, deferential, compliant spouse, seen but rarely heard, Bessie participated actively in Fred's political career, aware of its opportunities for her as well. She scanned the press and scrutinized the Commons Debates, commented on public issues, encouraged Fred's interventions, and monitored his voting record. She suggested, warned, and informed him. And Fred listened even when he failed to heed. He appreciated her "solicitude" and the "kind things" she said about his "speaking ability" and teased her about her vigilance: "I cannot forbear a smile at the closeness with which you watch my political movements. I wonder if all my constituents are as watchful – no doubt some of them are, but from vastly different motives." Your "judgment," he continued, "might not be the same if you were less interested. Love is blind & I might add credulous."[10]

Bessie was neither blind nor credulous, nor did she lack affection for Fred. She wrote to him every few days when she was absent from Ottawa, with comments and suggestions, exhorting him to "nail his colours to the wall" and not "compromise" himself. Nor did love blind her to Fred's omissions, such as his failure to vote on David Mills's proposed amendments to the Scott Act (Canada Temperance Act of 1878), criticisms he later confessed had been "right after all." While Fred appreciated "the quantity & quality" of Bessie's letters, he cautioned her that "Rome was not built in a day," and justified his actions by invoking St. Paul's recommended "reasonable cultivation" of expediency, and promised to do better in the future since "I dearly *want to please you* & have you *proud of me*."[11] Fred consulted and confided in Bessie, relating privileged information, including (later) cabinet discussion, confident of her discretion and judgment.[12] Not only was Fred impressed with Bessie's beauty, charm, and sophistication; he respected her intelligence and judgment, conscious of her role in his success.

Bessie understood the local nature of political power, its social cleavages, sensitivities, and values. She recognized the complicity of business and political power, and maintained a watching brief on local issues that might advance or impair Fred's constituents' welfare. She worried that the sale of the Cornwallis Valley Railway, in which Fred had a principal interest, to the Windsor and Annapolis Railway, in 1892, would cause Canning to become subservient to other parts of the Valley. She joined Canning's recently formed Epworth League, and insisted Fred join as well, and held him to his promise that his name would be recorded in debates on all of David Mills's future amendments to the Scott Act.[13]

Bessie made politics a family business. She discussed politics with her children. Their correspondence mirrored her interests and language.[14] They wrote their father of Mr. Holmes's painting their pantry and bathroom, and Mr. Northrup's neglect of their cow. They reported on the local weather, crops, weddings, and the progress of the Salvation Army in Canning. They shared their mother's outrage at "Mr. Dug Woodworth" [D.B. Woodworth], who they dismissed as "an unmitigated scoundrel."[15] Politics, however, rarely trumped the children's updates on their grandmother's canary, their dog Pluto's habits, their cat's health, and the antics of their unruly cow.[16]

Bessie accompanied Fred to Ottawa and participated in Parliament's opening social rituals, as Julia had done. Upon Fred's re-election in 1891, and the children safely installed in boarding school or college, Bessie and Mrs. Clarke moved to Ottawa for the 1892 parliamentary session. "I came, I saw, I conquered," Fred wrote triumphantly to Bessie after having "ransacked" Ottawa for suitable lodgings, explaining that he had just secured rooms at "$50 per month for both of us & $20 per month for your mother" at No. 8 Cliff Street. The lodging, he reassured Bessie, came complete with "conveniences," certified by Sir Charles and Lady Tupper's occupancy "a few sessions ago." Even better, he teased her, the lodgings were owned by good Methodists.[17] Unfortunately Harold's illness prevented renewal of the lodging the following year.

Bessie enjoyed Ottawa and quickly mastered its social protocol, "leaving cards personally," and never calling except on "at home" days.[18] She especially enjoyed the pageantry of parliamentary openings, followed by the Governor General's ball, the ladies dressed in evening gowns and the men in formal attire. She visited the House of Commons, especially in Fred's absence and reported on its debates, spiking her reports with information and admonition.[19] She lunched with members' wives, and established a national network of friends. Although excluded from male political culture of heavy drinking (which Fred had come to enjoy), lively music, and rowdy entertainment, her dress and deportment, her knowledge of books, theatre, and art, her patronage of orchestral societies, and her recreational interest in golf, tennis, and riding facilitated her access to refined Ottawa society.

She and Fred attended Dominion Methodist Church, located on the corner of Metcalfe and Queen Streets, reputed to be the largest Methodist church in the country, and later became a close friend of their distinguished ministers, Reverend George F. Salter, a popular lecturer and art critic, and Reverend James Henderson (1849–1923), the renowned early social gospel preacher. And it was she and Fred who introduced Laurier to Henderson at one of their dinner parties and accompanied him "incognito" to Dominion Methodist to hear Henderson's eloquent orations.[20]

Absorbed in pursuing his public career, Fred relied on Bessie's ability to manage family crises, such as Harold's deferred enrolment at Mount Allison in August 1893. Terrified that Harold's chest pain was the onset of tuberculosis, Bessie and Fred prepared to place their lives on hold. To relieve Fred's worries Bessie eschewed the 1893 parliamentary session and remained at home with her mother to supervise Harold's recovery, managing their large, drafty Old Place with very little domestic assistance. Although confident that Bessie was more than equal to the occasion, Fred urged her to secure more help and promised to return at any moment should Harold's condition become serious.[21] Bessie persisted, nonetheless, not wanting to revive Woodworth's charge that Fred neglected his parliamentary duties.

Fred's recruitment of a popular young McGill graduate, Dr. Kirkpatrick, to maintain his Canning medical practice during his parliamentary absence underscored Fred's commitment to Ottawa, a decision endorsed by his Liberal merchant friends who helped fund his 1891 purchase of the *Western Chronicle* (with a circulation of 1,750) to promote the federal and provincial parties.[22] Meanwhile Fred attended every parliamentary session, including evening sessions. A devotee of Samuel Johnson (1709–84), Fred loved repartee, controversy, and debate, especially on the estimates, "my forte – if I have any," and was "deeply interested in free trade with the United States.[23] Politicians on both sides of the House noted his assiduity and growing political prominence, and he was hailed as one of the "notable" young men who had been re-elected in 1887.[24]

Observers remarked on Fred's growing friendship with Wilfrid Laurier (1841–1919), the Liberal Party's new leader, whose temperament and policies Fred and Bessie preferred to those of "Master" Edward Blake (1833–1912), Laurier's able but aloof predecessor. Brilliant as Blake was, this "one man" party lacked appreciation of Atlantic Canada's priorities and politics. In fact, Fred preferred Sir Richard Cartwright, Blake's Ontario counterweight in the party, despite Cartwright's embarrassing dismissal of Atlantic Canada as the "rags and patches of Confederation." At least Cartwright was a freetrader and avowed opponent of the iniquitous National Policy.

Personality, policy, and style cemented Fred`s friendship with Laurier. Fred, only six years his new leader's junior, and Laurier first entered Parliament in 1874; they resided during several parliamentary terms at the Russell Hotel, and worked together for the next four decades. Pragmatists, they shared an inclusive approach to the economic, religious, and linguistic tensions that bedevilled the country.[25] Both had distanced themselves from their secessionist provincial colleagues. They were well read and educated in the classics. They were mannered and courtly; they enjoyed music, theatre, history, literature, and beautiful gardens, as did their wives, and over time they became close colleagues, neighbours, and friends. They both had an eye for attractive, intelligent women, such as Madame Émilie Lavergne and Bessie.[26] Laurier especially admired Fred's and Bessie's style and culinary sophistication, and on one occasion asked them to find him a suitable cook in England.

No one ought to have been surprised, then, by Fred's emerging prominence under Laurier's watch, especially after the party's 1891 defeat. Impressed by Fred's intelligence, industry, organizational abilities, and his reasoned, often humorous, political interventions, in 1890 Laurier made Fred the party's Nova Scotia spokesman, a role Fred used to champion provincial issues and mobilize the party's regional forces. He created the Nova Scotia Liberal Association, hired a provincial organizer, and arranged Laurier's 1891 tour of Nova Scotia. During the 1893 national Liberal convention in Ottawa, he founded the Maritime Liberal Association, with the three Liberal premiers as presidents and himself as vice-president, initiatives designed to dilute the influence of the fractious Ontario Party and strengthen Laurier's leadership.[27]

In Parliament Sir Richard Cartwright's free trade crusade made Fred a natural ally. Together they denounced the National Policy as a ploy to fill "the pockets of the combines,"[28] and the 1891 census as a colossal fraud to justify Macdonald's "bankrupt" National Policy. Fred's dismantlement of the 1891 census" findings" in Kings County so impressed Cartwright that he reprinted portions of Fred's Commons speech in his *Reminiscences*.[29] Despite Cartwright's dismissive comments on Atlantic Canada, he and Fred forged a political friendship that served Fred's national aspirations.

The party seconded Cartwright's good opinion of Fred. In 1894 it published his humour-laced speech on the budget, defending his party's "consistently patriotic" trade policy, its commitment to a revenue tariff, and its preference for parliamentary institutions, in contrast to the "cumbersome congressional system" and defunct House of Representatives."[30] In Parliament, Fred denounced the government's scandal-ridden administration, targeting the Tuppers, father and son, for their involvement in the Soulange Canal scandal. During debate on the government's Manitoba Schools Remedial Bill, he excoriated Sir Charles's hypocrisy, contrasting the bill with Tupper's 1864 Nova Scotia Free School Act, which effectively abolished French and Gaelic schools by depriving them of public funds. Labelled "the Nova Scotia interpretation of the Remedial Bill," Fred's pamphlet invited Tupper's retaliation. That, too, enhanced Fred's national profile.

As the decisive June 1896 federal election approached, Elizabeth, Harold, and Maude monitored their father's political activities with excitement and apprehension. So fearful had the faltering Conservative Party become that it had recalled Sir Charles Tupper from his high commissionership in London to lead the party into the electoral fray. The children's blood relationship to the new Conservative prime minister, and his efforts to unseat their father in Kings, made the 1896 election a public event and family contest.

Tupper's initial refusal to accept his government's defeat on 23 June 1896 prolonged the family's excitement and public speculation on Laurier's cabinet's composition. Meanwhile Laurier pondered his options. Even the Tory *Halifax Herald* conceded that Fred would enter the cabinet, but without portfolio.[31] Once Tupper capitulated and the Governor General asked Laurier to form a government, Fred was among the first to receive a portfolio. He was to be Laurier's minister of militia and defence, a position sought by more than one of his party's recently elected members, though Fred himself would have preferred trade and commerce. That post went to his friend, Sir Richard Cartwright.

Fred's appointment required a reordering of family life, a task that fell largely to Bessie. Fred and Bessie understood political life's social imperatives, to hear and be heard, to see and be seen, to receive and dispense hospitality. They knew, too, the unforgiving perils of absence. That meant managing local and national claims, coordinating their residence in Ottawa, where Bessie's social skills counted, with personal and constituency considerations, so important in retaining a solid local base. Above all, they resolved to keep the family together.

Finding proper family quarters to accommodate Fred's almost continuous presence in Ottawa raised important questions. Should Canning or Ottawa be their principal residence? If it were to be Ottawa, where and what sort of accommodation would be required? Should they have a house or a flat? Should they rent or buy? Would Mrs. Clarke accompany them? And how would they maintain and care for the Old Place during their Ottawa residence? And what would they do with their recently incorporated F.W. Borden Company, the corporate umbrella that sheltered their family's local business activities and funded their family economy? And all these considerations were affected by the family's regional sense of belonging and the precarious nature of politics.

A compromise solved their dilemma: they would maintain two residences, at least for a time. Ottawa would be their principal residence during the parliamentary session. They would rent rooms in Ottawa until they could find a suitable house. Meanwhile, Mrs. Clarke would maintain their Canning residence, and they would spend as much time there as they could spare, especially during the late spring, summer, and early fall. As for the family business, it would be renamed the R.W. Kinsman Company and be managed, or, rather, mismanaged, by Richard Kinsman. Despite the company's new name Fred remained its principal shareholder and Kinsman its temporary administrator, until that time in which Harold could assume a larger role in shaping its direction.[32]

The children were now young adults, though still dependent on the family's material support. Lizzie was almost twenty-two and remained at home after completing her year in Boston, a hostage of gender and class that placed most public careers beyond the pale of elite women. Harold was twenty and about to begin his last year at Mount Allison before entering McGill's Faculty of Medicine. At seventeen Maude had just completed her first year at Mount Allison's Ladies' College. While Bessie and Fred agreed to keep the family together, Bessie managed the exigencies of domestic life, foreseen and unforeseen.

Fred found the transition from Opposition MP to minister more taxing than he had anticipated, not because he lacked administrative ability, but his department came with an aged, though respected, deputy minister who was set in his ways, often ill, and committed to policies that Fred wished to change. More frustrating still, Fred's deputy minister had installed friends and relatives in key positions in the department. Recalled to Ottawa almost immediately after taking his oath of office for a short parliamentary session to approve the government's outstanding estimates, Fred spent much of the 1896 summer visiting militia camps. The rest of the time he spent in his West Block offices, with his private secretary, Henry Whidden Brown, his twenty-eight-year-old maternal cousin, and former bank clerk,[33] mastering the intricacies of his job, establishing a departmental library, and responding to a voracious horde of patronage seekers.

Little more than six months after Fred entered the cabinet, a rail accident prolonged his transition, obliging him to remain in Canning for an extended, painful convalescence. On 26 January 1897, upon his return to Ottawa from a meeting in Halifax of the Tariff Commission, the Inter-Colonial Railway's express train left the track at Palmer's Pond about two kilometres from Dorchester, New Brunswick, and plunged over a fifty-foot embankment, killing two persons and injuring many others.[34] Badly cut about the head and face, Fred was taken to Memramcook's Windsor Hotel, where Dr. Edouard Gaudet (1857–1920) bandaged his cuts. Anxious to continue his trip to Ottawa to attend to Bessie, who was ill, Fred downplayed his injuries. Expecting to be back to work in three weeks, he soon found that his injuries were more severe than he had imagined, leaving him with severe back pain and a neck injury, accompanied by neuralgia and toothache (teeth were a family problem)[35] that kept him from his office for six months. The prime minister advised Fred to take time to recover, a year if necessary.

The press was less patient than Laurier, and began speculating on Fred's retirement and possible replacements, rumours spread by the Opposition and hopeful Liberal replacements. Their speculation fuelled Fred's determination to return to Ottawa as soon as possible, and earlier than his doctors advised. In the interim W.S. Fielding, the minister of finance, followed by Richard Cartwright, his close friend and colleague, directed his department and kept him informed, aided by his private secretary, and Major-General William Julius Gascoigne, the militia's general officer commanding.

Meanwhile, Bessie monitored Fred's health, sensitive to his desire to minimize his injury, avert press speculation, and return to his office in three months. "Poor Daddy is suffering most awfully from tooth ache and neuralgia," Bessie wrote to Harold. She noted that his teeth were loose, and that he was often "almost crazy with pain" and unable to work or sleep. "Tonight," Bessie explained, he became "so pale that I ordered brandy & gave him a lot & at least it helped him sleep." Dissatisfied "with the way" Fred was "getting on" and with Canning's medical services, toward the end of February Bessie made an executive decision.[36] They would go south to Laurel-in-the-Pines, a popular winter resort in Lakewood, New Jersey, where Fred could obtain better medical care.[37] Fred's convalescence afforded him time to consider ways and means to remedy his department's deficiencies, reorder his personal affairs, disengage from his Canning banking arrangements, and put the Kinsman Company on the right track.

His return to Ottawa was prolonged further by Parliament's prorogation after a West Block roof fire soaked his and other ministers' books and papers.[38] Even more regrettable, Fred's accident prevented him and Bessie from attending London's spectacular Diamond Jubilee planned for June 1897 to mark the sixtieth anniversary of Queen Victoria's accession to the throne. One of a growing number of popular public spectacles focused on royalty, history, and tradition, the Jubilee was to be staged with pomp and pageantry, a spectacle designed to bolster support for the monarchy, and inspire and reinforce loyalty, pride, and patriotism.[39] Fred and Bessie loved pomp and circumstance. Moreover, Joseph Chamberlain, the British colonial secretary, had planned a Colonial Conference during the Jubilee in which the empire's defence was to occupy a central place on the agenda; it would have been an ideal occasion for Fred to learn and contribute. Fred and Bessie's only consolation was that Harold had been selected to join Canada's Coronation Contingent and would represent the family.

Chapter Seven

Harold

The family's expectations of Harold were clear from birth. They had named their 161-ton sailing ship, built in 1890 at Baxter's Harbour, the *Harold L. Borden*. When the ship came to port in Halifax in 1892, Fred insisted that Harold and Bessie meet him there, to christen the vessel.[1] Harold had little difficulty fulfilling his family's expectations. An example of occupational heredity, Harold had shadowed his father's educational and vocational trajectory. He had joined the militia when he was only seventeen years old, written partisan articles for the Liberal *Western Chronicle*, and helped manage the family business, overseeing work and workmen.[2] And he intended to follow his father, grandfather, Uncle Gus, and Great Uncle Edward Brown into the medical profession. He also had an interest in public service and business.

Harold's appointment to the Canadian Jubilee Contingent sparked predictable charges of favouritism from political opponents and disappointed applicants. Explain as Fred might that the selection committee had chosen Harold during Fred's convalescence and without his intervention, few people believed him. And, given the selection committee's composition, Fred's intervention had scarcely been necessary. Even so, Harold was not an unreasonable choice. A keen, educated young officer in the county's Canadian Hussars, Harold had joined the Hussars as a private in 1893 and had attended every subsequent summer camp (following the 1897 Jubilee he had obtained a first-class certificate from the Royal School of Calvary and been commissioned a second lieutenant).[3] What seemed less defensible was the selection of three Kings County candidates, Harold, E.M. Beckwith, and William Dorman, all from certified Liberal families.[4]

Affordability was a consideration. Clothing for the Jubilee cost Harold's family an estimated $68.13[5] (equal to about $1,000 in today's purchasing power) including Jubilee uniform, jacket, trousers, pantaloons, hose, and miscellaneous items procured from the military tailors, Hamburger Roger and Company, at London's 30 King Street. There were also supplementary personal expenditures, entertainment, and family gifts, including a scarf for his mother. Since the pageant was scheduled for June 1897, Harold wrote his final Mount Allison examinations under great pressure before joining the Canadian Jubilee Contingent's training camp, unaware of his examination results and graduating from Mount Allison *in absentia*.

An adventurous, idealistic young man, Harold was deeply impressed by the Diamond Jubilee's celebration of physical and cultural power. Staged in the heart of imperial London, the capital of the "world's greatest empire," the Jubilee warned a hostile world of the strength and solidarity of the Queen's domain, its success vindicated by its size, wealth, diversity, and allegiance. The spectacle's triumphant rhetoric, patriotic iconography, and intoxicating martial music (and Harold loved music), called for bonding and commitment and causes that appealed to Harold's muscular Christianity and the empire's potential "power for good."

Wilfrid Laurier, Canada's newly minted prime minister, was in his element. He had once contemplated an acting career, and during the Jubilee he played his scripted role with a skill, elegance, and conviction that captivated the British public. The Jubilee represented Canada, the empire's senior dominion, as an example of enlightened imperial rule, a country in revolt when Queen Victoria ascended the throne now happily united under Laurier, its loyal, eloquent, Catholic, francophone prime minister, recently knighted and the embodiment of the empire's virtue and promise.

On 22 June 1897 Sir Wilfrid Laurier, accompanied by a contingent of Canada's scarlet-clad North-West Mounted Police and two hundred cavalry troops, dressed in scarlet tunics, blue serge pantaloons, and stiff brimmed, peak hats, headed the colonial component of the climactic royal procession as it marched from Buckingham Palace to St. Paul's Cathedral. Trading upon his popularity, Laurier exhibited comparable leadership at the Colonial Conference on imperial defence, trade, and political unity that followed the Jubilee, skilfully extracting maximum advantages for minimum commitment.

Harold's Diamond Jubilee venture was a source of family pride and inspiration. His Jubilee medal, his descriptions of the intoxicating spectacle, and his personal experiences fed the family's royalist sentiments. They savoured Laurier's recognition of Harold during the event, drawing him out and chatting with him. Carefully tutored by Bessie in the rules of courtly decorum, Harold was a conscientious student who assured his mother that he had tried to avoid any errors in "social etiquette."[6] For the next few years Harold remained at the centre of the family's aspirations, his story told largely through his small daily diary.

Upon Harold's return to Canada in July 1897 he spent the rest of that summer at militia camp before registering in McGill University's Faculty of Medicine for a four-year undergraduate program leading to an MD, CM degree. Harold was one of 403 students registered that year in McGill's medical faculty, the university's largest faculty. A quarter of the faculty's students (92) came from the Maritime provinces. Medical degrees from McGill, the premier medical faculty in Canada, were recognized at par, without examinations in Britain and Ireland, and its students benefited from its recently expanded and renovated facilities,[7] gifts from two of its wealthy benefactors, John Thomas Molson (1837–1910) and Lord Strathcona (1820–1914), the university's chancellor. Situated close to the newly constructed (1893) Royal Victoria Hospital, its medical faculty boasted laboratories for pathology, physiology, histology (with 50 microscopes), and pharmacology, a dissecting room, anatomical museum, bone room, and library.

McGill's medical reputation, and its Maritime connections (specifically its scientific ties with Mount Allison), made McGill an obvious place for Harold's medical education. No less important was its proximity to his family in Ottawa. Fully recovered from his rail accident, Fred had returned to Ottawa, where the family had rented and eventually purchased a house on Wilbrod Street. They had also rented a house with a suite of rooms in Montreal at 111 Stanley Street for Harold during his first year at university. The accommodation came complete with meals, a housekeeper, laundry service, quiet study space, and place to receive friends for tea, dinner, or a chat. So congenial were Harold's arrangements that he and his friends considered renting comparable quarters the following year, as an alternative to a standard student boarding house.

If Harold's parents' protective instincts explain his enrolment at McGill, Fred and Bessie underestimated their son's maturity and survival skills. He had spent several years in boarding school and in college and university residences, and months in summer military camps. Nor had he any difficulty finding a standard boarding house, on 57 Union Street, when the Stanley Street lease expired. A social animal, Harold was soon surrounded by a coterie of former Mount Allison classmates, including his good friend William Edgar Rowley, from Marysville, New Brunswick.[8] Moreover Bessie, Lizzie, and Maude had not hesitated to leave Harold to his own devices for several weeks during their winter escape to Baltimore and Washington, DC, in 1898.[9]

But whether in Canning, Montreal, or Ottawa, Harold's family was never far away. Six daily trains linked Ottawa to Canada's dynamic economic, social, and cultural metropole, providing transportation, opportunity, and visibility for Canada's socially ambitious elite. The Stanley Street house was also a family facility that housed Bessie, Lizzie, and Maud during their visits to see Harold, to shop, or to entertain or be entertained by their friends.[10] Occasionally even Fred stayed at the Stanley Street House when he had a Montreal meeting or dinner party, or was just passing through. Normally he stayed at the Windsor Hotel if he were between trains.

Harold's McGill diary provides insight into his character, routine, education, and family life. It records his financial, social, and intellectual activities. It lists his expenses on dress, health, hygiene, religion, education, travel, entertainment (even visits to a fortune teller), gifts, and postage, a record that he tallied weekly, monthly, and yearly, and from which he compiled his financial reports to Bessie, the family banker, justifying his expenditures and making his financial requests with the precision of an accountant. While none of Bessie's children lacked funds to meet their physical needs and social aspirations, all were prudent and thrifty, and were required to account for their expenditures.

Harold's diary was also an itemized moral inventory of his personal failures and his resolutions for reform, an introspective analysis more typical of his mother than his father. Contrary to the entertaining stereotypes of late nineteenth-century medical students as unruly pranksters,[11] Harold was a disciplined, conscientious student who routinely "plugged" six to eight hours a day on his courses, relieved by brief lapses that lay heavily on his conscience. Studies in physiology, dissection, and bone anatomy occupied a large portion of his time and interest. Dr. Francis Shepherd's lectures on anatomy and histology were frequent casualties of Harold's battle with early morning classes. Novels were a favourite distraction, an indulgence he renounced for weeks to compensate for occasional neglect of his studies. His literary temptations were contemporary British authors, especially those who wrote about adventure, morality, history, and religion,[12] whose books he bought or borrowed from libraries in Montreal and Ottawa. As he browsed bookshops, he kept a sharp eye for rare editions for his father.[13]

Harold's physical stature and gregarious, genial personality gave him the air of a friendly giant. Restless and athletic, he craved physical activity. He played tennis, football, and hockey. He bicycled, fished, golfed, and was known as "a particularly fine horseman." During the Canadian Amateur Athletics championship games held in Montreal in September 1898 he competed in running, jumping, and the hammer throw.[14] In the cold months, Harold spent hours at the rink with his friends, sometimes skating twice a day. When Lizzie, Maude, and his mother visited they joined him at the rink. Harold often met young women at the rink. True to form, he maintained a careful inventory of his skating partners, their names, the number of times he skated with each, and those he walked home, respectfully identified as Miss Archibald, Miss Davies, Miss Monk, Miss Finley, and Miss Thompson.

Harold enjoyed theatre and concerts and accompanied his girlfriends to the Montreal Art Gallery.[15] Handsome, well-mannered, and well-connected, he was a popular dinner guest, euchre partner, or participant in parlour games, welcomed to the homes of hopeful parents. He responded to invitations in writing, and wrote letters of thanks, as Bessie had taught him. An equally welcome guest at coeducational parties, on one occasion, a Charles Dickens Party, he won the prize for his knowledge of one of his family's favourite authors.[16] Matrimony was never far from Harold's fantasies. He pondered several possibilities in Montreal, Ottawa, and St. Andrews, New Brunswick, though Madam Amene, the Montreal fortuneteller he and William Edgar Rowley had consulted, predicted he would not marry until he was thirty-three![17]

Harold became a founding member of the McGill chapter of Delta Upsilon (DU). Since membership entailed additional expenditures, Harold agreed to membership only after receiving his father's blessing and extra funding. That secured, Harold represented McGill at the DU convention in Philadelphia held 19–22 October 1898, the convention that accepted McGill into its fraternity,[18] where he enjoyed the convention's literary session and banquet at Swarthmore, more for the "nice girls" that he met than for the food and drink.[19] Meanwhile he maintained an active correspondence with girlfriends, former Mount Allison classmates, and chums from home and militia camps, and housed friends travelling through Montreal.

Most Sunday mornings and evenings Harold was found in church, whether he was living at home, militia camp, or university. In Montreal Harold worshipped at St. James Methodist church, the large dynamic Methodist congregation on rue Sainte-Catherine, sometimes accompanied by a former Mount Allison classmate. Harold enjoyed church music and congregational singing and was especially sensitive to Christianity's social imperatives. He budgeted for regular offerings, church fairs, and mission Sundays. Although he smoked a pipe, his diary provides no indication that he drank. Strick Methodists, however, were unlikely to have condoned his purchase of alcohol and cigars for Christmas gifts. Harold shared his father's and mother's belief in a patrician moral economy in which privilege entailed social responsibility and service, an obligation to lead and contribute "in proportion to our blessings."[20] As the son of a notable family, committed to a caring profession, civic duty, and with a penchant for business, Harold remained acutely conscious of his family's expectations and political obligations. At university he scoured his fraternity's papers for political news, and at militia camp he retained a "listening brief" for political intelligence useful to his father, aware that people saw him as a conduit to his father.

Bessie financed Harold's room, board, tuition, laboratory fees, equipment, books, and allowance. But she was more than his generous banker. A special affection bound her to her son. They corresponded regularly. She visited him often and advised him frequently. When she came to Montreal they skated, attended the theatre, and had long talks. Her affection carried a heavy weight of obligation as well. When he offended, as he rarely did, her disapproval was painful until she was appeased. Bessie was generous, understanding, and slow to anger, but when she was offended, she was not to be crossed, a rule the family respected, not least her equable husband and affectionate son.

Chapter Eight

The Grand Tour

Preoccupied as Bessie was with the demands of Harold's upbringing, she was no less attentive to that of her daughters. Education, E.P. Thompson has written, is an important instrument of middle-class "cultural hegemony,"[1] a measure of a family's social reach, and an investment in its children's future. Bessie and Fred were determined to provide their children with a broad education, appropriate to their gender, class, and interests, an investment in their formation and a favourable marriage. For that, Lizzie and Maude's education included "the grand tour."

Once a ritualized rite of passage for aristocratic children, in the nineteenth century the grand tour had become accessible to the sons and daughters of the affluent middle class, facilitated by more convenient, affordable transportation, accommodation, and "packaged" tours, notably those offered by Thomas Cook & Son, and guidebooks such as *Baedeker's*. Grand tours were even endorsed by Canadian Methodist leaders.[2] Tailored to specific incomes and interests, tours were class markers designed to sharpen a sense of identity and belonging and provide a conversational knowledge of art, literature, music, and history.[3] The "Canadian" grand tour focused on Britain, and its classical Western European roots, with little regard for contemporary European politics.[4]

Information on Lizzie's and Maude's grand tour is fragmentary, derived from a few extant letters, their scarcity a casualty of Bessie's habit of sending "a batch" of correspondence to absent family members, notably Harold in Montreal and Fred in Ottawa. According to these fragments, Lizzie and Maude left Boston in April 1899 aboard the *S.S. New England* for Liverpool, their Boston departure preceded by a large family party that included their father, mother, Grandma Clarke, Harold and his classmate George Johnson, Uncle Gus, Aunt Hattie, William

North, his wife, and their son and daughter, with whom Lizzie had boarded in 1894. There Fred and Bessie were relieved to meet Greta Finlay, "an English born woman from Montreal," a "Heaven sent protector," whose cabin adjoined the girls' and who promised to see them placed safely in the care of Miss Price, their English chaperone and tour guide.[5]

Lizzie and Maude's year-long, grand tour began and ended in England. Upon their arrival in Liverpool, a "mature" Miss Price met and brought them by rail to London, where she booked accommodation, guides, tours, and educational, cultural, and recreational activities. After a brief stop in London, Miss Price escorted the girls to Bournemouth for a few weeks to get their "land legs," choosing a destination and program that reflected her age and tastes rather than Elizabeth's and Maude's.[6] Situated about 150 kilometres southwest of London, Bournemouth was "in the process of becoming" a Hampshire health and sea resort, a place that Elizabeth described as having been "a fine sand heap sixty years ago." By 1899 the town boasted beaches, gardens, an "invalid walk," and a small artists and writers' colony, though much to the girls' disappointment there were few shops, historic sites, or young men.

According to Maude, a glance at the town's denizens explained why "young men don't thrive well here," populated as it was by elderly "damsels" and "bushels of invalids," captains, majors, and colonels, bishops, and bishops' brothers. All seemed to be in good health but "ancient and reduced in circumstances," individuals who passed their days discussing wills and what they and their friends might expect as small legacies from great uncles and maiden aunts, and who considered a "person of thirty almost too young to go out alone."[7] Maude did not like to contemplate their combined ages.

Clearly Elizabeth and Maude were not much taken with Bournemouth, an impression reinforced by meeting a recently married homesick American woman from Baltimore who was delighted to talk to someone "from the other side," especially two young women who had spent the past winter in Washington and Baltimore and were familiar with the Walter's Art Gallery. A weekend visit from Miss Price's adored brother, Hermie, confirmed Elizabeth and Maude's gloomy assessment of social life in Bournemouth: he was an "'haffable" man, Maude explained to her mother, "who lifted his head only once or twice an hour," and then only when spoken to. All of which drove Elizabeth, not one to "shilly-shally," back to her guidebooks to negotiate an agreeable escape.[8]

Well-schooled in British history and literature, Elizabeth and Maude chose the Isle of Wight, to see Alfred Tennyson's summer house and

Carisbrooke Castle, where Charles I had been imprisoned, a choice fortified by economic considerations. Cheaper room and board on the Isle of Wight might enhance their chance of extending their tour to Italy, the mecca of all grand tours. After the Isle of Wight, they travelled to Scotland, as planned, spending most of their time in Edinburgh and St. Andrews, visiting historic sites, hiking, putting on the links, shopping, and taking a short sewing course taught by a Mrs. Jack, who wrote with a quill.[9] Edinburgh and St. Andrews offered other curious characters, younger males, and opportunities for flirtation; according to Harold, Maude was especially adept at "conquests."[10] All served as grist for entertaining letters home, retailing tales of the "upper classes," and those aspiring to that status, all "bristling with good manners."

One of Maude's favourite stories entailed golfing alongside "the great [A.J.] Balfour[11] and Mr. and Mrs. [Margot] Asquith."[12] Lizzie and Maude watched closely as Margot, dressed in her pale green suit, upheld her reputation as a "terror" on the golf course. Amused by Mrs. Asquith's reputation, Maude recounted a much-told tale of a grumpy old gentleman's opinion that three things ought to be forbidden on a golf course were women, dogs, and Margot Asquith. Similarly, they related the the apocryphal story that Margot Asquith was the suffragette model in E.F. Benson's popular novel *Dodo: A Detail of the Day* (1893),[13] and that, during a luncheon with Benson, Margot responded to his mention of the novel with "Did you indeed write a book? How clever of you."[14] All were stories to amuse her parents and Grandma Clarke.

In early January 1900 Lizzie and Maude returned to London with Miss Price and five or six other girls. In London Lizzie and Maude were received by Lord and Lady Strathcona and probably other family acquaintances.[15] More memorable was the imperial city's patriotic reaction to the outbreak of the South African War in October 1899, and London's tribal response to the British defeats of "Black Week" (10–15 December 1899), an imperial moment, comparable to Harold's Diamond Jubilee venture. But, judged by their fragmentary correspondence, Maude and Lizzie were more interested in London fashions, and their escape from the city's flu epidemic.[16]

Details of Lizzie's and Maude's continental journey are sparce. We know only that in February 1900 Elizabeth, Maude, and Miss Price left London for Brussels, and stopped over in Bruges, on their way to Paris where they remained for several weeks, *en pension* at the Hôtel Jean Bart, on rue Jean Bart in the Quartier Latin. In Paris Thomas Cook guides secured tickets for them to visit galleries, museums, churches, and historic sites, and Maude and Lizzie practised their French and enrolled in a cooking course.[17] In leaving Paris they had only two regrets:

their failure to visit the academy of Rodolphe Julian (1839–1907)[18] and the art studios of William-Adolphe Bouguereau (1825–1905), and the brevity of their Parisian stay, too short to perfect their French, as they had hoped. Here, Lizzie wrote her mother, "a person is hardly considered educated who cannot speak two or three languages"; a deficiency they resolved to remedy in the years ahead.[19]

In April 1900 Lizzie and Maude were back in London, to arrange and await their passage home, though still under Miss Price's surveillance. Before they left England, they made an overnight trip to Bemerton, Wiltshire, to see St. Andrew's Church and Wardour Castle, Tilbury. Their visit, Lizzie wrote her father, included enjoying a pleasant tea, gathering primroses and bluebells, visiting St. Andrew's Church: George Herbert's old church and rectory gardens, and St. John's neo-Gothic church nearby, a "familiar" romantic architectural style reminiscent of Ottawa's Parliament Buildings.[20] So impressed were they by St. Andrew's bell tower, its ancient "leper window," and the rectory garden, they renounced dinner for evensong.

The next day a train and a two-mile hike brought them to Wardour Castle, a reconstructed medieval structure partially destroyed during the English Civil War, restored by the Arundel family in the eighteenth century as an eclectic tourist site that displayed paintings by Rubens, van Dyke, del Sarto, Michelangelo, and Titian, as well as Crown Derby and Royal Worcester plates, books, furniture, and silver. It also included a lock of Queen Elizabeth's hair, which Lizzie felt would interest her parents. Lizzie and Maude even managed to evade Miss Price's vigilance to "investigate some of the old curiosity shops" and learn more about English china. There, Lizzie saw a violin, inscribed with the date 1770, for only 95 shillings, certain it would interest her father.[21] A budding anglophile, Elizabeth was impressed with English people "of a certain class" and their knowledge of art, artifacts, and Italy, which they seemed to know better than their own island. There was, she concluded, "something behind English titles."[22] Her father and mother needed little convincing, though their appreciation of English society was more pragmatic and nuanced than that of the young, exuberant Elizabeth.

Enthralled as Elizabeth was with English life, she considered the English often "a little behind the times," her criticism tinged by a certain patriotic nostalgia. It was apple blossom time at home, and while Lizzie enjoyed English birdsong, wildlife, and gardens, she felt nothing compared to Nova Scotia mayflowers, roses, and apple blossoms. In her view English spring flowers, though generally pretty, had "no perfume." English birds, she conceded, at least their skylarks and thrushes, could probably sing better than Nova Scotia birds.[23]

During Lizzie's and Maude's absence Fred, Bessie, and Grandma Clarke wrote regularly of home, family, friends, and "the goings on in Ottawa."[24] Harold's letters recounted college gossip, and teased and chided his sisters. Fred and Bessie had planned to join the girls in Europe for Christmas, but the South African War made that and their alternative trip to Boston impossible.[25] Even Bessie's promise of a large Christmas box with food and family presents (to which Harold had contributed) became a war casualty owing to the girls' uncertain location. Instead, they simply dispatched "filthy lucre."[26] The war had made their father a captive of his Ottawa office, especially after the government's mid-December decision to send a second instalment of troops to South Africa, a mounted unit. And this time Harold's offer to join the contingent had been accepted.

Lizzie and Maude knew that Harold had volunteered to join the first contingent, but they were shocked to learn that his offer to join the second contingent had been accepted. Only ten days or so before Harold's fateful decision, he had written them a Christmas letter, teasingly addressed to Lizzie and "the cherubic enfant," as he called his younger sister, owing to her cheerful round face. His sixteen-page letter, penned from his fraternity house on 26 McTavish Street, betrayed no sense of restlessness or desire for military service. It was simply a gossipy "college man's letter," peppered with Latin references, teasing Maud for "trifling with human affection" in Scotland, and recounting his own military, sporting, cultural, and romantic exploits. He welcomed the first snow, the cold weather, and the rink's opening, ending with greetings from their mutual friends, and affectionately signed "Votre frère toujours aimé."

After Harold's breezy Christmas letter, Lizzie and Maude could scarcely believe that their "pride" and "treasure"[27] was in Halifax awaiting dispatch to South Africa. Their first instinct was to return home, to see Harold before he left, but the difficulty of procuring immediate passage persuaded them they could never reach Halifax before Harold's departure, and they resigned themselves to continuing their tour.[28] Suddenly the war had become a disturbing, personal reality.

Harold's enlistment ought not to have been a surprise, given his sense of family responsibility and his earlier attempt to volunteer. A little more than a month before the war began Harold had replaced Major J.W. Ryan in command of his cavalry unit during their summer camp at Aldershot and had been commended for his excellent work.[29] A recently minted militia major in Kings County's Canadian Hussars,[30] Harold had volunteered immediately for Canada's first contingent.

Much to his parents' relief, however, that oversubscribed infantry contingent needed no cavalry.

"Where is the son of the Minister of Militia?," the *Halifax Herald* had asked in accusatory bold, black letters the day following the dispatch of Canada's first contingent. Harold had been stung by the *Halifax Herald*'s veiled accusation of cowardice, even though he knew that the *Herald*'s taunt was designed to rekindle criticism of his selection for the Jubilee Contingent, to attack Laurier's initial reluctance to send troops to South Africa, and to remind its readers that both he and Laurier had marched in the Diamond Jubilee parade. Not only had Harold marched in the parade but he had identified with the empire's might and moral mission, reinforced by stories of heroic adventure, located in Africa, and rewarded with patriotic gratitude.

No sooner had the Canadian government authorized a second contingent than the *Herald* renewed its attack, targeting Harold once again, publishing his name in large black print as one who ought to go to the front.[31] Affronted by the newspaper's accusation, Harold volunteered at once for the second contingent, a unit composed of two cavalry battalions (mounted infantry) and a field artillery brigade. Once more Harold's parents tried to dissuade him, arguing the folly of disrupting his medical studies and risking injury and permanent disability.[32] But Harold remained adamant; his parents became resigned but never reconciled to his decision, his father haunted by a premonition that things might go badly. Harold had also recruited ten summer comrades from his unit to accompany him to South Africa and for whom he felt responsible, men who admired him, moved by his promise never to ask them to do anything he would not do himself.

Harold was as good as his word. Assigned to the First Battalion, Canadian Mounted Rifles (redesignated the Royal Canadian Dragoons in August 1900), Harold served under the command of François Lessard. He knew and respected Lessard, as did most of Lessard's officers and men. Lessard's battalion consisted of two squadrons, each containing four troops, each commanded by a lieutenant, half of whom were drawn from the permanent militia. Lessard knew Harold from militia camps and had no hesitation asking him, an active militia major, to command B Squadron's Troop 4 with the rank of lieutenant, and subsequently named Harold the B Squadron's second senior lieutenant. Harold's forty-man troop came from Sussex, Saint John, and Canning. B Squadron's other troop commanders were Francis Young, Charles Van Straubenzee, and Richard Turner, under the command of Major Victor A.S. Williams.

Elizabeth and Maude had no idea how long it would take to dispatch Harold's unit. The second contingent's mounted composition and the shortage of troop transport delayed the dispatch of the contingent's 1,230 men, 18 guns and 1,124 horses, which were shipped in three instalments, with Harold's unit among the last to leave. Even after Harold's transport, the *Milwaukee*, a bare, iron-decked freighter, reached Halifax on 7 February, it took more than two weeks to refit it. Had Lizzie and Maude known of the delay, they would have had ample time to see their brother before he left Halifax on 21 February, a month after his contingent's first instalment had sailed.

Harold's delay enabled him to drill his troop on the Halifax Common and visit his maternal Great Aunt Julia [Brown] and her husband, Dr. H.O. McLatchy, a prominent Halifax physician.[33] It also gave him precious time with his apprehensive parents, each time they came to the city for a troopship's departure, including the vessel carrying the "Strathcona Horse," recruited at the same time as the second contingent. Harold's delay also gave the *Halifax Herald* time to circulate false rumours of tensions between him and his squadron commander, Major V.A.S. Williams.[34]

Nothing made Harold's final departure easier for his parents, seeing their only son leave with his favourite horse and his dog, which he had stowed aboard;[35] their anxieties were magnified by the Canadians' costly casualties at Paardeberg Drift on 18 February, just days before Harold sailed. That battle and its sequel a week later were Canada's bloodiest military engagements since the War of 1812. Added to all this was Fred's unshakable sense of forboding. Harold tried to relieve the tension of the final moments by confiding to his mother that "the goal and ambition of his life" was to earn a Victoria Cross.[36] So fearful were Bessie and Fred for Harold's safety that Fred cabled Lord Strathcona, asking him to have Harold transferred to some safe noncombatant position,[37] a futile intervention and one that Harold would not have appreciated.

Fred and Bessie had other worries as well. In fact, the first seven months of 1900 made it a veritable *annus horribilis*.[38] Lizzie and Maude would not return to Montreal until 19 May 1900, aboard the Dominion Lines' 5,700-ton passenger ship *Vancouver*. Meanwhile Fred was absorbed in the dispatch of more troops, managing the political fallout, and coping with personal, financial, and administrative crises that threatened to drive him from public life, leaving Bessie to cover and compensate for his oversights, absences, and heavy drinking. Fred was no longer a member in good standing with Canning's Temperance Society.

Fred and William Mulock, the postmaster general, had led the cabinet faction insisting on a Canadian contingent. Their success left Fred with the formidable task of supervising the recruitment, equipment, and dispatch of Canada's first expeditionary force, all accomplished in less than three weeks. Fred was in his element. Although a man of almost inexhaustible energy, his task was made more difficult by his department's skeletal, inexperienced administrative staff and its quarrelsome general officer commanding the Canadian militia, Major-General E.T.H. Hutton. The Opposition, too, was relentless in its criticism and calls for his resignation and replacement, citing his poor health, exhaustion, and conflicts of interest.

Fred had barely recovered from this bruising ordeal when the government authorized a second (the Canadian Mounted Rifles and Artillery), then a third consignment of troops (the Strathcona's Horse). Both contingents were mounted units, which meant securing men, horses, and transport. The fatigue, strain, and responsibility of mobilizing a first, second, and third contingent stretched Fred's nerves and tolerance to their limit, which he sought to relieve with drink. Meanwhile, his relationship with General Hutton had reached a point of no return. Either he or the general would have to go. In the ensuing political contest Fred placed his career on the line and Hutton left.[39] Fred had triumphed, but his victory exacted a heavy toll.

At the same time, Fred's R.W. Kinsman Company, the corporate entity that funded his family's increasing financial requirements, was in difficulty, a casualty of its under-capitalization and the neglect and misjudgment of its manager, Richard Kinsman. Fred liked to keep a hand in things, but the war left little time to advise, monitor, and constrain Kinsman. All he could do was to postpone decisions and finance the company's operating shortfalls from his limited personal resources and from war contracts. Fred's back-up plan was to replace Kinsman with Harold as soon as Harold completed his medical studies.

Grief and conflict added to Fred's distress during the early months of 1900. His Uncle Andrew's death on 28 March, at the age of 85, broke a link with his father's generation. For Fred, family mattered deeply, and his Uncle Andrew was his favourite uncle and proxy parent following his father's death in 1875. An unshakable political ally, his Uncle Andrew had supported him even when his son, Robert Laird Borden, contested a Halifax seat for the Conservatives in 1896.[40] Nor did Robert object to his father's choice. In comparable circumstances Robert might have done the same.

Then just as things seemed to settle down, and Lizzie and Maude had returned from their grand tour, the Conservative member of Parliament for Jacques Cartier, F.D. Monk, rose in the House of Commons to accuse Fred of "gross and culpable negligence" in ordering and supplying

Canada's second contingent with adulterated vegetable protein emergency rations. Although Monk did not accuse Fred of profiting personally from the transaction, Monk's nineteen-point indictment held Fred constitutionally responsible for fraud and demanded his resignation. Denying any knowledge of the fraud, Fred agreed to place all papers before a parliamentary committee.

On the eve of a general election, only days short of the termination of the fifth and final session of the Seventh Parliament, the bipartisan committee's highly publicized, politically charged hearings resulted in a report exonerating the minister and his department. The report passed the Commons by a very slender majority, a measure of its unpopularity even within the Liberal Party. In finding evidence of fraud, but without assigning blame directly, the report gave the Opposition a tactical victory that left Fred alone to defend his ministry's failure.[41] Fred claimed his negligence was due to overwork and misguided confidence in his advisers, but neither explanation assuaged his political opponents.

Eleven days after the Commons voted on the controversial committee's report, Fred received the most devastating blow of his life. Harold had been killed in action at Witpoort on 16 July 1900. A week or so before his death, Harold had been hospitalized with enteric fever and had left the hospital the evening before the battle. He had been sufficiently unwell the next morning to ask Richard Turner to take over his duties. But when his squadron was ordered to support the embattled Royal Irish Fusiliers, who were attempting to repel an attack led by General Louis Botha, Harold insisted on leading his men into battle, as he had promised before leaving Canada.

Leaving their horses at the bottom of a ridge, his squadron crawled up the boulder-strewn ridge that separated them from their enemy, finding temporary cover at the top, only about 200 yards from their opponents' firing lines. Two troops, Harold's and Lieutenant John Edward Burch's (Burch was temporarily in charge of F.V. Young's second troop), were ordered to relieve the Irish. Harold and Burch stood up to lead the counterattack, and were killed, Harold instantly and Burch subsequently. Their squadron's counterattack came "at a most crucial moment" and forced the Boers to retreat, and "doubtless saved many lives,"[42] but exacted a terrible price.[43]

Feelings of shock, anger, bitterness, and vengeance spread through Harold's troop, squadron, and battalion, quickly infecting the Irish and supporting imperial troops. Quite apart from Harold's public prominence, the only son of Canada's minister of militia had earned the respect and admiration of his men and his fellow and superior officers.

In early May, Harold and Richard Turner had led five men across the Vet River, swimming across the river under fire, with their rifles above their heads, to drive Boer snipers from positions, impeding their units' progress. Their courage and leadership had been recognized in military dispatches. Later that month Harold had been mentioned again in dispatches for his part in the capture of three Boer wagons at Driefontein. His squadron's commanding officer, V.A.S. Williams, described Harold as one of his most competent, reliable, and popular officers. Even General E.T.H. Hutton, who had no love for Harold's father, had twice brought Harold's "intrepid and gallant conduct" to the attention of the commander-in-chief, Lord Robert.[44]

The next evening, in a moving lantern ceremony conducted by the brigade's chaplain, Reverend Gardiner, Harold and Burch were buried near a farm at Rietvlei, wrapped in "Canadian flags," which Lieutenant-Colonel T.B.D. Evans had procured in Pretoria.[45] Canada's two mounted battalions attended the "sad and impressive scene" together with representatives from imperial units, especially the Irish Fusiliers, their anger fed by rumours, bitterness, and solemn vows of vengeance. One unsubstantiated story contended that Harold had been shot by an Irish American sniper, fighting with the Boers, who the Canadians captured subsequently and handed over to the Irish Fusiliers, who executed the captive without trial.

The next day, Lord Roberts, whose only son had been killed earlier in the war, cabled the awful news to the Governor General's office, followed shortly by a personal note to Fred. Given the Governor General's temporary absence, his military secretary sent Roberts's cable directly to the militia department. A brief discussion persuaded the deputy minister, Colonel L.-F. Pinault, and the director of stores, Colonel D.A. Macdonald, that Laurier should break the news to Fred.[46] It was late afternoon, toward the end of the long, seven-month, tension ridden Fifth session of the Seventh Parliament; Fred was still in the House fielding Opposition questions on the war when he was called to the prime minister's office, near the parliamentary library. Devastated by the news, Fred's first thought was for Bessie, and he left immediately for home, not wanting Bessie to hear the news from any other source. Bessie had been ill for several days and Fred knew how deeply she would feel the loss of her son, the family's "treasure."[47]

The news of Harold's death spread through the House well before Laurier interrupted its proceedings to confirm the tragic news and move an adjournment out of respect for the family. In moving the resolution Laurier described Harold as a "model boy in every way," being of "great promise, athletic in figure, bright, intelligent and courageous."

In the absence of Sir Charles Tupper, the Opposition leader (and Harold's first cousin twice removed), Nicholas Flood Davin seconded the prime minister's resolution, declaring in his extravagant way, that the whole world served as an appropriate mausoleum for the heroic officer.[48] The stunned House postponed its evening's deliberations and adjourned immediately. Perhaps Robert Borden best captured the magnitude of the family's loss when he later described Harold as "a splendid young man of great promise" and "the hope and delight of his father."[49]

The House was prorogued the next day, and a devastated Fred and Bessie left for Canning with Lizzie, Maude, and Mrs. Clarke to cope with their grief. Their last family gathering had had been in Boston before Maude and Lizzie's departure for England.[50] In the absence of a body and funeral service, the family sought consolation and meaning from the flood of public and personal communications, from family, friends, neighbours, colleagues, and Harold's comrades. Newspaper headlines and black-bordered photographs announced Harold's death to the Canadian public, the partisan rhetoric and reportage suspended temporarily. In the British House of Lords, Lord Lansdowne, the British secretary of state for war, praised Harold's gallantry, and Joseph Chamberlain, the colonial secretary, seconded Lansdowne's sentiments in the Commons. The British press took up the lament. Laurier dispatched the cabled messages to Fred and Bessie in Canning. Even Queen Victoria's secretary conveyed the queen's personal condolences, noting that she had "read with great pride of his death," and requested a photograph of Harold.[51]

Public figures, journalists, neighbours, friends, relatives, and citizens expressed their sentiments in the ritualized, contemporary language of sacrifice, duty, patriotism, and loyalty to God, country, queen, and empire. They hailed Harold as a lion among men. They described his death as "the supreme honour given to martyrs," that of a true soldier who fell with his face to the enemy to bring liberty to a distant continent. They assured the bereaved family that Harold had passed from "the Army of Britain to the Army of God," and though his "light had gone" out his "halo and reflection will last through generations."[52] Poets joined the dirge proclaiming Harold an immortal hero of Canada.[53]

More personal letters came from Harold's comrades, officers, soldiers, and civilians who had worked closely with him.[54] The battalion's commanding office, François Lessard, described Harold as a quiet, unassuming, intrepid young officer. B Squadron's officer commanding, V.A.S. Williams, referred to Harold as his second-in-command, and the brigade's popular British commanding officer, E.A.H. Alderson, reaffirmed their assessments. Harold's close friend and "private banker," the Canadian Mounted Rifles' Methodist chaplain, the Reverend

William Lane, who had been the minister at Harold's Canning's Methodist church from 1884 to 1887, penned a detailed personal letter to his former parishioners.

Lane assured Fred and Bessie that Harold had been a good person who avoided the "habits of camp life," whose conduct was above reproach, attentive to religious services and interested in "the higher life." He described Harold as "an "ardent" soldier "beloved by his men," and who Lane had reason to believe the military authorities had slated for a Victoria Cross. This was Fred and Bessie's first indication that Harold had been considered for the very award that he had sought. Harold, Lane explained, had left two valises of clothes and money in Lane's safekeeping that Lane promised to return to Fred, together with three photographs taken in Cape Town by Harold's former Acacia Villa classmate, a Mr. Patterson, as well as Harold's dog, who had gone missing.[55]

Others, notably Major T.B.D. Evans, Fred's friend, and the First Canadian Mounted Rifles' able second-in-command, and E.B. Biggar, the Canadian commercial agent in South Africa, recounted Harold's last days, his death and burial, and promised to collect and return Harold's effects and care for his grave.[56] The retrieval of Harold's belongings proved more difficult than Lane, Evans, and Biggar had imagined, since several fellow officers had divided his kit among them in search of souvenirs. Some returned what they had taken, others did not. Harold's dog was never found. A few men claimed they had left money in Harold's keeping. But Lane had kept a close account of money owed to and by Harold and warned Fred to beware of unscrupulous claims.

However well-intended and helpful, the solemn rhetoric and flood of condolences failed to diminish the family's pain and sense of loss. For Bessie the most searing story was a nurse's report that, during Harold's recent illness, "in his dreams and delirium he was constantly calling for his mother."[57] For her, Harold's death was deeply personal, her only consolation was her belief in an afterlife, and her search for spiritual meaning or a higher purpose to explain her cruel loss. No amount of spiritual consolation, professional detachment, or patriotic pride could assuage Fred's loss of his only son and heir, his grief deeply grounded in their mutual affection and Fred's confidence in Harold's promising future.

Both parents sought consolation in memorialization, attempts to perpetuate Harold's memory and give meaning to his death. They began by requesting that his South African grave be marked by a proper marble headstone rather than a simple white wooden cross. The more impressive Canadian granite stones would come later.[58] They promised as well to donate a silver cup (valued at $500, and $100 to the recipient) to the Dominion Rifle Association for a memorial sharpshooting competition.[59] More ambitious plans would follow and continue until and after their own deaths.

Wherever Fred and Bessie went and whatever they did, Harold's memory haunted them. Exhausted by the chaotic seven-month parliamentary session, overwork, emotional strain, and personal anxiety, Fred and Bessie sought relief and escape, time and space, to regain perspective and rethink their lives. After a month and more in Canning, responding to the flood of condolences, Fred and Bessie left for Britain in search of rest and distraction, to travel, and to indulge their interest in history, art, and ancestry, and to reassess their personal and political future. The Opposition's persistent rumours of Fred's retirement seemed now an attractive option.

Although Fred and Bessie registered at Central London's elegant Hotel Metropole, mourning protocol precluded theatre, concerts, opera, museums, and galleries. Consequently, Fred and Bessie indulged their (largely Fred's) passion for book collecting, genealogy, and distant Kent relatives. They visited churches, cemeteries, and record offices in search of aristocratic lineage, as if to restore the broken male bloodline. The highlight of their search was a pilgrimage to the ancestral village of Burden in Kent, where Fred's family reputedly received land in the wake of William the Conqueror's victory, and where Fred procured a copy of Oliver Goldsmith's "oldest poems" from "the old Bordens in Headcorn in Kent."[60]

Lord Strathcona, Canada's sympathetic high commissioner, ever attentive to important Canadian visitors,[61] welcomed Fred and Bessie to London, sensitive to their grief. In September, he invited them to his recently (1895) constructed four-storey country house, Glencoe, situated on a ten-acre Scottish country estate, and discreetly alerted London's official and Canadian communities to the grieving parents' presence in the city. Both communities responded with invitations to private dinners, teas, and country house weekends, their sympathies fed by the intense imperial war fever, casualty lists, defeats, and victories that marked this stage of the war.

Harold's death was never far from Fred and Bessie's thoughts. In September Fred wrote a personal letter to the queen's secretary, Captain Frederick Ponsonby, who had requested a photograph of Harold (said to be one of two requests for a photograph of a Boer War casualty), providing the queen with a detailed summary of Harold's service.[62] He and Bessie also found time to choose a design for the Harold Borden Memorial Challenge Cup, which Fred had promised the Dominion Rifle Association: they chose a silver cup with medallions bearing Harold's image, which they commissioned from a London engraver.

Chapter Nine

Lady Borden

A cable announcing the dissolution of Canada's Eighth Parliament ended Bessie and Fred's British sojourn, obliging them to consider their political future. Already Kings County Conservatives had named a star candidate for the federal election on 7 November 1900, confident they could defeat Fred. Educated at Dalhousie (BA) and Harvard (LLB) and two years younger than Fred, Barclay Webster had been warden of Kings County from 1886 until 1891 and was currently serving as a stipendiary magistrate. An able solicitor, with the Dominion Atlantic Railway and the Bank of Nova Scotia as his clients, Webster was the son-in-law of Levrett de Veber Chipman, the avaricious head of the Chipman clan who Fred had defeated in 1874. Webster's son had served in South Africa (and died on his way home), and given the government's initial reluctance to dispatch troops, its dismissal of General Hutton and the emergency food ration scandal, the war was certain to become a central electoral issue in Kings. W.S. Fielding, the federal minister of finance, Harry Wickwire, King's member of the Legislative Assembly and Fred's business ally, and Harry Brown, Fred's private secretary, asked Fred to return immediately.

Fred's response was no surprise. Honour, loyalty, and courage were not his only considerations. Politics had shaped his world for a quarter of a century. His life needed structure, now more than ever. Public life had whetted his ambitions, extended his reach, benefited his business, and enhanced his and Bessie's status. It had opened doors, in both Canada and Britain, that combined private advantage with public service. Bessie and Fred agreed that he must stand and fight. But, as they left Liverpool on 27 September aboard the Montreal-bound Alan Line's 10,000-ton *Tunisian*, neither could have imagined how their decision would transform their lives.

The Conservative Party, goaded by its partisan and insensitive *Halifax Herald*, and other "lying and villainous" newspapers like the *Montreal Star*,[1] displayed an unusual interest in Kings. Their disorganized party lacked the Liberals' access to provincial and federal patronage. Nor was their obsession with what the *Herald* called "the dog biscuit" scandal particularly effective in Kings.[2] The suggestion that Fred had sent Harold's contingent into battle with defective emergency rations seemed indecent to those who knew Fred and his pride in his son. The county's electorate, buoyed by the country's general prosperity, was equally forgiving of Fred's failure to advance prohibition and free trade. Well-organized and armed with a stack of party pamphlets, such as *Facts for Farmers*, and his Baptist colleague Fielding's speech on prohibition,[3] Fred made a "house to house" canvas of his constituency,[4] seeking out the party faithful and eliciting their residual sympathy.

Fred's constituency responded convincingly, handing him 54 per cent of the vote. Had the campaign continued another week, Fred was convinced that his majority would have been "considerably larger."[5] Equally encouraging was the nationwide success of the party, returned with eleven more seats than at dissolution. Five of those seats came from Nova Scotia where the party won fifteen of the province's twenty seats, a success that enhanced Fred's and Fielding's political credibility. Fred's cousin, Robert Borden, one of province's few Conservative survivors, considered his party's performance a "national disaster."[6] Among their party's national casualties were some of Fred's fiercest critics, including George Eulas Foster and its bellicose leader, Sir Charles Tupper, who experienced his first personal political defeat.

Three months after the Conservatives' defeat their fractious caucus named Robert Borden its leader, an appointment that enhanced Fred's influence on both sides of the House. Not only did the 1900 election resuscitate Fred's political career, but it brought his party a sense of security, and a more civil parliamentary culture, shaped by Laurier's courtly manners and Robert Borden's stolid decorum. The election also rid Fred of a few of his battle-hardened Liberal rivals, such as James Domville. Better still, Fred returned to his department free from its obstructionist military and civilian heads.

Gone was Fred's theatrical, self-important general officer commanding, Major-General E.T.H. Hutton, replaced by Major-General Richard O'Grady-Haly, a conciliatory, cooperative officer whose father, General William O'Grady-Haly, had been stationed in Halifax as the general officer commanding British forces in North America (1873–8). Equally important was the retirement of Fred's tired old deputy minister, Charles-Eugène Panet, and his replacement by Louis-Félix Pinault

(1852–1906), a skilled publicist and responsive provincial politician. To these Fred added two of his able cousins, John William Borden (Robert Borden's brother) and Charles Henry Brown, who he placed in strategic departmental positions. Fred now had a team. He also had an agenda.[7]

The South African War had placed imperial questions at the centre of Canada's political agenda that enhanced Fred visibility. In 1900 the glossy Toronto monthly, *The Canadian Magazine*, published a five-page "Canadian Celebrities" article on Fred, replete with a photograph of him and Harold.[8] In June 1900 the University of New Brunswick granted him an honorary LLD. That same year the United States' Association of Military Surgeons named him an honorary corresponding member. The following year the British Army Medical Corps appointed him an honorary colonel. And, in January 1901, the Ontario College of Physicians and Surgeons made him its first honorary member.[9] All were tokens of respect and recognition that facilitated his and Bessie's access to a wider world.[10]

More remarkable was Fred's improved relations with Rideau Hall. During their recent passage of arms over General Hutton's dismissal, the Governor General had castigated Fred as corrupt, weak, intemperate, and incompetent, and twice urged Laurier to replace him with a "more competent' person."[11] Freed of Hutton's toxic influence, the Governor General's relations with Fred improved dramatically. Soon the Governor General informed his friends that Fred was a "thoroughly pleasant, agreeable man," "a very good friend," "always ready to meet my views," and "quite the best minister they have had here."[12] In short, the Governor General came to consider Fred an ally in promoting military reform, though they often disagreed on the exact blueprint.

Vice-regal favour brought Fred and Bessie invitations to Rideau Hall dinners, receptions, and parties.[13] Fred became a president of the Ottawa Cricket Club, whose clubhouse was located on the Rideau Hall grounds, and vice-patron of the Ottawa Lawn Tennis Club.[14] Bessie's relative youth and her enjoyment of winter sports, especially skating (for which Lady Minto had a passion and reputation), tobogganing, and skiing made her a welcome guest at vice-regal winter sports events. [15] Minto shared Fred's penchant for well-dressed, athletic women. Bessie and her attractive, articulate daughters enjoyed summer "class sports" as well, such as lawn bowling, croquet, tennis, golf, and riding, which made them welcome guests at Rideau Hall. Nor was Maude's close friendship with Miss Lola Powell, the Governor General's "flirtatious, snobbish" special friend a social liability.[16] It was Harold's death, however, that finally thawed Fred and Minto's frosty relationship.

Greeting Canada's returning soldiers and distributing service medals and civic gifts to war veterans steeled Fred and Bessie's determination to honour Harold. During McGill's 1901 convocation, Dr. Thomas Roddick (1846–1923) had reminded graduates of Harold's absence from their graduation list. Their brave alumnus's patriotism was lauded at the King's College convocation, as it had at the Mount Allison convocation. In January 1902 Mount Allison had unveiled a marble memorial plaque in its chapel. McGill faculty and students had begun a subscription for a "handsome memorial tablet" for its Medical Building to honour Harold and gunner Patrick O'Reilly. And in October 1901, Fred had accepted Harold's service medal from the Duke of Cornwall and York during the duke's departure ceremonies in Halifax. There Fred and Bessie had watched as the duke had laid the cornerstone of the province's impressive Boer War monument on the north side of the Legislative Building, commemorating thirteen Nova Scotia fatalities to date, with Harold's name among the fallen, and unveiled one of its three bronze plaques depicting the Battle of Witpoort.[17]

Harold's desire to win a Victoria Cross preyed on his parents' minds. They brooded over their correspondence from Harold's fellow officers and commanders, including Lord Roberts, lauding Harold's leadership and bravery at Vet River and Driefontein. Other correspondents reinforced Lane's speculation that Harold would have received the Victoria Cross had he lived. Fred and Bessie wondered if an exception might be made to the award's restriction to the living, or if Harold's service and sacrifice could be recognized in some other way. After all, military dispatches had lauded both Harold and Richard Turner for swimming the Vet River under fire, but only Turner had received the Distinguished Service Order.

Fred was aware of Minto's efforts to honour Canada's war veterans. And scarcely ten months after Harold's death he felt sufficiently confident of the Governor General's good will to seek his assistance, representing himself simply as "an aggrieved father." Minto was more than receptive. He endorsed Fred's request and sought the support of Lord Roberts and his War Office friends.[18] Not content to entrust the project entirely to Minto, Fred wrote Lord Strathcona, providing the high commissioner with a full dossier of correspondence from Roberts, Alderson, Hutton, Lessard, Williams, Otter, and Colonel Reeves, the commanding officer of the Royal Irish Fusiliers, all testifying to Harold's distinguished service, documents that Strathcona brought to the attention of Sir Edward Ward, the War Office's Permanent Secretary.[19] Sir Edward's response was not encouraging, citing the fact that to date the Victoria Cross had not been awarded posthumously. Nor was Sir

Edward's reply sufficiently conclusive to deter Fred from making a personal, though futile, appeal to the War Office's permanent secretary.[20]

Fortunately, the Governor General had a back-up plan, within his own power to achieve. Convinced that "we will not light upon a better min of militia,"[21] one with "the right point of view,"[22] Minto decided to reward the Borden family's imperial service and sacrifice with a knighthood (KCMG), an investment in Borden's imperial utility. Minto's initiative met no opposition in Canada or Britain. Nonetheless, it required vigilance, prodding, and timing.[23] The South African War's end seemed an auspicious occasion to recommend Fred's knighthood. To signal his larger intent, Mino recommended a comparable honour for William Mulock, who together with Fred had pleaded Canada's case for participation in the South African War.

Past and potential imperial service weighed heavily in Minto's decision to honour Fred, as did class. After all, the British Empire was "first and foremost a class act," a layered, hierarchical social structure designed to replicate and complement British society, a project in which class was a sine qua non.[24] Title identified one's place in that stratified society, open to those who possessed the social attributes and material means to sustain its form and function. Manifested by education, language, dress, deportment, and what Lord Shaftsbury (1671–1713) once described as "the dextrous management of words and actions," class entailed hospitality, philanthropy, and public service.

Fred and Bessie's social credentials, their decorum, service, and philanthropy, were persuasive. Quite apart from their charitable contributions to churches, libraries, universities, and choral and symphonic organizations, they worked with various social and cultural agencies. Bessie was a director of the Ottawa Women's Morning Music Club, the YWCA, the National Council of Women, a vice-president and member of the Victorian Order of Nurse's board of management, and vice-patroness (along with Lady Strathcona) of Lady Minto's Soldiers' Wives League.[25] Fred was a generous donor and director of the Canadian Red Cross, the Order of St. John of Jerusalem, the Tuberculosis Association, the Association for the Advancement of Science, the YMCA, and various historical societies, not to mention his numerous memberships in private clubs in Canada, Britain, and the United States.[26]

Laurier knew Fred and Bessie "more intimately than anyone else in his cabinet" and could testify to their credentials. A colleague, neighbour, friend, and frequent guest at the Borden home, Laurier was impressed with Fred and Bessie's social skills and ability to move within the highest levels of society. He appreciated Fred's political fidelity, intelligence, and style, his tall, "handsome presence and immaculate attire that made him an outstanding figure in parliamentary and court functions."[27] Laurier was no less impressed by Bessie. He fancied intelligent, elegant women with whom he could discuss books and ideas, and who, unlike Zoe, relished political discussion. Laurier recognized, too, the importance of appearances and social diplomacy.

Lord Minto had not always shared Laurier's or Fred's imperial agenda. But the Colonial and War Offices' failure to follow his advice or assessments of his ministers had obliged him to reassess his ministers' qualities. During Minto's reassessment, he came to recognize Fred's place within the cabinet and presumed influence on Laurier, especially on imperial issues. In briefing his brother-in-law and successor, the Fourth Earl Grey (1904–11), Minto advised Grey of Fred's imperial importance, advice that Grey appeared to follow, careful to introduce Fred to visiting imperial missionaries, such as Sir Frederick Pollock,[28] and to secure Fred's support for "saving" the Plains of Abraham and celebrating Quebec City's Tercentenary.[29]

Rumours of Fred's impending KCMG grew with news that the Grand Prior of the Most Venerable Order of St. John of Jerusalem would confer on Fred its title of "Knight of Grace" during his London visit to attend Edward VII's coronation in June 1902. A member of the St. John's Ambulance Association, an organization closely associated with the militia, Fred had donated generously to its care of the sick and wounded.[30] He and Bessie loved to dress up. They also relished the pomp and ceremony promised by the Venerable Order's May 1902 conferment ceremony during which the order's Grand Prior touched the shoulder of the fully robed recipient with a sword. Although knights of the order were not entitled to the prefix "Sir," they could wear its robes and the Maltese cross, one of its four arms representing temperance, not one of the future knight's conspicuous virtues. The fact that knights, however, could apply for a coat of arms, was especially important to Fred.

Fred's greater honour, the KCMG, was to be conferred the next month, following Edward VII's coronation, scheduled for 26 June 1902. Designed to rival the Diamond Jubilee, Edward's coronation once again cast Canada in a central role. This time Fred and Bessie would occupy seats in the choir stalls of Westminster Abbey, before attending a luncheon in the House of Lords.[31] The colonial secretary, Joseph Chamberlain, had planned a Colonial/Imperial Conference as well, hoping to capitalize on the South African War's end to reorganize the imperial estate. The conference's focus on imperial defence was especially important to Fred, serving as Laurier's principal military adviser. The coronation, the Imperial/Colonial Conference, and Fred's knighthood gave Fred and Bessie unprecedented exposure, and put their social skills and stamina to the test.

The Order of St. John of Jerusalem's May conferment obliged Fred and Bessie to leave Canada for London on 8 May 1902, a good month before the departures of Sir Wilfrid and Lady Laurier and other Canadian coronation guests, and three weeks before the end of the South African War. Preparation for their visit drew on Bessie's extensive organizational skills; she packed six trunks, a uniform case, two hat boxes, two leather bags, a larger leather bag, a hold-all leather bag, and a dressing case to accommodate their lengthy visit and a daily social agenda that might require changing clothes four times a day.[32]

Their rigorous preparations were prescient since only two days before his scheduled coronation on 26 June 1902, Edward suffered a severe attack of appendicitis that required surgery and a convalescence that delayed his coronation until 9 August. The coronation's postponement gave Fred and Bessie time for private business, personal interests, and social engagements. Even before its postponement, Fred and Bessie had endured a staggering schedule of official, public, and private social engagements, the scale of which the Canadian press described as "far reaching and splendid."[33]

Imperial entertainment was as deliberate as it was political, designed to encourage colonial elites' allegiance, deference, and replication. Encouraged by the Colonial Office and managed largely by imperial hostesses,[34] imperial hospitality permitted colonials "to rub shoulders with the aristocracy" and feel at home.[35] Entrepreneurial imperial hostesses went to extravagant lengths, convinced that colonials were "especially sensitive to these personal considerations."[36] Generous and intentional as was their hospitality, the political returns rarely matched expectations, as Lady Borden's experience demonstrated, the mixing of colonial and imperial troops during the South African War.

Class, function, and purpose determined who, where, and why colonials were entertained. Fred and Bessie faced a particularly charged social agenda. It included Lord Strathcona's grand Dominion Day dinner in the presence of the Prince of Wales and Field Marshall Lord Roberts; the British Empire League's coronation banquet at the Guildhall on 11 July, chaired by Joseph Chamberlain; the Prince and Princess of Wales' dinner (fresh from their imperial Canadian tour); the king's royal garden party at Windsor; the foreign secretary Lord Lansdowne's dinner; and the Lord Mayor of London's banquet. Apart from official obligations Sir Frederick and Lady Borden accepted many semi-official invitations, such as Lady Aberdeen's garden party, Leopold Rothchild's reception, Lady Strathcona's "at-home," and the invitations from public persons such as the notorious Boer War journalist William Burdett-Coutts[37] and from London's extensive Canadian community. More entertaining were invitations from Mr. Herbert Beerbohm Tree (1852–1917) and his wife to Her Majesty's Theatre and Sir Henry Irving's (1818–1905) reception at the Lyceum.

Meanwhile, London teemed with Canadian friends and colleagues who required attention. Canadians were everywhere: the Governor General; federal, provincial, and territorial ministers of the Crown with their wives and assistants;[38] honours recipients,[39] business magnates,[40] and other notables[41] who had secured invitations to the coronation; in addition to numerous curious Canadian tourists and travellers, and the 657 soldiers of the Canadian Coronation Contingent, a unit that constituted more than a quarter of the Colonial Coronation Contingent.[42] Lest anyone overlook the Canadian presence in London, Clifford Sifton's Department of the Interior had erected a fifty-foot high Canada Arch on Whitehall opposite the Horse Guard, adorned by maple leaf and wheat motifs that proclaimed Canada the "future granary of the world," an invitation to soldiers, settlers, investment, and business to join Canada's last, best West.[43]

The coronation's social agenda inflicted casualities. Laurier, for all his old world charm, found London's social demands exhausting and sometimes overwhelming. Besides, he was unwell at the time, and after the Coronation he sought medical attention in Paris. Although Fred was more resilient than Laurier, he too found London's sumptuous "dinners every night or afternoon – even sometimes twice a day" played havoc with his "insides." Yet, as he complained to Bessie on an earlier occasion, in London you "might as well say *keep warm*" as escape the excesses of British hospitality.[44] Bessie, however, withstood London's social and gastronomic assaults on her constitution.

Whether it was public business that taxed Fred more heavily than Bessie or his lack of stamina or restraint (notably his weakness for alcohol), he was sometimes indisposed and preoccupied, leaving Bessie to explain or cover up for his absence. Often, too, she was on her own while Fred attended official duties, personal and semi-public business, such as the Royal Navy Review at Spithead,[45] the Duke of Connaught's awarding of war medals to colonial troops at Alexandra Palace. Fred had also to prepare for the Colonial/Imperial Conference on imperial defence and defend his decision to adopt the Ross rifle and secure its manufacture in Canada the backbone of his citizen militia.[46]

Bessie was in her element, managing their social responsibilities, conscious of her role in supporting Fred's career. Sensitive to contemporary class codes governing dress, deportment, and protocol in the public and private spheres, Bessie demonstrated her capacity to move at the highest level of imperial power. In private she was generous, warm, considerate, open, and sympathetic with her extended family and friends. But in public she could be conspicuously regal, conversing only with those to whom she had been introduced, or in her words, those of her "speaking acquaintance."[47]

Comfortably installed at the huge, stately Hotel Cecil, the imperial visitors' nerve centre, located between Embankment and Strand Streets, Bessie and Fred occupied a double bedroom suite, sitting room, bathroom, and two small bedrooms. Each morning she organized and coordinated their activities, planning, preparing, and supervising their dress and logistics, responding to invitations to luncheons, dinners, garden parties, receptions, "at homes," and country weekends, and penning gracious "bread and butter" notes, communications in which her linguistic sensitivities and close attention to protocol proved immensely useful, and ably assisted by Fred's private secretary, Harry Brown, who had accompanied them to London.

Although sumptuary laws no longer existed in the nineteenth century, they were replaced with socially enforced dress codes, dictated by gender, class, occasion, season, and time of day, a labyrinthine system that Bessie negotiated with authority. Located in a city that she regarded as one of the two fashion centres of the world, the coronation gave her licence to indulge in fashionable dress and jewellery. It even justified her purchase of a tiara, which she reserved for state occasions in Canada and Britain.[48] Her dignified bearing, and her broad cultural reference, acute observations, and informed, diplomatic conversation made her a welcome guest, and opened doors, grounded friendships, and facilitated access to power and influence. It was during this extended visit that she and Fred established their imperial social network, one based on identification, recognition, and trust, social capital upon which they drew heavily in the years ahead.

The coronation's delay created problems. Not least was the Canadian coronation troops' growing restlessness. Confined to barracks at some distance from central London, in persistently damp weather, the men worried about their civilian employment and escalating personal expenses. Even their deep-pocketed commanding officer, Henry Pellatt, Fred's wealthy friend and financial adviser, who had agreed to cover some of the contingent's expenses, began fretting about the costs. In the end, they sent unhappy men home and retained only a representative handful of willing Canadian volunteers for the delayed coronation's march past.[49]

Fred took advantage of the coronation's postponement to research his family's "noble" Norman origins, his passion for genealogy reignited by his entitlement to a family coat of arms under the Order of St. John of Jerusalem. After extensive research, aided by a distant relative bearing Fred's exact name,[50] and J.A. Glen, a professional genealogist, Fred obtained an authorized family coat of arms, and immediately placed orders with Selfridge and Company Limited's stationers and printers for letterhead, calling cards and nameplates for their extensive library collection, all bearing the family's coat of arms. By 1905 Sir Frederick's ancestral claims had so impressed the Borden Parish's (Kent) *Monthly Magazine* that it declared the Borden family to be "now represented by Sir Frederick Borden, K.C.M.G., a member of the Government of the Dominion of Canada."[51]

Fred and Bessie, like other Canadians, visited the continent following the coronation, and Fred's investiture. Six days after the coronation Fred boarded the Royal Navy's recently constructed 4,700-ton Royal Yacht, *Victoria and Albert*, at Cowes, to be invested with the KCMG and to take lunch with the king. Four days later he and Lady Borden left London by rail for Dover and crossed the Channel to Calais on their way to Paris. There they joined Sir Wilfrid and Lady Laurier at the recently (1898) opened Hotel Ritz,[52] a palatial hotel overlooking the Place Vendôme, where the city's premier hotel provided en suite bathrooms, telephones, electricity, and a gourmet table.

After four days in Paris, Sir Frederick and Lady Borden boarded a train for Geneva, to begin their whirlwind western European tour, to celebrate their social elevation and relax following their exhausting imperial venture. Celebrate they did; relax they did not. From Geneva they travelled to Bern and the Interlaken by boat to Bregenz, then by rail to Lucerne, Milan, Rome, and Venice. In Rome they lunched with Sir James Rennell Rodd (1858–1941), first secretary of the British Embassy.[53] While they devoted only two full days to *The Stones of Venice*, it was there that Lady Borden's art books and Mount Allison's art courses took on new life.[54] On 30 August they reluctantly left Venice by rail for Verona, Innsbruck, Munich, Mainz, and Cologne, down the Rhine to Brussels, then to Ostend, arriving in London on 7 September. Four days later they boarded their transatlantic transport at Liverpool for their return to Montreal, armed with their memories, gifts, and treasures, ready to play a larger role in Canadian public life. After four months' absence, Sir Frederick needed two weeks of intense office work in Ottawa before they could return to their "country seat."

Chapter Ten

Borden Place

Canning's Young Liberal Association planned a cordial welcome for their newly titled residents: an expensive, "males only" banquet in the village's Drill Hall for the evening of 7 October. To greet their guests, they draped the Drill Hall with flags and bunting, and "festooned" autumn leaves "artistically around bayonet wheels." They arranged four long "nicely appointed" tables the length of the hall, perpendicular "to the prettily decorated" head table,[1] and hung a banner across the centre of the hall with the dates "1874–1902," the years of Sir Frederick's public service. An impressive number of celebrants came from Halifax, Yarmouth, Pictou, Windsor, and Wolfville, and from as far away as Gaspé. They included Premier George Henry Murray, Attorney General J.W. Longley, military personnel, business associates, professional colleagues, clergy, educational leaders, and local notables.

As the guests assembled for a seven-course meal catered by Halifax's R. Pearson and Company, a cash bar offered cigars and cigarettes and a selection of pre-banquet drinks, champagne, Croft's port, sherries, brandies, whiskies, ales, and liqueurs, along with lemonade, ginger ale, and mineral water for the abstemious. While the banqueters drank and chatted, Canning's recently formed brass band serenaded the guests with "a good program of popular airs which the guests frequently encored." It was 10:30 pm before the banquet's presiding officer, Sir Frederick's friend and provincial MLA, H.H. Wickwire, welcomed the guests, read greetings and regrets from absent friends, and proposed "an eloquent tribute" to Sir Frederick. After the audience cheered "for several minutes," Sir Frederick responded with "an exceedingly happy and eloquent speech."[2] The evening continued with lengthy toasts, and responses, to the king, the empire, the dominion, the province, the municipality, the learned professions, and the absent ladies.

Sir Frederick and Lady Borden were delighted with Canning's demonstrative celebration of their title, conscious of its promotional, social, and political importance. In Canada's ruling elite's replicative British world, hierarchy and titles delineated a layered social system, reinforced by courtly manners, salutations, deference, and forms of mutual recognition. They instilled confidence and respect and enhanced the recipient's social authority and opportunity for material advantage.[3] They were no less part of an unwritten reciprocal social contract that entailed leadership, philanthropy, and example, a contract that Frederick and Lady Borden understood and honoured.

Sir Frederick and Lady Borden seemed to regard politics as a performance art, a means to cultivate, exercise, and retain economic and social power. They appreciated the place of language, gesture, costume, and staging, and played their roles with grace and skill, aware that "beautiful dressing and fine living" gave one "a peculiar power to lead."[4] Initially, Fred had discounted rumours of his knighthood, pleading that he was too poor and too democratic. Once rumour became reality, however, neither poverty nor democratic instincts constrained his and Lady Borden's efforts to fulfil their perceived social duties and obligations.

Upon learning of his impending knighthood, Fred engaged the prestigious firm of Halifax architects William Critchlow Harris to plan and supervise extensive renovations to the Old Place. The result was a large wooden shingled "cottage," reconstructed in the popular Queen Anne revival style, marked by ornamentation, asymmetrical forms, hipped roofs, towers, and verandas, a retrospective style that "appealed to the burgeoning, prosperous middle classes in Britain and Canada who sought affordable houses that were also showy."[5] Once the renovations were completed, the Old Place was renamed Borden Place, a personalized designation suggestive of social and dynastic aspirations.

Although Sir Frederick and Lady Borden enjoined old "friends" and "family" to omit the salutation "Lady" and "Sir,"[6] titles frequently prevailed, except for very close friends, since many friends and acquaintances derived as much satisfaction from the salutation as the recipients. Residences and named homes had a similar purpose. Both were sources of civic pride and "commercial benefit," exemplified by contemporary postcards depicting the Canning "Home of Sir Frederick Borden" and the "Residence of Sir Frederick Borden." Borden Place became the community's most impressive home, the resort of distinguished guests and a focus of local curiosity that branded the village.

Borden Place occupied a spacious ten-acre estate between the steep banked Habitant River and Canning's tree-lined east-west Main Street. An elegant circular carriageway defined by well-manicured hedges and gardens gave visitors access to Borden Place from the village. Guests from away, arriving by rail, reached Borden Place by a spur of the Cornwallis-Kingsport Railway, which passed "between rows of apple trees" along the north side of the Habitant River, some of the orchards belonging to Sir Frederick. Borden Place's grounds accommodated two ice houses, a carriage house, stables, croquet and tennis courts, and vegetable and flower gardens. In 1910 Sir Frederick and Lady Borden insured Borden Place for $20,000 ($500,000 in contemporary purchasing power) and its contents for $10,000; it was clearly more than a modest country cottage.[7]

The ground floor of their renovated twelve-room "cottage" had a spacious foyer with a large stone fireplace, a dining room, a library, and a drawing room that extended the width of the house, all panelled in natural teak, with birch ceilings, and wood or tile floors, as well as a large pantry, kitchen, and maid's room. Family bedrooms occupied the second floor, including a 29′ x 28′ southwest-facing bed-sitting room where Mrs. Clarke, and later Lady Borden, spent a good deal of their time. The third floor had bedrooms for guests and live-in servants. Receiving rooms had stained-glass windows and contemporary furniture, paintings, vases, and *objets d'art*, collected during their New England and European tours. Their great-granddaughter, who lived at Borden Place during the late 1940s and 1950s, while Lady Borden was still alive, explained that Sir Frederick and Lady Borden were "notorious for buying cheap or getting a bargain" and many of their purchases were "of little value."[8] Nevertheless, they were useful props for projecting style, affluence, and power.

Sir Frederick and Lady Borden were particularly fond of portraits, oil, charcoal, and photographic, and patronized some of the most renowned contemporary portrait photographers in Canada and Britain, such as William J. Topley (1845–1930),[9] William Notman (1826–1891), Alexander Henderson (1831–1913), Lallie Charles (1869–1919), William Downey (1829–1915), Joseph Elliott (1835–1903), Clemence Fry (1840–1897), and Louis Saul Langfier (1859–1916).[10] The Bordens' fascination with portraits reflected the period's obsession with individualism, heroes and hero worship, represented in contemporary history, novels, short stories, and portraiture,[11] as examples of social and moral values.[12] Their fascination with portraiture underlines their attention to personal appearance and discreet self-promotion; the subjects' dress, pose, and setting a reminder of their position, influence, and family connections.

In September 1902, soon after Sir Frederick and Lady Borden returned from London, the freshly knighted Sir Frederick visited Boston and sat for a three-quarter-length oil portrait of himself, painted by Frank Hector Tompkins (1847–1922), a fashionable Boston artist.[13] In 1910 Tompkins painted an oil portrait entitled "Elizabeth Borden Hewitt: Pink Shawl."[14] This portrait may have hung in Elizabeth's home after her marriage. If so, it returned to Borden Place following her husband's untimely death and is currently reputed to be in private hands.[15] A full-length oil portrait of Sir Frederick in court uniform greeted guests who entered Borden Place. In the dining room, on the panelled wall behind the chair where Sir Frederick hosted dinners, hung a large framed photograph of Sir Frederick seated pensively with a book in his hand. The photograph had been taken in London by William Downey, a "royal" photographer. On the wall opposite hung a richly framed, full-length Downey photograph of Lady Borden, standing, regally posed, and elegantly attired. Their messages were unmistakable.[16]

Although neither of Sir Frederick and Lady Borden's two residences rivalled the grand mansions of Montreal and Toronto's very rich,[17] their homes served comparable purposes; they were places to impress, reward, and cultivate friends, colleagues, and visitors invited for teas, luncheons, dinners, and receptions.[18] During formal dinners, Lady Borden presided over a large dining table lit by a pair of eleven-inch sterling silver candlesticks placed between an impressive epergne. Royal Doulton or Royal Crown Derby dinner and dessert plates were framed by Shreve, Crump & Low (Boston) Iris-patterned sterling knives, forks, and spoons (they possessed a setting for 24),[19] cutlery that Lady Borden wielded with dexterity and a strict eye for propriety.

Guests invited for tea gathered in Borden Place's large drawing room, decorated with seasonal flowers, where Lady Borden poured from a sterling teapot crowned by a silver eagle. Her tea set consisted of a two-handled, silver sugar bowl, cream jug, and tray that had been made in Sheffield, England (valued at $1750 in 1967). Guests drank from Aynsley dark blue and gold English bone china cups, while they conversed and enjoyed instrumental or vocal music. After 1908 a Victrola record player, Lady Borden's gift to Sir Frederick the previous Christmas, often supplied the music. Guests could scarcely avoid being impressed, especially those from the village.

Adjacent to the dining room was a large library, replete with dark leather chairs, fireplace, and some 3,000 books and journals. The books were on history, literature, art, travel, and science.[20] The journals, such as the *Manchester Guardian*, *Public Opinion*, *London Illustrated News*, *Atlantic Monthly*, the *British Weekly*, the *Western Chronicle*, the *Halifax Chronicle*, the *Kentville Advertiser*, and *Young Canada* dealt variously with military affairs, contemporary literature, international and national politics, local news, and opinion. After 1908 each book contained a nameplate displaying the family's heraldic coat of arms. Family photographs and travel souvenirs occupied the mantle and small side tables.

Borden Place was heated by a large coal-burning furnace and twelve wood-burning fireplaces and was lit by electricity after the 1902 renovations. It was served by three and a half bathrooms, one located in the master bedroom. During peak summer season at least seven servants cared for Borden Place. The servants consisted of two maids, a cook, a housekeeper, and a gardener/chauffeur; other staff included a stoker, a cleaner, and stable hand (to care for the horses, cows, sheep, hens, ducks, and turkeys). Some servants possessed dual roles, employed seasonally or as causal workers. Household management required planning, organization, and supervision, for which Lady Borden was chiefly responsible.

A year after Sir Frederick and Lady Borden completed their renovations of Borden Place, they solidified their local visibility with an impressive public memorial to Harold, unveiled during a ceremony that attracted national attention. Among the invited guests was Dr. George Roy Johnson (1871–1956), Harold's old Mount Allison classmate and family favourite. At sea serving as a ship's doctor, Johnson deeply regretted his inability to attend the ceremony on 23 September 1903. "Time," Johnson wrote Lady Borden on 30 August 1903, "might heal but cannot reconcile one to the death of dear old Harold."[21]

Not only had time failed to erase Sir Frederick and Lady Borden's memory of "dear old Harold" but they had never accepted their failure to secure greater public recognition of his service and sacrifice. Each unveiling of a South African War monument (and there were many) or commemorative ceremony reminded Sir Frederick and Lady Borden of their failure. A marble tombstone in South Africa, commemorative plaques at McGill and Mount Allison, the small stone cross over Harold's empty grave site in the iron fenced family burial plot in Canning's Hillaton Cemetery seemed too little and too private. Even the generous competitive cup and medallion they donated to the Dominion Rifle Association seemed too small and specific. To right this wrong Sir Frederick, Lady Borden, and Lieutenant-Colonel Edward Manning Beckwith, the commander of Harold's old regiment (and Diamond Jubilee companion), formed a monument committee with "friends" from "Kings County and elsewhere" to erect a handsome public monument to Harold's memory. The location was as deliberate as it was significant: in the centre of Canning, at the crossroads of Main and North Streets, opposite Bessie's old home and not far from Borden Place where Harold had spent his childhood. No one could pass through the community without seeing the monument.

By September 1903, the monument was in place, a several-metre-high structure crowned by a bronze bust of a uniformed Harold, mounted on a layered rectangular granite pedestal. The bust had been sculpted by Hamilton McCarthy (1846–1939), one of three of Canada's most popular Canadian Boer War sculptors. McCarthy's son had also been killed during the war. On two sides of the rectangular pedestal, just below the bust, bronze plaques depicted episodes in battles in which Harold had distinguished himself: his swimming the Vet under fire and his heroic death charge at Witpoort (a replica of the bronze McCarthy had sculpted for the province's statue next to the provincial legislative building). The bronze plaque on the third side gave a biographical summary: Harold's place and date of birth, his parents and maternal grandparents, his education, military service, Diamond Jubilee participation and medal, and summary of his war service twice (the twice underlined) mentioned in dispatches. On the fourth side of the rectangular pedestal was a lion's head fountain and basin supplying clean water to "man and beast," a reminder of Harold's love of animals and Sir Frederick's campaign to provide Canning with clean drinking water. Founded in New York by the Henry Bonnard Bronze Company, the impressive monument was a forceful tribute to the life and patriotism of Harold, a native son who had made the supreme sacrifice for country and empire, a lasting reminder of his family's public service.

Perhaps only a minister of militia could have commandeered an unveiling ceremony that quadrupled Canning's population. Many of the participants were militia, under the command of Lieutenant-Colonel Beckwith, including members of Harold's old regiment, together with a detachment from Aldershot representing "various other arms of the service." Out-of-town guests included high-ranking officers from militia headquarters in Ottawa, political friends, business partners, and "delegations from Halifax and the rest of the province"; all were met at the train by Beckwith's forces, lining both sides of Main Street and the side street leading from the station. At about 2 o'clock, Sir Frederick, Lady Borden, Elizabeth, Maude, and Mrs. Clarke took their seats on the newly constructed, flag-draped platform, followed by the general officer commanding the Canadian militia, Lord Dundonald, his aide-de-camp, and his entourage. An honour party composed of Hussars, having left their horses outside the town, "slow-marched" solemnly through the town, their arms reversed as in a funeral procession, and formed a square around the monument while the seated official party and standing spectators rendered their religious, patriotic, political, and family tributes.[22]

When the official party was assembled, the local 68th Militia's band played and the audience sang "Nearer My God to Thee"; this was followed by a prayer from Reverend Doctor Wilson, Canning's resident Methodist minister. The band then led the audience in several stanzas of "The Maple Leaf Forever." Lieutenant-Colonel Beckwith, the monument committee's chairman, welcomed the audience, reminding them of Harold's service, patriotism, and leadership. He then introduced Lord Dundonald, who descanted on the imperial significance of the war, Harold's rapid, patriotic response, and his family's "British" loyalties, assuring the audience that the family's great patriotism and sacrifice would forever be "cherished here and throughout the Empire." Lord Dundonald then unveiled the monument while the militia "stood at the present" and the band played Handel's "Dead March in Saul." Lady Borden received the first tumbler of water from the fountain and the band played "Rule Britannia."

After Lord Dundonald's "splendid speech," the president of Mount Allison University, David Allison, spoke of the Harold he knew as a boy and a man, always a sterling character, model student, and gallant soldier. An unidentified person read a poem entitled "The Khaki Corps." The Reverend Professor E. M. Kierstead from McMaster University and J.L. Longley,[23] the provincial attorney-general, followed with remarks that "the large concourse greeted with breathless attention." "God Save the King" ended an event that the *Halifax Morning Chronicle* described as "the most memorable [day] in the history of Kings County."[24] Coloured postcards and ceramic plates depicting the statue memorialized the occasion. If commemoration is largely "an act of self-invention,"[25] the statue affirmed Harold's family's sacrifice and public service.

Well over a year later, on 3 November 1904, Sir Frederick and Lady Borden returned to the monument in a carriage drawn by a noisy crowd of Liberal celebrants behind a hastily improvised band. Earlier that evening Canning citizens had gathered in front of Borden Place to await the results of the 1904 federal election.[26] News of Sir Frederick's overwhelming electoral victory induced the jubilant partisans to draw Sir Frederick and Lady Borden to the monument to mark Sir Frederick's stunning electoral success, a contest in which Sir Frederick's dismissal of Lord Dundonald had been a central issue. Those who remembered Lord Dundonald's address over thirteen months before, and his lavish praise of Sir Frederick's "British" loyalty and patriotism, enjoyed the irony, as did Sir Fredrick and Lady Borden.

So confident had Sir Frederick been of his 1904 re-election that he had spent very little time with his old friends in Kings. Instead, he had campaigned for Liberal colleagues in Nova Scotia and New Brunswick, notably E.M. Macdonald, his Pictou friend.[27] Fred had received 64 per cent (2,594) of the votes cast, the largest percentage of his career, a majority unsurpassed by any other Liberal candidate in the province, where the party had captured every seat.[28] They had even defeated Robert Borden in Halifax. Sir Frederick was at the height of his political career. He and Lady Borden had clearly established their local political and social hegemony.

In 1982 Emily Eaton recalled seeing Sir Frederick and Lady Borden at the height of their local power, on "one of the grand days of my childhood." She was uncertain if it had occurred in the summer of 1909 or 1910. All she remembered was that it was a very hot summer day and her father had sent her on an errand to Mr. Isaac Chipman at Chipman's Corner. Since horses were "the chief mode of transportation," Emily rode her family's big Clydesdale mare bareback, "bare headed and bare footed," with only a sheep skin for a cushion, and wearing "knee pants forced well up toward my thighs, and only a thin shirt." As she approached the sandy Burial Ground Hill leading to the Baptist church in the direction of Middle Dyke, she was obliged to slow down. And just as she "turned to go down the hill" she recognized "Sir Frederick and Lady Borden's carriage and pair of horses" at the bottom of the hill. As they met, Sir Frederick stood erect and "bowed with, I am sure, all the courtesy he would have accorded the Governor General himself." Emily realized she was only a few hundred yards from her grandfather's farm and that Sir Frederick "had a good idea which house she belonged to" and "may even have known the horse I was riding."[29] For Emily the age of Camelot had come to Chipman's Corner.

Chapter Eleven

A National Class

For Sir Frederick and Lady Borden, however, local projects were not enough. Titled, affluent, and popular, a friend of the rich and powerful, Sir Frederick aspired to something above the rank of a second-tier politician, something that combined material profit and public service, and a certain immunity from public scrutiny. In 1904 Sir Frederick had been in politics for thirty-one years. His reputation and ambitions had outgrown his constituency's borders. He had exhausted much of his reform agenda. Life had become comfortable, routine, and increasingly claustrophobic. As he explained to a friend after the 1904 election, he was losing his appetite for elections.[1] Lady Borden, too, had become tired of "grubbing."[2]

Together they weighed their options. Although their entrepreneurial efforts funded their family's comfortable lifestyle, their wealth paled in comparison to that of many of their contemporary friends and associates. Inspired by their friends' wealth and privilege, Sir Frederick and Lady Borden nursed several financial dreams and schemes, postponed or hijacked by political priorities. Twice Laurier had offered Sir Frederick the lieutenant-governorship of Nova Scotia, and twice he had declined it in favour of Laurier's promise of the prestigious high commissionership, where he might broker his own interests and those of his friends. That post, once occupied by his old rival Sir Charles Tupper, was currently held by the aged Lord Strathcona, and best secured by remaining in politics.

Sir Frederick and Lady Borden remained attached to Borden Place. They returned often, though business and travel shortened their stays. At Borden Place they relaxed, entertained friends and relatives, and promoted and patronized Canning's churches, charities, and library. When their Methodist church burned on 8 February 1909, they paid 20 per cent ($1,500.)[3] of its reconstruction costs, and Mrs. Clarke donated the pulpit furnishings. Sir Frederick's constituency also benefited from important public works, such as Kentville's military Camp Aldershot and its Dominion Experimental Farms, and Canning's Armouries and its improved dock facilities, known locally as Borden Landing.[4]

Attached as Sir Frederick and Lady Borden were to Borden Place, Ottawa had become their epicentre, their home away from home. Easily accessible to Montreal and Toronto, Ottawa was populated by many of Sir Frederick and Lady Borden's friends and relatives, notably members of the Brown and Borden families, including the leader of the Opposition.[5] Moreover, the growing power of the state and the nationalization of the country's economic, religious, and intellectual life had enhanced Ottawa's stature, a place where its leaders endeavoured to transcend local and regional borders, and affirm their national and imperial standing.

Sir Frederick and Lady Borden might not have seen themselves as part of a national class. But as managers, custodians, and beneficiaries of their country's governance, resources, and interests, they and their colleagues defined and defended their decisions with national myths rooted in geography, history, and institutions, their explanations often brittle and divisive.[6] More generic, conspicuous, and cohesive was the power of material culture, represented by houses, dress, deportment, recreation, and state rituals, in which family played a prominent role.

The Borden's purchase of Stadacona Hall, a large grey limestone "gothic cottage" in Ottawa's fashionable Sandy Hill, suggests their personal and political aspirations. Built in 1871 by John A. Cameron, an affluent Ottawa lumber baron, Stadacona Hall had been John A. Macdonald's home (1878–83) before he moved to Earnscliffe, and it was still considered one of the city's most prestigious homes. In 1912 Sir Frederick insured his house for $75,000[7] and in 1908 its furnishings for $4,000.[8] Stadacona Hall's proximity to Sir Wilfrid and Lady Laurier's home nurtured Sir Frederick and Lady Borden's friendship with the prime minister, and fuelled favour-seekers' confidence that Sir Frederick had special influence with Laurier.

From their stately Ottawa mansion, Sir Frederick and Lady Borden dispensed their courtly hospitality, their style, décor, and menus inspired by their imperial visits, scaled to their resources and the Canadian context. Elegant, informed, and articulate, Lady Borden was in her element. She loved food and fashion, maintained a rigorous sense of etiquette and decorum, and enjoyed entertaining. She cultivated an "Ottawa accent," expunging any taint of parochialisms, determined to project an urbane image. One Ottawa reporter described Lady Borden "at home" in Stadacona Hall, seated in her morning room with sunlight streaming "through the large window facing south." The "delightful situation" of the room, the reporter speculated, "might be even more 'cheery' in the late afternoon, "when the light comes from huge logs burning in the wide old-fashioned fireplace, where Lady Borden serves her guests with fragrant cups of tea," surrounded by "flowers and books in this pleasant room."[9]

Lady Borden's Stadacona Hall became renowned for its dinner parties, its food, conversation, and political opportunities. There ten and occasionally twelve guests enjoyed a five-course meal in her "handsome mahogany-panelled dining-room,"[10] beginning with oysters on the half shell, followed by soup, a fish course, meat (beef, mutton, or turkey), and a desert, normally ice cream and fruit.[11] Mackenzie King was a frequent beneficiary of Sir Frederick and Lady Borden's hospitality. He was especially fond of Sir Frederick and Lady Borden, who were also good friends of King's wealthy patron, Sir William Mulock. Convinced that Sir Frederick wielded influence with Laurier, King looked to Sir Frederick to counterbalance and protect the young, ambitious politician from more conservative cabinet colleagues, such as W.S. Fielding, whose cautious policies King did not always support.

At Stadacona Hall King might meet many useful political, business, imperial, and foreign leaders. He might dine next to a senior cabinet colleague, such as Andrew Blair, Sydney Fisher, Clifford Sifton, or Sir Wilfrid. He might converse with influential public servants such as Joseph Pope, the Bordens' friend and neighbour, or clergy such as Reverend Doctor George F. Salton, Dominion Methodist's popular lecturer and art critic,[12] or businessmen such as Sir Sanford Fleming or Sir Henry Pellatt, the "King of Casa Loma," the athletic, eccentric Toronto capitalist, military enthusiast and Sir Frederick's sometime investment adviser and business partner.[13] Sir Henry and Lady Pellatt frequently stayed at Stadacona Hall.[14] Although absent, Mackenzie King might have enjoyed another of Sir Frederick and Lady Borden's dinner party in May 1909, for the visiting British entrepreneur, Wesleyan Methodist and Liberal imperialist MP, Sir Robert William Perks. That party included Sir Wilfrid and Lady Laurier, Mrs. Clarke and the Reverend James and Mrs. Henderson, who spent the evening discussing issues of war and peace.[15] King might also have enjoyed the Bordens' dinner for the Japanese consul general and his wife.[16] He may even have weighed the odds of a marriage to one of Sir Frederick and Lady Borden's attractive daughters, who were roughly his age.

Ownership of two substantial houses required hiring, training, and supervising competent household staff, a task complicated by the family's seasonal migration and public responsibilities. The parliamentary session's social season required residence in Ottawa during the late fall, winter, and early spring. During the cold winter months Lady Borden usually escaped to New Jersey or Maryland for several weeks. In the late spring, summer, and early fall she preferred Canning and her gardens and meals served outdoors on her large wicker table. Even assisted by two maids and a cook, the family's biannual pilgrmage was an ordeal, though skeleton staff in each house could dispatch missing items. After construction of the Kentville-Kingsport rail spur, Sir Frederick's ministerial railcar made transportation more convenient, even permitting transport of their family cow!

In Ottawa and elsewhere club memberships were investments in elite bonding, exclusive multipurpose sites for relaxation, confidential conversation, news, and gossip. They offered rooms for reading, smoking, drinking, dining, and overnight accommodation. Many clubs espoused occupational, political, sporting, or social objectives, and their patrons were often wealthy, influential titled persons. Clubs were especially convenient for a socially mobile, national class, exclusive venues to receive and reciprocate hospitality, transact business, and share interests. Modelled on British seventeenth- and eighteenth- century gentleman's clubs, these Canadian equivalents became particularly popular in the late nineteenth and early twentieth centuries, as did their contemporary compares, the country clubs that provided recreational facilities, and were often open to female and family participation, unlike rustic male hunting and fishing clubs.

Sir Frederick's club memberships suggest his and Lady Borden's geographic range and social reach. The Halifax Club, the Garrison Club (Quebec), the Laurentian Club (Montreal), the Albany Club (Toronto), the Intercolonial Club (Boston), the Canadian Club (Boston), the Calumet Club (New York), the Royal Automobile Club (London, England), and the Travellers Club (London, England) were but nine of the twenty clubs in which Sir Frederick held memberships, not to mention courtesy memberships he and Lady Borden enjoyed during official London visits. Since Ottawa had become the centre of their private and public life, many of their clubs were located there, including the Petawawa Fish and Game Club (which elected Sir Frederick its patron in 1911), the Ottawa Hunt Club, the Ottawa Golf Club, the Rideau Club, and the Connaught Jockey Club. Identified by the *Ottawa Citizen* as one of the city's "upper ten" gentlemen, Sir Frederick was also a founder, in 1907, of the Ottawa Country Club, and his son-in-law its honorary secretary.[17]

Although all were "gentlemen's clubs," ladies enjoyed restricted access to dining and special events, and many country clubs offered recreational facilities for families. The Ottawa Country Club, established on "the historic Ashworth homestead" and modelled on Montreal's Forest and Stream Club, offered family members "exclusive" facilities for bathing, fishing, tennis, bowling, and golf,[18] activities enjoyed by Lady Borden and her two athletic daughters. Lady Borden, Elizabeth, and Maude swam, rode, and golfed, and patronized the Ottawa Hunt Club and the Ottawa Golf Club. Clubs sponsored balls and social occasions useful for parents seeking suitable partners for their children. And Sir Frederick and Lady Borden had two attractive, cultivated daughters.

Family played an important role in Sir Frederick and Lady Borden's cultivation of social power. Once Elizabeth's formal education ended, she lived at home, migrating with her family from Ottawa to Canning, and often accompanying her parents on their travels abroad. British hostesses invariably included her in their invitations. Elizabeth loved formal ceremonial occasions, music, art, history, books, and education, and joined her parents in church, community, and social activities. She especially enjoyed travelling with her father. A well-dressed, informed conversationalist with broad interests and conscious of her family's standing, Elizabeth was devoted to her father's endeavours, protective of his reputation and ever ready to assist her parents' social diplomacy, attend dinners and club activities, and occasionally substitute for her mother as hostess.

As Sir Frederick and Lady Borden became more committed to public, business, and social obligations in Ottawa, and elsewhere, Elizabeth oversaw projects in Canning. She supervised inside and outside workers, her parents confident that things would be done well under her exacting watch. Practical, entrepreneurial, and decisive Elizabeth was a micro-manager, like her father, though more uncompromising. Although she was kind and charitable, her employees may have found her demanding and authoritarian.

In contrast to Elizabeth, Maude led an active Ottawa social life. Her friends included Lucy Crowdy, the daughter of the Governor General's secretary; Elsie and Dorothy Cotton, the daughters of her father's colleague Colonel H. Cotton, quartermaster of ordnance (1901), who in 1912 succeeded Colonel Otter as inspector-general of the militia, and who apart from his daughters had several eligible sons. Another of Maude's close friends was Lord Minto's theatrical, snobbish, and flirtatious "special friend,"[19] Miss Lola Powell. More lasting, though severely tested, was Maude's relationship with Leslie Macoun, the man she married in 1906. Leslie was the Irish-born second child of John Robert Macoun (1835–1923), a successful Irish linen manufacturer, and Wilhelmina Moorhead Dawson, who came from a "better family" than he.[20]

Leslie's migration to Canada was somewhat shrouded in mystery. Born on 31 July 1874,[21] Leslie Stuart Macoun arrived in Quebec City on 27 June 1890 as a steerage-class passenger aboard a ship sailing from Londonderry. He was then one month short of his sixteenth birthday. At the time, Canada had become a popular destination for British clerks and farm labourers. The ship's passenger list identified Leslie as a clerk (many of the ship's young male passengers claimed to be farm labourers or clerks). In retrospect, Leslie's self-designation seems to have been opportunistic or aspirational.

Family records explain Leslie's migration as an escape from an unhappy home and an old-fashioned "flogging' school." His home, "Woodburn," located in Belfast's exclusive Malone Park, was ruled by his stern, materialistic, religious (Church of England), and class-conscious father who had enrolled his eldest son in the King William's College for boys on the Isle of Man, a renowned but tyrannical school from which his father refused to remove his unhappy son. A strong-willed, independent boy, Leslie decided to flee his oppressive school and father. While home on holiday he stole some of his father's valuable old coins, went to the docks, found a ship destined for Quebec City, spent the night on the beach and left for Canada the next day. According to his daughter, her father's first year in Canada "was pretty grim." Although her father spoke little of his first year, she knew that he had worked on a farm in Ontario "for five dollars a month & board & milked cows [though] he had never been on a farm before,"[22] employment he may have secured through his association with his fellow steerage passengers.

Once Leslie's parents located their son, family played a larger role in his sustenance and advancement than his storybook venture might suggest. That Leslie's initial destination was Ottawa may not have been a coincidence, since Ottawa was home to his influential relative John Macoun (1831–1920), the Dominion Botanist, then assistant director of the Geological Survey and a "prominent figure in the city's social and intellectual circles."[23] A year after Leslie arrived in Ottawa, he left his life as a farm labourer for more lucrative and adventuresome employment as a chainman with the Geological Survey for $1.25 a day.

According to Leslie's daughter, her father was more forthcoming on his western adventures, regaling his family with tales of roughing it in western Canadian logging camps, mapping, and prospecting, dependent on Indigenous guides, while living on pork and beans and battling hordes of black flies. Meanwhile he re-established contact with his father who begged him to return, complete his education, and assume his family responsibilities as the eldest son. Attractive as his father's long-distant entreaties appeared to a low-paid linesman, a few months back in Ireland convinced Leslie "that he couldn't stand Belfast or his domineering father ... and he returned to Canada." He had been on his own too long to accept his family's constraints.[24] In later life, he liked to see himself as a self-made man, scornful of formal education.

Upon his return to Ottawa in 1895 Leslie secured a position at the Dominion Experimental Farms for the next seven years, first as a clerk then assistant accountant,[25] or bookkeeper. According to his later testimony, he owed his bookkeeper's position "entirely to the kindness of Dr. William Saunders,"[26] the director of the Dominion Experimental Farms and a colleague of Leslie's cousin, the Dominion Botanist. The farms' regular bookkeeper had become ill, and Saunders chose Leslie as his temporary, then permanent, replacement, though Leslie's bookkeeping was of a "very elementary level"; as was his salary. During that time Leslie lived in various Ottawa rooming houses on Metcalfe, Cooper, and Gloucester Streets. Upon the death of Leslie's mother on 2 January 1898 (at age fifty-two), Leslie returned briefly to Ireland. There, or upon the settlement of his mother's estate, he may have received some small inheritance, since his subsequent decision to remake his career as a manufacturer's agent and broker was unlikely to have been funded by his "savings" as a chainman or an ill-paid junior clerk at the Experimental Farms.

Whatever the source of Leslie's funding or good fortune, in January 1902 he advertised himself as a manufacturer's agent, insurance broker, and importer, and according to his daughter he soon became "quite well off." Indeed, before his marriage in 1906 Leslie possessed sufficient cash or credit to purchase, together with his friend George F. Macdonnell, an Ottawa solicitor, the old military hospital building on Wurtemburg Street, backing on the west bank of the Rideau River, which they transformed into two well-appointed semi-detached residences with back gardens terraced down to the river.[27] Number 197 Wurtemburg belonged to George and 199 Wurtemburg to Leslie. Gables, as Leslie named his residence, became one of his most profitable investments. In April 1906 (a month before Maude and Leslie were married), Maude's cousin, Robert Borden, the leader of the Conservative Party, and his wife Laura, bought Hayter Reid's house at 201 Wurtemburg Street, and named it Glensmere. Robert and Laura became and remained Maude and Leslie's neighbours and friends.[28]

Leslie's social remake was rapid and successful. Ambitious, incisive, and well-mannered, Leslie was an amusing conversationalist, with a rich, descriptive vocabulary and a caustic sense of humour; he moved with confidence and authority in Ottawa's socially mobile, layered British world. He joined the Princess Louise Dragoon Guards, a unit closely connected to Rideau Hall and popular with the city's elite and aspiring elite during Canada's "moment of militarism," that decade before the Great War when the presence of uniformed soldiers and martial music was a prerequisite of formal or official occasions.[29] A confident rider, good-looking and colourfully attired in his scarlet tunic, silver-coloured helmet, and white horsehair plume, Leslie rose quickly to the rank of captain in the dragoons. His expensive uniform confirmed his relative affluence; militia officers defended their socio-economic class barrier by insisting individuals purchase their expensive uniforms. An athletic young man, at home in private clubs, Leslie was also an eligible bachelor, well-positioned to attract the attention of the fashionable, lively younger daughter of the recently knighted minister of militia, himself an entrepreneurial member of Ottawa's "upper ten." Maude was no stranger to Rideau Hall, and, like Leslie, was athletic, independent, and resourceful.

In keeping with contemporary class customs, Lady Borden insisted on chaperoning Maude and Leslie, assisted by Sir Frederick's two dogs, one a Great Dane who took a dislike to Leslie. Known for his quick temper, Leslie solved his dog problem by delivering a violent kick to the dog's throat. And since unchaperoned riding was acceptable and Leslie and Maude were good riders, they found a more pacific solution to Lady Borden's vigilance, Leslie on his "big chestnut coloured horse "Paddy" and Maude on her small light grey Arab horse "Chumby," Maude riding side-saddle of course.[30] A year later, on 22 May 1906, Maude and Leslie were married in the large Dominion Methodist Church in Ottawa by its recently installed minister, Reverend Doctor George F. Salter, with Elizabeth and Arthur Wellesley Appleton, an Ottawa Bank of Montreal clerk, as witnesses.[31]

The *Ottawa Citizen* proclaimed the wedding a "Brilliant Social Event" and devoted two page-length columns to the wedding reception at Stadacona Hall, "the handsome residence of the popular Minister of Militia and his charming wife." In keeping with custom, the *Citizen* focused on the "rich gowns" worn by eighty-four of the reception's "beautifully gowned women." There were probably about 200 guests, a list of "prominent men" and "their wives" that read like an Ottawa who's who, beginning with the prime minister. The list included current and retired judges,[32] cabinet and ex-cabinet ministers,[33] senators, Sir Frederick's departmental colleagues,[34] notables and neighbours such as Joseph and Minette Pope, and Maude's girlfriends, notably Miss Lola Powell.

The press continued its effusive description of Maude and Leslie's reception in Stadacona Hall's spacious drawing room, decorated with "sheaves of American roses," where their guests "inspected the gifts of furniture, silver, cut glass, jewellery, ornaments etc.," gifts that came "from all parts of the Dominion, the United States and England." Unrecorded in the press were gifts of books, as well.[35] The offerings were so numerous that they overflowed "the room allotted to their display," the overflow consigned to tables and large cabinets in the hall, the number and quality of the gifts a measure of the parents' and guests' social standing.

After inspecting the gifts, the guests moved to the dining room and verandah for the "delicious refreshments so generously provided," for the toasts. In proposing a toast to the bride, Sir Wilfrid Laurier, witty and eloquent as ever, invited the guests to say goodbye to "Miss Maude Borden" and welcome to "Mrs. Macoun," adding that given such a charming wife her husband would have no difficulty keeping his vows to "cherish and love." But the bride, the prime minister mused, may not find it so easy to keep her vow to obey, "unless she is certain that her husband is in the right and she is the one to decide if he is in the right," a jocular reference to Maude's independence. The groom responded to the toast, and the best man proposed the health of the bridesmaids, after which the bride and groom left the room to prepare for their departure for Montreal. The bride and groom descended the stairs, and in contemporary fashion the bride tossed her bouquet to "a group of pretty girls standing in the hall below," after which the couple was showered with rice as they made their way to the carriage. A "large horse-shoe of white and pink roses that had been suspended over the hall" had been fastened to the carriage. The couple then drove to the train station accompanied by the younger guests.[36]

Altogether the wedding provided a snapshot of Sir Frederick and Lady Borden's place in Ottawa society, the picture of a family headed by what the *Ottawa Citizen* liked to call one of the City's "upper ten gentlemen," a familiar guest at Rideau Hall, a friend and neighbour of the prime minister, whose Brown and Borden cousins occupied prominent public positions including that of leader of the Opposition.

Their daughter's marriage to an ambitious young businessman extended Sir Frederick and Lady Borden's presence in the city. Sir Frederick and Leslie developed a warm, "affectionate," trusting working relationship. They shared an interest in the military, investment, politics,[37] and horse racing. Sir Frederick treated his son-in-law as a junior business associate and surrogate for Harold. They exchanged political gossip, investment advice, and on one occasion Sir Frederick sent Leslie to Europe in search of capital for a projected Gaspereau River hydro development. Sir Frederick brought Leslie into the family business, introduced him to business friends and government agencies, and endorsed his commercial initiatives, arrangements that aroused the Conservative Opposition's suspicions.[38]

Lady Borden's relations with Leslie were more reserved, correct, and cordial and never particularly warm. Leslie was a "man's man," crisp, respectful, and confident, more comfortable in gendered spheres, where men attended to business, politics, sports, and soldiering. Lady Borden admired Leslie's industry, ambition, and apparent administrative competence. She appreciated his deference, good manners, and verbal eloquence, and his appreciation of dress, decorum, and ceremony, and was reassured by Fred's confidence in him. But Lady Borden and Leslie shared few interests, certainly not religion, music, books, education, or art. Nor in the early years did Lady Borden perceive Leslie's penchant for pugnacity and cutting sarcasm, which ultimately had such a chilling effect on their relations.

Chapter Twelve

Courting London

Although Canning and Ottawa were a long way from London, Sir Frederick, Canada's minister of defence, and Lady Borden were strategically located to demonstrate their imperial credentials during Canada's "moment of militarism."[1] But even during this era of high imperialism those credentials required proof and persistence. With neither mentor, rulebook, nor guarantee, Sir Frederick and Lady Borden set out to convince Ottawa and London of their ability to negotiate Canada's controversial imperial interests, a gamble that required political skill and social diplomacy, with no assurance of success.

Ever since Queen Victoria's Diamond Jubilee in 1897 Canada enjoyed an enviable reputation in imperial London, hailed by imperialists as a vindication of imperial rule. The British immigration and investment that flooded Canada during the decade and a half before 1914, reinforced British confidence in Canada's future and its centrality to the imperial project. No meaningful reordering of the imperial estate could proceed without Canada's participation or compliance, a maxim Laurier quickly grasped and used to extract maximum benefits at minimum cost. To sustain this strategy Laurier needed a skilled, credible associate who shared his notion of liberal imperialism.

Laurier's choice was his minister of militia. Colleagues for decades, they were now close friends and neighbours. They shared intellectual, social, and political interests, and were pragmatic and committed to religious and linguistic diversity, a perspective they brought to national and imperial politics. Both believed in a country and empire based on diversity and autonomy and opposed imperial centralization. In their view empire began at home, each nation governing its part of the imperial estate. Laurier had watched his minister of defence at home and in

London. He appreciated and trusted Sir Frederick's loyalty and persistence and admired his growing influence in London.

Laurier understood the importance of social diplomacy in imperial London with its intoxicating talk of "Empire, Empire, Empire," but feared its magnetic appeal of "royalty, aristocracy, and plutocracy," and how easily it turned "weak men's heads." He had watched Sir Frederick at the 1902 Colonial/Imperial Conference and had appreciated his private and public defence of their shared imperial agenda. He had admired his social skills and style, how Sir Frederick's tall, "handsome presence and immaculate attire had made him an outstanding figure in all Court and Parliamentary functions."[2] Nor was Laurier blind to Lady Borden's sophistication and commitment, and her contribution to Sir Frederick's success. He had little hesitation, therefore, entrusting Sir Frederick with Canada's imperial dossiers, especially as defence came to trump trade and political reorganization on the imperial agenda.

Imperial defence made Sir Frederick a familiar figure in London, charged with negotiating Canada's needs, costs, and modalities. In the decade before the Great War, financing the Anglo-German naval rivalry sparked a vigorous British debate on imperial management, its nature, price, and priorities. The debate spawned numerous plans for imperial reorganization, some that challenged the Canadian government's commitment to a liberal empire. Manoeuvring within the debate's treacherous national and imperial shoals and cross-currents required knowledge, skill, and sensitivity, and the social capital to purchase access to imperial decision makers.

Imperial policy was not Sir Frederick and Lady Borden's only interest in London. Equally important was the city's capacity to advance their personal and material interests. Pre–Great War London was a mecca for ambitious, entrepreneurial Canadians, including prominent Maritime entrepreneurs and politicians such as Charles Tupper (1821–1915), James Dunn (1874–1956), and Max Aitken (1879–1964), men whose aspirations outgrew local, regional, and national borders, and who, like Sir Frederick, saw imperial access as a path to personal advantage. Whatever constraints imperialism may have imposed on Canada's constitutional development during the apex of British imperialism (1880–1920), London was the financial, political, and cultural centre of the world, a magnet for Canada's ambitious and socially mobile public men and women in search of personal and material advancement.

The age of imperialism and militarism coincided with a golden age (1902–14) of British capital investment in Canada, when Canada replaced the United States as Britain's single largest borrower, "absorbing perhaps a third of British lending."[3] As an ambitious entrepreneur Sir

Frederick nursed several private projects that sought British markets and capital. His apple orchards, which represented 15 per cent of his capital investment, benefited directly from access to the large, expanding British produce market, and imperial London was an obvious capital market for his cold storage, hydroelectric, and traction interests.[4]

Association with imperial power brought recognition, prestige, and influence at home and abroad. It promised titles, deference, and patronage, rewards often out of proportion to a person or colony's power and importance. Whether imperial bonding was fired by a sense of blood and belonging, public interests, or simply private profit, it expressed itself in rituals, imagined affinities, and efforts to coordinate shared interests in defence, trade, and governance. Given the contemporary complicity of private, personal, and public interests, entrepreneurs with material objectives and personal aspirations craved imperial visibility and endorsement.

Late Victorian and Edwardian Britain seemed especially receptive to socially ambitious Canadians as class distinctions within the upper echelons of British society became more blurred and permeable.[5] The erosion of British agriculture and land wealth had pried open British class stratification to its commercial and industrial classes, enabling the nouveau riche to purchase access to its freemasonry of imperial power. Colonial title seekers seemed to enjoy even easier access to its upper echelons than British residents; their colonial social antecedents more easily disguised by wealth, and their social mobility facilitated by post–Boer War British imperialists' efforts to recruit colonial elites to their causes and encourage colonial replication of British society. Perhaps no better contemporary example existed of a colonial's success than Canada's "naturalized" high commissioner, Lord Strathcona.

Sir Frederick and Lady Borden had little difficulty replicating British ruling-class customs and culture. Both were familiar with the structure and practices of British elite society, shaped by their reading of British history and literature, and their knowledge of its local aadaptations. They understood the complicity of public and personal life, of social and political power, and of the seasonal cycle of political life and entertainment dictated by the court and Parliament.[6] They appreciated, too, the instrumental role of political hostesses in the imperial project, the strategic social interventions of wealthy, well-connected women who negotiated hospitality, recognition, and opportunity, arranged marriage alliances, and stage-managed public life. As Julia Bush has written, political hostesses were effectively "unelected Lady politicians,"[7] with their own agendas, who lobbied for their causes, "veiling their self-assertiveness and success behind men."[8]

Although Lady Borden performed on a smaller stage, she played her role with skill and conviction, never doubting the efficacy of social diplomacy and the ethical propriety of complicit public and private interests. She also had the formation, aptitude, and ability to hold her own in that imperial world. Since few British upper-class ladies "went to school,"[9] Lady Borden's formal education was probably more extensive than that of many of her British compares. She had a knowledge of and interest in art, literature, music, history, and travel, a passion for fashion, and a meticulous regard for language, manners, and deportment. She had demonstrated her social skills during the 1902 coronation festivities, skills that British ladies often found lacking in "colonials," a consideration that weighed heavily in Edwardian London.[10] She also had the physical stamina to withstand their drawing room receptions, teas, dinners, garden parties, "at homes," and visits to clubs, country houses, gardens, museums, galleries, theatres, and concerts halls. In short, imperial London offered Lady Borden an opportunity to live and test her imagined world against the realities that grounded her life.

To demonstrate and enhance their imperial credentials, Sir Frederick and Lady Borden sought a social bridgehead in London, an objective that depended on perception and contingencies that made progress difficult to measure or predict. Nor was London won easily or immediately. Success required regular correspondence, visibility, and personal contact. Sir Frederick and Lady Borden had launched their well-timed initiative during their lengthy 1902 London sojourn. The coronation, Sir Frederick's "double" knighthood and the Colonial/Imperial Conference had introduced them to a range of influential policy makers, gentlemen capitalists, and their wives. Fred's membership in the Royal Colonial Institute, the Cobden, United Services, and United Empire clubs garnered introductions and social contacts, opportunities to listen, learn, and appreciate the imperial agenda's complexities and strategies. The coronation introduced them to titled imperial enthusiasts such as the Duke of Devonshire (1868–1938), the Duke of Connaught (1874–1942), and the Duke of Norfolk (1860–1917), and enhanced Sir Frederick and Lady Borden's imperial standing, and reinforced by allusions to their recent personal sacrifice. References to imperial occasions and titled persons were no less useful back home.

Central to Sir Frederick and Lady Borden's imperial project was London's sizable Canadian community, its epicentre the Canadian High Commission, directed by Lord Strathcona, Canada's wealthy high commissioner, whose political and financial tentacles permeated Canadian and British society. Sir Frederick and Lord Strathcona were no strangers. They had sat opposite one another in the House of

Commons for many years. Their personal relations were unmarred by any personal or political conflict. They also shared a certain dislike of Sir Charles Tupper. Since then, personal, political, and private interests cemented their relationship and dissolved residual partisan suspicions.

During Fred's first official visit to London in December 1897, the high commissioner had demonstrated his legendary reputation for wining and dining visiting Canadian dignitaries.[11] He had invited Fred to spend Christmas dinner with his family, and later, when Lizzie and Maude visited London in 1899, he had entertained them and assisted them in securing scarce wartime return passage.[12] During Fred and Bessie's subsequent visit to recover from Harold's death, Lord and Lady Strathcona had received them at their impressive Glencoe estate and alerted the Canadian community to their presence in London. Lady Borden and Lady Strathcona were also joint patrons of Lady Minto's Soldiers Wives League.

Even before Harold's death, Lord Strathcona had a favourable opinion of Canada's minister of defence. Fred's thoughtful response to the high commissioner's offer to raise a small battalion of Canadian scouts for service in South Africa, and the minister's flattering insistence that it be named the Strathcona's Horse, had worked their spell. Had Strathcona any residual doubts about Fred's dependability, Sam Hughes, the Conservative party's military critic and friend of the high commissioner and the minister, would have reassured Strathcona of Fred's ability and good will. Fred admired the high commissioner's business acumen, political power, and deep pockets, and invested in some of Strathcona's enterprises,[13] though given Strathcona's entrepreneurial tentacles they would have been difficult to escape.[14] Subsequently, Fred never hesitated to seek Strathcona's advice or solicit his financial, political, and personal support, nor was he ever disappointed.[15]

Old colonial hands constituted the core of London's Canadian community. That included past Governors General, their families and entourage,[16] general officers commanding the Canadian militia, and general officers commanding the British North American Halifax Garrison, as well as Canadian businessmen, writers, and expatriates.[17] Among former Governors General, Lord Lorne and Princess Louise, and Lord and Lady Aberdeen were particularly attentive to Canadian visitors, as was Lord and Lady Aberdeen's daughter Marjorie Sinclair (1880–1970), Baroness Pentland, who maintained an active interest in Canada and its history. Later, whenever Sir Frederick and Lady Borden visited London, they received invitations from Sybil Mary Grey, the 4th Earl Grey's only daughter and her husband, Arthur Morton Grenfell.

Sir W.J. Gascoigne,[18] Richard O'Grady-Haly,[19] and Lord William Seymour; all had enjoyed working with Sir Frederick and provided hospitality and useful introductions.

Favour-seekers were conspicuous among Sir Frederick and Lady Borden's British social network, influence peddlers who mixed private and public interests, a market in which Sir Frederick was both benefactor and beneficiary. Arms salesmen were especially solicitous. They included Sir Charles Henry Augustus Frederick Lockhart Ross, the 9th Baron of Balnagown, who had persuaded the Canadian government to substitute the militia's standard Lee-Enfield for his Ross rifle. Representatives of Vickers, Sons & Maxim, the large arms, ammunition, naval, and (later) aeronautic company paid court – men such as Sir Arthur Trevor Dawson (1866–1931), the company's managing director, who was also a director of Vickers' Canadian affiliate.[20] The network included men with private financial interests such as Sir Robert William Perks (1849–1936), the outspoken Liberal imperialist, and the 4th Duke of Sutherland (1851–1913), the large British landowner interested in shifting his land-based wealth to western Canada.

As an engaged partner in imperial statecraft, Lady Borden occupied a strategic listening post. An informed, acute observer, attentive listener, articulate conversationalist, and shrewd analyst, Lady Borden knew when to speak and not to speak and to whom. Although she held strong personal views on public issues, she was discreet and ecumenical, and understood the power of political intelligence. And, as Susan Mann has pointed out, female "purposeful gossip" constituted an important information network, a language of power and control that many women managed with skill, and with benefit to themselves, their husbands, and their family – a language that Lady Borden mastered with distinction.[21]

As a recipient and contributor to this information network, Lady Borden was subtle, acute, and poised in public, though forthright and incisive in private, a person who could pierce the mask of political rhetoric and posturing. Nor did she hesitate to employ these qualities to assess imperial schemes and schemers, influence peddlers, and favour-seekers. In her semi-public role as consort, she often reversed the role of passive listener and assumed a more active role by cultivating "useful" friendships with women such as Polly Ross, Sir Charles Ross's wife; Lulu (Louise Grant) Dawson, the wife of Sir Trevor Dawson; Edith Perks, the wife of Sir Robert Perks;[22] and the 7th Countess of Jersey, Lady Margaret Elizabeth Jersey,[23] the regal wife of a wealthy Glyn, Mills & Company banker, and one of London's most assiduous political hostesses.

Among Lady Borden's "useful" friends and hostesses were the wives of cabinet ministers and public servants. Mary Ethel Harcourt, the imperialist wife of Lewis Vernon Harcourt (1863–1922),[24] the Liberal MP and secretary of state for the colonies (1910–15), was perhaps Lady Borden's closest friend next to Lady Jersey, both anti-suffragists whose views posed no barrier to their friendship. Generally, Lady Borden's coterie was wide and inclusive, extending to women such as Madeleine Middleton (1856–1942), the wife of St. John Brodrick, the secretary of state for war (1900–3);[25] Consuelo Vanderbilt, the 9th Duchess of Marlborough, whose husband was under-secretary of state for the colonies (1903–5),[26] all well-connected, cross-party associates. Her rapport with these powerful ladies netted invitations to clubs, concerts, conversaziones, dinners, flower shows, and country weekends, occasions that facilitated the sharing of information, instilled confidence, and eased access to persons and opportunities.

Lady Borden, however, was more than simply a human resource, Sir Frederick's "manipulative" stage manager, fixer, and escort. Many of her British female friendships were based on companionship and reciprocal interests. She enjoyed the company of the "well-bred," their culture of food, dress, decor, and gardens, a world of intelligent, talented women with whom she shared an appreciation of music,[27] art,[28] gardens, literature, travel, and public affairs. Those who shared her passion for gardens, music, and theatre provided invitations to flower shows, concerts, and operas,[29] all tokens of power, respect, and confidence. Many of Lady Borden's elite female friends were accomplished public persons, often more interesting than their husbands.[30]

Few of Lady Borden's lady friends were more imperious and influential than Lady Margaret Elizabeth (Leigh Child-Villiers), 7th Countess of Jersey (1849–1945) and sister of the Duke of Westminster. A prominent political hostess, philanthropist, traveller, imperialist, and author, she was knighted in 1927 for her war service; her husband was a colonial administrator who had attended the Ottawa Conference in 1894. Coveted invitations to the Jersey's elegant Osterley Park estate, its home designed and decorated by Robert Adam, promised interesting guests, stimulating conversation, and extravagant hospitality.[31] Lady Borden not only received invitations to Osterley Park but to Middleton Park, Lady Jersey's 330-hectare eighteenth-century Oxfordshire estate (with instructions to dress informally); indeed their friendship continued beyond Sir Frederick and Lady Borden's active public lives.

How precisely Lady and Sir Frederick Borden's jointly constructed social network advanced their private and public agendas remains presumptive and circumstantial, difficult to prove or deny. But in

December 1903, less than a year and a half after Sir Frederick and Lady Borden had established their social beachhead in London, Sir Frederick had an opportunity to demonstrate his diplomatic skills to his Ottawa colleagues. His London mission was to obtain imperial support for his proposed amendments to the Canadian Militia Act, to make it "a Canadian law, first, last and all the time."[32] The task pitted his agenda and powers of persuasion against those of Lord Minto, the Governor General, and Lord Dundonald, the officer commanding the Canadian militia, who bombarded the Colonial and War Offices with advice, warning them against Sir Frederick's proposed amendments, an opposition that bordered on obstruction.

The Governor General and the general officer commanding had often disagreed on Canadian military matters but on this occasion, both sought to block three items in Sir Frederick's proposed new Militia Act. They rejected Sir Frederick's decision to vest the position of commander-in-chief in the king rather than in the Governor General, to open command of the Canadian militia to an officer of Canada's permanent force, and to omit the statutory provision to place the Canadian militia under the King's Regulations in the event of service with British troops. Before the minister struck these provisions from the Militia Act, Minto insisted that Sir Frederick secure the approval of the British government's Committee of Imperial Defence, confident that the British would reject Sir Frederick's proposals and the minister would return, having been seduced by imperial splendour and the wiles of social diplomacy.[33]

For Sir Frederick the stakes were high. But he was prepared, arriving in London in good time to renew acquaintances and to attend clubs and meetings. Trading on his recent knighthood, and personal sacrifice, he interviewed ministers and officials in the War and Colonial Offices and reached an informal understanding well before the Committee of Imperial Defence's official meeting. Fortuitously, Alfred Lyttelton (1857–1913) had replaced Joseph Chamberlain as colonial secretary only months before and was more open to a decentralized empire than Chamberlain. Much to Minto's disappointment, Sir Frederick returned to Ottawa with much more than he had asked. Not only had the British approved his reform proposals, but they had agreed to recognize the equality of Canadian militia ranks with those of the British regular force, to reserve six senior staff positions for Canadians at the British staff college, and to transfer the British garrisons at Halifax and Esquimalt to the Canadian government. In addition, they had named Sir Frederick a member of the Committee of Imperial Defence.

Astounded by Sir Frederick's verbal account of his success, the Governor General doubted its veracity, after a draft of the Committee of

Imperial Defence's minutes appeared to contradict the minister's report. Sir Frederick, however, lost no time dispelling Minto's doubts, writing privately to Alfred Lyttelton, the secretary of state for the colonies, who obligingly confirmed Sir Frederick's recollection, regretting that the War Office secretary had "composed the minutes on the theory that what he conceives ought to have been arranged was arranged."[34] This was not the last time Sir Frederick's private intervention secured editorial favours from colonial office secretaries.[35] Given the colonial secretary's response, Minto could do little but rant to his diary about the colonial secretary's unbelievable "stupidity," unable to admit, at first, Sir Frederick's success.

Perception was everything. Sir Frederick's success, however, had less to do with his diplomatic skill or social influence than with the Committee of Imperial Defence's strategic decision to withdraw the North American fleet to "home" waters and trust to Anglo-American good will. Nonetheless the British authorities were sufficiently supportive of Sir Frederick's larger blueprint for militia reform to reserve coveted positions for Canadians at the British Staff College and relinquish imperial control of the Halifax and Esquimalt garrisons. They were also sufficiently persuaded by the minister to reject Minto's and Dundonald's efforts to sabotage his London mission. Nor were they obliged to offer Sir Frederick "membership" in the Committee of Imperial Defence, the first "Colonial so honoured," even if membership was an amorphous honour owing to its functional composition and distant meetings. Nevertheless, Sir Frederick saw his appointment as a personal honour, as did his family, who had it chiselled on his tombstone.

Back home, Sir Frederick's appointment met with mixed reactions. Imperialists and their opponents agreed that Sir Frederick's 1903 appointment to the CID was a "precedence of great importance," even if they disagreed as to its desirability.[36] Hopeful imperialists praised the CID as the nucleus of more ambitious imperial governance, while anti-imperialists feared it as a dangerous precedent that required vigilance. Imperial centralization was not Frederick's objective. What he sought was a pragmatic, cooperative constitutional equality, a liberal empire, in which Canada managed its own portion of the imperial estate.

The next year Sir Frederick reinforced his imperial credentials during his explosive dismissal of Lord Dundonald. Not only did Sir Frederick enjoy the Governor General's private sympathy, and the understanding of the British War and Colonial Offices during the dispute, but he had little difficulty "in getting his way" on the troublesome officer's replacement, in contrast to his failure to secure Percy Lake's services after Hutton's departure in 1898, even with Lord Strathcona's intervention.[37]

Each imperial success enhanced Sir Frederick's colleagues' confidence in his diplomatic skills and cooperative imperialism, a success recognized by several scholars.[38]

Yet even during this era of high imperialism, London readily forgot colonial politicians. And in Ottawa colonial diplomats' imperial triumphs were easily overshadowed by pressing domestic issues. To avoid amnesia or indifference during imperial doldrums and domestic distractions, Sir Frederick and Lady Borden continued to refine their imperial credentials and explore ways and means for reordering the empire, with an eye to Canada's advantage within that fancied world. They corresponded, read, and travelled. Not only was travel a congenial pastime, it enhanced their imperial visibility and domestic authority.

Lady Borden had not accompanied Sir Frederick to London for his short, focused meeting with the Committee of Imperial Defence in December 1903. But on 1 September 1906, following Maude and Leslie's elegant May wedding, Sir Frederick, Lady Borden, and Elizabeth sailed from Montreal for Liverpool aboard the Allan Lines recently constructed 10,000-ton R.M.S. *Virginian* for a six-week visit to Britain and the continent, a sea voyage, enlivened by the company of Sir Hugh and Lady Andrew Montague Allan, accompanied by their maid, servants, and chauffeur. Otherwise, the voyage was a rough, dreary seven-day passage, relieved only by their anticipation of London's social season, political life, and friendships, and subsequent visit to the continent.

Arriving in Liverpool on 7 September 1906, Sir Frederick, Lady Borden, and Elizabeth reached "dear old Chester" by train, just in time for the Harvard-Cambridge boat race. Sportsmanship and college loyalty dictated their support of Sir Frederick's alma mater despite Harvard's defeat. Comfortably settled in the Grosvenor Hotel, Sir Frederick and Lady Borden set out on foot to show Lizzie their old Chester haunts, including restaurants and tea houses that they had so enjoyed in 1900. Their itinerary included Eaton Hall, the Duke of Westminster's country house and gardens, and evensong at Chester Cathedral. An unrepentant anglophile, Elizabeth was charmed by Chester, "so full of historic interest, so full of life & good cheer, so busy & happy & so self-satisfied."[39]

Elizabeth's enchantment grew next day as they drove to Lichfield, Staffordshire, to visit its three-spire medieval cathedral and to meet its bishop. In Lady Borden's opinion Lichfield's Cathedral was "the Queen of English Cathedrals." But for Sir Frederick their visit to the birthplace of Samuel Johnson, his favourite author, was the highlight of their visit. Their sentimental journey continued in the afternoon as they drove to Warwick and stayed at the Warwick Arms, close to the castle as they had done in 1900, Sir Frederick and Lady Borden sleeping in a four-poster bed and dressing by candlelight. A ten-mile drive the next morning brought them to "beautiful Stratford on Avon," where they spent a "delightful day" visiting Anne Hathaway's "simply fascinating" thatched house. Their only regret was having to leave for London late that afternoon.[40]

London meant an exuberant schedule of shops, theatres, and galleries. Their Ebury House Hotel in Belgravia was within walking distance of Parliament, Buckingham Palace, and the recently opened National Gallery of British Art (the Tate Gallery). As soon as they unpacked, they enjoyed a quiet afternoon viewing the Tate's "beautiful paintings," especially *The Doctor*, by Samuel Luke Fildes (1843–1927), which Lady Borden described as "more than up to [her] expectations." The next day they lunched with the recently minted Lord Northcliff (1865–1922), the British newspaper magnate, and Edward "Ned" Mortimer Macdonald (1865–1940), Sir Frederick's old friend and Liberal MP for Pictou. In the afternoon, Lady Borden and Elizabeth passed the rest of the day at the newly bequeathed Wallace Collection of eighteenth- and nineteenth-century European painting and furniture, collected by Sir Richard Wallace (1818–1890).

The next morning Lady Borden and Elizabeth shopped on Oxford Street while Sir Frederick searched Christie's_for antiques and collectibles. In the evening, all three attended Arthur Wing Pinero's (1855–1934) four-act play at St. James's Theatre, entitled *His House in Order*, the story of a virtuous young woman's marriage to an older man who was living in the shadow of his beloved but secretly adulterous deceased first wife, a production that Lady Borden considered "very fine indeed." The next day Lady Borden and Elizabeth shopped at Kensington's high-end shops such as Derry & Toms, where they lunched before rushing back to their hotel to collect Sir Frederick for the evening performance of Joseph Comyns Carr's (1849–1916) *Tristan and Iseult*, a pseudo-Arthurian legend of knightly adultery, which Lady Borden again found "perfectly splendid," especially Edith Wynn (Mattison) Kennedy's (1875–1955) performance of Brangwaine.[41] Lady Borden had a curious fascination for themes of infidelity and adultery in contemporary theatre.

Sir Frederick, Lady Borden, and Elizabeth rose early the next day, Sunday morning, and motored to Windsor, Ascot, and Sunningdale, about 40 kilometres west of London, then lunched and spent the afternoon with Mr. and Mrs. Frederick Williams-Taylor (1863–1945), the Moncton-born, recently appointed London manager of the Bank of Montreal and a close associate of Lord Strathcona. In keeping with her fascination with Edwardian society, Lady Borden noted that the couple were "very pleasant but very worldly in a very open way." After lunch, a Mr. Puddie drove them to Lord Roberts's Ascot home and garden (a poignant occasion in that Roberts also lost his only son in the South African War), before returning to their hotel for a "nice little supper" and a welcome fire on a cold damp Sabbath night.[42]

On Monday morning they packed their bags, purchased travel tickets, maps, and tour books for their continental travel, and after lunch searched old book shops on High Holborn. During the next day's motor trip to Headcorn, Kent, their putative "family seat," Elizabeth and her father discussed family history, while Lady Borden watched the countryside, the "prettiest drive I have had." Eventually, at 8 pm, they reached what Lady Borden described as "the funny old place, where they spent the night, their arrival the cause of great "excitement over the motor coming." Elizabeth was especially "delighted with the place & people"; and more so the next morning as they toured the church and admired the recently (1904) installed window to commemorate the Borden family, donated by an American, Lavinia Borden.[43]

After a "nice little afternoon feast" early that afternoon, they left for Dover and boarded the ferry for a "most wretched trip" to Ostend. Their destination was Bruges, "the charming old city – with canals running in every direction," where they were welcomed to "a most comfortable hotel" by "all the servants male and female." Next morning, they toured the city by auto, visited churches, and viewed their artworks and "wonderful carving on wood." Mid-afternoon they left for a three-hour drive to Antwerp's Grand Hotel. After a substantial dinner of "splendid cuisine," the intrepid tourists searched for a music hall. When they finally located one Sir Frederick found the music too loud, and overcome with exhaustion they returned to the hotel.

The next morning's agenda only left time to view the museum's "pictures," largely by Peter Paul Rubens (1577–1640), whose sensuous nudes and Catholic Reformation pictures Lady Borden found "especially good," before motoring to Amsterdam and registering at a comfortable hotel with "a bathroom and every comfort." The city itself appeared "very modern & everything up to date," in many ways "a modern Venice – all canals" and houseboats. Although Lady Borden spotted some "quaint people in quaint clothing ... with wooden shoes & dogs working like horses," the city seemed less quaint to her than Bruges. The highlight of her visit was the queen's palace, "a large handsome building, with some splendid rooms," including a "dining room lighted by 400 wax candles" and "wonderful paintings." They then drove to the "Jewish quarter" and to the docks, and in the evening Sir Frederick went off alone to a "very fine" concert.

Although Lady Borden's travel diary ends on 23 September 1906 at Amsterdam, they visited Paris before returning to London, where they remained for the next three weeks, for business and pleasure, cultivating their social network and enhancing their visibility in the imperial capital, before boarding the *Virginian* in Liverpool for Montreal on 20 October 1906; they disembarked with their acquisitions, their fashionable clothes, household furnishings, and gifts for friends and family, together with their memories and conversational knowledge of their wider world with which to regale friends and colleagues.

Lord Grey, Canada's new Governor General needed little convincing. Lord Minto had already advised his brother-in-law and successor that Sir Frederick was a very influential cabinet minister, close to the prime minister and knowledgeable on imperial affairs. In espousing his various imperial causes, preserving the Plains of Abraham, staging the Quebec Tercentenary, and receiving imperial visitors, Grey was careful to include Sir Frederick, convinced that he was only one of two members of the Canadian cabinet who had any knowledge of "foreign affairs."[44]

Chapter Thirteen

Our Lady of the Snows

Although disenfranchised, many late nineteenth- and early twentieth-century Canadian elite women had significant influence on civic life. The nature and impact of their influence, however, are often obscured and ignored, owing largely to its oral, privileged, personal, and undocumented character. More difficult to ignore or deny is their commitment to "social politics" and their personal access to power and influence.[1] Moreover, a growing body of British and Canadian historical writing, based on diaries, memoirs, and correspondence, has demonstrated the success of elite women in shaping public policy.[2] The task, then, is to identify the nature, objectives, and methods of their contribution, and to recognize their success.

Not all of Lady Borden's elite female contemporaries agreed on the propriety and efficacy of women's participation in civic life. Much depended upon their commitment, access to power, and how well the existing system served their interests. Those women who viewed public affairs from a privileged position, confident "of their ability to influence male power-holders," practised what Anne-Marie Kinahan has termed "transcendent citizenship."[3] These were women who were content to elect and inspire good public men, rear public-spirited sons, and serve as "well-informed and respected advisors,"[4] rather than seek female enfranchisement or engagment in public advocacy, an approach favoured initially by many women in Canada's National Council of Women. The debate on elite women's public participation, then, is more about means than ends, and the nature of their convictions, character, and opportunity.[5]

Churches, service organizations, and reading clubs were sites for elite women to consider and address contemporary issues. Teas, "at homes," and mixed-gender dinners were also venues for genteel exchange on current affairs and the means to effect change – a grown-up version of

Mount Allison's topics nights! Congregants at Lady Borden's Dominion Methodist Church in Ottawa, acclaimed as the "Mother Church of Canadian Methodism" or the "Mars Hill of Canadian Protestantism,"[6] heard sermons on topics such as "science and religion" and "Christian socialism," and claims that Jesus was the greatest socialist of all time. The church's Epworth League sponsored an array of progressive speakers, including Newton Rowell (1867–1941), Nellie McClung (1873–1951), Ralph Connor (1860–1937), and John Wilson Bengough (1851–1923), who lectured on social reform, women's rights, church union, the single tax, citizenship, and immigration. Lady Borden's dinner guests discussed war and peace, the place of women in Japanese society, the Reciprocity Agreement, and the Naval Bill. Her "at homes" were sites of gentle advocacy, often in the presence of Laurier, who enjoyed listening to and chatting with engaged, intelligent women.[7]

Lady Borden read contemporary journals, political history, and biography, and attended House of Commons debates. Her support of social causes was inspired by her Christianity, her reading of Charles Dickens and John Ruskin, her sense of noblesse oblige, and her belief that "to whom much is given much is required." A friend of Lady Aberdeen during the latter's residence in Ottawa (1893–8), Lady Borden worked with the National Council of Women and served as a vice-president, and joined the Victorian Order of Nurses' board of management.[8] Both were active social service organizations founded by Lady Aberdeen and led by elite women. Like many of her peers, Lady Borden shared their "patrician" social perspective, and though interested in the condition of women at home and abroad,[9] she was not a vocal advocate of women's enfranchisement. She did not enjoy public speaking.[10] She preferred private influence, serving as a "well informed and respected advisor,"[11] discreetly exercising her influence through her husband and content to groom her son for public life.

Nonetheless, Lady Borden appreciated the spectacle of power and public service, its purpose, and its possibilities. Public service appealed to her missionary instincts, inherited from the Tuppers, and Methodist commitment to social betterment and education tempered by a shrewd sense of human frailty and folly, and informed by history and literature. She understood the potential of her privileged position, of soft power, and how titles, honours, and ritualized deference facilitated influence. Aware of the pitfalls of her position, and the need for discretion and diplomacy, she was uncomfortable with public advocacy, preferring to support other women's public interventions, women such as Dr. Helen MacMurchy, Professor Edna Victoria Moffatt, or her daughter Elizabeth.

Popular, contemporary debate on empire and nation was not confined to men. Elite women participated in the debate and discussion of their country's character, mission, and future. Nor were their ideas any more homogeneous than those of elite men.[12] Lady Borden's Canada was neither founded nor refounded on the Plains of Abraham. Of proud "Planter" ancestry, she had little time for theories that founded her country exclusively on its Loyalist, anglophone, and Protestant heritage. She was especially sceptical of crusading imperial, religious, or ethno-linguistic societies and their divisive rhetoric as it applied to her "binational" country's mixed ethnic and religious composition. During the apotheosis of British imperial power and proselytizing, her name is conspicuously absent from membership lists or executive positions in imperial organizations. Her absence is even more striking given her imperial visibility and friendship with aristocratic ladies such as Lady Jersey and Edith Lyttleton (1865–1948).[13] London's imperial ladies' failure to recruit her to their causes underlines her reticence, and suggests the "complex interplay of colonial nationalism, imperialism and gender."[14]

Lady Borden's Canada was a European settlers' project, composed of people of Norman and Saxon extraction, proud of their language, literature, culture, and rights.[15] Sir Frederick Borden, too, insisted on his Norman origins in the design of his coat of arms. Theirs was a political project defined and enriched by its duality, though blind to its Indigenous heritage. Among Lady Borden's non-negotiable settlers' rights were autonomy and diversity, rights that she believed settlers carried with them and were secured by allegiance, not subjection.[16] And, in Joseph Howe's stirring rhetoric, British settlers asked for nothing more, but would be satisfied with nothing less. Lady Borden's liberal imperialism mirrored Rudyard Kipling's memorable, contemporary characterization of Canada in *Our Lady of the Snows*: "Daughter am I in my mother's house, / But mistress in my own. / The gates are mine to open, / As the gates are mine to close."[17] Her empire and its monarch were a shared property, not the United Kingdom's private possession, a symbol of that wider imperial family of nation states, represented in contemporary imperial iconography as sisters or daughters. Canadian identity, therefore, did not demand imperial rupture or mindless mimicry, nor did it preclude building a "Better Britain" in Canada.[18]

While Lady Borden, like her elite Montreal compares,[19] sought social betterment, she was also interested in economics, war, national, and imperial (international) politics, especially Canada's evolving imperial relationship, one that promised Canadians a privileged, profitable access to a larger world. She shared her husband's instrumental approach to London's social clubs and civic organizations, such as the United Services Club, the British Empire League, Royal Colonial Institute, and Cobden Club. She accompanied him to many of their debates and discussions focused on profitable imperialism, such as the Pacific Cable, Penny Postage, Fast Atlantic Steamship service, the Home Scholarship Fund, and the Imperial Commercial Club. She, like he, preferred forms of cooperative imperialism promoted by organizations such as the National Council of Women, the Victorian Order of Nurses, the Soldiers Wives League, all of which promoted Canadian interests, responsibility, and autonomy, in contrast to the Imperial Order Daughters of the Empire (IODE).[20] Nor was she prepared to restrict her political interests, ideas, and actions to hospitality, fundraising, and what Charlotte Whitten once dismissed as "social trivialities."[21]

Lady Borden focused on larger national and imperial issues. She had seen her province and country transformed by Confederation. She had felt its tensions and imagined its promise. She had listened to the tumultuous debate on federal and provincial relations, and its animated, self-interested rhetoric. She shared her husband's and Laurier's reservations on the centralizing "new imperialism" that threatened to erode her country's autonomy and diversity. Nor did she hesitate to incite Sir Frederick to defend that heritage with vigour and determination, her spirited interventions an example of elite women's interest, access to, and participation in governance and policy formation, her views documented by two letters.

The first letter was written by Lily (Griffith) McConnell (1880–1972) to Lady Borden in April 1926, at the height of the controversial W.L.M. King–Julian Byng constitutional crisis over Governor General Byng's rejection of Prime Minister King's advice to dissolve Parliament, a decision that led to Byng's subsequent departure and the redefinition of the Governor General's role in Canadian government. The second letter was written by Lady Borden to Sir Frederick during the controversial 1907 Imperial Conference. Lily McConnell was the wife of John W. McConnell, a devoted Liberal and imperialist, whose husband had been a friend and business partner of Sir Frederick. From her Beau Rivage hotel in Lausanne Lily wrote to Lady Borden in 1926 that she was distraught by Governor General Byng's rejection of King's request to dissolve Parliament, and fearful that the subsequent constitutional crisis would damage irreparably Canadian imperial relations. The daughter of a Methodist clergyman, Lily "loved Canada" and the empire. She regarded the empire as nothing less than "the instrument of Christianity" and Canada as "the pivot" of the empire, and believed she possessed the power to dispel the ominous misunderstanding that threatened to sour Canadian-imperial relations. But she needed Lady Borden's assistance.

As Lily McConnell explained to Lady Borden, she had spent a good part of the previous year (1925) in London and Switzerland, mixing with the British political elite and "talking with people who are now framing empire policy," men such as Leo Amery (1873–1955), the Conservative colonial secretary (1924–9); Stanley Baldwin (1867–1947), the Conservative prime minister (1923–9; 1935–7); and Sir John Simon (1873–1964), the deputy leader of the Liberal Party (1922–4). Disturbed by the British Conservative government's negative opinion of King during the political controversy, Lily decided she could and must defend her Canadian Liberal prime minister.

Lily's magic potion was a story told to her by Madame Marguerite Thibaudeau Lamothe,[22] which Lily felt would explain Mackenzie King's constitutional position if only British political leaders knew it, a story that entailed royal favour that would dispel misunderstanding. But she needed Lady Borden's confirmation, confident that Lady Borden would remember the details that Lily McConnell required before she could intervene with her well-placed British political friends and set things right. Madame Lamothe's dramatic story dated from the explosive Imperial Conference of 1907.

Initially Laurier had resisted attending the 1907 Imperial Conference. He disliked crossing the ocean, "an uncomfortable voyage for a poor sailor," and the conference's social routine that "would wear down a body stronger than mine,"[23] and found the political negotiations tedious and exhausting. Since imperial defence organization and funding was to be at the core of the 1907 conference's potentially acrimonious discussions, a debate fuelled by Anglo-German rivalry, Laurier was confident that he could entrust negotiations to Sir Frederick, who liked working with numbers, was a good sailor, a "bon vivant," and a skilful negotiator. However, the Governor General, Lord Grey, persuaded Laurier to attend the conference as a courtesy to the newly elected British Liberal government. Although Laurier attended, he found it a most unpleasant conference, and at one point left the conference in anger.

Initially Sir Frederick bore the brunt of British wrath for Canada's refusal to be stampeded into funding the Admiralty's one big navy. Sir Frederick had learned from Laurier, the master,[24] and during his tense discussions on imperial defence, Sir Frederick "withstood all pressure" and effectively "torpedoed" the imperial centralist defence agenda, much to the chagrin and disgust of the British government. In fact, Sir Frederick so infuriated Sir John Fisher, the tactless, remorseless First Sea Lord and obsessive advocate of "one navy," that Fisher threatened to abandon any plans for Canada's defence, a country he dismissed as composed of "an unpatriotic, grasping people, who only stick to us for the good they can get out of us."[25]

As Marguerite Lamothe related to Lily McConnell, Laurier's 1907 encounter with the imperial authorities had been equally unpleasant. H.H. Asquith (1852–1928), the chancellor of the exchequer (1905–8), and Winston Churchill (1874–1965), the brash under-secretary of state for the colonies (1905–8), had been so "astonishingly rude" to the Canadian prime minister that at one point Sir Wilfrid left the conference in anger, deeply offended by their bullying tactics. Laurier returned to the Hotel Cecil, where the Canadian delegation was staying, and told Sir Frederick and W.S. Fielding, the minister of finance, to pack their trunks, as they were leaving London tomorrow, "never to return." While they were packing their bags Edward VII's secretary came by, saying that the king had heard of Laurier's abrupt departure and wanted to dine with him before he left. After their dinner Edward VII took Sir Wilfrid by the arm and said, now let us have a talk, during which the king informed Sir Wilfrid: "I consider you as much my Prime Minister as the man in Downing Street and I shall never rest until the Empire is joined against our enemies." In return, the king asked Laurier not to break up the conference, as he wanted it to end amicably. Consequently, Laurier returned to the conference, and it ended on a false note of solidarity.[26]

Since Lily McConnell considered Edward VII's 1907 constitutional position identical to Mackenzie King's in 1926, she was convinced that if Baldwin and Amery knew of Edward VII's constitutional reading of empire they would understand W.L.M. King's view and the imperial misunderstanding would evaporate. Lily and Marguerite Lamothe's interest in public life, their access to information, and their confidence that Lady Borden had and would share that information, suggest the nature and potential influence available to elite women. Unfortunately, the record is silent on Lady Borden's response.

Lady Borden had not accompanied Sir Frederick to London for the 1907 Imperial Conference. Maude was in her last months of pregnancy, and Lady Borden and Sir Frederick and Elizabeth had been in London only six months previous, touring Britain, Holland, Belgium, and France. Lizzie had been only too willing to replace her mother and accompany her father to the April–May 1907 Imperial Conference, especially as she and he planned a post-conference visit to Paris. Given Lady Borden's enjoyment of imperial occasions, it must have been with regret that she said farewell to Fred and Lizzie as they left for Saint John in April 1907, to board the CPR's *Empress of Britain* for Liverpool.

Lady Borden was far from indifferent to the 1907 Imperial Conference's outcome, however. Nor did she confine her interests to personalities and human interest stories. During Sir Frederick's absence, she foraged the newspapers for information on the 1907 conference's political dynamics, and corresponded frequently with Sir Frederick and Lizzie, vicariously engaged in the conference's discussions. Unrestrained in her private correspondence with Sir Frederick, Lady Borden left no doubt of her views on imperial pretensions (suggesting what she might have said and more, had she been present). She informed Sir Frederick she was delighted that "Sir Wilfrid [was] holding his own and not missing matters," and proud that he was "getting good backing from his Minister of Militia." But, she insisted, much more was needed to puncture British pretensions and insularity. "Someone," she continued, ought to reverse the moralizing British rhetoric and "make a few remarks" as to "what Canada has done for the motherland." And in her view, "It would make a pleasant variety. One grows so tired," she complained, "of hearing how much we owe, when all I can think of is how much we have given."[27] Harold may have been uppermost in her mind as she penned these bitter lines.

Clearly things needed to be set right. If not, Lady Borden saw little future for the empire, at least an empire directed from London. Nor did she fail to deplore the sharp behaviour of a nation of shopkeepers. "Mark my words," she wrote, "there will never be a really satisfactory understanding as our English cousins are far too dense and too conceited to ever see things from any but the narrowest point of view. Little Englanders they certainly are – greedy little wretches who want to swallow us." While Canada might accept the role of daughter in her mother's house, Canada would not become the empire's Cinderella. Henri Bourassa could not have put the case more bluntly!

Laurier had no reason to fear that Lady Borden's head might be turned by the "magnetic appeal of 'royalty, aristocracy, and plutocracy.'"[28] Much as she enjoyed London and its social derivatives, this Lady of the Snows remained grounded and determined. She had no intention of surrendering her liberal empire without a struggle. "You dear man," she incited her husband, "you must do your best and imagine you are doing something big, great and lasting,"[29] advice "from the home front to the war front" that Sir Frederick would follow in his own time and manner.[30]

Lady Borden's vicarious participation in the 1907 Imperial Conference, together with Lily McConnell's attempted intervention in the aftermath of the 1926 King–Byng constitutional crisis, suggests how three elite Ladies of the Snows managed the interplay of nationalism, imperialism, and gender. All were discreet and averse to public advocacy. All occupied strategic listening posts; they mixed with power brokers and were committed to building a "better Britain" in Canada, one that conformed to their aspirations of a liberal empire in which Canada played a central, autonomous, exemplary role. Nor were the three ladies' political interventions singular in contemporary Canada or Britain.[31]

Chapter Fourteen

Scandal

Gossipmongers' tales of Sir Frederick's drinking, partying, marital infidelity, and conflicts of interests began to compromise Sir Frederick and Lady Borden's political ambitions, especially as Canadians came to demand higher standards of public and private morality from their representatives. While Sir Frederick and his friends might dismiss opponents' charges of political patronage as partisan hypocrisy or simply an occupational hazard, public accusations of drunkenness and infidelity were a personal embarrassment and political liability that threatened to compromise his access to higher office and imperial service.

Lady Borden was neither censorious nor prudish; nor was she a moral crusader. A devout Methodist, she undoubtedly espoused temperance, but total abstinence was not an article of her faith. She served and drank wine at dinner and enjoyed beer with pub meals. For her, drunkenness was a behavioural lapse, a venal rather than a mortal sin. What she thought of adultery is unclear. She was fascinated by contemporary theatre and literature and its focus on marital duplicity, but she was also shrewd and pragmatic, and often indecisive. In Nova Scotia adultery, desertion, and cruelty were grounds for divorce. But, proof of adultery was gendered,[1] humiliating, and difficult to establish, and divorce usually resulted in economic hardship, social stigma, and religious exclusion.[2] Moreover, "patrician adultery" was often shrouded in secrecy and hypocrisy, and less corrosive of married life than one might expect.[3]

Rumours of Sir Frederick's amorous relationships circulated for years but had failed to threaten his public career until 1894, more than a year before he joined Laurier's cabinet. At the time, Fred and other Nova Scotia members of Parliament were living at Mrs. Allison's boarding house on Russell Street. During that time, Fred had signed Mrs. Allison's daughter's application to a nursing program in Montreal.

According to Mrs. Allison, Fred had enticed her daughter to Montreal, where he subsidized her rent and visited her weekly. To buttress her accusation, Mrs. Allison claimed that her daughter had been but one of Fred's victims. Another alleged victim was her neighbour, Mrs. McParland, whose home he had "broken up." Fred explained Mrs. Allison's charges to Bessie as a "blackmailing business," designed to extort $2,000 for her silence. At the time Fred considered taking legal action, but Bessie dreaded the publicity.[4] His decision, however, simply delayed public exposure.

In 1904 the Conservative Party, stung by its electoral defeat and loss of five seats, launched a crusade against what the partisan press described as the Liberals' penchant for "wine, women and graft." While Sir Frederick appeared to be an obvious target, he had been shielded somewhat by his cousin, Robert ("Rob") Borden, the leader of the Opposition,[5] who had sought and received political favours from Sir Frederick and whose brother, John William, administered the militia's sensitive contracts department.[6] Rob's shield was not impenetrable, however, nor could it save Sir Frederick from moral regulators and political mavericks outside Rob's influence.

But it was only in 1907 that Sir Frederick's private life became a collateral damage of Robert "Bob" Edwards's (1860–1922) vendetta against Clifford Sifton, Laurier's former minister of the interior. In an article in his *Calgary Eye-Opener*, "an amusing but disreputable little weekly" that specialized in "slander and smut,"[7] the Scottish-born editor cited Sir Frederick's antics at a Toronto mess dinner as typical of the decadence corroding Laurier's government. According to Edwards, an intoxicated Sir Frederick had executed a sword dance between the decanters, after which he was sighted in the company of "two ladies of easy virtue," from whose thrall he emerged two days later, devoid of his Windsor uniform and unable to attend a public function. Given the *Eye-Opener*'s unsavoury reputation, Edwards's penchant for fanciful, hypocritical charges (Edwards's own life was not above reproach) and his Conservative sympathies,[8] Sir Frederick ignored the charges at first, convinced that no one ever won a war against a skunk.

To friends, Fred explained Edwards's scurrilous article as the work of "a small clique of low down politicians," whose rantings lacked "the slightest foundation or justification."[9] Less easy to dismiss was a sulphurous exposé by Henry Hamilton Fyfe (1869–1951) in the British journal *Nineteenth Century and After* of the "foul and miasmic depths of corruption" in Canada, beginning with the Pacific Scandal, citing Edwards's allegations as a contemporary example.[10] While Fyfe did not name Sir Frederick, the *Toronto World* (a Conservative journal outside of Rob's control) did, citing as evidence Mrs. Allison's letter to the *Eye-Opener* charging Sir Frederick with corrupting her daughter.

Given Sir Frederick's desire to succeed Lord Strathcona, he could scarcely ignore the *Nineteenth Century and After*'s allegations, and after consulting Laurier he retained the services of the renowned London solicitor Sir Charles Russell (1863–1928), the son of Baron Charles Arthur Russell (1832–1900), the former chief justice of England (1894–1900). Baron Russell had been counsel to the Bering Sea arbitration (1893) and had become a warm friend of Joseph Pope, the Canadian under-secretary of state, a friend and neighbour of Sir Wilfrid and Sir Frederick.[11] Sir Charles won an immediate apology from the *Nineteenth Century and After* that the journal printed in its December (1907) edition, repudiating the article, and regretting "any such unfortunate and scurrilous gossip should have been quoted in these papers." The journal accompanied its apology with £250 (about $32,000 in today's purchasing power) plus costs "for any injury."[12] Although a welcome vindication, Sir Frederick's tribulations had just begun.

A looming general election turned the last session of Canada's Tenth Parliament into a carnival of accusations and recriminations. Each item of Sir Frederick's department's estimates[13] was scrutinized for any taint of corruption, especially Sir Frederick's interests in a government-subsidized cold storage scheme. His son-in-law, Leslie Macoun, was called before the Commons' Public Accounts Committee to account for his $74,000 copper contract with the Quebec Arsenal.[14] George Eulas Foster, Sir Frederick's cranky old political antagonist, whose own "shady dealings" had been documented by a Royal Commission,"[15] was relentless, bitter, and personal, even raising the subject of Mrs. Allison's letter to the *Eye-Opener*. The *Halifax Herald*, the *St. John Telegram*, the *Toronto News*, and other "scurrilous yellow rags" joined the fray with searing attacks on the minister.[16] Sir Frederick was best when he was provoked, and gave as well as he got, though it took a heavy toll on his health and family.

An unusually charged summer separated the Tenth Parliament's tumultuous session from the chaotic general election on 26 November. Paramount on Sir Frederick and Lady Borden's summer agenda was Lord Grey's spectacular Quebec Tercentenary, a singular opportunity to advance their imperial campaign. During the last two weeks of July "Lord Grey's Imperial Masquerade"[17] drew an estimated 100,000–150,000 visitors to Quebec City, "ablaze with flags and bunting," its streets lined with soldiers and sailors, and its hotels, residences, and official spaces swarming with guests and visitors and their entourages. Distinguished guests included the Prince of Wales, British noblemen and ladies, army and navy brass, senior Admiralty, War Office and Colonial Office civil servants, imperial representatives from Australia, New Zealand, and South Africa, and foreign countries such as France and the United States.[18]

The two-week celebration focused on the Prince of Wales's arrival, activities, and departure, his dedication of the Plains of Abraham, and his grand review of the troops, its success praised by British military brass including Field-Marshall Lord Roberts, who attributed its success to Sir Frederick's administration. Even the Prince of Wales penned a personal note of thanks and commendation. Only Frank Lascelles's eight-part historical extravaganza rivalled the Prince of Wales's presence, a historical pageant on Canada's "founding" with Jacques Cartier and "re-founding"(!) on the Plains of Abraham, a spectacle that commanded a cast of some 4,000 participants. The tercentenary included a naval regatta, a pontifical high mass, meetings of the Royal Society, balls, banquets, dinners, receptions, and concerts. Despite the rigorous schedule, it was a welcome relief from the carping of the recent parliamentary session, an occasion to meet, greet, and impress imperial power brokers, and a respite before the turbulent election to come.

In retrospect the long, contentious 236-day parliamentary session was but a dress rehearsal for the raucous 1908 federal election, a campaign described variously as "one of the most unpleasant of Canada's federal elections," and a continuation of the "gutter politics" of the previous parliamentary session.[19] Frustrated by their several failures to dislodge Sir Frederick from Kings, the local Conservatives nominated a "non-partisan" candidate to contest the 26 October 1908 federal election, a tactic they had employed successfully in June 1906 to defeat H.H. Wickwire, Sir Frederick's friend and provincial counterpart. Designated as the "United Reform Party" and backed by some thirty or so local clergy calling for purity in politics,[20] the Conservatives were certain they could repeat their political success against such an obvious "sinner" as – the corrupt, intemperate, womanizing Sir Frederick!

The Tories underestimated Sir Frederick. Uncertain at first of his opponents' strength, Sir Frederick soon had their measure, exposed their "non-partisan" claims, political inexperience, and lack of organization. His straitlaced Baptist colleague W.S. Fielding, the powerful minister of finance, canvassed Kings on his behalf once again, and when the polls closed Sir Frederick found that he had garnered 55 per cent of the votes cast. Sir Frederick, however had not escaped unscathed.[21]

Early in the campaign Sir Frederick decided to confront the *Eye Opener*'s and the *Nineteenth Century and After*'s charges by waving a copy of the latter's public apology, and promising to use the monetary indemnity to establish a scholarship for Kings County students.[22] At the same time, he made it clear that he would prosecute any person who continued to spread scurrilous stories about his private life. For years William Carruthers had blamed Sir Frederick for his 1883 dismissal "for certain irregularities" as Kentville's postmaster and superintendent of its Savings Bank.[23] Carruthers decided, however, to disregard Sir Frederick's threat, and six days before the election he was charged with criminal libel, and a preliminary hearing was set for 10 November. During the preliminary hearing E.M. Beckwith, the local justice of the peace, found sufficient evidence for Carruthers's prosecution. Carruthers was released, and a trial was scheduled for the Nova Scotia Supreme Court's Kentville assizes in June 1909.

Meanwhile, Sir Frederick became the object of a barrage of accusations and insinuations that no person aspiring to a prestigious public office could ignore. During this painful ordeal Lady Borden appeared a pillar of composure and support. Whatever her private feelings, she seemed more deeply concerned for Fred's health than with any personal injury. Even before the election Lady Borden decided they would vacation in Europea to recover from the stressful parliamentary session and compensate her for her inability to accompany Sir Frederick and Elizabeth to the 1907 Imperial Conference.

An unresolved imperial dispute provided a pretext for their 1908 transatlantic journey. The conflict stemmed from Sir Frederick's failure to challenge the 1907 Imperial Conference's agreed credentials for membership in a proposed Imperial General Staff and its reporting mechanism. Try as he had for months to rectify his oversight by corresponding with the War Office, nothing had been resolved. Fred decided, therefore, to speak directly to Richard Haldane, the secretary of state for war, and the British Army Council during his visit.

On 30 November 1908, five weeks after the tumultuous general election, an exhausted Lady and Sir Frederick Borden left New York for Liverpool on a seven-week business vacation in Europe, returning to Halifax on 22 January 1909. Early December was not the pleasantest season to cross the North Atlantic or visit Britain, especially for Lady Borden, who disliked cold, dark, damp climates. Nor was she a good sailor, especially as heavy autumn seas confined her to her cabin for much of the voyage. British hospitality, however, soon dispelled her gloom and discomfort.

Arriving in London well before Sir Frederick's 15 January meeting with Haldane, Sir Frederick and Lady Borden made their rounds of clubs, dinners, at homes, and country weekends, entertained by old friends and acquaintances including many of those whom they had met during the previous summer's Quebec Tercentenary. In keeping with their London routine they toured museums and galleries, attended concerts and theatres, searched bookshops, and purchased small gifts and souvenirs for family, friends, and constituents.[24] They also attended club meetings devoted to imperial causes in which Canada had a material stake or Sir Frederick had a private interest, such as Sanford Fleming's all-red cable route.[25] Then just after Christmas, Sir Frederick and Lady Borden fled England for southern France and Italy's sunnier climate, returning to London in mid-January for Sir Frederick's meeting with Haldane and the British Army Council.

Rest had been a justification for Sir Frederick and Lady Borden's European travel. Although Cook's agents arranged their travel, no agent could curtail Sir Frederick and Lady Borden's energy and curiosity. Incorrigible tourists, they spared neither time nor energy in pursuit of historic sites, galleries, concerts, good restaurants, and shopping, mixing business with pleasure. For Lady Borden no Italian tour was complete without a visit to Florence with its monuments to the Medici merchant princes' wealth and influence in church and state, art and architecture. Registered at the Hotel Savoy, the great stone luxury hotel on the Piazza della Repubblica, not far from the Cathedral of Santa Maria del Fiore, their primary Florentine mission was the Uffizi and the Palazzo Petti, including the royal apartments with their rooms displaying Renaissance and Baroque masterpieces of sensual, allegorical art, so unlike Lady Borden's own quiet, pastoral watercolours. Their imitation and invention, classical and religious references, celebration of nature, discovery, and progress appealed to her intellectual curiosity, and her love of colour, costume, conflict, and drama. Nor did she fail to note the synergies of art, wealth, and leadership. Lady Borden's long walks and visits to galleries and good restaurants confirmed her unbounded affection for the city.

Rome extended their artistic pilgrimage, their first stop being the National Gallery of Modern Art. But for Sir Frederick imperial Rome's architectural remnants were the city's chief attractions, especially the ruins of the Appian Way from the Forum to the Colosseum, to which he returned alone on several occasions, and in the rain, to visualize the setting of his classical studies of statecraft, rhetoric, and war. Together Sir Frederick and Lady Borden strolled through Rome's Pincio Gardens and attended a production of Richard Wagner's *Die Walküre* at the Grand Opera, which Lady Borden considered "the greatest performance" she had ever seen.[26] In Rome they lunched with the British ambassador, as they had in 1902. More memorable was Sir Frederick's audience with Pope Pius X (1835–1914),[27] an event Sir Frederick subsequently added to his biographical references. That year the pope had refused to meet Theodore Roosevelt, who was on his way to an African safari, owing to Roosevelt's association with the city's Methodists' anti-Catholic crusade.[28] Sir Frederick and Lady Borden were also Methodists, but neither had any tolerance for anti-Catholic crusades.

By 15 January 1909 they were back in London for Sir Frederick's meeting with the British secretary of war, Richard Haldane, and the British Army Council, along with Major-General John Charles Hood of Australia, to discuss the contentious criteria for appointment to the Imperial General Staff and the nature of its communication with colonial governments. For Sir Frederick these issues struck at the heart of Canada's cooperative imperial relationship. When the British remained intractable on both questions Sir Frederick broke the impasse on imperial communication, insisting the Canadian government be copied on all communications between the Imperial General Staff and its Canadian representative, otherwise he would create a separate Canadian General Staff, a threat the War Office believed "tantamount to a declaration of military independence."[29]

Although the War Office blinked on the communication issue, it refused to alter its appointment criteria to the Imperial General Staff. Whereupon Sir Frederick called their bluff. When he returned to Canada, he nominated Brigadier-General William Otter, chief of Canadian General Staff, as Canada's representative on the Imperial General Staff. And, when the British objected to Canada's recommendation because Otter lacked British General Staff College credentials, Sir Frederick offered no other recommendation, leaving the Imperial General Staff "stillborn,"[30] to use Colonel C.P. Stacey's words. The British soon learned that they "could not push Borden too far."[31] And this time Lady Borden was in London, close to the action.

Travel and statecraft, however, failed to silence Sir Frederick's home-grown detractors. In his absence moral crusaders continued to denounce the plaintiff in partisan private and public discussions. Nor did the Nova Scotia Supreme Court's hearing in June 1909 end Sir Frederick's purgatory. During the court's selection of jurors, Sir Frederick's counsel, H.H. Wickwire and W.E. Roscoe, were so clearly outmanoeuvred by their legal opponents, R.E. Ritchie and A.E. Dunlop, that Sir Frederick's counsel sought and secured the court's postponement until 12 November 1909 to provide additional witnesses, a move that prolonged Sir Frederick's public prosecution.

Meanwhile, Dr. J. Pringle launched an intemperate assault on Laurier's government during the Presbyterians' General Assembly in Kingston, Ontario, in June 1909, singling out Sir Frederick for special abuse, whose name Pringle charged, was simply "a synonym for lust." When Pringle's colleagues attempted to restrain the outraged divine, he dared Sir Frederick to "bring any action" against him in the courts.[32] Closer to home, the Reverend Joseph A. Spidell, a disappointed member of the ephemeral Union Reform Party, condemned Sir Frederick in comparable language. Still stinging from his failure to dislodge Sir Frederick, he informed members of the Central Baptist Association that constituents "rose from their knees where they had been praying Thy Kingdom Come ... and went straight to the polling booth and cast their vote for a man whose name ... has become a stench in the nostrils of the right-thinking people from Halifax to Vancouver."[33] The *Halifax Herald* joined the fray, demanding Sir Frederick refrain from imperial negotiations until he had cleared his name.

Sir Frederick carried on, confident of Laurier's support. And a month after the Nova Scotia Supreme Court's postponement of Carruthers's trial, Sir Frederick and Lady Borden were back in London, accompanied by Louis-Philippe Brodeur (1862–1924), the minister of marine and fisheries, tagged to become Canada's minister of naval services in May 1910. Their mission was to procure British assistance for Canada's nascent navy. Remembering his unpleasant 1907 battle with imperial authorities, Laurier realized that the British remained "farouchement" opposed to an autonomous Canadian navy, despite Parliament's bipartisan parliamentary resolution of 29 March 1909 endorsing a Canadian navy.[34] He asked Sir Frederick, therefore, to accompany Brodeur to London, to open doors, to defend Canada's naval autonomy, and to secure the requisite materiel and professional assistance. Aware of Sir Frederick's enthusiasm for a Canadian navy, Laurier was confident of Sir Frederick's negotiating skills. Even the Opposition acknowledged Sir Frederick's credentials, branding him Canada's "First Lord of the Admiralty and Minister of Militia," to undermine Brodeur and underline Sir Frederick's "unhealthy political interest" in the naval project.

Sir Frederick and Lady Borden were delighted to escape the harrowing partisan press. Since Elizabeth planned to accompany them, Gus's wife, Hattie, came to Canning to stay with Mrs. Clarke. And, on 10 July 1909, Sir Frederick, Lady Borden, and Elizabeth boarded the CPR's recently launched 14,000-ton *Empress of Britain* in Montreal, destined for Liverpool, with a return booking to Montreal on 30 September, twelve days before resumption of Carruthers's trial. Aboard the *Empress of Britain* was a large party of Sir Frederick's family, friends, and advisers, including Louis-Philippe Brodeur and his wife, Emma; Robert and Laura Borden; Robert's brother, John William Borden, and his wife;[35] Charles Panet, Sir Frederick's private secretary;[36] Major-General Percy

Lake; and Rear-Admiral Charles Edward Kingsmill.[37] Contrary to the moral pariah painted by the Tory press, Sir Frederick presided over a genial "naval conference" of those who wished to listen, learn, and opine, a gathering that included the leader of the Opposition whose party had agreed to the fragile bipartisan parliamentary consensus on building a Canadian navy.

The voyage was not all business. Among the ship's 301 first-class passengers, Lady Borden found many persons of "speaking acquaintance,"[38] including Sir Frederick's eighty-two-year-old Nova Scotia friend, Sir Sanford Fleming, accompanied by his fifteen-year-old grandson. Sir Sanford was still game to join Sir Frederick for an evening concert organized for the 1,200 second-class passengers. Lady Borden was no sailor but once the ship passed the Newfoundland fog banks into smoother waters and sunnier climes, she spent many hours on deck, long enough to become quite sunburned. It "is well I have not been in Canning," she joked to her mother, "or some rash conclusions might be come to in reference to my having been drinking heavily."[39]

Arriving in Britain on 16 July, Sir Frederick, Brodeur, and their advisers had less than two weeks before their official meetings. In London Sir Frederick and Lady Borden confronted a stack of invitations,[40] and made good use of their time, creating a favourable private and public reception to promote Canada's place in a participatory, liberal empire. Sir Fredrick spoke at the Guildhall Banquet and the British Empire Club, and arranged an interview with the *London Standard*. His message was familiar and reassuring: Canada enjoyed British rights and freedoms, was attached to Britain by sentiments and shared values, and was committed to relieving Britain of the cost and responsibility for Canadian defence by taking over the Halifax and Esquimalt garrisons and dockyards. Canada could call upon a potential land force of 50,000 men, Sir Frederick assured his audiences, and with its proposed naval force it was ready to defend its portion of the imperial estate, an agenda that had been endorsed by a bipartisan parliamentary resolution.

Laurier was right. The Admiralty had never digested the 1907 Imperial Conference's endorsement of colonial navies and used every means to reverse the decision. Its case was familiar, a reminder of Canada's vulnerability, disparaging warnings against autonomous "two penny–half-penny" colonial navies combined with a porous promise of protection in exchange for a financial contribution to the Royal Navy's race with Germany, a combination of threat and bribery that one author has called "a game of brinkmanship with the Dominions."[41] The Royal Navy had made its case during the Quebec Tercentenary, but it had failed to persuade Sir Frederick, Sir Wilfrid, or Brodeur. Unmoved by the Admiralty's warning, promises, and urgency, Sir Frederick and Brodeur listened politely, insisting that Canada have its own navy under Canadian control, their model being the Canadian militia. In rejecting the Admiralty's arguments, the Canadian ministers reminded the Admiralty of the 1907 Imperial Conference's endorsement of colonial navies and the Canadian Parliament's non-partisan resolution of 29 March 1909 endorsing a Canadian navy. And should the Admiralty doubt the resolution's non-partisan unanimity, it need only consult the leader of the Canadian Opposition, Robert Borden, who happened to be in London and still supportive of the non-partisan parliamentary resolution. Despite their successful rejection of the Admiralty's "Big Navy" obsession, Sir Frederick and Brodeur extracted the materiel and instructional support they had requested. Laurier was delighted with their success, and temporary "domestic felicity."[42] The fragile bipartisan domestic felicity, however, soon fractured, but that was for another day and by then out of Sir Fredrick's hands.[43]

Sir Frederick had little time to savour his and Brodeur's success. Ten days after his return from London he was back in court facing the sordid details retailed by Carruthers's witnesses during the six-day trial from 12 to 18 October 1909, a form of judicial theatre that commanded a national audience, including many of Sir Frederick's fearful cabinet colleagues. Since Carruthers had claimed during his preliminary hearing that his electoral intervention had been based on his confidence in Mrs. Allison's allegations, the plaintiff's counsel focused on the falsity of Mrs. Allison's claims and Carruthers's use of her testimony to pursue a vendetta over his dismissal from the Kentville Post Office.

Those with seats or standing room in the crowded Kentville courtroom were well entertained by the plaintiff's first witness, Miss Charlefour, Mrs. Allison's forty-year-old daughter, the alleged victim of Sir Frederick's "seduction." Testifying under oath Miss Charlefour assured the court that she had never received Sir Frederick in her apartment or anywhere else or had Sir Frederick provided her with financial assistance. But when the defence counsel asked her to identify a photograph of herself and Sir Frederick, the theatrical Miss Charlefour grasped the photo and tore it to shreds "sending the fragments of cardboard flying through the court."[44] The plaintiff's second witness, Mrs. McPharland, whose marriage Sir Frederick allegedly had broken up, denied knowing Sir Frederick, having laid eyes on him only once in her life.

The defendant's chief witness, Mrs. Allison, maintained her version of Sir Frederick's relationship with her daughter. She restated her previous claim that Sir Frederick had signed her daughter's nursing application, subsidized her residence in Montreal, and visited her weekly. She also repeated her claim that Sir Frederick had broken up Mrs. McPharland's marriage and had hidden "in a pile of old boxes near the house," waiting for her husband to leave for the evening.

The defence made a tactical error in recalling Miss Charlefour to the stand. For, in her second appearance she cut a wide swath. Not to be upstaged by her mother, Miss Charlefour, still under oath, confessed that she had a closer friendship with Sir Frederick than she had admitted initially, adding that she had been "on very intimate terms with a number of men." At the same time, she dismissed her mother as a quarrelsome, litigious, conniving person who had left her second husband, committed her son to a mental institution, and pressed charges against him for "indecent language." Miss Charlefour explained, too, that her mother had induced her to blackmail Sir Frederick for $2,000.[45]

The plaintiff's counsel pressed its advantage. It recalled Carruthers to the stand to recount his quarrel with Sir Frederick over his dismissal from the Kentville Post Office. The jury took little time to reach its unanimous verdict: Carruthers was guilty as charged. The defence counsel pleaded with the judge for a lenient sentence since Carruthers was the sole support of his sister, "an elderly lady and subject to heart trouble."[46] The judge gave Carruthers the choice of a fine of $100 (about $2,600 in today's purchasing power) or six months in prison.

Fresh from the Carruthers victory, Sir Frederick decided to clean his slate. He entered a $25,000 libel claim against William Cotton, editor of the *Cowansville Observer*, who had published and commented on the *Eye-Opener*'s charges. Cotton apologized at once, pleading editorial inexperience.[47] The Opposition press, fearing other libel suits, and/or their leader's displeasure, gave Sir Frederick a clean bill. Although legally vindicated Sir Frederick realized the pyrrhic nature of his victory since, as he liked to say, one never quite won a war with a skunk.

Notwithstanding his legal success, in October 1909 Sir Frederick's future appeared uncertain. He and Lady Borden had hoped that the 1904 election would be their last, a desire magnified by the unpleasant 1908 election and resultant Carruthers trial. Both had become tired of political life. In April 1907 during a visit to Gables, Lady Borden watched Robert Borden in shirt sleeves, the parliamentary session ended, helping his worker spread earth and "working like a good one." She wished it were Sir Frederick with her beside him. "How glad I shall be when the time comes for us to live & cease to grub," she wrote Sir Frederick: "The game we are playing is not worth the candle – it takes too much & gives too little."[48]

Yet neither Sir Frederick nor Lady Borden seemed entirely convinced of public life's futility. After all, public life had always been about more than just business and politics. It had been about what Thorstein Veblen called "human nature," about purchasing recognition, power, and position.[49] And neither Sir Frederick nor Lady Borden was yet willing to relinquish that quest. They had invested too much in their imperial project. And surely, before the next general election Canada's eighty-eight-year-old high commissioner would retire, and London would be theirs. "None of us can look very far ahead, Sir Frederick wrote gloomily to Gus, "but at the present moment it looks as if I might remain in politics for some time."

Chapter Fifteen

Their Imperial Sunset

In May 1910 Lady Borden was only forty-seven years old. She, like Samuel Johnson, had never tired of London. She knew and loved its energy and unapologetic self-importance, its theatre, music, art, fashions, and shopping. "London," she wrote nostalgically some years later, "is as ever the very most wonderful & satisfying city in the World. I can quite understand how so many come here to end their days. I think I could leave almost any place without regrets to come to London." That was high praise, given Lady Borden's attachment to Borden Place. Sir Frederick appreciated London's appeal as well and was tempted by its opportunities, but he was sixty-three and beginning to feel his age, though not yet ready to retire.

Once the embarrassing Carruthers trial ended, Sir Frederick's threats of legal action against other "slanderers" brought retractions and apologies. The public's absorption in more important public issues, such as the naval debate, refurbished Sir Frederick's imperial ambitions. In May 1910, during debate on the Naval Service Act, Sir Frederick seconded the bill (owing to Brodeur's illness), answered questions on the London conference, and fielded financial details that Laurier assured the House his minister of militia understood better than he.

More absorbing still was the promise of another coronation following the death of Edward VII in May 1910. Sir Frederick and Lady Borden had met Edward VII's successor, George V (the Duke of Cornwall and York) on several occasions, during his 1901 tour of Canada, his father's 1902 coronation, and the 1908 Quebec Tercentenary, and would certainly be invited to his coronation, after a year of ritual mourning. Once more they would occupy front seats at a coronation and attend an Imperial Conference as spectators and participants. This was no time to leave public life.

Sir Frederick and Lady Borden had more than a year to dream, ponder, and plan before receiving the Lord Chamberlain's "Royal command" to attend the coronation. Invitations were limited. Mrs. Clarke, Maude, and Rosamond were unable to accompany them to London, Mrs. Clarke because of her age, and Maude owing to her commitment to serve as matron of honour at Miss Lola Powell's wedding to Charles Eric Charles of the Royal Engineers in Christ Church Cathedral, Dublin, on 20 April 1911.[1] Maude could not justify a longer absence from home. A place was found for Leslie, a good, decorative, and accomplished rider, as aide-de-camp to Colonel H.A. McLean, the officer commanding the Canadian coronation contingent, which included thirty-eight representatives of Canada's recently created navy. An inveterate monarchist, Lizzie, though recently engaged, could not be restrained. A place had also to be found for Sir Frederick's secretary Charles-Louis Panet. Again, they would stay at the Hotel Cecil, along with other colonial delegations.

And once again, Sir Frederick and Lady Borden faced a formidable social calendar. It began with their London arrival, a good month before the coronation, their arrival announced in the *Court Journal*. The pace accelerated as the coronation approached and continued until they left London, almost two months later. The formalities began with éclat on 22 May with Lord Chamberlain's summons to attend a court reception "in full dress with feathers and train," followed by a luncheon hosted by the king. The Buckingham Palace luncheon was for some fifty guests, ten guests seated at each table. The king and his entourage occupied Table 1. Lady Borden sat at Table 4, on the left of Prince Christian and to the right of the Duchess of Connaught, the wife of Canada's new Governor General. In the evening the British prime minister, Herbert Asquith, and Mrs. Asquith, held a dinner for forty-eight guests at 10 Downing Street. Laurier sat on Asquith's right, and Sir Frederick between Lord Milner and Winston Churchill. The following day they again met Asquith and Mrs. Asquith at the Asquiths' garden party. On 24 May Queen Victoria's younger son, the Duke of Connaught (1850–1942), Canada's new Governor General, held an "at home" at the Royal Colonial Society. Two days later he hosted a luncheon at Clarence House. And on 27 May the 8th Countess of Granard (Beatrice Mills, the American heiress) celebrated the king's birthday with an "at home." And on it went, relentlessly.

Lady Borden's papers retain 109 invitations from their 1911 coronation sojourn, invitations to banquets, dinners, at homes, country weekends, receptions, conversaziones, theatre, opera, concerts, galleries, museums, flower shows, historic sites, historical re-enactments, boat

(Oxford and Cambridge) and horse races (Ascot), not to mention club meetings and official activities. Seven of the invitations were from members of the royal family. Eleven invitations were from nobility, and several were from cabinet ministers (Colonial Office, War Office, Foreign Office, and Prime Minister's Office). The rest were from friends and titled notables. There were invitations as well from institutions and societies, vintners, grocers, innkeepers, haberdashers, fishmongers, goldsmiths, and ironmongers to banquets, receptions, and re-enactments of their "ancient rites and privileges," invitations that competed with those from old and new friends, all to be fitted into a crowded agenda.

Conflicts required choices, often at the cost of personal preferences. Royal invitations were "in the nature of a command that must be obeyed." Friends were flexible and understanding, and generously included "Miss Borden." Whenever possible, Sir Frederick and Lady Borden indulged their passion for music, history, and pageantry. The Royal Opera at Covent Garden on 30 May was a must. So too was the Inner Temple's concert at Queen's Hall, featuring the Hall's orchestra and the Temple Choir, conducted by Henry Walford Davies (1869–1941), in a program of Wolfgang Amadeus Mozart, Edward Elgar, Felix Mendelssohn, and Richard Wagner. They also found time for St. Paul's special "Great Organ" recital and for theatre.[2]

Lady Borden supervised their schedule, as she had in 1902, working closely with Charles-Louis. Each morning they sorted the post, consulted family, and decided which invitations to accept or decline, and the appropriate language. They then chose stationery, composed carefully worded replies to invitations and thank you notes to hosts and hostesses for the previous day's hospitality (and handwriting was *de rigueur*), and arranged the day's dress and logistics. Sir Frederick's public obligations drove the family's social agenda. Most invitations included Lady Borden. Others required only Sir Frederick's attendance; these included the Prince of Wales's inspection of the colonial troops in Alexandra Park on 27 June, the king's review of the Fleet at Spithead on 24 June (where Canada's naval representatives from the *Niobe* and *Rainbow*[3] were present), the Boy Scouts' march past the king on 4 July 4, the Bisley Rifle competitions, and the post-coronation Imperial Conference.

While Sir Frederick fulfilled official engagements, Lady Borden and Lizzie visited galleries and museums, attended club meetings such as the Ladies Empire Club, and shopped. Sir Frederick's health kept him from several social obligations. Whenever possible Lady Borden and Lizzie covered for his absence, often in debilitating, record-breaking summer heat, when temperatures at one point reached 100 degrees Fahrenheit, and air-conditioning was rare.

Once again Canadian participants and spectators were everywhere, owing to its "proximity to the heart of the Empire."[4] Apart from the 965-strong Canadian coronation contingent, there were 135 Canadian Boy Scouts and 100 official Canadian coronation guests, comprising public figures and honours recipients (including forty-eight special guests of the Imperial Parliament), a delegation of Manitoba teachers, a team of Canadian athletes, IODE representatives, and an untold number of Canadian tourists and travellers. Official representatives and guests enjoyed extraordinarily generous hospitality. Lord Northcliffe's Festival of the Empire hospitality committee oversaw its social extravaganza. Lord Roseberry chaired a committee to entertain the guests of the Imperial Parliament. General Sir Ian Hamilton supervised hospitality for the colonial troops, and Captain Arthur Morton Grenfell (the 4th Earl Grey's son-in-law) chaired the scouts' reception. London abounded in formal and informal entertainment, much of it organized by various imperial ladies' organizations.[5]

The coronation entailed more than the crowning of a king. It featured a political spectacle whose inescapable, didactic message was empire, its size, diversity, governance, industrial strength, artistic expression, moral purpose, athletic prowess, and military might.[6] The king opened the Festival of Empire on 16 May on the 200-acre Crystal Palace grounds (at Sydenham), a spectacle that lasted until October. An electric railway transported visitors on an "All Red Tour" to three-quarter size replicas of the parliamentary buildings of the self-governing dominions and India, reminding visitors of the success, wisdom, and geographic reach of British governance. Inside each replica, examples of the natural resources, industry, and transportation facilities advertised their country's economic potential. Artistic and literary expression was also on display, including the popular Canadian painting *The Water Carriers*, by Maurice Cullen (1866–1934). The "Women's Work" exhibition of arts, crafts, nursing, and charity work recognized the increasingly visible and vocal women's movement.[7] Membership in the Terrace Club, a special pavilion overlooking the royal pavilion, enabled Lady Borden and Elizabeth to view the exhibition at a more leisurely pace.

The highlight of the Festival of Empire was a dramatized pageant depicting the empire's history, mission, and grandeur, organized by Frank Lascelles (1875–1934), an actor and sculptor who had served as aide-de-camp to the Canadian Governor General, Lord Minto (1898–1904). Known as the maste' of imperial pageantry, Lascelles had staged the Quebec Tercentenary (1908) and the Union of South Africa Pageant (1910). His 1911 coronation pageant featured a four-part, four-day performance, held on successive days, eulogizing the steady, heroic progress of imperial power, accompanied by stirring music written by 20 different composers, played by 50 military bands, and sung by a 500-voice choir. Another festival event was the Inter-Empire Sports Competition, a precursor to the British Empire and Commonwealth Games, designed to demonstrate the empire's athletic prowess – a contest won by Canada's team, thanks to its gold medallist sprinter Frank J. Halbhaus (1887–?), swimmer George Richie Hodgson (1893–1983), and John Lindsay "Wonder Boy" Tait (1888–1971), a middle-/long-distance runner.

Among the complementary coronation events none was more successful than the Woman's Coronation Procession on 17 June, held five days before the coronation. Mrs. Emmeline Pankhurst, the seasoned suffrage advocate, headed thousands of women of all ages, many clad in white (Canadian representatives among their number), as they marched from Trafalgar Square to the Royal Albert Hall, with bands playing and banners flying, their call for women's rights cast in terms of duty, sacrifice, patriotism, and motherhood, symbolized by a float with an enthroned "Mother of Empire" dressed in neoclassical attire. Less numerous, though distinguished, were the dignitaries attending the Duke of Devonshire's Coronation Meeting for Men, held at the Queen's Hotel on 20 June to hear the bishops of London and York, Lord Roberts, Baden-Powell,[8] and others discuss ways and means to establish "the imperial and Christian religion's place in Empire,"[9] their objectives deeply embedded in the imperial project.

None, however, upstaged the coronation on 22 June in Westminster Abbey. As official guests, Sir Frederick and Lady Borden were already seated in Westminster Abbey as the king and queen, in "stately splendor"[10] began their procession from Buckingham Palace to Westminster Abbey, their golden carriage led by the North-West Mounted Police. Following at a respectable distance behind the golden carriage were the carriages of the "royal guests" (family members and state representatives), including Laurier, the only Canadian "royal guest," who shared a carriage with Andrew Fisher (1862–1928), the Australian prime minister. Streets of crowded, curious spectators cheered the royal party as it moved toward the Abbey, their route lined by some 50,000 troops, including representatives from Canada's militia, NWMP, and newly formed "autonomous" navy.

By the time the king reached Westminster Abbey Sir Frederick and Lady Borden and some 6,000 guests (including 100 Canadians) had been seated in the Abbey for over three hours on specially made Chippendale-style chairs with their names carved on the back of each chair, souvenirs that they might purchase. For Sir Frederick and Lady

Borden the coronation's music, theatrical ritual, and affirmation of allegiance must have more than compensated for the tiresome wait for the king's arrival, compromised by their concern for their son-in-law's condition following his serious accident the previous day.

During the coronation rehearsal parade, Colonel A.H. McLean, the officer commanding the Canadian contingent, had asked Leslie, McLean's aide-de-camp, to test his horse. They were on Pall Mall. It was raining and the street was slippery, and when the massed band struck up "God Save the King," Leslie's horse reared. Leslie leaned forward holding his drawn sword. The horse's hind feet slid on the pavement and Leslie fell backwards. The horse fell on him and broke his arm, pelvis, and ribs; injured his right leg; and fractured his skull, causing a concussion. For several days his life was reported to be in danger.[11] After the coronation Sir Frederick moved Leslie to a better hospital than he had been assigned and where he remained for several months, visited by members of London's Canadian network, including the Duke and Duchess of Argyll. For the rest of his life Leslie remained deaf in one ear and slightly lame, and suffered pain in his right leg.[12]

Eight days after the coronation Sir Frederick and Lady Borden enjoyed their own personal coronation! It began with The King's Coronation Honours List, which named Sir Frederick an honorary surgeon-general to the king. That meant attendance at court for the King's Royal Banquet on 25 June, followed by an invitation to the King's Garden Party on 27 June. But for Sir Frederick and Lady Borden nothing surpassed Lord Strathcona's Dominion Day Banquet on 30 June. Lord Strathcona's elegant, gold-embossed invitation with the Canadian coat of arms, a crown on top and a maple leaf on the left below, summoned eighty guests to the Imperial Institute in South Kensington to celebrate Canada's forty-fourth birthday. The banquet began at 10 pm, on the eve of 1 July, the guests serenaded by Pitman's Blue Imperial Orchestra playing patriotic airs, including "The Maple Leaf Forever" and "Vive la Canadienne."

Lord Strathcona presided at Table 1, which included Elizabeth, the Prince of Wales, and the Duke of Connaught. Sir Frederick and Lady Borden sat at Table 2 with Laurier and Mackenzie Bowell. In his welcoming remarks, the aged high commissioner surprised his quests by informing them that this was his last Dominion Day banquet as Canada's high commissioner: the news that Sir Frederick and Lady Borden had waited for years. In thanking the high commissioner for his long, distinguished service, Laurier delighted Sir Frederick and Lady Borden further by informing the banqueters that they had in their midst Strathcona's successor, Sir Frederick Borden. Sir Frederick had been tagged to toast members of the Royal family, though he might have been excused if his mind were elsewhere.

This most prestigious appointment in the gift of the Canadian government was all but his, one that he and Lady Borden had coveted for years and held recently by his erstwhile rival, Sir Charles Tupper (1888–95). Sir Frederick had not been the only aspirant to the office,[13] but twice Laurier had promised him the position whenever it became vacant. Twice Sir Frederick had refused the lieutenant-governorship of his province while he awaited the aged high commissioner's resignation. The high commissionership would crown Sir Frederick's public career.

The emotionally charged, post-Coronation Imperial Conference confirmed Laurier's confidence in the high commissioner designate. Together he and Sir Frederick faced an array of imperial schemes and suggestions that would have taken a year or more to debate.[14] Some were useful, others politically dangerous. At home Canada's imperial advocates, critics, and sceptics scrutinized the press, in search of political ammunition. Sir Frederick understood the political perils. He listened, learned, and assisted, as Sir Wilfrid skilfully manoeuvred among the several and conflicting proposals on offer, selecting what he thought beneficial to Canadian interests and rejecting what he considered detrimental or politically unwise, a tactic that increasingly irritated imperial well-wishers on both sides of the Atlantic, but played well to a home audience that offered him a triumphant return.[15]

The press's announcement of Sir Frederick's proposed appointment elicited a flood of congratulations and social invitations, though Sir Frederick and Lady Borden now had even less time for social activities. There were so many decisions and things to do in preparation for their move to London. Sir Frederick discussed his appointment at length with Laurier before the prime minister left London, and Laurier made clear that the date of Sir Frederick's appointment depended upon Lord Strathcona's formal resignation and cabinet approval. Cabinet approval was little more than a formality since Sir Frederick's replacement of Strathcona had been an open secret for years. Waiting was more difficult.

Sir Frederick's appointment required important personal and political decisions. Appropriate living space in London was a priority, including accommodation for Mrs. Clarke, a decision best settled before they left London. Then there were the usual questions, how to maintain Stadacona Hall and Borden Place during their absence, and who would manage their farms and local business. Would and could Leslie and Maude, or Elizabeth and her fiancé, manage things under Sir Frederick's long-distance supervision? More immediate questions entailed political timing and convenience. When ought Sir Frederick to withdraw from cabinet and transfer his ministerial responsibilities to his replacement, whose identity was no secret?[16] Sir Frederick's friend, E.M. Macdonald, the Liberal member of Parliament for Pictou, was Laurier's choice. The sooner Sir Frederick cleared his office for Macdonald the better. Sir Frederick also wrote to H.H Wickwire, his obvious federal replacement in Kings, and only recently re-elected to the Nova Scotia Assembly, advising him to delay accepting a provincial cabinet position. That done, Sir Frederick, with a palpable sense of relief, reassured Lady Borden that "there will be no more elections for us."[17]

Strathcona was in no hurry to resign, and to press him would be indecent. Meanwile Sir Frederick returned to Canada immediately after the Imperial Conference, to prepare things for E.M. Macdonald, leaving Lady Borden in London to plan their move and oversee Leslie's recovery. As much as she enjoyed London, Lady Borden, too, was anxious to return to Canada to supervise their move and prepare for Elizabeth's marriage. Elizabeth's wedding had been planned for early October at Borden Place, and she and Sir Frederick wanted to make it a memorable occasion. After waiting in London for two weeks, and still no response from Lord Strathcona, Lady Borden left for home with her coronation medal,[18] memories, and dreams, her departure announced in the 14 July 1 *Court Journal*, accompanied with a photograph and a promising "au revoir."

Chapter Sixteen

Lady Alone

At home, Canadians were still debating the controversial Reciprocity Agreement with the United States, which W.S. Fielding had announced so triumphantly in January 1911. During Sir Frederick and Lady Borden's two-month's absence that debate had grown in intensity and complexity, especially among Toronto's wealthy Liberal business community, increasingly organized and lavishly funding the Conservative-led Opposition.[1] As the acrimonious debate droned on week after week, tempers flared and patience frayed. Finally, Laurier threatened to end the Conservatives' filibuster by dissolving the House, confident that he could win a majority. The Opposition called his bluff; Laurier dissolved the House and called for an election on 21 September 1911.

Lord Strathcona still had not submitted his resignation. Sir Frederick had no desire to re-offer. To contest his constituency, and then resign during or immediately after the election, seemed a waste of energy, resources, and good will. In the short run, all he could do was to await a decision. Only when he could delay no longer did he bow to Laurier's plea to contest his old constituency, convinced that reciprocity would "carry the country hands down," especially in Kings, where he faced a glib "young stripling" from Canning, Arthur de Witt Foster, a twenty-five-year-old schoolteacher and student at Acadia College.[2] Sir Frederick misread his constituency. Notwithstanding Kings County's historic free trade proclivities, and Laurier's triumphant tour of the Valley (where he spent overnight at Borden Place), the young stripling defeated Sir Frederick by 151 votes. Worse still, the government's defeat ended Sir Frederick's chance to succeed Lord Strathcona as high commissioner, the potential reward that had kept him in politics.[3]

Family and friends were sympathetic and generous in their praise of his career, as was the new prime minister, who seemed almost to resent his cousin's defeat. Colleagues, commentators, and even opponents praised Sir Frederick's contribution to public life, especially his military reforms, many repeating the British military magazine *The Broad Arrow*'s earlier assessment that "no Minister of Militia has ever done so much toward making the Canadian forces so thoroughly effective and ready for the field as he."[4] That 1901 assessment seemed even more valid after a decade of significant military reform. His departmental staff thanked and honoured him with gifts and testimonials. Sam Hughes, Sir Frederick's old friend and Conservative replacement as minister of militia, followed his leader's example and expressed "his deep regret at your going down"[5] and vowed to consult Sir Frederick and welcome his advice.

Composed and stoical as Sir Frederick and Lady Borden appeared in public, defeat was not how they had imagined their release from political life. Nothing conformed quite to those dreams of a time when they might lead "their own lives, to speak regardless of what the world or society might think." Sir Frederick had talked for years about returning to private life to devote more time to business. His doctors had warned him to slow down, counsel that Lady Borden had endorsed to no avail. The high commissionership had promised him the benefits of private gain and public service together with the "consideration and good opinion that wait upon riches." That option no longer existed.

Sir Frederick and Lady Borden brooded privately for a month or more, each trying to console the other and dissimulate their disappointment. During sleepless nights they pondered what might have been, regretting the loss of public office with its exceptional social and material opportunities.[6] Of the two Sir Frederick may have suffered less. He realized that his defeat meant the end of "all further honours or distinctions derivable from political life." He even professed mixed feelings about the high commissionership: "I would, I must confess, have liked to have tasted of the High Commissionership for both our sakes, but I never really cared to go farther than to taste."[7] He was sixty-four, tired, in poor health, and had several promising entrepreneurial projects closer to home. What hurt more was the thought of Bessie's disappointment.

Sir Frederick thought of Lady Borden's contribution to his political success, and her desire to play a larger role. In excellent health, Bessie was in her prime, able, ready, and willing for the challenge, now cruelly denied. Although Sir Frederick once described himself as "too poor and too democratic" to accept a knighthood, he resented newspaper speculation on Laura becoming another Lady Borden. "I was under the impression there had been a Lady Borden for going on 10 years," he wrote Bessie, "& still is one in good standing!!," adding, "I only hope the second one will do her part as well as No. 1." Of course, he conceded, "if they make Rob G.C.M.G. he will take precedence. But who cares? Not we. I really think if Rob has his way he will prefer to remain plain Mr. I should if I were he." Clearly Sir Frederick did care, at least for Bessie.[8]

Lady Borden reciprocated his sympathies, justifying her feelings in more practical terms. She reminded Sir Frederick of his precarious health and need to slow down. She assured him that he had paid his dues to society, that it was time to enjoy life, engage in other activities, travel, and lead a quieter life. As for imperial service she remained sceptical of its utility. Behind its rhetoric she saw little real benefit for Canada. To alleviate her own disappointment, she turned to her faith for meaning and purpose. After all God moved in mysterious ways.

What Lady Borden failed to extract from Sir Frederick was a firm promise to end his political career. The day after the election Laurier called a cabinet meeting for 26 September and Sir Frederick left Canning immediately for Ottawa, spending overnight in Montreal with E.A. Robert, before travelling to Ottawa the next day. Laurier, Sir Frederick wrote Lady Borden, was "in great form" as he met his full cabinet (all except Oliver and Templeman) for an all-day meeting, astonishing them by announcing that their first duty would be to fix a date for Thanksgiving Day!!" He then made clear that he would remain leader and asked his defeated cabinet ministers to find seats in the House "to present a unified front." While many of his colleagues wanted to "get out" as soon as possible and "presumably early next week," Sir Frederick guessed that others – Fielding, King, Graham, and Fisher – would re-offer. Sir Frederick assured Lady Borden that he had "said most unequivocally that he was out & [would] remain out." Yet, he added, "if I thought Sir Wilfrid really needed me, I would not care to be obstinate or obdurate. But I feel that I can be very well spared & in any case I can always give a little advice by letter when necessary – as to military matters."[9] Sir Frederick's qualification was not reassuring.

Lizzie's imminent marriage was an immediate, therapeutic distraction. Scheduled for 11 October 1911, only three weeks after the government's defeat, Lady and Sir Frederick Borden intended to make it a memorable occasion. They had watched Lizzie's maturing friendship with Dr. Charles Gordon Hewett, the Dominion Entomologist, with hope and anticipation, delighted by Lizzie's engagement and choice of fiancé. A handsome woman, sophisticated, educated, and well-travelled, Lizzie was an informed conversationalist with broad literary and artistic interests. She was active, socially engaged, organized, and forthright. Casual acquaintances may have found her forbidding, but behind her mask lay a shy, sensitive, generous romantic.

Lizzie had lived comfortably at home, sharing her parents's life and causes. "Ask Lizzie," was her father's reflex response to farm or household workers seeking direction during his absence. She loved travelling with her parents. She had accompanied them to London in 1902, 1906, 1907, 1909, and 1911. She especially enjoyed travelling with her father, whose energy, curiosity, and sense of adventure she shared. In early September 1905 she and Maude had joined their father and Lieutenant. General Percy and Mrs. Lake on a month-long military promotional tour cum vacation in Western Canada to promote Sir Frederick's citizen army. Unable to accompany the party owing to illness, Lady Borden received ecstatic letters from Sir Frederick and Elizabeth describing the splendours of Lake Louise, Emerald Lake, the Kicking Horse Gorge, Laggan, Fields, Kamloops, Mount Hector, Temple, and Cathedral, all "quite equal in grandeur … to anything we saw in the U.S.," as well as their camping, riding, and hiking, Elizabeth out-walking everyone, "going up hills with scarcely an effort."[10]

Elizabeth's 1908 return to the West with her father confirmed her unqualified enthusiasm for Western Canada. Once again Lizzie revelled in the contemporary West's "go-ahead," energy, growth, and optimism. It appealed to her drive and sense of purpose, reinforced by the warmth and hospitality of her father's political friends and business associates. She was particularly impressed by the young migrants she met, many of them young maritime migrants and acquaintances such as Ethel Davies Hayman, the daughter of Sir Louis Davies, the former PEI premier and her father's former cabinet colleague (1896–1901). Edmonton and Calgary, she concluded, were towns where "one might live without longing for the east," and Calgary was clearly the "prettiest town in the west."[11]

Lizzie had a modest circle of female friends, but few male suitors. Charles "Gordon" Hewitt was her happy exception.[12] She had met Gordon soon after he arrived in Canada in September 1909. Ten years her junior, Gordon had been born near Macclesfield, England, on 23 February 1885. A prize student, he had been educated at Macclesfield (King Edward VII) Grammar School,[13] and Victoria University of Manchester, where he obtained a BSc (1902), MSc (1903), and a DSc (1909) and been appointed an assistant lecturer (1902), lecturer (1904–7), and demonstrator (1907–9) in "economic zoology."[14] He was only twenty-three years old when he arrived in Ottawa, having just completed his doctoral studies in zoology, and where he promised to stay for one year.

Lizzie changed Gordon's plans. Within a year of his arrival Gordon and Lizzie were hopelessly in love. Lizzie saw herself as a born naturalist, who "always panted for fresh air" and had an "obsession for parks & gardens," a passion second only to her love of books.[15] It was a "match made in heaven," based on shared interests in literature, art, music, travel, gardening, and community service. Lizzie and Gordon's relationship was no less fortified by his fortuitous Canadian career prospects. The November 1908 death of Dr. James Fletcher (1852–1908), the Canadian "Father of Economic Entomology,"[16] two months after Gordon's arrival in Canada, opened an important position in an expanding government service dedicated to research and dissemination of information on harmful insects and noxious weeds in agriculture, Canada's principal export. An organized, energetic research scientist, Gordon was an ideal replacement for Fletcher. Nor was Gordon's career hindered by Sir Frederick's friendship with Sydney Fisher, the minister of agriculture, a staunch conservationist.[17] Gordon was also a scholarly, idealistic crusader, all qualities that appealed to Elizabeth. He adapted quickly, sensitively, and enthusiastically to his new home, and all thoughts of returning to England vanished.

Gordon's colleagues in the Department of Agriculture saw him as a "scholar and a gentleman," reserved, and somewhat "aristocratic" in manner. Sensitive to the qualities and opportunities of his new home, Gordon was a "great admirer of the French language in arts and science" and insisted on "using the French language while speaking at public meetings in Quebec ... to give a public example," an initiative Elizabeth applauded.[18] Gordon shared Elizabeth's fascination with Canada's great potential, its last best west, this booming part of the imperial estate, where the future of "our Empire" was being decided, a mission he embraced with youthful zeal and liberal imperial conviction.

During a triumphant three-week inspection and speaking tour of Western Canada in October 1910, scarcely a year after his arrival in Canada, Gordon visited provincial boards of horticulture, ministers, and deputies, deeply impressed by the region's sheer energy and optimism. In speech after speech, he pleaded with evangelical zeal for the protection of "our wildlife and natural heritage," preaching a gospel of 'health over wealth' to packed halls and enthusiastic audiences. As he boasted to an appreciative Lizzie, his audiences responded by "drowning the end of my sentences with applause."[19] The press took up his cause and converts joined his crusade. According to Gordon, one unidentified person, who "had been responsible for rolling most of the large boulders that came my way," confessed that he had been "entirely converted," and the premier of British Columbia, Richard McBride (1903–15), Sir Frederick's Conservative friend, "privately" declared Gordon "a public benefactor."[20] Lizzie needed no persuasion. Given Gordon's triumphant tour, his career prospects, and his blossoming relationship with Lizzie, how could Gordon imagine leaving Canada after only one year?

Gordon and Lizzie were chronic romantics.[21] During his three-week western tour in 1910 they corresponded frequently, passionately, and at length. Occupied and successful as Gordon's Western tour may have been, Lizzie was never far from his thoughts. As he confided to her on his way back to Vancouver from Victoria, he carried her letters with him to read at dinner, having first asked the orchestra to play Jacques Offenbach's "Belle nuit, O nuit d'amour."[22] He then retreated to a quiet spot on the ferry boat to pen an enamoured response to her last letter. "As I came across from Victoria this afternoon & tonight, he wrote:

> I felt like some of the seagulls that instead of keeping with the boat flew ahead of it. They were anxious to reach the port. I wanted your letters. In the westward was a glorious sunset over the sea & behind the mountains of Vancouver Island. When it had gone I went to the Eastern side & the moon sailed there. Now it is helping to light this page, for my window is wide open facing the East. And I found not one but two letters-the one ... forwarded. Can't you send me the one I missed at Regina? It is mine.

Their letters' more cryptic messages suggest an advanced relationship and commitment. "I can't say how happy [the letters] made me to know you are now happier. You made me so & I helped to make you. No," he continued, "we will not let people spoil happy days. I agree, but I wish I could say this to you instead of writing-still keep this one sentence – & you have it in writing if ever you see the world & people threatening to spoil it. It shall be our true compact. It will be hard to keep; you know how hard, but it will be less hard than before. I wish you were here to talk to."[23] Less than a year later they were married.

Gordon appreciated Sir Frederick and Lady Borden's prominent social standing in Ottawa, and its access to power and influence. He regaled his proud parents with tales of his social and professional success, political gossip, and stories of Sir Frederick and Lady Borden in their "ancient mansion," of his singing to their distinguished guests during an "at home" at the Bordens', his solo interrupted by a short visit from Sir Wilfrid, his discussion on the Conservatives' Naval Bill at Sydney Fisher's "at home," and his call on Maude, Leslie, and Rosamond, where he chatted about gardening, caterpillars, and pest control with the newly minted prime minister, Robert Borden, in shirt sleeves, who had dropped by for a chat.[24] Clearly Gordon's access to power and advancement was uninterrupted by the 1911 change of government, his civic reputation enhanced by his volunteer work with Ottawa's

Boys' Home, Boy Scouts, and Humane Society. Within a very short time, then, Gordon was well and comfortably installed in Ottawa, infatuated with Lizzie and her important family. Lizzie's family were no less charmed by Gordon; Lady Borden was especially taken with him: he was such a striking contrast to her more formal, hot-tempered son-in-law.

Although the family planned "a quiet home wedding"[25] at Borden Place, tailored to Lizzie's and Gordon's taste, it soon became a carefully staged event, a timely distraction and outlet for Lady Borden's social and artistic sensibilities. A day before the wedding an excited Gordon arrived by rail from Ottawa. Overwhelmed by Lady Borden's preparations, he savoured every detail of her "most beautiful idea." As he exulted to his father and mother after the wedding, the site was the drawing room at Borden Place, a long rectangular room extending across the length of the house. Guests entered from the central door into the foyer to the drawing room. Cleared of all its furniture the drawing room had been rearranged to resemble a private chapel with an imitation communion rail in front of a window at one end of the room. And knowing how fond Gordon and Lizzie were of "the woods and nature," Lady Borden had decorated the wall behind the "communion rail" with pine, spruce, and ferns. In front of the window, she had created "a curtain of green moss ferns with large pink roses to resemble a natural stained-glass window." The piano was placed at the other end of the drawing room and covered with ferns, roses, and large bowls of chrysanthemums, as was the spacious entrance hall with its great open fireplace.[26]

On that "glorious sunny autumn day" of Wednesday, 11 October 1911, about thirty or so guests entered Borden Place from Canning's bunting-decorated Main Street for the wedding ceremony, which began at 10:30 am. The small number of guests, Gordon reassured his parents, was quite intentional as was the absence of real friends since "it would not have been possible to draw the line & at the same time have a small wedding." Consequently the "only people who were invited were relatives & the chief people in the village & neighbours."[27] Canning's Methodist minister, the Reverend Arthur Hockins presided, assisted by Reverend William Ainsley, their former minister and old family friend from Bridgewater. The bride and groom were accompanied by Maude, Leslie, and Rosamond, Lizzie's four-year-old niece as flower girl.

Gordon could not have imagined a service to "have been so beautiful." Apart from Lady Borden's "most beautiful idea" of simulating "the woods and nature," Gordon's fondest memory was of the music. The service began with Richard Wagner's "Wedding March" from

Lohengrin, followed by Schumann's "Dedication" (*Widmung*), as the wedding party made its slow progression to the "communion rail." A small choir of three girls sang "O Perfect Love," after which the Reverend Hockins, assisted by the Reverend Ainsley, read the service. Gordon and Elizabeth pronounced their vows and Reverend Ainsley spoke for five minutes. Mendelssohn's "Wedding March" accompanied the bridal party as it left for the dining room, where they received guests and enjoyed a wedding breakfast, the guests seated at small tables. When the wedding breakfast ended about 12:15 pm, the couple changed their attire, said farewell to their family and guests and left for their honeymoon. To Gordon "the sun seemed to be everywhere and in everyone's face and heart and especially in ours."[28]

In Gordon's world the whole Valley was "flooded with autumn sunshine" as they slowly made their way for seventy miles by motor to Annapolis Royal, where they spent the night. Next day a team of horses drove them thirty-five miles, their luggage strapped to the buckboard, to the Kedgemakooge Kejimkujik Rod and Gun Club's landing, where a boat brought them to the recently constructed clubhouse. They were assigned one of the club's three log cabins. The recreational club had been established in a forested water system in south-central Nova Scotia by wealthy American sportsmen, to fish and shoot moose, bear, and deer in rustic comfort. Gordon and Lizzie spent the next five nights at "Kedge," in their log cabin overlooking the lake, the cabin equipped with a huge fireplace and a pile of logs outside, and only five or ten minutes from the clubhouse where they took their meals. It was a romantic's paradise, especially for naturalists delighted with its "out of the wayness."[29] On Tuesday 17 October, they returned to Annapolis Royal, took the Dominion Atlantic Railway to Yarmouth (the railway's general manager had provided passes), where they boarded the railway's Yarmouth Steamship ferry for Boston and remained there for five days before returning to Ottawa.

Sir Frederick and Lady Borden were delighted with Lizzie's marriage, deeply impressed by Gordon's "brief but brilliant"[30] scholarly, administrative, and public career. A prolific research scientist and public advocate, during Gordon's eleven years as Dominion Entomologist he authored 130 publications, reports, monographs, and scientific articles on public health, conservation, and preservation. His most notable treatise was entitled, *The House-Fly: Musca domestica* (1914).[31] Two years before this illustrated treatise appeared, Cambridge University Press published a popular edition entitled *House Flies and How They spread Disease*, which advised covering liquids and solid foods, and protecting infants' faces from disease-carrying flies.[32]

Gordon was a member of the Entomologist Society of America, the Economic Entomologist Society of America, the Entomologist Society of Ontario, the Ottawa Field-Naturalist' Club,[33] all of which he served as president, and the Royal Society of Canada, of which he was honorary treasurer. He was a fellow of the Entomological Society of London, the Zoological Society of London, and the Royal Society for the Protection of Birds, and secretary to the Canadian Wildlife board. An enthusiast, imbued with liberal imperialist dreams, in August 1912 Gordon represented Canada at the Second International Conference of Entomologists in Oxford.[34] After the conference he met with representatives of the "self-governing Dominions" and the colonial secretary to plan an international agreement on pest control. Much of Gordon's professional activity required travel, usually accompanied by Lizzie.

A tireless advocate of the conservation of nature and wildlife, game preserves, and bird sanctuaries, Gordon drafted Canada's Destructive Insect and Pest Act of 1910 to govern inspection and insect control, and negotiated the Canadian American Migratory Bird Treaty of 1916, for which he received the Royal Society's 1917 gold medal for the protection of birds. As president of the Ottawa Boys' Home, counsellor of Ottawa's Humane Society, and advocate of the Boy Scouts, he directed their conservation efforts and encouraged amateurs to collect data on flora and fauna.

Gordon was also an efficient, effective administrator who knew how to "distribute work, organize research, obtain results," and secure resources for his branch. During his eleven-years tenure as Dominion Entomologist, he transformed his small division within the Experimental Farms into a separate branch with four, well-equipped divisions, one headed by Germain Beaulieu.[35] Anxious to encourage cooperation and avoid duplication, he urged each province to establish entomological laboratories devoted to regional issues.[36] He also found time to serve as the Civil Service Professional Institute's founding president. In 1975 the Entomological Society of Canada honoured his memory by establishing the C. Gordon Hewitt Award for scholars who, within ten years of completion of their doctoral degree, had made a distinguished contribution to the field of entomology.

Lizzie's marriage and Sir Frederick's electoral defeat forced the question of Sir Frederick and Lady Borden's Ottawa residence, less difficult in 1911 than it had been in 1896; they quickly resolved the matter in favour of selling Stadacona Hall, while remaining in Ottawa, close to their daughters, granddaughter, relatives, and friends. That meant a smaller Ottawa residence, especially since Gordon and Lizzie sought a house of their own, an issue easily resolved by Lizzie and Gordon purchasing 17 Blackburn, from Lizzie's cousin, John William Borden, and Sir Frederick and Lady Borden purchasing 15 Blackburn, next door to Philip Buck,[37] a clear demonstration of their intention to remain in Ottawa.[38]

Family, colleagues, and friends facilitated Sir Frederick and Lady Borden's return to private life. In the late spring and summer Sir Frederick and Lady Borden continued to migrate to Canning, where their extended family joined them for weeks. There Rosamond commanded the attention of her "Aunta" and Uncle Gordon, her adoring grandparents, and great-grandmother Clarke, all caring, generous, and fascinated by her development. Rosamond was scarcely five years old when her family began worrying about her distinct limp. An Ottawa physician speculated that the cause of Rosamond's limp was a "malevolent fly bite." Sir Frederick insisted on a second opinion from his friend, Dr. Edward H. Bradford, the dean of Harvard's Medical School (1912–18), an orthopedic specialist who concluded that the limp was the "influence of habit ... a little girl's appreciation of her grand-mother's peculiar method of locomotive," a defect easily rectified by a series of exercises twice a day. Maude delegated the exercises' supervision to Rosamond's governess, who decided Rosamond was too tired for exercises after her school lessons. Whereupon Leslie, who seemed to have had a relatively low regard for formal pedagogy, decided that lessons had to go, since he thought physical exercises were more important than learning that 2 plus 2 equalled 4 or spelling cat.[39] Sir Frederick disagreed. In his view education was non-negotiable. Nor could he see any incompatibility between exercise and education,[40] a rare but defining difference between the two men.

For all of Sir Frederick and Lady Borden's family distractions, politics retained its adhesive grip. Robert Borden, the new prime minister, acknowledged Sir Frederick's public service and rebuked his detractors. He invited Sir Frederick and Lady Borden to the opening of Parliament and other public events.[41] He sought Sir Frederick's advice on Sam Hughes's cabinet appointment and the management of "British officialdom."[42] Robert and Sir Frederick continued to exchange investment information and family history, to seek and grant favours.[43] Robert and Laura were very fond of Maude, Leslie, and Rosamond, and enjoyed discussing conservation and landscaping with Leslie, Lizzie, and Gordon, all avid gardeners, and conservationists.

Sam Hughes followed his leader's example. He promised to consult Sir Frederick, though consultation was never Hughes's strength. He granted Sir Frederick favours and dampened overzealous Conservative criticism of Sir Frederick's military legacy. Whoever was responsible, in January 1912 Sir Frederick became an honorary associate member of the national committee for the Celebration of the One hundredth Anniversary of Peace among English Speaking People.[44]

Laurier, too, appreciated Sir Frederick's political utility, and once Laurier had absorbed his party's defeat, he named Sir Frederick to a small political reconstruction committee that included Sydney Fisher and Mackenzie King. The corporal guard's agenda drew Sir Frederick back to the political fray, reorganizing the party as he had done in 1891–6. Sir Frederick's perceived access to the new prime minister enhanced his political utility on both sides of the House, and during the Liberal Senate's filibuster of the Conservative's naval bill in May 1913, Sir Frederick attempted but failed to break the impasse.

Sir Frederick and Lady Borden's reflex response to defeat was travel. On 27 April 1912, while contractors were completing the extension and renovation of 15 Blackburn, Sir Frederick and Lady Borden boarded the CPR's *Empress of Ireland* in Montreal for a three-week visit to Britain, to enjoy the English spring, and from there travelled by train ferry to France. No longer bound by public business's exigencies, they were now tourists, welcomed by old friends and associates, though reminded of what might have been. Upon their return to Ottawa in August 1912 they joined Sir Wilfrid and Lady Laurier, and Mr. and Mrs. Edmund. Robert, for a visit to New Hampshire's White Mountains.[45]

Sir Frederick now had more time for his deferred entrepreneurial dreams and schemes. Of these none was more ambitious, fraught, and potentially lucrative than E.A. Robert and John Wilson McConnell's plan to electrify Halifax by harnessing the Gaspereau River. Although negotiations began well before Sir Frederick left office and required more effort and political acrobatics than he had imagined, he mustered the energy and exercised his cross-party clout, including that of Sir Robert Borden, to assure the project's success.

Friends began to note Sir Frederick's declining energy.[46] Lady Borden's worries had begun well before his electoral defeat. During his last years in government, Sir Frederick seemed strained, tired, and anxious. In the fall of 1910 Lady Borden persuaded him to consult his doctor, who advised him to slow down and stop worrying "about business affairs,"[47] advice that Lady Borden seconded but Sir Frederick ignored. Soon after the outbreak of World War I, Mackenzie King, Sir Frederick's ambitious young friend who had a morbid interest in his colleagues' health, noted Sir Frederick's disturbing physical appearance. Four months later King was alarmed. "Sir Frederick looks a much-shattered man," King wrote in his diary, "I doubt he has much longer to live.

Certainly, he will have to give up forever the thought of returning to public life."[48]

Sir Frederick relinquished neither his entrepreneurial activities nor his political aspirations. They were part of his daily routine, even if he paid them less attention than they required. Although he had difficulty letting go, he fostered his dynastic aspirations by casting Leslie in a role he had planned for Harold. Soon after Maude's marriage he named Leslie managing director of the Nova Scotia Produce and Supply Company, which "owned" the family's property and marketed its produce.[49] He made him chairman of the Cornwallis Trading Company's board and effective owner of his Woodside-Bell Hill farm. Sir Frederick had secured the Woodside-Bell farm from C. Bigelow with a personal bond, serviced and redeemed by its farm profits, and it was where Leslie, Maude, and Rosamond spent their summers.[50] Sir Frederick also transferred his controversial interests in the New Brunswick cold storage company to Leslie to smokescreen his involvement in the government-subsidized project. Nor did anyone believe Leslie was more than the proxy for Sir Frederick's interests in the Blomidon Railway Company Limited, incorporated in 1911 and capitalized at $250,000 to build a railway from Canning to Cap Blomidon to market the "land of Evangeline."[51] Similarly, after Lizzie's marriage, Sir Frederick named Gordon to the Supply Company's board, to represent and protect Lizzie's interest. While Gordon loved the family property, redesigned its gardens, and possessed administrative ability, business and finance were not his primary interests. He tended to trust people's good will and integrity. In fact, Lizzie was probably a better guardian of her own interests, being shrewd, demanding, and less confident of human virtue.

The outbreak of war in August 1914 changed Sir Frederick and Lady Borden's world. Their leisurely prewar Ottawa life became more hurried, ordered, and impersonal. It restrained non-essential European travel, redirected capital investment, restricted consumer goods, raised prices, absorbed labour, and increased wages. War work competed with household and farm labour and cut into profits. At times, it was difficult to hire anyone at any price. Projects requiring private or public capital or authorization were postponed. Inflation and escalating costs required watchful management. While the war offered golden opportunities for shrewd, energetic entrepreneurs with political connections, life became more taxing for an aging man in declining health.

War reshaped politics as well. When war began Laurier returned to Ottawa, cancelled his planned transcontinental political tour, and called for a political truce to curtail "all party strife." During Parliament's first emergency session he pledged his party's support for all war measures for as long as danger remained. Mackenzie King, who had become the party's full-time information officer and editor of the *Canadian Liberal Monthly*, invoked the political truce to accept John D. Rockefeller's lucrative offer to head his foundation's Department of Industrial Relations.

The political truce and King's departure created a political vacuum, filled shortly by a younger generation of Liberals. Restless under their party's aged leadership and anxious to exploit the Conservative government's blunders and increasing unpopularity, the younger Liberals attempted to rejuvenate the Liberal Party and champion the country's changing demographics. Laurier recognized the younger generation's desire to reorder the party but paid little attention to their suggestions. Sir Frederick and Fisher retained access to Laurier, "comfort friends" who supported and reassured him but who possessed no real influence, though both intended to stand for election to Canada's Twelfth Parliament.

Sir Frederick's chances for re-election were promising. Arthur de Witt Foster, the Conservative "stripling" who had defeated him in 1911, had relinquished his parliamentary seat after having been charged with corruption and expelled from his party. Sir Frederick's constituency's Liberal Association had unanimously acclaimed "their distinguished leader" as their candidate.[52] Sir Robert Borden, who seemed never to have taken to Foster, was unlikely to resist Sir Frederick's return to the House. In July 1916 the government named its large new military base Camp Borden to honour Sir Frederick's military contribution, an initiative Sir Sam Hughes had undertaken with Sir Robert's blessing.

Early Saturday morning, 6 January 1917, Sir Frederick died in his sleep at Borden Place, four months short of his seventieth birthday. Lady Borden had monitored his health closely during the last two years, aware that he was seriously ill.[53] Appearances notwithstanding, Sir Frederick remained remarkably resilient. Only ten days before his death, he had been in Halifax attending to business and visiting friends. A week after he returned from Halifax, he suffered a paralytic stroke and was confined to bed. Three days later he was dead. Lady Borden was alone with only her mother and the servants at the time. Elizabeth, Maude, and their husbands left Ottawa immediately for Canning. Leslie took charge. He informed Sir Frederick's extended family, political friends, and business associates, consulted Lady Borden, and made funeral arrangements. He sent telegrams to Sir Robert, Sir Wilfrid, Sydney Fisher, Mackenzie King, and others announcing Sir Frederick's death.

Major Canadian, British, and American dailies reported Sir Frederick's death, the articles often accompanied by a photograph and a biographical summary of his career. Some published editorial tributes, noting his militia reforms and their contribution to Canada's performance in the current war. Many repeated the familiar claim that he had been Canada's best minister of militia to date,[54] his recently discredited successor, Sam Hughes, still fresh in the public mind.

Although the war, the season, and public business constrained attendance, Sir Frederick's funeral service on 9 January 1917 was an impressive event. It was a calm, fine day and flags flew at half-mast in Canning and Kentville, and throughout the county. Special trains ran between Kentville and Canning to accommodate the hundreds[55] of out-of-town guests. The county's municipal council adjourned its semi-annual morning meeting in Kentville to permit the full council's attendance at the afternoon funeral. Only a small number of "the immense crowd"[56] of friends, neighbours, and the curious gained entrance to Canning's Methodist church, its interior draped in black and packed with floral tributes from friends, colleagues,[57] and municipal, provincial, and federal institutions, and other public bodies. A large Union Jack covered his casket. Another hung behind the pulpit.[58]

Public and private obligations kept several prominent persons from attending the funeral. Only days before the opening of the decisive 1917 parliamentary session, the pressure of public business kept Sir Robert Borden in Ottawa. Rob's "favourite brother," Henry "Hal" Clifford Borden (1870–1943), represented him.[59] Sir Wilfrid was detained in Ottawa for similar reasons but sent a warmly worded tribute to his old friend. And according to Mackenzie King's diary, only his mother's illness, requiring around-the-clock care, kept him from going to Canning.[60] Other colleagues who knew and loved him were absent, such as Sir William Mulock, who was vacationing in Florida.[61] A.K. MacLean, the Liberal MP from Halifax, represented the Canadian government, E.H. Armstrong, the Nova Scotia Legislature, and M.H George its Legislative Council.

After a brief, religious service at Borden Place, faithful family employees accompanied Sir Frederick's flag-draped casket to the church and placed it at the front, amid lavish floral tributes. Despite its public nature, the church service retained a family character. Sir Frederick's cousins, the Reverend Dr. Byron Crane Borden, the president of Mount Allison University, and the Reverend Dr. Arthur Cummings Borden, the renowned retired Methodist missionary to Japan, assisted two of the family's favourite ministers, the Reverend William Ainsley, from Kingsport, and the Reverend Arthur Hockins, from Grand Pre, who conducted the religious service. After the opening prayer and hymn, "How Firm a Foundation," the Reverend Arthur Hockins read Psalm 23 ("The Lord Is My Shepherd"), the Reverend Mr. Wright (Kingsport) read Psalm 46 ("The Lord Is My Refuge and Strength"), and the Reverend Mr. Bell (Cunard) read John 14 ("Let Not Your Heart Be Troubled"), the congregation sang "Strong Son of God." In his tribute the Reverend Doctor B.C. Borden read Laurier's message to the rapt congregation: "I have lost one of the truest and most devoted friends I have ever had ... a true patriot and wise counsellor," words that the family had chiselled on Sir Frederick's monumental headstone.[62] A long, solemn entourage of family, and political and public figures, including university representatives (Kings, Acadia, Mount Allison, and Dalhousie) followed Sir Frederick's remains to the family burial plot in the Hillton Cemetery (the site of the former Wesleyan Methodist Church), which had been enlarged in 1911, thanks to land Sir Frederick had donated to the church. There Sir Frederick was interred, next to his first wife, with space on his other side for Lady Borden, and close to the empty plot marked by a stone cross as a memorial to Harold, whose body remained in South Africa.

Lady Borden was now alone and would have to remake her life. She was alone except for her bedridden, eighty-eight-year-old mother, who was attended by two nurses. Sir Frederick had often reminded Gus of the unshared burden of his mother's care. Lady Borden maintained her composure for several days, long enough to oversee the funeral arrangements, receive condolences, and thank those who paid homage to her husband. Then, immediately after the funeral she "collapsed" and was confined to bed under doctor's care until mid-February, suffering from what doctors described as a "nervous break-down." For several weeks she left her room only for meals.[63]

During Lady Borden's convalescence she tried to rethink her life. Elizabeth and Maude were married and lived in Ottawa, and though Lady Borden enjoyed Ottawa, she could think of no reason to retain her Ottawa residence. The girls and their family would join her in Canning in the summer, and she could visit them regularly in Ottawa. But for a restless, autonomous woman, accustomed to occupying her own space, the restrictive status of guest had limited appeal. Sir Frederick's death underscored how much their friends, interests, and lives had become interdependant. She was now more vulnerable. She would have to assume greater responsibility for the family's material assets. Her mother's care and uncertain health, however, made planning difficult.

On the other hand, she was fifty-four and not without personal and material resources. She had no desire to become one of those affluent, "parasitic" older women who, according to Agnes MacPhail, made no contribution to society.[64] She had many relatives, friends, and neighbours whose correspondence, invitations, and shared interests could help her remake her life. She retained a keen interest in public affairs. Mary Grew (nee Brown), Sir Frederick's politically engaged cousin and matriarch of Ottawa's influential Brown clan, plied Lady Borden with Ottawa political news.[65] Gus and Hattie urged her to visit them in Wetmore, Colorado. Travel, however, was out of the question during the war, in the dead of winter, with her mother's illness and her need to settle Sir Frederick's estate.

Chapter Seventeen

Administrator

Ten days after Sir Frederick's funeral Lady Borden was still in bed, unable to participate in a family council to discuss the estate's settlement. Elizabeth attended, armed with a list of her father's securities. She listened carefully, a vigilant guardian of her family's material interests, her father's reputation, and her mother's welfare. Everyone assumed Sir Frederick had left a will, though their search proved futile. Sir Frederick had died intestate. The family was obliged, therefore, to petition the probate court to name an executor to itemize his real and personal assets, pay his debts, and distribute the residue of his estate among his three heirs-at-law, Lady Borden, Elizabeth, and Maude. The probate court suggested that Lady Borden execute Sir Frederick's estate, but Lady Borden declined, as did Elizabeth and Maude.

Leslie chaired the family council and expected to become the estate's executor. He had worked with Sir Frederick and was familiar with his entrepreneurial activities. He currently managed the family's Supply Company and chaired the board of its Cornwallis Trading Company, two of the family's principal sources of income. He had taken over Sir Frederick's controversial stake in the New Brunswick Cold Storage Company,[1] and had become his proxy for other politically sensitive interests. He was an investment broker and Sir Frederick's portfolio was mined with investment stocks. Everyone agreed that Leslie ought to become executor, subject to Lady Borden's consent.

A week later, just before Maude and Leslie returned to Ottawa, Leslie met Lady Borden in her bedroom to discuss the estate's management and disposition. Leslie recounted the family's earlier discussion, and the suggestion that he become the estate's executor. He reminded Lady Borden of his knowledge of the estate and his accounting experience at the Experimental Farm and the Ottawa Country Club. He also promised to consult the heirs except "for quick decisions," and to provide a "true inventory of the estate's effects within three months" and a "just and true account of my administration" in a year to eighteen months.[2]

Leslie reassured Lady Borden that he would have no difficulty maintaining his Ottawa business, as broker and manufacturer's agent, spending three to six months of the year in Ottawa and the rest of his time in Canning, travelling between the two locations, as necessary. He also agreed to continue administrating the estate, taking decisions on its assets, management, and enhancement, apparently oblivious to the potential conflict between his administrator's and executor's responsibilities. Lady Borden noted Leslie's repeated assurance that he "did not expect the full executor's commission provided by law," since the family already paid him to administer their estate.[3]

During their bedroom conference, Leslie warned Lady Borden that he might need temporary funds to cover succession duties and other exigencies, and Lady Borden had agreed, conscious of the estate's complexities. At the time, she had "absolute faith" in Leslie's business acumen and ability. Her only suggestion was that he consult Edmund A. Robert, who had generously offered to assist the family with their corporate portfolio. Lady Borden's solicitor later informed the probate court, however, that Lady Borden was then in no position "to bring intelligent judgment on matters of finance," since she was still suffering "25% mental impairment."[4]

Leslie was pleased with Lady Borden's confidence. An ambitious entrepreneur, his executor's duties promised greater visibility within his fraternity of corporate agents. The appointment might even prove useful to the estate. Neither Leslie nor the family anticipated the potential conflict in his dual role as estate administrator and estate executor. Both overestimated his credentials and underestimated the estate's complexities. Nor was Leslie sufficiently appreciative of local sensitivities; people were often offended by his brisk manner and impatience. In his haste to begin his duties, he and Maude left for Ottawa immediately after his discussion with Lady Borden, armed with packets of estate papers, three weeks before his formal appointment as executor on 24 February 1917.

The family's immediate concern was Lady Borden's care and financial security. All agreed that she continue to occupy Borden Place and 15 Blackburn and have the use of their contents, stables, carriages, and automobile until the estate was settled, and that she retain the option to purchase either or both properties. They agreed, too, that the estate pay for the houses' maintenance, taxes, two maids, household, and outdoor labour (a projected annual cost of $2,225), and that the Supply Company extend credit for her groceries and supplies until the estate was settled.

Lady Borden was not destitute. She had personal income, principally from her lucrative shares in International Nickel and her 6 per cent Supply Company bonds and mortgages, supplemented later by an inheritance following her mother's 1919 death. As portions of the estate were liquidated, she received her just portion. While the exact amount of Lady Borden's disposable income is unclear, by 1923 she had received some $24,255 of her share of the estate's liquidated assets,[5] altogether sufficient to maintain her social standing, travel, and entertainment.

Lady Borden was vulnerable in other ways, however, from persons with exaggerated notions of the family's wealth. For example, about twenty months after Sir Frederick's death, Lady Borden received a letter from Dr. Victor F. Connor, a Canning physician, holding her personally responsible for damages to his car and loss of income, caused by her chauffeur the previous Sunday morning. Three days before Dr. Connor wrote to Lady Borden, his Kentville lawyer, John J. Porter, had assured him he could extract considerable compensation from Lady Borden from her chauffeur's car accident.

According to Dr. Connor's carefully scripted 8 September letter to Lady Borden, he and a fifteen-year-old boy, Roland Spicer, were driving east along Main Street about 10 am on Sunday morning, well before the church traffic, when they were struck by Lady Borden's Cadillac emerging from her driveway, Walter C. Wallis, her chauffeur and gardener, allegedly having failed to sound his horn as was required by Nova Scotia law. Connor had taken his damaged car to Mr. Smith, a garage mechanic in Wolfville, who itemized his car's damages. According to Connor his car was a Ford, "new last May" and "in perfect running order," and he sought compensation for the car's repair, his loss of income, and car hire "essential to his profession" during its repairs.[6]

Lady Borden immediately consulted Leslie, the estate's administrator. The next day she replied to Connor by registered letter, politely regretting Connor's accident but declining to accept responsibility. The car, she explained, belonged to her deceased husband's estate, and although she had been granted its use, paid its provincial licence, and agreed to purchase it upon the settlement of the estate, the vehicle currently belonged to the estate. Moreover, the car had not been employed on estate business at the time of the accident. She had loaned the car to Walter C. Wallis to visit his cousin in White Rock in the Gaspereau Valley, who had been conscripted for overseas service, on the condition Wallis pay for the gasoline.[7]

Dr. Connor took two weeks to reply to Lady Borden's response, long enough to consult two "leading legal authorities in Halifax." Upon their advice, Connor suggested to Lady Borden a "friendly arrangement," to avoid the "unpleasantness" of court costs and proceedings.[8] Lady Borden and Leslie were outraged. They regarded Connor's suggestion as "a hold-up game" designed to bluff Lady Borden "into paying him a certain sum" and agreed to face him in court if he persisted. Lady Borden thanked Connor for his "kind suggestion" but insisted that she was "entirely free from any liability."[9] Meanwhile, Leslie submitted the matter to the estate's counsel, William P. Shaftner, J. Frank Outhit, and James L. Ilsley.[10]

Shaftner, who took the case, learned that Porter was on "the warpath for heavy damages," and had tempted the penurious, underemployed Connor with the prospect of a generous court award.[11] And, on 21 December 1918, Connor's lawyer filed a case with the Supreme Court of Nova Scotia against Leslie S. Macoun, the estate's agent for $3,000 damages, citing Wallis's "negligence in managing, driving and operating the estate's motor vehicle," resulting in great damage, large expenses, injuries, and loss of medical practice.[12] A trial was set for June 1919 in Kentville.

Leslie was furious. Already he felt overwhelmed, dealing with four other estate court cases, maintaining two offices, managing the estate's complexities, and was conscious of the rapidly approaching deadline for the estate settlement. All required more time than he had imagined: identifying, and persuading, witnesses; securing, assessing, and reviewing evidence and arguments with counsel. Each lawsuit had its irritants, of which Connor's claim was but a tedious example. Witnesses were elusive, indecisive, and ambiguous, and some required payment. Lady Borden`s maids, two of Leslie's more reliable witnesses, were in Ottawa as he was preparing the case and their evidence had to be taken there.[13] Then in January 1919 Leslie's own health broke. He contracted the Spanish flu, followed by "a severe nervous breakdown."[14]

Short-tempered, caustic, and irritable, Leslie vented his frustrations to his counsel, paying little deference to verbal courtesies. In Leslie's ad hominem assessment, Dr. Connor was a worthless physician of dubious professional ability, "a very inefficient person" who "might possibly be employed by someone in a veterinary capacity" if one "did not greatly value the animal." Otherwise, Connor was simply an underemployed, layabout physician who spent his time "loafing around the verandah of Waverley House," where he boarded, and who his colleague, Dr. James S. Miller, sent to patients he did not wish to see or to places on the mountain that he did not want to go. According to Leslie, Connor had been "run out of Hants County" and had "possibly inherited" his father's "addiction to lawsuits."[15]

More relevant was Leslie's attempt to establish the facts. According to Leslie's witnesses, on the fated Sunday morning Wallis had emerged from Borden Place's driveway onto Main Street, having first sounded the horn, and was partially on the sidewalk when Dr. Connor, travelling at a "high rate of speed" on the wrong side of the street to avoid a mud puddle and having failed to use his brakes "slammed into him," doing $50–$60 damage to the estate's car. These were Leslie's facts. Opposing counsel questioned the cars' location at the time of the collision, accused Wallis of sounding the horn after, not before emerging from the driveway, and demanded compensation for Connor's injuries, car damage, and loss of income.

Leslie was incensed by Connor's monstrous monetary claims: $500 for damages to his car, $1,000 for personal injuries, and $1,500 for loss of professional income at a rate of $20 a day. According to Leslie's information, Connor's car had cost only $650, and he had driven it for some time. In fact, the car was in such fragile condition that the Wolfville mechanic feared damaging it during its repair, and Connor subsequently sold the car in Wolfville for $250.[16] As for Connor`s personal injuries, he was seen only "a few minutes after" the accident helping pick up the glass, and later that afternoon he was spotted driving to Kingsport. Nor was the boy travelling with Connor hurt by the accident.[17] Moreover Leslie was convinced that Connor had never earned $20 a day in his life since his stock-in-trade was largely births and deaths. To Leslie this was a comic opera at best, and an irritating distraction from his executor's duties.

Dr. Connor was not Leslie's only administrative irritant. At times he felt he was surrounded by thieves who were "protected by the law," and who "flourish here like the green bay tree."[18] No sooner had Leslie settled the Connor affair than he complained to Lady Borden that Wallis had "absolutely wrecked" her Cadillac during his two years in her employ, "starved" and abused her favourite horse "Dolly," "stole" all the tools in Borden Place[19] and owed the estate $190.10 for a harness and old victoria they had asked him to sell. According to Leslie, Wallis was a man who they thought was honest and "an exception to the local rule" but who deserved "a good whipping."[20] Moreover, their estate's handyman, Lynk, was "frightfully lazy" and worked only under supervision (in Leslie's view it was a family failing), and only occasionally paid for the rent of his estate-owned house. Lynk's replacement, Charlie Dorman, was little better, not strong enough for the work, and had to be replaced by another man who was a "reformed" drinker.[21] Meanwhile 300 to 400 bushels of oats disappeared from the farm, the prime suspect a "prominent member of the Baptist church in Kingsport."[22] At times, even Lady Borden seemed an irritant.

Leslie's frustration was complicated by his overlapping duties as executor and administrator. The heirs-at-law's rights and responsibilities to suggest, direct, or veto the decisions of an administrator of an intestate property were ambiguous and easily confused with a legatee's material interests. As the surviving spouse and agreed occupant of Borden Place and 15 Blackburn Avenue, Lady Borden assumed a custodial responsibility for the estate's maintenance and administration. A vigilant, exacting custodian, she seemed to see Leslie as an estate factor, her paid employee, responsible and answerable for the estate's well-being, and subject to its owner's direction and consent. This was not a role that Leslie found reasonable or comfortable. But as a member of the family, and dependent on Lady Borden's good will, he tried to accommodate her requests, suggestions, and questions.

Meticulous and sensitive to Borden Place's appearance, Lady Borden worried Leslie about repairs, painting, and the maintenance of steps, veranda, windows, door trimmings, the sewing room floor, and the property's fences. She advised him on their colours and design and insisted upon her approval. She sought explanation for his removal and replacement of hedges, flowering shrubs, and pear trees, and worried about their "artistic" effect on the driveway and its perennial borders. She questioned his disposal and sale price of sleighs, carriages, and harnesses, and insisted upon the retention of her horse, Dolly. She instructed him to readdress or cancel journal subscriptions.[23] She fretted about a lost key found two years ago by one of her servants. She consulted him on the execution of her mother's will and was no less attentive to the productivity of the Borden Place farm, its apple orchards, potato and hay fields, and the estate's securities.[24] She insisted upon explanations for the sale of lands and made her consent conditional upon her approval.

Leslie tried at first to remain respectful, deferential, and friendly. He explained his decisions in detail and assured her that the rusted bird cage would be restored, and the barn floor would be replaced before hay-making season. He reported on the number of acres planted in potatoes and the estimated number of barrels of apples they might harvest and the prices they might fetch. He informed her of his efforts to sell various properties, including houses in Canning and Kingsport, and his difficulties collecting from the estate's numerous "swindling scoundrels."[25]

Initially Leslie's responses were full, frequent, and scathingly entertaining, his communications marked by familiarity and complicity. Soon they became punctilious, defensive, restrained, and abrupt. He complained of overwork and inadequate compensation, invoked his executor's responsibilities, reminded her of her "life interest" in Borden Place and her limited control over the disposal of the estate's assets. He was especially miffed by Lady Borden and Elizabeth's refusal to give him power of attorney or even their address during their travels, and her "absurd" worries over a key, lost years ago.[26] More ominous was Lady Borden's insinuation of his favouritism in distributing the estate's assets.

Chapter Eighteen

Executor

Leslie found estate administration more demanding and tedious than he had anticipated, and he came to resent his role as general factotum, subject to the beck and call of the heirs-at-law. Above all it distracted him from his principal task of compiling an inventory of Sir Frederick's assets and liabilities and determining their market value and obligations. Meanwhile he had to confront predatory creditors, reluctant and duplicitous debtors, some of them Sir Frederick's former partners, and a few of dubious integrity. Altogether, it was an exhaustive, fraught assignment, and was not completed until 1920.

When Lady Borden applied to the probate court in 1917 she cited Leslie's initial evaluation of Sir Frederick's estate, which he had estimated to be $300,000: $270,000 in movable and $30,000 immovable property.[1] By 1920, Leslie had revised his categories and estimates, reckoning that Sir Frederick's estate possessed $461,032 in assets and $347,683 in liabilities, leaving approximately $113,348 to be shared among its heirs.[2] Among the estate's liabilities were $1,346 of uncollectible promissory notes, $7,710 of uncollectible court decisions, and $150,000 in loans and liabilities to the Bank of Montreal, secured by shares and bonds in various enterprises, such as Nipissing Mines ($8,000) and the Lockport and Buffalo Railway ($6,581).[3] Leslie also discovered that Sir Frederick's stock in 47 of his 73 companies was worthless promotional stock in failed or failing enterprises. Nor was the market value of his investments obvious, since only 18 companies in his portfolio were listed on a stock exchange, eight on the New York Curb, and three on an unnamed "regular exchange."

Among other surprises bedeviling Leslie's bottom-line calculations were promissory notes, obligations attached to stock options and the shady antics of some of Sir Frederick's former partners. Perhaps none of Sir Frederick's shady partners surpassed Freeman I. Davison, the Nova Scotia-born Boston "thug" who worked the international border to his advantage, and with whom Sir Frederick had several risky dealings.[4] The antics of Davison and others required costly, lengthy litigation, complicated by the need to navigate cross-border jurisdictions, and whose uncertain outcomes delayed settlement and skewed Leslie's initial calculations.

Quite apart from demonstrating the material fragility of Sir Frederick's estate, Leslie's investigations documented Sir Frederick's informal business practices. Leslie discovered that Sir Frederick maintained no proper ledgers, cash books, or journals. He had borrowed and loaned money and pledged assets as collateral, often secured by verbal understandings.[5] Altogether, he had spun a complex web of financial obligations, grounded on political and personal relations, mutual trust, and benefit, arrangements more familiar to a rooted rural society than an impersonal world of financial capitalism, and particularly ill-advised for an elderly man, in declining health, in a world disordered by the Great War.

Leslie ought not to have been surprised by Sir Frederick's unruly affairs. He had warned Sir Frederick of the carelessness, irregularities, and petty larceny of many of his "overstaffed," "overpaid," and poorly supervised Supply and Cornwallis employees. Although a micromanager by nature,[6] Sir Frederick had become overextended, distracted, and overwhelmed by his bifurcated ambitions, balancing his business and political interests. Three large dossiers illustrate Sir Frederick's disordered affairs, and Leslie's challenges as executor.

The bedrock of Sir Frederick's entrepreneurial project had been his Supply Company, the corporate umbrella that sheltered his assets, secured many of his investments, and underwrote his family's material welfare, its history a tale of business and political complicity. A year before Fred joined Laurier's cabinet in 1896, he had incorporated his diverse businesses under the name of the F.W. Borden Company, with ambitious powers and a capitalization of $50,000. Two years later, he recapitalized the company at $250,000 and renamed it the R.W. Kinsman Company, after its manager, to avoid the appearance of political conflict of interest, though Borden remained the company's "sole owner" of its preferred stock, and "by far the largest owner" of its bonds.[7]

Well-positioned in Laurier's cabinet to win friends, secure investments, and expand markets for his company from his Halifax and Toronto political associates,[8] Borden pledged his company's substantial landholdings as security for the loans and mortgages essential to his company's activities. His political friends responded cautiously, unconvinced of his company's viability and wary of its inflated capitalization.

Borden had even less success micromanaging the R.W. Kinsman Company from Ottawa, and within two years his company escaped bankruptcy only by Boer War patronage, two timely insurance claims,[9] and the intervention of Ontario's premier, George Ross, and Senator George Cox, who persuaded the Temperance and General Life Insurance Company to invest in Borden's reorganized Supply Company.[10]

Undaunted by his company's near-death experience, in April 1901 Borden reorganized and renamed his company the Nova Scotia Produce and Supply Company and capitalized it at $500,000, its bonds marketed by the National Trust Company. In July 1901 he mortgaged (indentured) his previous company's property to the National Trust for $85,000, using the money to purchase the new company's bonds as insurance against his property's loss. Apart from Alfred Potter and Captain W.R. Potter, and Borden's fellow Canning merchants and neighbours, his new company attracted little new capital.[11] Even Borden's gift of $25,000 of the new company's inflated, preferred stock to Thomas White failed to persuade the wily National Trust's president of the reorganized company's long-range viability.

White was right, and within two years the Nova Scotia Produce and Supply Company was in trouble, and the recently knighted Sir Frederick Borden appealed again to his Toronto friends. Their conditional support obliged Borden to reduce the company's capitalization to a more realistic $200,000, remove Richard Kinsman, its general manager, and omit "Nova Scotia" from its name, to give the company wider appeal.[12] Sir Frederick accepted his political friends' conditions and reclaimed his property by a legal provision that Leslie would invoke in 1921. In May 1903 he and the National Trust petitioned the Supreme Court of Nova Scotia to foreclose and auction the old company's property, and since the law permitted the majority bondholder to bid for the property, Sir Frederick reclaimed his and Lady Borden's property with their bonds, assets estimated to be worth $150,000 at the time.[13]

Having reclaimed their property on 15 July 1903, Sir Frederick, "and Bessie Borden, his wife,"[14] again sold their title, property, privileges, and franchises in the Nova Scotia Produce and Supply Company to the "new" Produce and Supply Company for 1,210 shares valued at $100 a share and a $100,000 (6 per cent) first mortgage bond on the company's assets.[15] The Manufacturers Life Insurance Company increased its bond holding to $15,000 at 6 per cent, and Robert Boak,[16] Alfred Potter, and Captain W.R. Potter (Kinsman's replacement as general manager) transferred their investments to the new company, secured by the Borden's 5,177 acres of property.[17]

This time the restructuring worked, and the Supply Company remained profitable for more than a decade before the Great War, owing to its lucrative apple exports to England and its appreciating property values.[18] War, however, changed all this. The danger, cost, and scarcity of transatlantic wartime shipping (apples were not essential war materials), and the dearth and cost of farm labour, capital, and materials slashed Supply Company's profits, leaving it with expensive contracts with English suppliers, a crisis made more acute by the Halifax Explosion's devastation of the city's port facilities in December 1917.[19] By 1917 the Supply Company faced annual operating deficits of $20,000–$30,000, which it covered by selling and mortgaging properties.

Given the Supply Company's deficits, its land-based securities' declining value, and more competitive wartime investments (even the Supply Company was letting mortgages at 8 per cent) the National Trust and non-family bond holders urged foreclosure. Eight days after Sir Frederick's death Manufacturers Life sought redemption of its bonds, on threat of foreclosure. By 1921 National Trust estimated that the Supply Company's landholdings, valued at $150,000 in 1903, had fallen to $43,750.[20] By then, the Supply Company was an empty shell. Given the company's parlous situation Lady Borden considered selling the entire estate, retaining only what land the family needed for its use.[21]

Soon after the Great War, Leslie had tried but failed to sell the estate. He had advertised the company's land in Canadian and English journals such as *Land and Water, Country Life, The Army and Navy Gazette, The Field,* and *Canada,* directed toward a "class who might be interested and in a position to purchase one or more of the farms."[22] His advertisements elicited only one serious offer, from an Englishman, and even that fell through. Nova Scotia's land market was a casualty of its postwar depression, out-migration, loss of the English apple market, currency restrictions, steep interest rates, and sterling's devaluation (the pound dropped from $5 to $3).

Since the company was effectively bankrupt, Leslie replayed Sir Frederick's 1903 retrieval scenario. National Trust petitioned the Nova Scotia Supreme Court to foreclose and auction the Supply Company's real estate. J.L. Ilsley, the estate counsel, retrieved the land with the family's $95,000 bonds, and compensated National Trust with $3,000 in cash for twenty years of fees, services, and legal costs.[23] Upon Leslie's request, Ilsley delayed transferring the land "to the heirs-at-law," to shelter the transaction from inheritance tax, with the family signing warranty deeds for the property.[24] According to Leslie the property was worth $150,000,[25] his success proof of his executorial abilities.

Leslie's second major dossier as executor, the estate's Montreal Tram shares, was one of the family's most lucrative and complex assets, and another example of Sir Frederick's informal management style. In his search for capital Sir Frederick had extended his reach beyond Halifax and Toronto to his Montreal political friends. Like many of his contemporaries, Sir Frederick was mesmerized by public service investments in enterprises such as Montreal Tram, a commodity that traded unlisted on the Montreal Exchange. His investment in Montreal Tram grew out of his friendship with Edmund Arthur Robert, a Liberal partisan and vice-president of the Montreal [Canada] Light and Power Company, who worked in tandem with J.W. McConnell.

For years Sir Frederick had sought to exploit his extensive woodlands, infatuated by the rising price of newsprint and the future of hydroelectricity. In 1906 he incorporated the Gaspereau Power Company, and shopped about for capital and entrepreneurial skill to develop his waterfalls and woodlands. In February 1909 Robert expressed an interest in harnessing the Gaspereau River's power.[26] In anticipation of Robert's investment, Sir Frederick, and W. George Lambe, a Montreal businessman, borrowed $80,000 from the Albany Bank to purchase an additional 30,000 acres of Nova Scotia timberland.

Robert was a man of his time, a time of mergers and consolidations, spectacular profits, and imperial connections, represented by Max Aitken's buccaneering Montreal career. In October 1910 Robert became president of the Montreal Street Railway, evicted its management, merged it with his Canadian Light and Power Company, and incorporated a London holding company called Imperial Trust, which became the parent company of his amalgamated Montreal Tramway and Power Company.[27] Beguiled by Montreal Tram's impressive 1912 balance sheet of $2,932,689 net profits,[28] many investors expected even greater returns from Robert's plan to consolidate, monopolize, and manage Montreal's expanding residential and industrial market for hydro, gas, and transport facilities, their confidence buttressed by Robert's election to the Quebec Legislative Assembly (1912–19), and well placed to secure franchises, standard voltages, and protection from its competitor.

Robert's primary interest in the Gaspereau was not pulp and paper but the electrification of Halifax. To monopolize Halifax's tramway, gas, and electric power facilities, Robert needed Gaspereau's hydro and Sir Frederick's political influence. To procure both, he persuaded Sir Frederick to invest in Montreal Tram through a financial manoeuvre that netted Sir Frederick some $40,000. According to their agreement Sir Frederick was to purchase $100,000 of bonds in Robert's Canadian Light and Power for $20,000. In return Sir Frederick would receive

$100,000 worth of shares. The bonds and 600 shares were then sold back to the renamed Montreal Tram, leaving Sir Frederick with 400 shares (with a paper value of $40,000).[29]

A warm personal and political friendship cemented Sir Frederick's financial dealings with Robert. He and Lady Borden visited Edmund and Eliza Robert at their Beauharnois estate and Montreal residences, and occasionally vacationed with them. Friendship bred confidence, commitment, and dependence. And, in January 1913 Sir Frederick purchased an additional 1,300 shares in Montreal Tram on margin through the New York brokerage firm of Charles Head and Company (later taken over by the Montreal brokerage firm of O'Brien & Williams, a member of the Montreal Stock Exchange), secured by his 400 shares in Montreal Tram. In July 1916 Sir Frederick was so confident of Montreal Tram's future that he persuaded Leslie to invest in Montreal Tram, convinced its shares would increase from $50 to $75 once it received a municipal franchise.[30]

Predictably, Montreal's potentially lucrative transit market attracted a well-led, political rival, the Montreal Light, Heat and Power Company. In confronting its rival, Tram's fatal weakness was its "lack of electrical power for expansion" and its "deficiency of financial strength," a weakness exacerbated by Canada's trade recession (1913–15), European rearmament, and the Great War.[31] Despite Tram's difficulties, at the time of Sir Frederick's death, its future remained promising owing to the end of the trade depression, Tram's increased transit fares, and its prospect of a municipal franchise. Tram's subsequent failure to obtain its franchise stalled its momentum while it sought an interested buyer. Meanwhile the value of its shares fell. A month after Sir Frederick's death Tram's shares declined from $40 to $30. A year later, they traded for $23.50 on the Montreal Stock Exchange, still governed by wartime restrictions. When restrictions were lifted, its shares fell to $13.50. Meanwhile, the family's Montreal brokers demanded payment for the marginal shares Sir Frederick had purchased at the top of the market.

Leslie knew of Sir Frederick's marginal buying but he did not know its extent or terms until Sir Frederick's death. His brokers, O'Brien & Williams, lost no time in informing Leslie of Sir Frederick's $40,000 debt to their agency for his 1,300 marginal Tram shares. Upon Robert's intervention, Imperial Trust loaned Sir Frederick $6,000 to cover his initial payment, secured by his holdings in Nova Scotia Power. The second instalment ($4,000), however, came due on 1 February 1917 (before Leslie's official appointment as executor), followed by a third ($5,000) on 1 June 1917, and a fourth on 17 October 1917.[32] Hard-pressed to meet these and other obligations, Leslie negotiated a Bank of Montreal demand note in Lady Borden's name for $20,000 at 6 per cent, endorsed by all three heirs.[33]

While Lady Borden consented to the demand note to secure the family's marginal shares in Montreal Tram, she had no idea how Leslie had used the money. What seemed reasonable in the winter, spring, and summer of 1917 to protect an investment became a nightmare as Montreal Tram's shares deteriorated. As time passed disturbing rumours grew, and Leslie sought to reassure Lady Borden. But reality soon overtook Leslie's optimism, and in April 1919 Lady Borden asked Percy Borden, Sir Frederick's cousin, and prominent Ottawa businessman, to call a family council, with Percy as her representative, to decide what to do.

The meeting instructed Leslie to dispose of the estate's Tram shares and other questionable securities. In keeping with his instruction, Leslie persuaded Mark Workman, president of Dominion Coal and Steel and Sir Frederick's former business partner and recipient of militia clothing contracts, to accept $12,000 worth of Tram securities to cover the estate's debts. Leslie estimated that he had recovered at least $30,643 of the Tram's $40,000 investment in one way or another, and the rest remained on the estate's books and subsequently became profitable. Leslie's material interest in Montreal Tram and his failure to consult Lady Borden or "Mrs. Hewitt,"[34] however, bred suspicion and recrimination.

The third example of Sir Frederick's material legacy and complex business practices was what Leslie called the "Burgess mess," a maze of local projects, personal arrangements, and duplicity that took almost four years to clean up.[35] The "mess" described Sir Frederick's dealings with Arthur Stephen Burgess (1882–1920), the young, litigious son of Stephen Burgess, a prosperous Liberal Centreville farmer. Impressed by young Arthur's ambition, audacity, and imagination, Sir Frederick made Burgess a partner and managing director of his Cornwallis Trading Company Limited, a company that owned real estate and sold "Dry Goods, Clothing, Boots, Shoes, Flour, Feed; Hardware, Groceries Etc.," a business comparable to the F.W. Borden Company.[36]

Sir Frederick seemed to see Arthur Burgess as a dynamic young apprentice, whereas Burgess regarded Sir Frederick as a mentor, an insurance plan, and calling card, altogether a very open-ended relationship. Through inheritance, marriage, purchases, and mortgages Burgess acquired extensive property and other assets and liabilities. Impressed by Burgess's apparent success, Sir Frederick extended his business dealings with Burgess, seemingly blinded to the liabilities.

One of Sir Frederick and Burgess's joint projects was the Canada Food Company Limited, incorporated in 1913 and capitalized at

$100,000, with its bonds offering a return of 7 per cent,[37] a company that Leslie described as having had "a lurid existence of about three or four months,"[38] but generated years of conflict and litigation. The company's three partners were Burgess, Sir Frederick, and William H. Weatherby, a Halifax Hollis Street merchant with whom Sir Frederick had business and militia connections. The company's primary purpose was fruit farming tailored to the British market, and Burgess was its managing director.

Central to the Food Company's success was a 150-acre farm (including 12 acres of dyke land) purchased from Acadia College in Wolfville. Encouraged by the Nova Scotia Fruit Growers Association, Acadia College had founded a horticultural school in 1893. Two years later, its entrepreneurial president, Dr. Atwood Cohoon, established a farm to generate revenue and reduce Acadia's residential food costs. In 1911 Professor Ingram B. Oakes, MA, DCL, a former president of Acadia's affiliated Horton Academy and a member of the Acadia board's executive and investment committees, persuaded the college to sell some of its farm property. As president of the Kings County's Liberal Association and Sir Frederick's friend and sometime legal counsel, Oakes assured the board he knew a potential buyer.[39] Sir Frederick, Oakes reminded the board, was a proven entrepreneur, instrumental in establishing the Kentville Experimental Farm, and familiar with the transatlantic fruit trade.

On 23 December 1913 Acadia College mortgaged 150 acres of farmland to the newly incorporated Canada Food Company in return for a $15,000 promissory note at 8 per cent, signed "jointly and severally" by its partners, payable to Acadia on or before 1 March,1914.[40] Each partner agreed to pay $5,000 when the note came due, but only Sir Frederick and Burgess honoured their commitment, and Sir Frederick was obliged to secure the note's "temporary renewal" to address Weatherby's default. The Acadia board agreed to the note's extension on the condition that Sir Frederick pay the interest on Weatherby's defaulted portion of the note, and Weatherby remit his outstanding portion within sixty days, an agreement guaranteed jointly by Sir Frederick and Burgess. When Weatherby again defaulted, Sir Frederick covered the entire amount of Weatherby's outstanding note, and sought judgment against Weatherby in the courts on 18 August 1914,[41] confident that Burgess would recompense him for his portion of their joint endorsement of Weatherby's repudiated note.

Meanwhile, the Canada Food Company declared bankruptcy. Since each partner held 140 preferred shares and all possessed priority in the distribution of its assets, each had to await the court's disposition to reclaim his portion. Moreover, during its "lurid existence," the company had incurred other obligations and assets, including land in north-end Halifax for a warehouse it considered vital to its transatlantic project, now compromised by the Great War, a property subsequently expropriated by the Dominion government for $1,500.[42]

Leslie later claimed that he "never had any illusion" as to Burgess's lack of integrity and had warned Sir Frederick on several "occasions to cut loose from him" as he was a "thorough going scoundrel" who would not hesitate "to defraud us."[43] Leslie had reason to question Burgess's integrity. They had worked together in the Cornwallis Trading Company, Leslie as the company's board chairman and Burgess as its managing director. During that time Leslie had drawn Sir Frederick's attention to several irregularities, insisting they be brought into conformity with the law.[44] Only after Sir Frederick's death, however, did Leslie learn that Burgess owed the estate $17,000, in addition to repayment of a $1,000 short-term loan Sir Frederick had authorized a few weeks before his death, to enable Burgess to purchase feed for his animals.

Upon Sir Frederick's death Leslie had an opportunity to follow his own advice and "wind up Burgess,"[45] but he chose a gentler approach. Immediately after Sir Frederick's funeral, Leslie met Burgess to discuss his "heavy indebtedness" to the estate. During that meeting Burgess promised to reduce his obligation to the estate as soon as he secured additional investment capital. Leslie consulted "Dr. Hewitt" and they agreed to give Burgess every opportunity to meet his obligations. Their agreement included discounting Lady Borden's future purchases from Burgess's retail store against Burgess's debts to the estate, and a one-year repayment schedule for his recent $1,000 short-term loan. The family also offered to buy Burgess's apple warehouse near Canning for the price ($2,750) Burgess had asked of William Henry Chase (1851–1933), their Wolfville rival and the province's "apple king," a sale subsequently blocked by Burgess's inability to give Chase clear title owing to a $10,000 claim against Burgess's property resulting from the Canada Food bankruptcy litigation.[46]

In July 1917 Burgess accepted Leslie's generous agreement, with its one-year terminal date.[47] Burgess then mortgaged his store, warehouse, and surrounding property to the Borden heirs-at-law, made sporadic payments on his short-term debt, and debited Lady Borden's purchases from his retail store and the grain the Supply Company had taken from Burgess's fields. Burgess, however, found no new capital investment to relaunch his retail business. It was wartime, and capital was scarce and expensive for small mixed-farming operations. And Burgess soon faltered in his payments. Confronted by reluctant suppliers, credit costs, and impatient creditors, Burgess reduced his stock-in-trade, and sold and mortgaged property, further eroding his security and enhancing his creditors' anxieties.

Leslie's relations with Burgess deteriorated rapidly upon the expiry of their one-year agreement in 1918. Burgess's payments became sporadic. Leslie's attempts to enforce or renew the agreement became acrimonious, magnified by Burgess's repudiation of his portion of the Weatherby note and related misunderstandings. At first, Burgess pretended he had lost the Weatherby note, then claimed Sir Frederick had released him from its commitment, though just before his death Sir Frederick had instructed his solicitor to take legal action against Burgess, and the case was before the courts.[48] Burgess then billed the Supply Company for unspecified services.[49] Leslie countered by suing Burgess for non-payment of debts. Leslie attempted to garnishee Burgess's income from the sale of their north-end Halifax warehouse,[50] and refused to pay Burgess for twenty-one bushels of oats and barley the company had taken from Burgess's farm and had stored in the Supply Company's barns. Burgess then sued the Supply Company for non-payment.[51] In another case Burgess sued the Borden estate for Lady Borden's $151.56 purchases at his store from December 1919 to February 1920, and so it went.[52]

Patience was not Leslie's long suit, nor was it wise in dealing with Burgess, especially as his credit eroded and the number, and anxieties, of his creditors mounted. To stanch the estate's potential loses, Leslie foreclosed on Burgess's store, warehouse, and adjacent land, and assigned the mortgage to George A. Holt for $9,000 at 6 per cent.[53] Convinced that Burgess "would be safer in jail than anywhere else" and would stop at nothing,[54] Leslie feared Burgess might even torch his store to collect the insurance.

On 29 February 1920 flames consumed Burgess's shop, furniture, stock-in-trade, and records. Burgess had provided for this eventuality by insuring his assets with three different companies. He had insured the building with Phoenix Insurance of Hartford for $5,000, the building's refrigeration and furniture with Provident, Washington for $2,500, and his stock-in-trade with George A. Holt, a local agent of Thompson Adams & Company for $1,700.[55] At the time of the fire Burgess owed $20,000 in unsecured debts, including $5,200 to the Borden estate. He had borrowed smaller sums from other persons but had "forgotten" the amounts. And now there were no records. According to Leslie "99% of the population believed" that Burgess had converted "his property into cash through the medium of a fire."[56]

When a $500 reward for information leading to an arsonist's conviction failed to produce a claimant, Burgess collected his insurance money.[57] But even that failed to cover Burgess's debts, and on 16 June 1920 he declared bankruptcy and swore he owned no personal or farm property or assets. In his statement of bankruptcy, Burgess claimed he had spent $32,102 to clear his various debts and possessed only $15.96 cash to meet several unsettled lawsuits should they not go well.[58] To cover the claims of Burgess's other debtors, on 16 August 1920 the county sheriff auctioned Burgess's Centreville farm and stock. The sale included cows, horses, implements, machinery, seed, growing crops, and first and second mortgages. The insurance agent, George A. Holt, purchased most of Burgess's real estate, then offered to sell it to the Borden estate – as if the estate needed more real estate. Leslie considered the offer so outrageous given Burgess's outstanding debts to the Borden estate that he took legal action against Burgess, claiming the auction had been designed to defraud the Borden estate, Burgess's principal creditor.[59]

Burgess was not entirely destitute. Just before he declared bankruptcy, he transferred his house, mortgages,[60] life insurance, car, and real and personal property to his wife, Prudence Annie Burgess, leaving no money in his own accounts, claiming she had brought these assets into their 1908 marriage or obtained them through joint efforts. Even so, Burgess still faced several outstanding lawsuits against the Supply Company, the Borden estate, and Weatherby from which he might expect to receive income.

Soon Burgess's health became an issue. In August 1920, as Burgess's several trials approached, he sought medical advice in Montreal for an undisclosed illness. His lawyer, Barry Roscoe (the late W.E. Roscoe's son), then received a letter from Burgess's doctor certifying his patient's "precarious health," a letter that in Leslie's sarcastic words claimed Burgess suffered from "every known disease with the exception of croup and housemaid's knee"[61] and was unable to stand trial.[62] The case was adjourned until October. Meanwhile, Roscoe advised Burgess to drop his suits against the Borden estate and the Supply Company,[63] and pay the estate $5,000 and court costs for all outstanding claims.[64]

In return, Leslie agreed to withdraw his various suits against Burgess, though in doing so he felt he was "compounding a felony."[65] Already Leslie had received $5,000 from the sheriff's auction and $2,500 from Burgess's portion of Weatherby's dishonoured note and $275 from the grain stored in Supply Company barns. Leslie lost his case against Burgess for non-payment of his initial debts since the court found that Burgess never entirely ceased payment. Leslie realized he had nothing to gain from a bankrupt, penniless invalid except court costs and more grief.[66] Meanwhile, he assured Lady Borden that he had "increased the insurance on some of our buildings … in the event of any gratification of [Burgess's] unsatisfied proclivities we will be fully protected."[67] With that the Burgess mess ended.[68] And according to Leslie, Burgess "celebrated his freedom from litigation by one continuous drunk, which in his physical condition was hardly advisable."[69]

Leslie's liquidation of the Supply Company, reduction of the estate's Montreal Tram loses, and resolution of the "Burgess mess" were only three items on his charged executor's agenda. Leslie, however, considered them a vindication of his stewardship. He had also reclaimed some $70,000 through other litigation. Lady Borden and Elizabeth saw things differently, however, and Leslie had now to defend his integrity and management in the probate court, against two of the estate's three legatees.

Chapter Nineteen

Deaths and Delays

Personality and contingencies framed, fuelled, and prolonged the family conflict. In Leslie's view Lady Borden and "Mrs. Hewitt" failed to appreciate their estate's complexities, his administrative service, or his successes. Leslie was also blind to his own failures: his lack of knowledge, his inexperience, overconfidence, and paternalism, and his petulance and imperiousness Nor had Leslie or the family anticipated the effect of war, disease, and death on the settlement of their family's estate.

The province's Probate and Trustee Acts defined an executor's and an administrator's powers and responsibilities. The Probate Act charged an executor with identifying an estate's assets and liabilities, paying its debts, and distributing its assets to the heirs-at-law, whereas the Trustee Act instructed an estate administrator to care for and protect an estate's assets. Only on 21 August 1920, after Leslie had occupied both positions for three years, and faced legal challenge, did he seek professional clarification on his responsibilities and constraints.[1] Moreover, his Ottawa Agency added another complexity to his charge.

Leslie appeared blind or indifferent to the potential conflicts and ambiguities of his personal and professional activities. How and when, for example, was he to liquidate the estate's property and/or develop and keep it in saleable order, especially since the farms and some of its outbuildings "were in a deplorable condition"? To what account and in what proportion was he to charge the administrative costs of his sole secretary, working concurrently on the execution and administration of the estate and his Ottawa Agency? Was the maintenance of Borden Place and 15 Blackburn to be charged to the executor's or administrator's account? And from what account was he to draw funds to cover taxes, repairs, and mortgages on the family's Blomidon, Habitant, and Bell Hill farms, the latter currently "owned" and operated by Leslie for his family's benefit?

Equally vexed were the estate's multiple portfolio decisions pending its settlement: when and what to buy, sell, or reclaim before the courts to meet the estate's debts and protect or enhance the heirs' assets. Which financial transactions were subject to the executor's commission and at what rate? Subsequently the probate court examined 205 transactions on that question alone and referred 92 others to the judge.[2] Had Leslie initially sought legal clarification on his various roles he may have saved time, minimized the legatees' suspicions, and avoided court proceedings.

Leslie was a novice, an outsider by accent and manner, convinced he was surrounded by local "thieves." As he explained to Lady Borden, he did not aspire to "popularity with everyone," and in that he succeeded.[3] He had never executed an estate before, and though he had worked closely with Sir Frederick, managed the family's Supply Company, the Cornwallis Trading Company, and related ventures, he had little idea of the extent and complexities of Sir Frederick's investment portfolio and the estate's disorder. A man of action, Leslie acted first and consulted later. No less toxic were Leslie's feelings of being overworked, underpaid, and unappreciated, grievances enhanced by the deteriorating plight of his Ottawa Agency.

Gender, too, may have inflated personal tensions, though the issue was never mooted in those terms. Leslie preferred to work with men. He treated Lady Borden with respect and deference, assuming a protective role in keeping with contemporary class and gender codes. He informed and advised her, and dutifully honoured her instructions and supressed his growing impatience. Lady Borden understood the era's gendered class codes and initially accepted Leslie's manner, having then "complete" confidence in his business acumen, though she was accustomed to fuller discussion, especially on her investments and on the Supply Company, whose existence and development owed much to her inheritance. Very soon she came to resent Leslie's condescending, paternalistic "not to worry" response to her questioning.[4]

Elizabeth was even less inclined to defer to Leslie's judgment or submit to his dismissive manner. Leslie had consulted and informed Gordon on estate business, confident that Gordon spoke to and for Elizabeth. As Leslie later explained to the probate court, Dr. Hewitt was a director of the Supply Company charged with "looking after her interests."[5] Gordon was cooperative and agreeable, and Elizabeth appeared to trust him implicitly, but he was more interested in the farm's ecological and esthetic qualities than its business and financial transactions. As for Maude, Leslie claimed he spoke and wrote on her behalf and "consulted her over all major decisions."[6]

The estate's delayed settlement constrained the family's plans and activities, tested their patience, and created anxiety and apprehension. Very shortly, Lady Borden and Elizabeth began to suspect Leslie's motives, question his judgment, and seek alternative advice. Initially their irritations entailed small matters and delays in communications. But soon, substantial issues fractured their confidence in Leslie's judgment. Only eight days after Sir Frederick's death, Leslie was obliged to respond to Manufacturers Life's threat to foreclose on a $15,000 bond secured by the Supply Company's property.[7] Given the cost of war-inflated credit, Leslie recommended that Lady Borden sell her prized International Nickel shares to meet the creditor's demand. While Lady Borden accepted Leslie's advice, she remained unhappy with the decision.[8]

Leslie's second request, however, raised Lady Borden's suspicions. During their bedroom conference Leslie had alerted her to his need of a draft on her Bank of Montreal account to cover succession duties, "pressing liabilities," and general expenses. But it was not until O'Brien and Williams requested payment on Sir Frederick's marginal shares in Montreal Tram that Lady Borden realized that Leslie required as much as $20,000. Lady Borden signed the undated authorization on the assumption that $15,000 was to secure the estate's marginal shares. She had no idea how Leslie spent the rest of the draft, or of his arrangements with Robert. Only later did she learn that Leslie had written himself a $8,542.47 cheque on the account to redeem Maude's debt to him, fully intending to subtract the amount from Maude's inheritance.[9]

Lady Borden's solicitation of alternative investment advice signalled her growing concerns. Two of the persons she consulted were Percy Borden,[10] Sir Frederick's cousin and a businessman, and E.A. Robert, in whose Montreal Tram Sir Frederick's estate was heavily invested. In Robert's letter of condolence on Sir Frederick's death, he had "generously" offered to assist Lady Borden with investment counsel. And, both Lady Borden and Leslie had consulted Robert, oblivious to Robert's material interest in the estate's holdings.

For more than two years after Sir Frederick's decease, war, illness, and death limited Lady Borden's vigilance. The Great War had scarcely ended when Lady Borden learned of the death of Gordon's brother, a recently returned war veteran. In February 1919 Sir Wilfrid's sudden death evoked a flood of memories: the privilege of having "known Sir Wilfrid so well and to know that he loved and valued Fred so highly."[11] Except for brief visits to Ottawa, Atlantic City, and Baltimore, Lady Borden felt trapped in Canning, responsible for her mother's care. Wherever she went or for however long, her mother's failing health remained a worry. Mrs. Clarke's death on 27 June 1919 lifted that burden and eased the family's financial anxieties. Mrs. Clarke left an estate worth $22,471 after taxes (about $458,950 in current purchasing power), and a will that Lady Borden executed in the summer of 1919.[12]

Mrs. Clarke bequeathed $5,000 (about $68,500 in current purchasing power) to each of her surviving children, Gus and Lady Borden. A 1917 codicil to Mrs. Clarke's 1903 will provided an additional $2,000 to Lady Borden for her mother's lengthy care. Mrs. Clarke's granddaughters, Elizabeth and Maude, each received $2,500. Her great granddaughter, Rosamond, received $100 and Mrs. Clarke's jewellery.[13] Mrs. Clarke remembered Gus's wife Harriet with $2,000 and each of their two daughters with $1,000. Small sums were bequeathed to friends and relatives, and $500 to her church. The estate's residue was divided between Gus and Lady Borden.

By mid-August 1919 Lady Borden, having executed her mother's will, was free at last to visit Gus and Hattie in Wetmore, Colorado, except that the Spanish flu made travel unadvisable. This tragic Great War postscript claimed some 50,000 Canadian lives, only 11,000 fewer than were lost in the Great War. A grim time of death, fear, quarantine, and economic and social disruption, the flu epidemic closed schools, churches, public assemblies, and funeral parlours. Even the 1919 Stanley Cup play-off had been suspended after Game 5. Death rapidly followed infection. Persons between the ages of fifteen and thirty-five were especially vulnerable and survivors faced a lengthy recovery.

While the epidemic had abated by late 1919, public authorities advised against travel. But after her mother's death Lady Borden felt that she could not endure a winter alone at Borden Place and decided to take her chances. On 1 November 1919 she left Canning for her Ottawa residence, to be closer to Elizabeth and Gordon, Maude, Leslie, and Rosamond, and her Ottawa friends and relatives. She planned to remain there until the end of February 1920, then travel to Atlantic City during the colder weeks of winter and from there undertake her long-promised visit to Gus and Hattie in Colorado. But no sooner had she settled in Ottawa than she and Elizabeth contracted the flu and were confined to bed. Both recovered, though each remained under doctor's care for months.

Elizabeth was still ill when she confronted a greater tragedy. On 23 February 1920 Gordon returned home ill after attending the Canadian Commission on Conservation's meetings in Montreal. It was Gordon's thirty-fifth birthday. Elizabeth helped Gordon to bed, and they exchanged flowers from their separate beds. Gordon "never rose again."[14] He had contracted flu, developed pleural pneumonia, and died six days later. Elizabeth was devastated. Her idyllic decade had ended. She was now alone, and like her mother would have to remake her life. In her grief Elizabeth turned to travel, religion, and memorialization, determined to keep faith with Gordon's mission.

Gordon's funeral service was simple and befitting the man, the principal mourners' fragile health, and the tragic times: a small assembly of Elizabeth's family and Gordon's close friends and colleagues. Elizabeth asked the respected Quebec entomologist Georges Maheux (1889–1977)[15] to give the eulogy. Maheux spoke of Gordon's life as a scholar, administrator, conservationist, and gentleman. He described Gordon's personal qualities, his "warmth and affection," and his "great admiration for the French Language," concluding his remarks with "Nous déposons sur sa tombe un souvenir ému pour l'homme et un hommage d'admiration pour le savant."[16] Elizabeth was deeply touched by Maheux's remarks.

Convalescence gave Elizabeth time to mourn, review her happy decade, consider ways to honour Gordon's life and work, and plan for her own future. One thing was clear: she would publish Gordon's recently completed 336-page manuscript on the conservation of the wildlife of Canada. She would ask Georges Maheux's permission to print his moving eulogy, and she would write a short biographical appreciation of Gordon's life. Elizabeth could write, and in her affectionate, six-page memorial she recalled Gordon as a generous, gentle, joyous person who loved children, told them stories, and drew them pictures of nature and wildlife;[17] a veritable Hiawatha "'who learned of every bird its language."

By August 1921 Elizabeth had negotiated a contract with Charles Scribner's Sons and a generous $5,000 publication subsidy from the Canadian government. It helped to have a prime minister in court! She also resolved to continue Gordon's educational work, to teach Canadians the value of their natural environment and its need of conservation. In 1921, soon after the publication of Gordon's *The Conservation of the Wildlife of Canada*, the National Council of Women (NCW) asked Elizabeth to become national convenor of its conservation committee, an invitation she welcomed[18] and subsequently presented a report entitled "Conservation of Natural Resources" to the NCW's 1923 annual meetings.[19]

But where was Elizabeth to live? Ottawa seemed an obvious choice: a city of 107,000 people, where she would remain among friends and family and participate in familiar activities, and still enjoy summers in Canning. Her retention of 17 Blackburn made less sense. At first, she rented her house during the summer, but its size and expense, her uncertain finances, and her mother's residence in Canning argued against its retention. She may have pondered other options but all we know is that by June 1923 Elizabeth was living at 222 Buena Vista Road in Rockcliffe.[20]

Gordon's death lent a new urgency to the settlement of her father's estate. Gordon had left no inheritance. As Lady Borden later explained to the probate court, Gordon was a "scientific man" who had "practically nothing." Apart from 17 Blackburn, her grandmother's legacy, and Leslie's sporadic distribution of her father's assets,[21] Elizabeth's income was limited. More ominous was her growing impatience with Leslie's "shilly-shallying" and her eroding confidence in his competence and integrity, sentiments fuelled by her financial exigencies.

Elizabeth, the romantic, was also realistic, forthright, and practical. She understood the financial limits of her father's estate and the need to maximize her income. She was forty-six, relatively healthy,[22] energetic, ambitious, and inspired by the successful careers of contemporary women.[23] She could write and was interested in management and commerce. Her father had often asked her to supervise estate projects and she enjoyed that. She knew something of gardening, marketing, and the supervision of labour. After all, Gordon was an administrator and economic entomologist. How all this might fit together would have to await her recovery and the settlement of her father's estate.

Lady Borden faced Gordon's death with grief and stoicism. She liked Gordon immensely and shared his interest in literature, art, music, and gardening. She respected his scholarship and was proud of his professional success and public service. She appreciated his positive energy and his and Elizabeth's complicity. Their relationship had given Elizabeth's life direction and purpose. But what Elizabeth and her mother needed immediately was rest and distance. They decided to go to Atlantic City and Baltimore as soon as their doctor consented, then visit Gus and Hattie in Colorado. Since Lady Borden's medical authorization came first, she left for Atlantic City and Baltimore, to await Elizabeth's convalescence. When Elizabeth joined her in Baltimore the first week of May, Elizabeth was too weak to visit Gus that year.[24]

The next year Elizabeth and Lady Borden travelled in opposite directions, Elizabeth to England and Lady Borden to Colorado. Scarcely a year after Gordon's death, his mother became ill and Elizabeth rushed to Gawsworth, Cheshire, to assist her mother-in-law, confident that this was what Gordon would have wanted. Elizabeth believed in family and service and continued to brood over Gordon's death. It was also an opportunity to learn more of Gordon's early life and the society that had shaped "her darling." Once she was no longer needed at Gawsworth she visited Switzerland and Italy, to rest, think, and plan. Lady

Borden appreciated Elizabeth's sense of service but had no desire to accompany her. Nor was she as attached to Gordon's family and its stalwart middle-class culture. Indeed she and Sir Frederick had just too "much to do" to visit Gordon's parents during their 1912 sojourn in England and the continent.[25]

Lady Borden decided, therefore, to visit Gus and Hattie alone during Elizabeth's European absence. In early June 1921, after her usual late winter / early spring vacation in Atlantic City and Baltimore, Lady Borden left by train for Wetmore, Colorado. As she approached her destination on 3 June 1921, about thirty miles short of Pueblo town, an overturned freight train blocked the route. A flash rainstorm had flooded the Arkansas River, bursting the town's reservoirs, destroying houses, and sweeping rail cars into the rushing waters, leaving a reported 150 people dead and 3,000 residents homeless.

For the next several days, Lady Borden remained stranded and lonely, patiently awaiting the rail's restoration, with time to ponder and plan. On 13 June she recorded her sense of isolation in her brief travel diary. "Yesterday," she wrote, "was the anniversary of my wedding day. How long such days are without Fred – how long it is all the time – there is always the empty [?] in my heart – empty but full of memories." A more immediate, inescapable concern was Sir Frederick's unsettled estate, so vital to her family's material welfare, and the festering quarrel over its settlement. All were subjects she planned to discuss with Gus once she reached Wetmore. He and Fred had been classmates, friends, and business partners, and she could trust Gus.[26]

While Lady Borden waited, she reviewed the facts and pondered her options. Thirty-five months had passed since Leslie's promised deadline for settlement of the estate. She was aware of the estate's complexities, the postwar market, and the recession. She realized that Leslie and the legatees had been ill and preoccupied with personal problems. Nor were the legatees agreed on what to do with the Supply Company and its property, the family's principal asset, their equivocations both emotional and material. All worried about the company's long-range viability, its capacity to generate a reasonable family income, and the wisdom of maintaining all or some of the land. Yet delay simply bred suspicions and impatience, a situation exacerbated by Gordon's death.[27]

Lady Borden and Elizabeth suspected for some time that Leslie was delaying settlement to compensate for his losses from his anaemic Ottawa Agency. They began to question his personal and administrative expenses, his "unreasonable" travel and hotel bills, and his secretarial, supply, and rental costs, specifically how he billed his Canning office for the estate's business done by his Ottawa Agency and how he compensated his Canning office for agency work done in Canning. They also challenged his evaluations and disposal of personal property, and his "partial" distribution of assets.[28] Nor had they confidence in his investment decisions. Percy Borden had advised them to have nothing to do with "speculative stock."[29] Yet Leslie had retained speculative stock in Montreal Tram, stock in which he had a material interest. As the family's effective head, Lady Borden pressed Leslie quarterly for a firm settlement date.[30] After Leslie's July 1918 deadline for winding up the estate, she became more dissatisfied with Leslie's evasive responses. Finally, she insisted that Leslie meet the legatees in Montreal, with Percy Borden (1873–1922) as her representative, to resolve several issues.

Percy, Leslie, Gordon, and Elizabeth (though not Maude) met in Montreal on 2 and 9 June 1919. Their civil, informative meetings had covered a range of subjects and elicited questions, opinions, and counsel. Leslie had circulated a full list of the estate's securities and sought advice on each. They had agreed to sell their holdings in Montreal Tram, Noiseless Typewriter, and Maritime Trust, for a reasonable price and as soon as possible.[31] Since no one had voiced dissatisfaction with his administration, Leslie had left the meeting falsely reassured, but aggrieved that no one had broached the issue of his remuneration, though he had spoken to Lady Borden on several occasions.[32]

The Montreal meeting had been civil, but its message was clear: Leslie's management was being monitored. That became obvious the next month as Lady Borden executed her mother's will. Anxious to put her affairs in order, she had pressed Leslie to wind up the estate.[33] Leslie had responded that the family needed to decide on the disposal of their land. The flu epidemic had prevented travel and no formal meeting had taken place that year. During the summer Leslie had discussed the farm's business with Gordon.[34] But routine farm business was not the same as winding up the estate. Besides, Gordon was now dead, and Leslie had to deal directly with Elizabeth. Sensitive to Elizabeth's financial insecurity following Gordon's death, Lady Borden was becoming tired of Leslie's patronizing reassurances, his failure to explain the Supply Company's relationship to the farms.[35] Nor was she convinced that nothing could be done until they disposed of the farms. Finally, they agreed to meet in Nova Scotia that summer, but that meeting became impossible, owing to her and Elizabeth's health.

Later, in recounting his deteriorating relations with Lady Borden and Elizabeth to the probate court, Leslie blamed Lady Borden and Elizabeth for the meeting's failure, neglecting to mention their medical reasons. According to Leslie all had been ready in 1920, except for a decision on the property, and that was to be decided when they were all in Nova Scotia, but the "two ladies had gone to the southern states" and the meeting had been rescheduled for the following summer. That meeting had also failed becauseLady Borden had spent "a month in Atlantic City and some months in Baltimore" and then had gone to Colorado, and "Mrs. Hewitt had absconded" to Europe, and upon her return went directly to Ottawa and instituted legal proceedings "against me."[36]

What Leslie did not tell the court was that Elizabeth had difficulties of her own. Upon her return to Canada from Europe in 1921 she had learned of her mother-in-law's death. She had also learned that her house had not been rented out and the financial loss required her immediate attention in Ottawa.[37] But as Leslie explained later, this made little difference since Elizabeth had already decided that their only option was legal action.

Regardless of what Gus may have advised Lady Borden during her 1921 visit, family relations had become toxic. When Leslie returned to Nova Scotia in the spring of 1920 for the Connor trial, and before he and Maude opened their Bell Hill home, he had booked and billed the estate for a room and bath at Kentville's Cornwallis Inn.[38] Over the next several months Leslie's communications with Lady Borden became curt and sarcastic. Elizabeth became "Mrs. Hewitt," and letters to Lady Borden were signed "yours sincerely" rather than "yours affectionately," as formerly. Both women recognized the change in tone, though the letters' contents were sufficient notice. In January 1923 Leslie billed Lady Borden and Elizabeth $1,500 for "provisions and servants wages" during their seven-month residence at Borden Place, insisting each heir was responsible for a third of the expenditures, a bill that Lady Borden and Elizabeth returned, refusing "to allow their share to be charged against them."[39] By then Elizabeth and Lady Borden communicated with Leslie only through their lawyers.

In the late summer of 1921 Lady Borden and Elizabeth sought legal counsel from the prominent Halifax law firm of A.K. McLean, C.J. Burchell, and J.L. Ralston,[40] a move Leslie considered an "act of war." Tensions spread to their counsel. A.G. Parker, Lady Borden and Elizabeth's counsel, threatened to collect his outstanding legal fees personally from J.L. Ilsley, the estate's lawyer.[41] Finally, in the fall of 1922 Lady Borden and Elizabeth instructed their counsel to charge Leslie with mismanagement, obliging him to submit his accounts to the probate court on 10 January 1923. The court scheduled a hearing in Kentville for 3 May 1923.

Chapter Twenty

Lady in Court

The Borden case pitted two able Liberal law firms against one another. James Lorimer Ilsley (1894–1967), Leslie's counsel, was born in Somerset, Kings County, and educated at Acadia and Dalhousie Universities. Admitted to the bar in 1916, he had served as the estate's principal counsel since Sir Frederick's death.[1] Lady Borden and Elizabeth's counsel, Alexander Kenneth Maclean, was a senior partner in the Halifax law firm of Maclean, Burchell and Ralston, and was an old family friend and political comrade of Sir Frederick. He was also a member of Parliament and since the House's sittings conflicted with the trial's date, Maclean delegated litigation to an ambitious young colleague, Archibald G. Parker. The presiding judge, Barclay Webster, had been Sir Frederick's political opponent in the 1900 election.

The court sat for ten days, beginning on 3 May. In preparation for the trial, legal counsel formulated questions and answers, secured witnesses, and sought professional advice. Leslie and Lady Borden were the court's principal witnesses. Accused of mismanagement, conflict of interest, and defrauding the estate, Leslie attended every court sitting, whereas Lady Borden appeared only on 10 May 1923. The plaintiff called two witnesses, Colonel Byron Weston, founder and general manager of Eastern Trust, and Major J.F. Stairs, general manager of Royal Trust. The court focused on Leslie's management of the estate's assets, his executor's commission, and his expenses.

Prepared, forthright, and understandably defensive, Leslie was often testy and sarcastic. Whereas Lady Borden remained dignified, gracious, generous, and slightly vulnerable. She was nonetheless focused, conscious of the power of language, insisting upon her precise words during her exchanges with Ilsley. Counsel treated her with a measure of deference and indulgence, permitting her to construct her own narrative. In recounting the history, circumstances, and challenges of his executor's mandate, Leslie explained his deteriorating relations with Lady Borden and "Mrs. Hewitt," especially after Gordon's death. It soon became apparent that his executor's charges, administrator's compensation, estate administration, and their relationship to his Ottawa Agency had envenomed the dispute and had become so acrimonious and personal that they were prepared to fight publicly.

Although the probate court had no jurisdiction over Leslie's compensation for estate management, Leslie complained that his responsibilities as executor had devastated his Ottawa Agency. During the first four years of his mandate his agency's net annual income had dwindled from $8,431.13 to $791.84. The devasting first two years had prevented him from benefiting from the 1917–18 "banner years" for "his type of business." So reduced had his Ottawa business become by 1921 that he had relinquished his Ottawa office and secretary and retained only one client.[2] The heirs, he complained, were well aware of his "serious loss and had promised to take action to relieve it" but had "failed to do anything."[3] In fact, he received only $2,500 for his estate management, whereas he believed his services were worth twice that amount, a deficiency that justified his charging the maximum executor's commission permitted by law.

Four months before the hearing, Ilsley had consulted James McGregor Stewart (1889–1955), one of Canada's leading corporate lawyers, on executor's commissions. Stewart explained that probate court "invariably" permitted 5 per cent, though executors normally charged 3 tp 4 per cent.[4] But whatever the amount, executor fees were levied only on cash receipts for their actual amount, and on personal property bequeathed or assigned by the executor. Moreover, neither custom nor authority sanctioned a commission on real estate bequeathed to heirs unless the will specified or constituted the legatee a *pro tanto* trustee, in which case the remuneration was governed by the Trustee Act.[5] Stewart's definition encouraged Parker to contest every transaction, every administrative or personal expenditure, a course he pursued with forensic zeal.[6]

Three days after Leslie's opening remarks, Lady Borden told her story, a tale of broken promises, failure to consult, questionable investment decisions, conflicts of interests, and deception. She began by describing her solicitous care of Sir Frederick during his last two years of failing health, her shock at his sudden death, her resultant confusion, "nervous break-down," and confinement to bed, compounded by the inexplicable absence of a will. She confessed that she had little recollection of her bedroom conference with Leslie, except his promise to consult the heirs-at-law on all but routine issues and to wind up the estate within a year to eighteen months, and his explicit assurance that his duties would not interfere with his Ottawa Agency, nor would he expect to receive the "the full commission" permitted by law.[7]

Lady Borden assured the court that she had tried to be "kind and fair."[8] She commended Leslie's industry and conscientious effort to administer the estate and confessed her initial "absolute confidence" in his financial acumen and familiarity with the estate, adding that she herself had no knowledge of stocks, nor had Leslie ever sat down and explained the estate's assets and liabilities. Her only information had been Elizabeth's list of the estate's securities. She realized that she was "being shielded" by the family, owing to her condition. Yet on two subsequent occasions she had asked Leslie for money from the Supply Company, in which she held equity, to be told that she had to await the estate's settlement. She soon detected Leslie's lack of knowledge, objectivity, and judgment, his failure to consult or inform, her assessment confirmed by trusted family friends and financial experts.

In Parker's cross-examination of Leslie, he elaborated and reinforced Lady Borden's case. He dismissed Leslie's claim of inadequate compensation, and the ruinous effect of his estate responsibilities on his Ottawa Agency, reminding the court that Leslie had sought the responsibilities, agreed to his remuneration, and assured Lady Borden that his additional responsibilities would have no material effect on his Ottawa Agency. Not only was Leslie's plight self-inflicted but he had deliberately prolonged the estate's settlement to compensate for his Ottawa Agency's shortfalls.[9] From the start, Parker continued, Leslie had lacked the required qualifications, knowledge, and experience, as demonstrated by his dubious accounting practices.

Pressed by Parker's interrogation, Leslie admitted that he had no formal training as an accountant, bookkeeper, or auditor. Although he had been honorary secretary-treasurer for the Ottawa Country Club, he neither administered nor audited the club's accounts. His only other accounting experience had been assisting Lady Laura Borden, his next-door neighbour, with her local IODE branch's accounts. He admitted that he had not understood the difference between his executor's and his estate-administrator's responsibilities until 1923, and had no knowledge of the Trustee Act. Consequently, he had deposited farm profits from the sale, mortgage, and rent of land in the same account, and pledged land and securities for bank loans,[10] thereby confusing his dual responsibilities. He admitted that his accounting practices had been erratic. He had assigned as much as 75 per cent of the Supply Company's secretarial and overhead expenses to his executor's account and overcharged that account by as much as $11,250 over six years. He had also failed to compensate his Canning executor's account for 20 per cent of his agency's work done from his Canning office.[11]

Leslie explained his errors as oversights and misunderstandings, casualties of his overlapping responsibilities, the estate's chaotic accounts, and Sir Frederick's informal managerial style. Since Sir Frederick had kept no ledgers, cash books, and journals Leslie had to create them retrospectively. That took time and patience, to decipher Sir Frederick's multiple formal and informal arrangements, some written, others verbal, and many open to disagreement, and to deal with the wiles of some of Sir Frederick's unsavoury former partners. Sir Frederick, Leslie continued, had granted clients credit, signed promissory notes, let goods out on consignment, sub-let fields, and endorsed loans, often with several partners, and many with ambiguous deadlines and no indication of individual liability. Leslie reminded the court of the complexities of liquidating an estate in six provinces and several American states with differing laws on property, taxation, and litigation. All this explained his accounting oversights and delays in settling the estate. Leslie reminded the court, too, of his successes, of retrieving the family's mortgaged property from the National Trust and the recovery of $70,000 in other assets through litigation.[12] Contrary to Lady Borden's complaint that he had not consulted her sufficiently, he had believed she had understood, since she had asked no questions.[13]

Pleased with Leslie's admissions to careless and questionable accounting practices, Parker opened a second front, focusing on Leslie's "actionable" use of the $20,000 emergency loan that he had "extracted" from Lady Borden when she was suffering from "25% mental impairment," and unable to make rational decisions.[14] Leslie admitted that he had not informed Lady Borden of the purpose and subsequent use of the loan. But she had not asked. The bank note, however, had been signed by all the heirs, and they understood that it was a reserve.[15] Nor did Leslie see any reason to inform "Mrs. Hewitt" of his discussions with Lady Borden.

Parker, sensing Leslie's discomfort, pressed him to explain precisely how he had spent the $20,000 loan. Parker undoubtedly knew the answer. Under pressure Leslie conceded that he had used only $5,000 to meet O'Brien and Williams's second demand, and $1,000 for Supply Company business. The rest he had used for unspecified purposes. But what were these purposes? Parker insisted. At this point Leslie admitted he had written himself a cheque for $8,542.47 to cover money Maude owed him and which he intended to subtract from her inheritance, an admission that spoke poorly for his judgment and aroused graver suspicions.[16]

Parker's third line of attack centred on Leslie's "mismanagement" of the estate's Montreal Tram shares, which Parker insisted was an example of Leslie's fiduciary floundering, negligence, and conflicts of interest. According to Parker, Leslie had disregarded warnings against speculative stock and continued to throw good money after bad to protect his personal investments. To lend authority to this accusation, Parker called his two prominent Halifax witnesses, Colonel Byron Weston, and Major J.F Stairs, who predictably testified that the executor's duty was not to speculate with an estate's assets but to distribute them promptly.[17]

Well prepared for Parker's accusation, Leslie cited five reasons for his Montreal Tram decision: his confidence in the stock's growth once the company received a municipal franchise; the heirs' implied consent to the stock's retention; Lady Borden's recommendation that he seek Robert's advice, upon which he acted; the confidence in the security expressed by Mark Workman, "a large financial man" who had accepted $12,000 in Tram shares in payment for a debt; and his own confidence and judgment, demonstrated by his personal purchase and retention of 300 Tram shares that he "treated exactly as the others," and on which he had lost $15,000.[18] He admitted that his judgment may have been faulty, but it did not constitute incompetence, corruption, or conflict of interest. He reminded the court of his retrieval of $30,000 of the family's $140,000 investment in Montreal Tram. Parker had no interest in what Leslie had retrieved, only the $9,357 of family's assets he had lost, and why he had not acted sooner.

Slowly Leslie made his case, wading through a mass of information on his administration. His command of details enabled him to guide the conversation, put his gloss on events, and impress the court with the magnitude and complexity of his mandate. In telling his story he insisted on Sir Frederick's chaotic management, the difficulty of liquidating the estate, especially after the Montreal Stock Exchange restricted trading in the early months of 1918, a restriction that lasted until June 1919. He cited examples of his handling of other troubled items in Sir Frederick's portfolio. He explained how Toronto Power, one of Sir Henry Pellatt's projects, whose bonds were once depressed, had since recovered and yielded a reasonable postwar return of 6 per cent. And he reminded the court that the Buffalo, Lockport, Rochester Electric Railway Company's unlisted bonds had defaulted a year before Sir Frederick's death, and the the company had been placed in receivership and reorganized, and though its future remained uncertain its preferred bond holders continued to yield 6 per cent. He explained how Robert had reneged on his promise to redeem "at any time" Sir

The black box: The box containing Borden family papers.
Photo by Pamela Miller.

The family pillar, Bessie's mother, Elizabeth Tupper Clarke (Edwards, St. Stephen, N.B.). Courtesy the Julia Green MacKay Collection.

Bessie's enterprising father, John Hopson Clarke. Courtesy the Julia Green MacKay Collection.

A political partnership: Julia (Clarke) Borden, and Dr. Frederick William Borden, M.P. (Notman/Topley, Ottawa). Courtesy the Julia Green MacKay Collection.

Bessie's well-dressed children: Harold, "the protective brother," standing; Elizabeth, "the vigilant older sister," seated; and Maude, seated and "in her own world." Courtesy the Julia Green MacKay Collection.

Mount Allison, 1896: Harold, "the friendly giant," seated, his college friends, George R. Johnson, and H.A. Allison, standing behind. Courtesy the Julia Green MacKay Collection.

A student of art: Watercolour by Bessie (Clarke).
Courtesy the Julia Green MacKay Collection.

Lady Borden's 1902 court presentation. Courtesy the Julia Green MacKay Collection.

Their stage: Lady and Sir Frederick's newly renovated and re-named Borden Place, Canning, Nova Scotia (A.L. Hardy, Kentville, Nova Scotia). Courtesy the Julia Green MacKay Collection.

A town monument: The inauguration of the Harold Borden Monument (1903) in Canning, Nova Scotia: a military detachment surrounding the monument, the family's ladies discernible in their white dresses, seated front row centre on the Union Jack–draped reviewing stand, Sir Frederick seated to their left. Courtesy the Julia Green MacKay Collection.

Escaping Lady Borden's vigilance: Maude seated side saddle on "Chumby," and Leslie on "Paddy." Courtesy the Julia Green MacKay Collection.

Badge of achievement: Sir Frederick's coat of arms.
Courtesy Julia Leslie Green MacKay and Kenneth MacKay.

Capturing London: Lady Borden in London (Charles, Mayfair, London, c. 1906).
Courtesy the Julia Green MacKay Collection.

Elizabeth, an Anglophile, royalist accomplice (H.B. Henderson, 1903).
Courtesy the Julia Green MacKay Collection.

A family coronation: Elizabeth (Borden) Hewitt, c. 1911.
Courtesy the Julia Green MacKay Collection.

Elizabeth's "modest" wedding party: The wedding party photographed outside Borden Place. Standing left to right: Maude, Gordon and Rosamond, Elizabeth, and Leslie, with Lady Borden and Sir Frederick seated. Courtesy the Julia Green MacKay Collection.

Elizabeth's "darling": Charles Gordon Hewitt.
Courtesy the Julia Green MacKay Collection.

A family of readers: seated left to right, Maude holding Rosamond, and Mrs. Clarke reading a book, with Lady Borden standing between Maude and Mrs. Clarke. Courtesy the Julia Green MacKay Collection.

A family project: Rosamond, c. 1912.
Courtesy the Julia Green MacKay Collection.

Elizabeth's Ottawa home, c. 1920. The woman in white by the window may be Lady Borden. Courtesy the Julia Green MacKay Collection.

A dear neighbour: Sir Wilfrid Laurier, with Lady Borden and possibly Elizabeth, c. 1918. Courtesy the Julia Green MacKay Collection.

Blood is thicker than politics: Leslie and Sir Robert Borden, standing left to right, behind a garden bench. Lady Laura Borden, Maude, and Lady Bessie occupy the bench, left to right, with Rosamond seated on the lawn slightly to the right of Lady Bessie Borden, c. 1935. Courtesy the Julia Green MacKay Collection.

Salon de Tuileries: Rosamond, left, in Émile-Antoine Bourdelle's studio working on her "Femme Assise" for the 1928 Salon des Tuileries. To her right is an unidentified fellow student. Courtesy the Julia Green MacKay Collection.

Refurbishing her wardrobe. Rosamond in Brussels, 1936.
Courtesy the Julia Green MacKay Collection.

A site of hospitality: Rosamond's Stockholm residence, 1948–52.
Courtesy the Julia Green MacKay Collection.

Public service: A poor, unidentified Swedish newspaper clipping of Rosamond and Edmund welcoming the Scottish 1921 Nobel Prize physicist, Sir Andrew Noble, to Stockholm. Courtesy the Julia Green MacKay Collection.

Lady Borden's mantel of memories: Items from right to left: a photo of Gus; a watercolour (probably by Lady Borden); photos of Rosamond, and Sir Frederick. Courtesy the Julia Green MacKay Collection.

Frederick's 1,450 common shares in Halifax Tram at $40 a share, leaving the estate to absorb the loss in a falling market. Leslie summarized his defence by restating the magnitude of his task and the parlous condition of Sir Frederick's estate,[19] and urged the court to remember the messy Burgess saga and the estate's dealings with the "Boston Thug," all necessitating lengthy litigation to recover a net sum of $70,000.

Much of the court's time was spent examining Leslie's entitlement to an executor's commission, a sensitive exercise that challenged Leslie's administrative ability, integrity, and claim to having been underpaid. Fortunately, five months before the hearing, opposing counsel did a forensic audit, aided by an accountant that resolved many issues and saved court time. Even so, 92 of the 205 unresolved controversies were referred to the judge for decision.

After ten days of hearings, Webster submitted his decision to the probate court, though the court only released its decree on 9 June, more than three weeks later.[20] Webster acknowledged Leslie's lack of training and experience, his errors and overconfidence. He did not believe, however, that Leslie's faults were caused by negligence, mismanagement, or deception. Webster found it equally unfair to second-guess Leslie's investment decisions, fault his failure to consult the heirs on every decision, or hold him to his unrealistic settlement deadline. Nor did Webster link the estate's delayed settlement to Leslie's floundering Ottawa Agency or question his handling of the Montreal Tram dossier. Webster even suggested that some of the estate's assets had benefited by their delayed liquidation.[21] Webster found Leslie's 5 per cent executor's fee unreasonable, however, and reduced it to 3.5 per cent, except for the complex Montreal Tram transaction, where he permitted the full 5 per cent.

Lady Borden and Elizabeth were shocked by Webster's decision, their disappointment fanned by Parker's wounded pride. "I never heard a man talk so unreasonably," Ilsley informed Leslie upon meeting Parker in Halifax. After costs, only $8,381 remained of the estate's undistributed liquid assets on "the date of settlement."[22] What infuriated Parker, Lady Borden, and Elizabeth most was Webster's granting of "nearly all" of Leslie's personal expenses and the executor's full commission on the Montreal Tram shares.[23] Stinging from the court's stiff fees for judge, counsel, secretary, and shorthand reporter, Lady Borden and Elizabeth considered Webster's decision on the Montreal Tram commission a gross insult. Had not Leslie assured Lady Borden that "he did not expect the full executor's commission"?

Nine days after the court's decision Lady Borden and Elizabeth petitioned the Nova Scotia Supreme Court for permission to appeal a portion of Webster's judgment. Their petition contended that "the learned judge of Probate" had erred in finding the estate's value to have been "merely $32,313.78,"[24] and that his failure "to find the Administrator liable for losses in closing out the marginal account with O'Brian & Williams" allowed Leslie to pocket $7,000 in executor's commissions, having disposed of the Montreal Tram shares before the final settlement.[25]

Lady Borden and Elizabeth's appeal surprised neither Ilsley nor Leslie. The next move was Leslie's. Should he cross-appeal and face the litigants in court or negotiate a settlement? Leslie was headstrong and impulsive and hated to lose. His first instinct was to cross-appeal, to gamble, even if it meant bankruptcy. To cover that eventuality, he considered transferring Gables, his principal asset, to Maude.

While Ilsley agreed that a cross-appeal was an option, he considered further litigation to be sheer folly. In his view, the heirs' petition was little more than a "weapon to compel" Leslie to reduce his claims for remuneration on the Tram transaction. "If I were in your place," Ilsley counselled, "I would make the best settlement I could with the heirs ... [since] you may not be sacrificing very much in coming either part or all the way to Parker's terms."[26] It simply entailed keeping "what is in your hands now and calling everything square."[27]

Above all, Ilsley warned Leslie against transferring Gables "to your wife at this time," since it "could be set aside as fraudulent and void as against creditors in the event of the heirs obtaining judgment," more particularly in view of "a few [unspecified] undesirable features which you and I fully discussed." Better to give Maude security on Gables for the large sum Leslie owed her or sell all his Ottawa property, as money was "easily disposed of."[28] Moreover, Leslie ought to act only after advice from someone familiar with Ontario bankruptcy legislation.

Leslie's physical absence and limited material resources determined his decision. He was at "Woodburn," his late father's home in Malone Park, Belfast, when he learned of Webster's 'favourable' decision. His father had died on 2 April 1923, and he had left for Ireland after the trial to be with his family and oversee the settlement of his father's estate. There he remained until the last week of August, dealing with the trial's aftermath and his disappointing inheritance. Parker understood his client's risks as well and was prepared to await Leslie's return the end of August.[29]

Delay did little to resolve Leslie's economic plight. His father's estate had netted approximately $410,000, after stiff postwar British inheritance taxes ($60,000). Half of the estate went to Leslie's stepmother, Mary, who was much younger than her late husband. Each of his father's five grandchildren inherited $2,500, and his church and charities received bequests. The remainder was divided among Leslie and his seven siblings, each obtaining $35,000, but frozen in the United Kingdom by postwar currency export restrictions, which applied even to the capital's estimated $1,500 annual income.[30]

Since Leslie`s administrative and executor's duties had ceased, his only Canadian income came from his few securities and his struggling Ottawa Agency.[31] In 1919 his agency had declared a net loss, and though it recovered slightly in the following years it could not support his family.[32] To limit his expenses Leslie had reduced his agency's "office chambers" at 40 Elgin to one room, and replaced Miss Helen Brakin, his faithful secretary, with a stenographer who worked one hour a day. And, when these expenses became untenable, he worked from home.

Parker's terms were firm. Leslie must accept what he had received for his services prior to Webster's judgment and nothing more. Although Leslie remained recalcitrant even after he returned from Ireland, he had few options. He already owed Maude "a large sum of money."[33] Faced by these restraints, he capitulated finally to his finances' bitter logic. With his submission the family's legal battle ended, an armistice at best, and Leslie recast himself as a full-time gentleman farmer.[34]

Chapter Twenty-One

Maude

The trial sorely tested family civility and solidarity. Spectators and speculators had watched the family's public quarrel with amusement, curiosity and avarice. Naysayers had predicted the nascent dynasty's demise. Scavengers waited to pick up pieces of what Webster described as quite a large estate. The family, however, proved more resilient than the rapacious and the prophets of gloom had imagined, though family amity returned only with time. No family member faced a more difficult situation than Maude, during and after her family's painful six-year quarrel, trapped between her husband and her mother and sister.

Maude was a survivor, understanding and pragmatic, and a conciliator, anxious to contain rather than enflame conflict.[1] To hasten the estate's settlement and reduce its administrative costs, she had taught herself stenography and typing. She had loaned Leslie money to supplement his declining Ottawa Agency's income. She had even loaned the estate money to cover immediate administrative costs.[2] More remarkable, she had retained amicable relations with her mother and sister during the dispute and trial, though she had not escaped difficult decisions. While she permitted Leslie to represent her during family discussions, when the conflict went to trial, she refused to retain separate counsel or contest her mother and sister's claims, a stand that undoubtedly strained marital relations.

Everyone wanted to protect Rosamond from the trial's fallout. An only child surrounded by a closely-knit extended family, Rosamond was the object of their anxieties, and aspirations. Her slight limp remained a family concern. No medical remedy corrected the disability. One leg remained about two inches shorter than the other. Special shoes and alterations to skirts and dresses helped to disguise the discrepancy. Rosamond also had a slight curvature of the spine, for which doctors advised swimming and special exercises throughout her life.[3] Yet, none of her disabilities prevented her from hiking, dancing, skiing, riding, and acting. Attractive, lively, and engaging, Rosamond enlivened her home and Borden Place with her gardens, pets, theatrical performances, and conversation, "talking to every dog she met," or pretending she was "Robolund," an old lady who walked with a stick.[4]

Lady Borden was devoted to her granddaughter. When Rosamond was not in residence, Lady Borden said goodnight to Rosamond's photograph on her bedside table. She monitored her granddaughter's social and intellectual development, and encouraged her interest in music, literature, and art. "Aunta," as Rosamond called Lizzie, was equally enamoured of her niece. Rosamond's affection for her "Granny" and her "Aunta" was mutual; nor did it diminish her devotion to her father. She enjoyed her father's generosity, attention, and verbal jousting. They corresponded when they were apart; he addressed her as "Dear Dickie" or my "little peach."[5] The question, then, was how best to shield her from the trial's fallout.

Education seemed an appropriate and timely answer. Rosamond would be sixteen on 3 July 1923. She had had only "a very sketchy" formal education,"[6] schooled largely by tutors and a governess. Everyone agreed that it was time to extend her education, a formation appropriate to her class, interests, and aptitudes. At fifteen Rosamond had no fixed vocational plans. During her May 1921 tonsil surgery in Montreal, surrounded by flowers, gifts, "wonderful food," and "nice nurses," Rosamond thought she "would just love to be a nurse or doctor."[7] She was also interested in sculpture, fashioning three-dimensional forms, and had an eye for character, at once incisive and humorous, much like her father and mother. Paris was a familiar Canadian destination for art studies.[8] Its rapid postwar recovery made it an attractive, fashionable, inexpensive location. Two or more years in Paris promised to provide distance from residual family tensions. Study in Europe was also a class act, vocational and social, a twentieth-century version of the grand tour. All depended upon Maude finding the right school and housing, at the right price.

The date of Maude, Leslie, and Rosamond's transatlantic passage depended on the trial. As soon as the trial ended, Maude and Leslie packed and prepared Gables for rental, boxing hundreds of books to make room for tenants. On 1 June 1923, an "over-tired" Maude, a tense Leslie, and an excited Rosamond boarded the CPR steamer *Montnairn* for Liverpool, where Leslie left them for Belfast, while Maude and Rosamond proceeded to Antwerp, before heading by train to Paris.[9]

Although postwar Paris was inexpensive, Maude's finances were precarious. She calculated that it cost her and Rosamond $4,500 a year to live in Paris[10] (school tuition, room and board alone cost $1,600 per annum), a budget equivalent to the family's total annual income.[11] Gables' annual rental income ($2,500–$3,000) could cover part of that cost. The rest would have to come from Maude's fluctuating securities, occasional land sales, and profits from their 120-acre Bell Hill Farm. Income from Leslie's inheritance could purchase only British goods. Fortunately, that included transatlantic travel.[12]

Maude could manage money. She could maximize resources, match purchases to income, and secure value for money, while maintaining the requisites of class and standing. She could cook, clean, and sew. Although she lived frugally in Paris, often *en pension*, once she found a flat, she employed a cook and a cleaning woman or man. A seamstress or tailor fashioned and refashioned their wardrobes, and when resources were restrained Maude mended or wore "underclothes that were very much worn."[13] Maude had a penchant for bargains, including her and Rosamond's dental and ocular care, available in Brussels for a third the cost in Paris.[14]

Upon their arrival in Paris, Maude's most pressing priority was finding shelter, a sufficiently large, clean, heated, affordable flat in a convenient, reputable location. The task took longer than she anticipated, and entailed reading advertisements, consulting friends and agencies, and vetting "dozens" of flats, sometimes three a day. Everyone seemed to want to live in Paris.[15] But Maude was prepared to wait for the right flat at the right price. Meanwhile she and Rosamond lived a nomadic existence *en pension*, first at the Hôtel Pas de Calais, on rue des Saints-Pères, then at the modest Hôtel d'Alsace, on rue des Beaux-Arts (where Rosamond was delighted to learn that Oscar Wilde had spent his final days) until she found a pension on 21, rue Washington, a quiet location close to the Champs-Élysées, with a courtyard and garden, double room with wardrobes, fresh, bright dining and drawing rooms, and pleasant landlords. The food was another matter, but Maude endured the food "for a couple of weeks,"[16] in fact for five months until she found a flat in a four-storey stone building on 2, rue Meissonier.

Maude's rue Meissonier lodging was a bright, clean, furnished flat with tapestries on the wall and an open fireplace, owned by people who had "delightful manners" and had been "very much before the war" but still employed "immaculate servants," including an Australian au pair.[17] Madame Bidal, was a pleasant, accommodating landlady who served meals on request. Initially Maude and Rosamond were her only paying guests.[18] The flat cost more than their previous pension

(52 francs daily rather than 35), but the difference, Maude reasoned, was simply the cost of good French lessons, since Madame Bidal's children spoke only French.

Moreover, Madame Bidal's rental conditions permitted Maude and Rosamond to suspend rental payment and store their luggage while they travelled during school vacations, an arrangement that lasted until the end of Rosamond's term in boarding school. Equally convenient was the flat's location off the avenue de Villiers, close to the Wagram station, within reach of Rosamond's school and only a five-minute walk from Maude's close friend, Elsie Cotton. Proximity to Elsie had been a requisite of Maude's search. Both locations were near Parc Monceau, the elegant public park with banks of spring and summer flowers, a subject of Claude Monet's paintings.

While Rosamond's education was Maude's primary objective, Paris enabled Maude to reorder her own life. Her formal education had been more limited than her siblings' or parents' education and she had travelled less than they. Paris was an opportunity to redress these deficiencies. And by 1923 Paris had regained its eminence as the artistic, literary, cultural, and fashion centre of the world: "les années folles," with their infectious, creative, social, and political vitality, became a magnet for students, tourists, and temporary residents from Canada and elsewhere. There Maude might perfect her French, enjoy theatre, concerts, museums, gardens, and historic sites. From Paris she could tour France, Belgium, Switzerland, Italy, and England. For Maude and Rosamond, it was a postwar world focused less on Britain, and within Maude's constricted budget.

Paris allowed Maude to rethink her marriage as well, severely tested by six years of family tensions. While the Black Box contained no evidence of a matrimonial break, for over five years Maude and Leslie lived separate lives, except for Leslie's annual apple-marketing visits to England and Ireland, and his brief Parisian side trips to visit Rosamond. As marital relations improved Leslie extended his visits in France and included Maude. In their family correspondence Maude and Rosamond reported but did not elaborate on Leslie's stay in France, the brevity understandable given Lady Borden's and Elizabeth's feelings toward the man who had so "upset things."[19]

Maude was curious, and needed people and social activity. Even before she had settled Rosamond in school, she and Rosamond explored Paris, looked up friends, and joined associations. Together they visited churches, museums, markets, parks, and gardens, their tourist guidebook in hand. One morning they rose at 4 am to reach Les Halles at 5 am to watch the arrival of wagons loaded with flowers and produce.[20]

They attended concerts, theatre, and ballet and went on picnics and excursions. High mass at Notre-Dame was more an aesthetic than devotional exercise. Like her father, Maude enjoyed the cathedral's music and especially its grand organ. Once Rosamond's school began Maude enrolled in French conversation classes. Yet for all her activity, Maude was often lonely, but determined "to get used to it," drawing on her family's social capital.[21]

Shortly after they arrived in Paris, Maude and Rosamond registered at the Canadian Commission. Its long-serving (1911–28) commissioner general, Dr. Philippe Roy (1868–1948), a medical doctor, Liberal senator (1906–11), and former colleague of Sir Frederick's, recognized Maude's political antecedents, and added her and Rosamond to his guest list.[22] A conscientious host, Roy was assisted by his assiduous wife, Helen Young, who introduced everyone to everyone, often several times.[23] Thanks to Dr. Roy, Maude and Rosamond attended the commission's reception for Canada's all-male 1924 Olympic team, "clad in white … with a large red maple leaf design on their back … the best-looking lot of men" in the Olympics.[24]

Unapologetic royalists, Maude and Rosamond appreciated Dr. Roy's invitation to the British embassy's Olympic reception for the Prince of Wales, noting how much older the prince appeared than during his 1919 Canadian tour. Invitations to embassy receptions enabled Maude to renew acquaintances with the 4th Duchess of Sutherland (1867–1950), whom she had met in Canada.[25] Conscious of Maude and Rosamond's royalist sentiments, Roy invited them to the Prince of Wales's unveiling of a Great War memorial to British soldiers in Notre-Dame Cathedral, the enamel tablet displaying the coats of arms of Canada, Australia, New Zealand, and Newfoundland,[26] and to the prince's opening of the Maison des étudiants canadiens in 1926.[27] Dr. Roy also invited Maude and Rosamond to receptions for Sir Robert and Henry Borden and for Senator Henri-Severin Beland (1869–1935), Sir Frederick's former colleague. Maude registered at the Cercle de l'Union interallié, as well, a prestigious social club located at 10, av. Gabriel, founded in 1917 to facilitate inter-allied understanding, a project to which Roy was deeply committed. Overseas Parisian visitors enjoyed the Cercle interallié's excellent table, active lecture programs, and accommodations.

Postwar visits from family and affluent friends helped bridge the distance between Paris and home. During Lady Borden and Elizabeth's 1924 and 1928 Parisian visits they dined with Maude and Rosamond in "good and bad cafes and whenever possible." Maude was introduced to dressmakers and shops where they spent time and money. Maude joined them on tours to the Parc Monceau, the Bois de Boulogne, the

Russian Church, Sainte-Chapelle, and Notre-Dame. Other family members came to Paris on short or extended visits.[28] Many brought presents and all had news from home. Maude and Rosamond guided them to historic sites, restaurants, cafes, and shops, and entertained them, chatting and playing bridge.[29]

Travel was also a class ritual and Paris was a popular destination, and according to Maude, "lots of [other] Canadians" passed through Paris during these years, people who could afford to travel or live abroad. Many were on their way to or from destinations in France, Italy, Spain, and Switzerland.[30] Some were temporary Parisian residents, students, or custodians of relatives at finishing schools, language programs, or art studios. Others were friends, such as Ethel Fleming, the daughter-in-law of Sir Sanford Fleming; Mrs. Charles Cambie, the wife of the manager of the Bank of Commerce in Ottawa; Lucy Crowdy, the daughter of James Crowdy (1876–1934), the Governor General's secretary;[31] Winnifred McConnell and Bunty Peck, all welcome links to home.[32]

Among Paris's more permanent Canadian residents none proved more helpful than the family of the late William Henry Cotton, Sir Frederick's militia colleague.[33] Mrs. Jessie (Penner) Cotton was living more "comfortably and cheaper" in Paris than in Ottawa, with her daughters Dorothy and Elsie. Dorothy, a decorated Great War nursing sister, had served with the No. 3 Canadian General Hospital (McGill) and had seen action in Russia during the chaotic days of the revolution and was currently employed in France by the Rockefeller Foundation's Commission for the Prevention and Cure of Tuberculosis.

Dorothy's sister, Elsie, became Maude's closest Parisian companion, residing only five minutes from Maude's Meissonier flat.[34] Both Maude and Elsie were custodians, Maude for Rosamond and Elsie for her niece, Norah Rosamond, whose father had been killed in World War I. Sunday mornings Maude and Rosamond accompanied the Cottons to the embassy's Church of England chapel and dined with them afterwards.[35] Most days Maude and Elsie enjoyed long walks and talks in the Parc Monceau or the Bois de Boulogne, stopping at a cafe or returning to the Cottons for tea. Other days they visited museums, shopped, or just window-shopped.[36] Maude joined the Cottons and their friends for the Prix du drag, a steeplechase, where "everyone wears best clothes."[37] Not surprisingly Maude and Rosamond had Christmas dinner with the Cottons. Whatever the need, Elsie was a valued confidant who accompanied Maude through bouts of loneliness, and on one occasion loaned her money. When the Cottons left Paris, even for a short time, Maude missed them terribly.[38]

The Cottons introduced Maude to their circle of Canadian, British, and French friends and colleagues working for international agencies, such as Dr. Leon Bernard, one of the founders of the League of Nations Health Organization, and Dame Rachel Eleanor Crowdy (1884–1964),[39] a decorated British Great War nursing sister who headed the League of Nation's Department of Opium Traffic (1919–31), the only woman to head a League administrative unit. Occasionally the five women, Elsie, Dorothy, Rachael, Maude, and Rosamond, spent a summer evening dining at an open-air Montmartre café, enjoying the lights and sights of the city and watching the artists, celebrities, and "other wildlife."[40]

Deeply committed to community service, Dorothy recruited Maude to her social causes. One entailed the emigration of a young, former sanatorium patient named Bell to a fruit farm in the Okanagan. Bell's doctors had prescribed "outdoor work" following his release from a sanatorium, but the only work he could find was selling furniture. Bell's father had died "a few weeks ago," and his only living relative, his grandmother, was unable to support him. At Dorothy's behest, Major Hugh Neil Fraser (1885–1970), a Great War veteran like herself, and the son of a wealthy Liberal Ottawa lumber baron, known to Dr. Roy, the Cottons, and the Bordens, offered Bell employment on his Okanagan farm if Bell could fund his passage to British Columbia. Dorothy, Dr. Roy, and Maude solicited their friends and acquaintances. Maude secured contributions from her mother and Ethel Fleming, and the committee soon reached its objective, thanks to an anonymous donor.[41]

During Maude's long residence in Paris, her mother and sister became her distant lifeline. They corresponded regularly, exchanged Christmas and birthdays gifts, and visited twice. Lady Borden and Elizabeth's gifts consisted of sizable cheques, and Maude and Rosamond reciprocated with thoughtful Parisian purchases, fashion books, and catalogues. Lady Borden rarely waited for an occasion to send Maude or Rosamond a generous cheque, simply relying on "a feeling" that Maude or Rosamond needed something with the approach of winter, vacation, or a new school term. Maude worried lest her mother went "without things" to fund her, but that was unlikely.[42] Lady Borden and Elizabeth asked Maude to buy them prized Paris items, elastic corsets, hats, scarves, sunglasses, silk, lace, napkins, knives, and shades.[43]

No sign of tension marked their family correspondence. Nor was their correspondence confined to personal or domestic subjects. An obvious shared interest was Parisian visitors, especially if they were relatives, friends, and notables. And Sir Robert Borden was all three, as well as Maude's Ottawa neighbour. In April 1927 "Rob" and his nephew, Henry (1901–89), visited Paris on their return from their Italian tour and language course, and Maude invited them to dinner. Sir Robert had a penchant for ancient and modern languages, and had endeavoured to master French during the 1919 Paris Peace Conference, carefully recording his diary in French. In recounting Rob's visit to her mother, Maude reported that that Rob looked much older than she remembered but was still "remarkably acute and interested in everything" and "not as ponderous as he used to be." What Maude found more "remarkable" was his mastery of French, which he had continued to perfect after his retirement. In Maude's opinion, his French was now very "correct and quite fluent and not at all a bad accent." His nephew, a Rhodes Scholar, seemed a "nice boy as well, good manners and not bad looking."[44] Maude always had an eye for good-looking men.

Lady Borden and Elizabeth wrote Maude about health, home life, weather, farms, relatives, and public affairs. Maude reciprocated with news of her and Rosamond`s personal and domestic life, their health, travel, social activities, and, above all, Parisian fashion. "Skirts are very short, very little below the knees," Maude alerted her fashion-conscious mother in 1925, and "at least twelve inches from the ground, except if one were going to the United States, in which case they might be lower."[45] Nor were Maude`s reports on the novelty and ingenuity of Parisian advertising lost on a merchant's daughter. During this heyday of department stores, Paris's Louvre, Bon Marché, Galeries Lafayette, and Printemps window displays piqued Maude's fancy, particularly during the 1924 Summer and Winter Olympics.

The display Maude found most fascinating was a cyclorama entitled "Sports d'Hiver" created for the Winter Olympics in Chamonix, a region she and Rosamond had visited the previous summer. The cyclorama's snowy background scenery seemed especially realistic, as was its foreground's focus on three events: a curving miniature bobsleigh run with eight-inch figures that coasted down and "tumbled off" at the curves, an "enormous" ski jump with a toy man jumping every two minutes and landing "safely each time," and miniature skaters performing on a rink with "onlookers nodding and clapping at intervals." Equally remarkable were the miniature figures' flawless mechanical movements, expressions, and dress, "exactly like people would be dressed in such a place."[46]

All three women followed economic and public affairs. Maude scanned the *Guardian*_and the *Times* for Canadian political news and weather, fearful of windstorms and frosts that might affect their apple harvest. They discussed markets, investment returns, and how to obtain a favourable imperial tariff for Canadian apples.[47] They commiserated on Nova Scotia's "disastrous" June 1925 provincial election that ended the Liberal Party's forty-three-year dynasty, leaving it with only three seats. The defeat of their cousin, Allison Hart Borden, in Kings (despite Leslie's accompanying ten workingmen to the polls!) was particularly painful, his only attempt at public office.[48] Maude reported her discussion of the election with Mrs. Power, a Parisian visitor from Halifax, who agreed that the popular former commanding officer of the Nova Scotia Highland Brigade's defeat was a casualty of the Liberal Party's decrepitude, the province's postwar depression, the Liberal's mishandling of the Cape Breton coal strikes, and the Conservatives' maritime rights program's promise to negotiate trade treaties. More difficult for Lady Borden, Elizabeth, and Maude was the October 1925 defeat of the federal Liberal member of Parliament for Kings, Ernest William Robinson (1875–1952), by that "disgraced [Arthur de Witt] Foster man," an "outrage" fortunately avenged the following September by J.L. Ilsley, who returned Kings to the Liberal fold and held the riding for the next twenty-two years, a county record exceeded only by Sir Frederick.[49]

Occasionally Maude reported on contemporary French politics. In May 1925 she recounted the French government's handling of an anticipated May Day "Communist uprising," how residents had been warned to avoid the Bastille and Montmartre as "aeroplanes" monitored the crowds, communicating with police headquarters by wireless. The previous day the police had "discovered a communist plot" and rounded up the alleged troublemakers, and Paris enjoyed its calmest May Day in years.[50] Since the "communist threat" had only been postponed until the Fête de Jeanne d'Arc (10 May), the government again forbade a procession. Little affected by the political turmoil of postwar France, Maude and Rosamond considered the French government's response an overreaction, attributing it to their revolutionary history.[51] No subject, however, trumped their preoccupation with Rosamond's Parisian education.

Chapter Twenty-Two

Rosamond

Maude's choice of Rosamond's Parisian school was no surprise. Filippo Colarossi (1841–1906) had brought his Académie Colarossi to Paris in 1870, an innovative alternative to the more traditional, expensive, and less accessible École des Beaux-Arts. Unlike the Ecole des Beaux Arts, Colarossi's Académie required no "infamous admission competition" or "tough French language" tests and charged "modest registration fees." It also opened its live model classes to female teachers and students. Consequently, it attracted many Canadian female art students, including Mary Alexandra (Bell) Eastlake (1864–1951),[1] Emily Carr (1871–1945), Prudence Heward (1896–1947) and Frances Loring (1887–1968).[2]

For girls who lacked the École des Beaux-Arts' linguistic and cultural prerequisites, Colarossi's Académie suggested a private preparatory girls' school, conveniently located on 34, rue Mozart, close to Maude and Rosamond's flat on 2, rue Meissonier. Only after students had completed their preparatory school's program were they admitted to the Académie, located on 10, rue de la Grande Chaumière in the heart of the Parisian artists' quarter off the Boulevard du Montparnasse. There they had access to the Académie live models and instructors, including the distinguished French sculptor Antoine Bourdelle (1861–1929).

For two years (1923–5) Rosamond attended the Académie Colarossi's genteel preparatory school. Its headmistress, Mademoiselle de San Carlos, affected a noble lineage, a conceit she impressed upon parents during conversation and dinners (as she did Maude and Rosamond in February 1925), served from an impressive table of glass, plate, and silver embossed with her family's coat of arms.[3] Girls lived in a stone building surrounded by a large garden, where classes were often held. The school's curriculum focused on French language, composition, grammar, dictation, literature, art, history, drawing, and deportment.

Rosamond loved her studies. A bibliophile like many in her family, she read in French and English, and purchased and collected books to "an alarming" extent.[4] Twice a week she and three other girls, accompanied by a chaperone, attended lectures on history and deportment at the Sorbonne. The deportment class taught ladies how to stand, sit, enter a room, and how to speak to a person on the street, exercises that amused Rosamond so much that she had "difficulty keeping a straight face."[5]

The school year ran from October to July, and was divided into three terms of two and a half months, with vacations at Christmas, winter, Easter, and summer.[6] The day began with breakfast at 7:30, followed by lessons until 12:30; lunch and a walk until 3:30; drawing lessons until 4:30; tea until 5:00; study from 5 until 7, then dinner, bedtime at 9, and lights out at 10. The food was nourishing. To Maude that meant vegetables, fruit, and salads.[7] Monitored by the school's vigilant matron, Madame LaTouche, the girls spoke entirely in French, except on Sunday, when they might return to their homes. The matron animated her linguistic regime with a point system, one point per day for linguistic fidelity. Ten points entitled students to a visit to the cinema or a motor car excursion.[8] On Thursdays the school organized visits to Chantilly, Fontainebleau, and other sites, the girls transported by a *char à banc* (an open-topped horse-drawn or motor vehicle).[9] Each week they attended an opera, play, or concert.

Maude was pleased with Rosamond's linguistic progress. So, too, was the Académie which commended Rosamond for her proficiency and accent, and placed her in its highest level of instruction and assigned her a lead role in one of its plays.[10] And in the summer of 1924 it recommended that she serve as interpreter for a Norwegian diplomat's wife's visit to the Louvre.[11] Delighted with Rosamond's linguistic progress, Lady Borden reported her success to family and friends, and paid for her extra "expensive" elocution lessons given by an elderly Mlle de San Cailor, a Comédie-française tutor.[12] She even offered to fund the accompaniment of Rosamond's French teacher on their Swiss vacation, an offer Maude declined as excessive.[13]

At times, Maude fretted over Rosamond's social development, her shyness, her "tendency to underestimate herself," and her lack of friends "her own age," owing to her living too much in adult company, which Maude hoped Rosamond's boarding school would remedy.[14] At school Rosamond shared a room with two other girls. One of her roommates was Norah Rosamond (1907–1996), Elsie Cotton's niece. The other girl, Lily, was Belgian. Norah had attended school in England and spoke French as well as Rosamond, but Lily spoke no French at all, and was often "very muddled." The girls' lively sense of humour soon cemented their friendship.[15]

Very shortly Rosamond was surrounded by school and family friends. Two Ottawa girls enrolled in her school the following year: Sue Houston (whose mother was a Nordheimer) and Roma Ethel Vals Gilmour (1910–1991), who became Rosamond's lifelong friends.[16] That same year Rosamond's cousin, Gwendolyn, Percy and Eva Borden's daughter, registered in a nearby school, and Maude frequently invited her friends to tea or a concert.[17] Maude also cared for Gwendolyn for several weeks in 1926, when Eva returned to Montreal to assist a relative.[18] Another of Rosamond's lifelong school friends was Elizabeth (Betsy) Greenhill, who became a distinguished British decorative bookbinder.[19]

Maude also encouraged suitable male friendships, nice, well-mannered, well-spoken young men who invited Rosamond to the Louvre, the outdoor theatre at Place Saint-Sulpice, or dinners at the Cercle de l'Union Interallié, conditional upon their return by 11 pm.[20] Occasionally Rosamond's male friends stayed for dinner or Maude accompanied them to the Louvre. More congenial, perhaps, were the males she met on vacation who enjoyed swimming and fishing. Otherwise, Rosamond lived comfortably at home, supervised closely at her school, and preoccupied with her studies.

Rosamond, Maude explained to Lady Borden, had a "large dose" of "artistic temperament" and was unable to "keep much on her mind but her work."[21] Protected, provisioned, and contented at home and school, she had few practical distractions. Her mother planned, purchased, fashioned, and refashioned her wardrobe, anticipated her social and seasonal needs, including an opera gown and a winter coat made of Siberian deerskin.[22] What her mother could not fabricate or alter, owing to Rosamond's "hard figure to fit,"[23] she ordered from their tailor or seamstress, who knew how to accommodate Rosamond's "short, uneven waist, round rift and legs." Maude was equally careful of Rosamond's health and welfare, providing good medical, dental, and optical care at reasonable prices.[24] While Maude and Rosamond preferred female doctors, professional expertise trumped gender. A male Dr. Monchet recommended regular swimming sessions for Rosamond in the Clandee Hotel's "lovely big bath" close to their former pension on rue Washington[25] and rigorous Swedish exercises on the rue Saints-Pères to improve her posture and spinal curvature.[26]

Travel was an essential part of Rosamond's cultural and social formation, as it had been for the "grand tour." During their first two years in Paris, Rosmand's school calendar dictated travel times and locations.

The school's two-month summer vacation (July and August) was the most obvious time to travel, while its two-week Christmas, winter, and Easter breaks permitted shorter expeditions. Once Rosamond's formal schooling ended, she and Maude undertook an even more ambitious educational itinerary.

Each Christmas vacation Maude and Rosamond migrated to the Côte d'Azur, Monaco, or Menton to escape the damp, cold, overcast Parisian winters. A Parisian winter, Lady Borden agreed, was "not a climate one would choose," despite the city's "fine food and pleasant people,"[27] especially if the alternative was the Côte d'Azur. The interwar Côte d'Azur attracted a lively colony of artists, writers, and other "exotic" denizens, including Canadian, British, European, and American vacationers. Maude and Rosamond were inveterate people watchers, their world a live theatre and source of artistic and literary inspiration, a laboratory to refine a sculptor's eye, a writer's pen, and to entertain Lady Borden.

Maude and Rosamond enjoyed nature and physical activity. In July and early August 1924, they vacationed first at Spitz, an elite mountain resort on Lake Thun in the Interlaken Swiss canton of Bern, and then at Monnetier-Mornex in the French commune of Haute-Savoie. Installed in Spitz's elegant, art nouveau Grand Bellevue hotel, where Sir Frederick and Lady Borden had stayed in 1902 and Elizabeth in 1921, Maude reminded her "dearest mother" and "Lizzy" of the resort's dramatic beauty, peaceful comfort, and its fruit, vegetables, and pastries. She described its waterfalls, their five-mile hikes gathering cyclamen bulbs and autumn crocus, and the hotel's residents: a Persian prince and his family, the British ambassador to Constantinople, and a prominent financial adviser to the French government.

Their Monnetier-Mornex resort offered comparable beauty, located below the Saint-Arve Mountain within view of Mont Blanc. On one occasion so spectacular was its sunset and rising moon that Rosamond almost fell from the window watching the changing colours. The resort offered human interest as well. The League of Nations' Geneva meetings were only nine kilometres from Monnetier, and Rachel Crowdy sent her car to fetch Maude and Rosamond for dinner with her French friends and other "clever people," including Manley Hudson (1886–1960), professor of law at Harvard and later judge of the Court of International Justice, and twice nominated for a Nobel Peace Prize.[28] Only the need to prepare Rosamond's wardrobe for the school year prevented Maude from extending their Swiss vacation.

Other vacations provided comparable attractions. In April 1925 Maude and Rosamond joined Hugh Percy (1871–1942) and Ethel

Fleming (1881–?) and their daughter Margo (1901–93)[29] for a twenty-day motor tour of Normandy, Brittany, and Aquitaine. Although fascinated by the area's Anglo-Norman and Celtic history, their tour was largely a coastal vacation, with stops s at Avranches, Saint-Brieuc, Quimper, La Rochelle, Nantes, and Arcachon, where they spent Easter week at the Grand Hotel, enjoying sandy beaches, boat rides, fishing, swimming, and golfing with other vacationing Canadians and friends of the Flemings, including the *Titanic* "heroine," Lady Lucy Noel Martha Dyer-Edwards Rothes (1878–1956) and her "awfully nice" sixteen-year-old son Jock (John Wayland Leslie). When the Flemings left for Spain, Rosamond and Maude returned to Paris by train, after a day trip to Bordeaux to see the city's Gallo-Roman façades and its great Gothic Saint-André cathedral, which Rosamond had studied in her art history course at the Sorbonne,[30] followed by overnight in Angoulême and a tour of Charente's chateaux.[31]

The end of Rosamond's two-year schooling in July 1925 raised the thorny question of their return to Canada. Rosamond wanted to remain, to have access to Colarossi's studios, instructors, and "Professor Bourdelle, one of the greatest sculptors in France."[32] Maude, too, loved Paris and travel, but missed her family. Much to Rosamond's relief, family finances required Gables' extended rental until March 1926. That enabled Rosamond and her mother to devote the next year to travel and Rosamond's artistic formation.

Their travel itinerary began on 1 July 1925, when Maude left for Brussels to consult her oculist and endure extensive dental work. A week later Rosamond joined her mother, after a four-hour rail journey to Brussels with a teacher and a schoolmate.[33] Their pension was a "nice, new House," centrally located on rue de la Longue Haie, a recommendation of Rosamond's French teacher. The pension's managers, Mlle Given and Mlle May, offered their twenty-one guests good food and accommodation; an accommodation to which Maude and Rosamond would return and recommended to others. Their first recruit, Eva Borden, joined them in Brussels, a prime location for inveterate bargain hunters such as Eva and Maude. Fortunately, Eva's affection for Brussels' casino and "gaiety" enabled Rosamond and Maude to break free for a day trip to Bruges.

By 16 July Maude and Rosamond were back in Paris, preparing for a more extensive educational tour, serious entertainment focused upon history, architure, and art.[34] Their destination was Normandy's Atlantic coast, accessible by train from Paris, where they spent their summer exploring Normandy's familiar topography and Anglo-Norman history. After a week at Cocherel, a small commune in the Haute-Normandie's

Eure department, about 75 kilometres from Paris, they moved to Arromanches-les-Bains, Calvados, the popular Normandy seaside resort about 192 kilometres from Cocherel, where they occupied a "huge, sunny, ground-floor room with hot salt-water baths" at the Oasis, a Victorian stone villa bordered by a seawall hedge and garden.[35] The town promised romantic walks over old stone bridges and paths "trod by William the Conqueror," as well as good food, beaches, and an active social life.

Wherever Maude and Rosamond vacationed they met Canadians and guests who knew Canadians. A chatty, ever-restless Mrs. Power and her daughter, Kitty, greeted them at Arromanches-les-Bains, as did Mr. Stockton, an English assistant headmaster at the Northampton High School for boys and a former schoolmate of Gordon Hewitt. Mr. Stockton and his wife invited Rosamond to join them for shrimp-fishing and other ventures. Interesting, too, were their conversations with the "old painter" Leopold Franz Kowalski (1856–1931) and his "plump, comfortable wife, daughter and son-in-law."[36] Although Maude found the Atlantic water too cold, Rosamond spent much of her time on the beach after she met a Cambridge science student, John Evans. The son of a British Colonel in India, John was perfecting his French in Arromanches-les-Bains. Their friendship progressed sufficiently for Rosamond to agree to be Evans's guest during Cambridge's 1926 May Week's feverish end-of-term celebrations. That placed England on their travel agenda.

At the end of August, Elsie Cotton joined Maude and Rosamond for a three-week exploration of Anglo-Norman history, a story of territorial, dynastic, and religious battles, told by its castles, churches, and monuments. From their tourist bases at Caen, Mont-Saint-Michel, and Rouen they visited Creully, Bayeux, Saint-Lô, Coutances, and Avranches before returning to Paris via Rouen. Among their memories were the sixty-nine-metre Bayeux Tapestry depicting the Norman Conquest, Creully's great chateau, Caen's Abbaye aux Dames, built for Queen Mathilde, and Coutances' thirteenth-century Gothic cathedral. The monuments' stirring tales of the Hundred Years' War, the martyrdom of Joan of Arc (the recently canonized French Catholic cult figure), and the fragile reconciliation of church and state following Thomas Becket's murder left indelible memories. Equally memorable were Coustances and Avranches' botanical gardens and Mont-Saint-Michel's medieval abbey. Not to mention the region's renowned tides that Rosamond and Elsie rose before sunrise to confirm that they were no higher than the Bay of Fundy's! Not all their accommodations were comfortable, nor were all tables as renowned as that of Saint-Michel's Mère Poulard.

Indeed some lodgings were best forgotten, especially those they shared with fleas.[37]

Back in Paris Rosamond made the most of her access to the Colarossi studio before their annual Côte d'Azur winter retreat. In Paris Maude rented a large sunny room on rue Raspail, within walking distance of Rosamond's studio. A small stove heated their bedsitter, where they took their petit dejeuner. Otherwise, they lunched and dined with a French family down the street. Two resident sculptors encouraged Rosamond's sculpting, impressed by her plasticine animals and "great sense of form." During her next two months Rosamond rarely missed her classes, composed mostly of fifteen girls, who moved from room to room, taught by instructors and with access to live models.

"Fired with ambition," Rosamond continued her artistic and linguistic education during their extended (1925–6) Côte d'Azur residence. She enrolled in a Berlitz Italian class, sketched, and sculpted. She even secured a commission to sculpt Mrs. Hope Johnson's dog. Meanwhile, her mother served as her model, "posing each morning after her bath" as "Eve holding an apple." An "imperfect model," Rosamond 's complained to her Granny, as she was "too thin and her thighs too fat."[38] Recovering from surgery, Elsie joined them in Menton, and together, primed by lectures and guidebooks, they toured historic sites and gardens. Maude shared her father's interest in Roman ruins and her mother's fascination with gardens.

More significant was Leslie's six-week sojourn in Menton, which included Christmas and New Year's. Leslie's Ottawa Agency was practically moribund, and in the dead of winter his Bell Hill farm manager needed little supervision. To accommodate the family's temporary reconstitution, Maude rented a reasonably priced semi-basement flat in the Hotel Alexandra, a newly constructed, six-storey hotel in Menton, owned and operated by Swedes, reputed to be "the best hotel keepers in Europe after the Swiss." The flat came with a maid who cooked, cleaned, and did errands, for only eleven dollars a month.[39] The maid's culinary deficiency was easily remedied by the hotel's restaurant, which also offered visual access to its seasonal celebrites. That year's Christmas celebrity was King Gustaf V of Sweden (1858–1950), attended closely by the "perspiring hotelkeeper." Seated close to the king, Rosamond described Gustave V to her ever-curious Granny as "very tall, thin, not good looking, with wide mouth, open while he picked his teeth."[40] This would not be Rosamond's last encouter with Gustaf V.

More exotic sightings surfaced during their Christmas party, as Maude, Leslie, Rosamond, and Elsie dined and danced at the gaily decorated Hôtel de Paris in Monte Carlo. The guest list included the

Duke of Westminster (1879–1953) with Mlle Gabrielle Co-Co Chanel (1883–1971); the ex-Duchess of Marlborough (Consuelo Vanderbilt, 1877–1964, who Lady Borden had met years ago in London) with her new husband, Jacques Balsan (1868–1956) and his seventy-two year old stepmother, Lady de Bathe (Lillie Langtry, 1853–1929), the beautiful often-married actress and consort of British royalty and aristocracy, still "quite beautiful, grey hair, unlined face," and still dancing. Equally amusing to Maude, Leslie, and Elsie was Rosamond's vivacity, her dancing belying her alleged shyness, and only her age barred her from the casino.[41]

Rosamond and Maude had planned to visit Milan, Rome, Florence, Palermo, and Naples during their winter migration. But northern Italy's unusually cold winter grounded them in Menton for four months. That left little time for Italy and preparations for May Week. Better to postpone Italy for another year. On 3 May a bitter week-long British coal miner's strike threatened to derail May Week when the nervous British government recruited temporary civilian constables to ensure provision of essential services, and John Evans, Rosamond's summer friend, volunteered for service. The strike's brevity saved May Week, and the third week of May, Maude and Rosamond registered at the Strand Palace Hotel in Piccadilly Circus to prepare for the Cambridge festivities. Since they had planned a three-month visit to England, there would be time afterwards to explore London and the countryside, especially as Rosamond's friendship with Evans faded quickly after May Week.

Rosamond had never visited England before and did not like London at first. Certainly it could not compare to Paris. She found it "funny" speaking English after three years of speaking French in school and in public. Maude understood. She, too, felt "more at home on the continent than in England." Perhaps, she wrote her mother, one feels "lonely in an English-speaking country when one knows no one or practically no one than in a foreign land if one can speak the language moderately well."[42] While one may read too much into Rosamond and Maude's initial response to England, the Great War had replaced many imperial dreams with colonial realities, altered Canada's economic and constitutional relations, and extended Canadians' world view.[43] Maude and Rosamond took little time, however, warming to London's historic sites, galleries, concerts, theatres, and shopping. Maude warmed even more quickly. She loved theatre, and though they attended theatre in Paris, Maude's French comprehension was less acute than Rosamond's. She was delighted, therefore, to see "lots of plays" in London, as many as possible. Sean O'Casey's recently opened *The Plough and the Stars,* with its controversial criticism of the 1916 Easter Rebellion, deeply impressed both Maude and Rosamond, conscious of Leslie's Northern Irish sensitivities.

Elsie Cotton joined them in London but stayed with friends. Meanwhile Maude and Rosamond pursued family and historical interests, beginning with a day trip by bus to Canterbury Cathedral. They required overnight accommodation at the Fair Maid of Kent Hotel in Walmer to inspect Headcorn, Borden Hall, and St. Peter's and St. Paul's Church, with its stained-glass window and floor plaque memorializing their Borden ancestry, followed the next day by an exploration of "family" and Plantagenet history at Walmer Castle.[44] On 12 August Rosamond, Maude, and Elsie left for Brussels for dental work before returning to Paris at the end of September.[45] Aware of her mother's desire to return to Canada, Rosamond returned to Paris determined to take full advantage of access to her studio.

Chapter Twenty-Three

Return

As much as Maude had enjoyed Paris, she longed for the world she had lost. Lonely, ill, and often discouraged by financial restraints, she often felt overwhelmed by Rosamond's care. She tried to be stoic but at times she failed, overcome by memories of "apple blossom time,"[1] fresh strawberries, and "the joy of hearing English" during a London company's Parisian production of Bernard Shaw's *Pygmalion.*[2] Improved marital relations and the end of Rosamond's formal education seemed a good time to end her exile. Family finances, however, remained a worry. As she explained to her mother in the autumn of 1926, the strong franc, rising Parisian rent and food prices, and the instability of her family income threatened their continued Parisian residence. But neither could they afford to return, since the expense of their return journey, together with their loss of rental income and the cost of heating Gables, would leave them little to live on.[3]

Maude worried about Rosamond's health, her continual coughs, colds, and infections. Soon after they returned to Paris, Rosamond developed a persistent fever and fatigue. Doctors diagnosed her condition as anemia and prescribed a healthy daily diet and a two-hour afternoon rest. Maude appreciated the relationship of health and food, and prepared a menu of milk, beef, potatoes and turnips, and salads of lettuce and tomatoes, though no dessert, and insisted on a daily rest period, despite Rosamond's protests. No sooner had Rosamond recovered from her anemia than she contracted measles, and Maude was obliged to hire a nurse. Nor was Maude herself well. Apart from colds, she suffered digestive problems. She was "tired all the time" and vomited upon "the slightest provocation." Doctors diagnosed her ailment as "a gall bladder condition" and advised her to avoid fried food.[4] She also developed a skin rash that troubled her for weeks.

Maude missed her mother and sister. They had visited her in 1924 and she wanted them to return. In January 1926 she begged her mother and sister to join her and Rosamond on the Côte d'Azur, after Leslie's departure. "Why can't you sail to the Mediterranean," she pleaded; "it may be a little more expensive but you will have warmth and sunshine," both strong considerations with Lady Borden, as was the Côte d'Azur's proximity to Italy and inexpensive lodging in Menton.[5] But even Maude's description of almond, peach, and pear blossoms and the woods full of violets, hyacinths, and anemones, months before anything similar might appear in the Annapolis Valley, failed to convince her mother. Lady Borden needed Elizabeth as a travelling companion, and Elizabeth insisted on first visiting her English friends and Gordon's relatives. That meant England in January. Maude renewed her plea later that year, hoping to convince her mother to avoid England, owing to a rumoured coal shortage following the May 1926 strike, and to come directly to Paris via Cherbourg or Le Havre, where she might enjoy the comfort and cheap rates at the Pas-de-Calais, and so close to Notre-Dame de Paris.

Talk of returning unsettled Rosamond. She loved Paris, her art studio, and instructors, and was especially fond of Émile-Antoine Bourdelle. She had adapted readily to his monumental style, inspired by classical forms and subjects. Apart from his impressive reputation, Rosamond found him "awfully nice," supportive, humorous, and "terribly funny looking." He was, she wrote her grandmother, "very short 5 ft 2 perhaps not even that and absolutely square. His hair is white and sticks straight up on the top of his head in a sort of tonsure, and he has a funny looking beard that curls up to his mouth and he wears a grey tunic "of cloth corduroy and Oxford bags."

Bourdelle reciprocated Rosamond's good opinion. He "seemed delighted" with her work which he described as "very good," with "a lot of flame (I'm translating literally) and colour ... and very subtle." In fact he thought Rosamond's life-sized stone man "so powerful and strong he could not believe a girl had done it and asked her twice if she had done it."[6] So impressed was he with her stone man that he returned the next week (rather than the usual two weeks) to make certain that her man's "muscles were correct."[7] He also recommended that Rosamond be invited to exhibit her "femme assise" at the 1928 Salon des Tuileries's annual May exhibition, a flattering endorsement by a founder and vice-president of the Salon's Comité du Tuileries exhibition,[8] an invitation considered "the highest recognition for any foreign artist."[9] Consequently, the thought of leaving Paris simply "disgusted" Rosamond!

Maude understood Rosamond's feeling. Her school and studio had done her "a lot of good."[10] To enable Rosamond to maximize her remaining time in Paris, Maude promised to rent a flat close to Bourdelle's studio upon their return from London, a flat they would share with Elsie. Although Elsie's mother and sister had returned to Canada, Elise wanted to remain. How long she could stay depended on her application for the librarian's position at the American Embassy. Meanwhile, she and Maude signed a six-month lease for a third-floor flat on 47, Boulevard Garibaldi with four sunny front rooms, close to the Hôtel des Invalides and Rosamond's school's studio.

An ideal flatmate, Elsie was generous, congenial, and dependable. She shared the rent and housework and provided invaluable support during their illnesses. At first, they had only an afternoon "femme de ménage" to scrub and do dishes, until they found Richard, a twenty-five-year-old Polish man, with very "funny French," who dusted, polished floors, and cooked. In the interim Elsie kept the flat clean, and Maude prepared the meals, a task she "seemed to enjoy for a short time."[11] Although Rosamond chafed that her illness interfered with her studio time, after three years of hotel and pension food she relished her mother's home cooking.[12]

The impending termination of their lease in March 1927, Elsie's departure, and Leslie's annual visit revived the subject of family reunification. Maude's French landlord resolved her rent shortfall, created by Elsie's departure and the franc's appreciation, by extending Maude's lease for four months and reducing her rent to $100 per month.[13] The date of their return to Canada was more difficult to negotiate. Once again family finances persuaded them to extend David Gilmour's lease of Gables until October 1927 or the completion of his Rockcliffe house.[14] That meant another year in Paris. This was not the resolution Maude had hoped, but at least it was final. Leslie agreed to book their passage for next spring and return to help pack.

Rosamond welcomed the reprieve, and Maude managed the fallout. Maude repeated her request that her mother visit, alone if necessary and "as her guest" until Elizabeth could join them in the late winter or early spring.[15] Although Lady Borden was not convinced, she and Elizabeth detected Maude's distress and promised to visit in the late winter of 1928. Meanwhile time passed quickly as Maude and Rosamond travelled, entertained visitors, and prepared for their return, increasingly buoyed by improved marital relations and family finances.

No one had benefited more than Leslie from the family's retention of its lands. The role of gentleman farmer appealed to Leslie's skills and social aspirations, and his enthusiasm was buoyed by talk of an imperial preferential tariff. He enjoyed risks, was not afraid of hard work, and in 1924 he had few options. A long English summer drought in 1921 revived British interest in Nova Scotia apples. By 1924 the number of bushels of Nova Scotia apples shipped to Britain had almost doubled prewar records, an increase aided by the availability of refrigeration, and cheaper and faster transatlantic transportation.[16]

The failure of an imperial preference notwithstanding, Leslie decided to exploit the English apple market, employing scientific, managerial, and marketing methods. He substituted tractors for horses and employed commercial fertilizers and pesticides. He replaced his farm's manager with a literate, energetic person who monitored farm labour and instituted sound accounting and marketing practices. Conscious that Nova Scotia apples had dominated the English market more for their price than their quality,[17] Leslie paid special attention to their transport and packaging. He reduced spoilage by shipping and marketing his apples directly rather than through the United Fruit Companies,[18] except for the early apples, whose distribution benefited from the United Fruit Company's collective marketing. Very shortly Bell Hill Farm became a profitable enterprise. By 1942–3 Bell Hill Farm received $9,486.48 from the Nova Scotia Apple Marketing Board,[19] a sum that more than covered the $2,000 in expenditures on the farm's manager, day labourers, school taxes, hydro, telephone, bank charges, and travel.[20]

Bell Hill Farm's successful 1926–7 season began to dispel Maude's anxieties about "reclaiming" their lives,[21] her optimism grounded on her farm's increasingly lucrative apple market, and concomitant real estate prices. She monitored her farm's progress from planting to market, anxious about frosts, winds, and sales, hoping for a "good crop," and fearful of a poor one.[22] She scrutinized accounts and markets, advised Leslie on land sales and urged Elizabeth to lobby Neville Chamberlain, chancellor of the exchequer, and L.S. Amery, secretary of state for the colonies, for an imperial preference for Canadian apples.[23] If things continued Bell Hill Farm's profits and her securities ought more than cover Gables' loss of rental income. With the end of her Parisian expenses, termination of British currency restrictions, and the economies of a reconstituted family, they could now surely reclaim their lost world.

Meanwhile, Maude and Rosamond made the most of their time in Europe. As soon as Leslie returned to Canada in May 1927, Maude and Rosamond began their long-delayed Italian pilgrimage.[24] Maude's Ottawa friend Ethel (Gilmour) Fauquier had invited them to accompany her in her motor car as far as Lausanne. From there Maude and Rosamond took the railway to Montreux, Caux, Milan, Florence, Venice,

Rome, Naples (Capri), and Sicily. Occasionally they travelled second class, sometimes seated on their baggage in crowded cars, and stayed in ordinary hotels until they could find better. The absence of further information on their travels, however, obscures their precise itinerary.

True to their promise, Lady Borden and Elizabeth reached Paris in March 1928. For three weeks they lunched or dined with Maude and Rosamond, shopped, and visited their tailors. Madame Roy honoured Lady Borden and Elizabeth with a tea at l'Union Interallié, to which she invited twenty ladies, including Madame Le Grault and Madame Barmeau, who had sheltered Canadian soldiers during the Great War.[25] Lady Borden reciprocated with a tea at l'Union Interallié to thank Madame Roy and other Parisian friends for their hospitality. The highlight of their Parisian visit was Rosamond's invitation to exhibit her "femme assise" at the May Salon des Tuileries, an occasion which they celebrated with food and drink. After Paris, Lady Borden and Elizabeth spent a few days on the Côte d'Azur, before travelling to Florence, where Maude and Rosamond joined them for a week.

Meanwhile, Maude and Rosamond prepared for the May Salon des Tuileries, said goodbye to their Parisian friends, and packed their accumulated treasures. Then on 23 June 1928 they boarded the Red Star's *Arabic* in Antwerp, bound for Halifax, where they arrived on 2 July 1928. Leslie met and drove them to Canning. There Lady Borden and Elizabeth awaited their arrival, anxious to restore harmony in their reconstituted, extended family.[26]

Chapter Twenty-Four

Life with Lizzie

During Maude and Rosamond's absence, Lady Borden and Lizzie made two pivotal decisions: to cohabit and "return to the land." Lady Borden and Lizzie were not obvious cohabitants. Both had strong personalities. Elizabeth's executive, no-nonsense manner contrasted with Lady Borden's quiet, determined demeanor. Elizabeth liked to organize, direct, and advocate, whereas Lady Borden preferred to suggest and influence, to reign rather than rule. No less different were their attitudes to their land. Elizabeth was a pragmatic, hands-on farmer, who planned and directed her farm from seed time to market, whereas Lady Borden remained a vigilant rentier, appreciative of her land's material, social, and ascetic value.

Whatever their differences, Lady Borden and Elizabeth needed one another. Both were relatively young, lonely widows, whose lives had complemented those of their husbands. Both had large houses and limited income. Their six-year battle to defend their inheritance had cemented their relationship. They also shared friends, interests, and values, were committed to family, church, and public service and enjoyed their summers in Canning.

In 1926 Lady Borden was sixty-three. She had been widowed for close to a decade. Her mother was dead, Elizabeth was still in Ottawa, and Maude and Rosamond lived in Paris. She had sold her mortgaged Ottawa house, and, apart from her annual visits to Ottawa and winter excursions to the American eastern seaboard, she was alone and confined to Borden Place. Elizabeth faced a comparable dilemma. In 1926 she was fifty-two years old. She had been widowed for six years, had a small circle of Ottawa friends, and belonged to a few voluntary organizations. Since Gordon's death she had considered ways to supplement her income including writing, inspired by her reading of biographies of bold, accomplished "women who dared." Elizabeth now had a plan.

Six months before she reclaimed her portion of her father's estate, Leslie had informed Ilsley that Lady Borden and Elizabeth's only interest in their land was their bond.[1] However, within months of becoming the proprietor of 1,702 acres of farms, residential properties, and woodlots, including 248 acres of prime orchard land in Lower Habitant, Cornwallis Township, Elizabeth (and Lady Borden) asked Miss Annie Stewart, their friend and real estate agent, to find purchasers for their extraneous properties; their sale was designed to generate capital to develop their orchards and farms.[2] Elizabeth had decided to become a lady farmer in a male gendered occupation,[3] and make her lands the centre of an imagined British world, its full implementation contingent upon selling her Ottawa house.

The "Garland Cox property," the core of Elizabeth's Habitant Farm, encompassed over one hundred acres of apple orchards, making it one of the largest apple orchards in the Kings-Annapolis apple belt,[4] a farm from which she intended to extract a profit through scientific management and marketing, as Gordon had advocated and Leslie had practised, and whose examples she was determined to follow.[5] Nor did she intend to be a rentier or dilettante. She intended to be a hands-on lady farmer, a responsible community leader, and advocate, living her ideal, leading by example, as she believed her father had done, her style at once professional and personal.

Elizabeth interviewed potential farm workers; she evaluated their knowledge of farming, their "superiority of mind," energy, and "economy of time."[6] She "borrowed Jordan Zwicker's pig to tramp manure," talked about steers with Stanley France, and assisted Mrs. B., "a widow with three children," to move to a new house, loading up "bed and bedding, kitchen stove and sofa" and sending her a dinner of "cassarola & bread and oranges."[7] In her daily Chronicle she considered the benefits of salt licks, cornmeal drinks, and apple skins in the feeding and fattening of pigs, poultry, and livestock; the snow's effect upon trees; and the marketing of hay and apples.[8] As a hands-on farmer, she spent entire days consulting, surveying, and supervising farm work and workers. She would leave Borden Place on her horse "Seweey," clad in riding breeches, to consult her factor, Basil Ells, on hiring, budgets, monthly timetables and sprays.[9] At other times and seasons she joined her shipper, Eaton Dickie,[10] grading and selling apples, checking and directing teams of horses – sometimes as many as 68 in a day – hauling her apples to her warehouses for shipment abroad, working side by side with her male and female employees, addressing them by their first names and returning home late in the afternoon, feeling "better after being at the farm."[11]

Elizabeth had a mind for detail and an eye for profit, qualities her contemporaries gendered as male. She had little time for these conventions. During her conflicts with Leslie over her father's estate she had resented his failure to consult her on estate matters, a resentment made more inexcusable after Gordon's death. Her resentment was confirmed by her reading of contemporary literature on and by women, books such as *Pink Sugar* (1924) by O. Douglas (Anna Buchan, 1877–1948), in which men were peripheral to a world managed by kind, caring, able women.[12] Elizabeth was determined to be a woman who cared and dared and who faced realities, including the need for family reconciliation.

Although Elizabeth had resented Leslie's attitudes and had contested his management and his execution of her late father's estate, she admired his managerial methods (vindicated by his success), assured that Gordon would have agreed. Leslie's initiatives in packaging, shipping, and marketing apples, and getting apples to the United Kingdom in better condition, made good sense. Since she and Leslie sought access to the same market, the logic of jointly advertising and marketing in Britain, touting the superiority of Nova Scotia apples, could not be denied. Elizabeth was a pragmatist, ready to learn from Leslie's success and cooperate with his endeavours, but on her terms. She was now a farmer, and on an equal footing with Leslie. She would not be ignored or taken for granted. Leslie respected her terms. He did not require her affection. He too was a pragmatist.

Maude's return facilitated family reconciliation. A trusted, discreet, and judicious mediator, Maude was far from a passive landowner or spectator to her family's cold war. Quietly observant, shrewd, and entrepreneurial, Maude possessed knowledge, judgment, and interest in her farm's economy, its finances, marketing, and administration. It was her land, a reality Leslie did not question. She monitored its markets and sought to sell, rent, or mortgage her available properties, possibilities she discussed with Elizabeth, their mutual trust and confidence a bridge to family reconciliation.[13]

Whatever or whoever was responsible for the thaw, soon after Maude's return Elizabeth and Leslie began marketing their apples cooperatively. Employing their telling corporate label, The Borden Fruit Company, Growers and Suppliers of Apples, Canning, Warehouses, Woodside,[14] they designed and produced attractive labels and boxes and displayed their apples at the annual Imperial Fruit Show. Success validated their strategy, and the Borden Fruit Farm's three attractively labelled barrels of Baldwins won first prize in the Canadian Championship Section of the October 1935 Imperial Fruit Show in Cardiff, Wales, a success they repeated in 1936 with three half-barrels of Cox's Orange Pippin, and in 1937 with three barrels of Golden Russets. Moreover, cooperation enabled them to monitor dishonest English marketers.[15]

For Leslie Britain was a familiar remunerative market, as well as a restrictive world tainted by unhappy memories, a world in which he reserved the right to accept or reject whatever part of its class system and values served his purpose. But for Elizabeth Britain was more than a market. It was an ideal, a replicable model and a cause, tailored to Canadian exigencies. She identified herself as British, a chameleon category based upon her ancestral, institutional, and cultural heritage, and reinforced by her reading and search for identity and meaning.[16] She was also a romantic and an activist who sought to retain or restore an idealized world represented by her late father and husband, whose imagined legacies she was determined to defend and promote.

Elizabeth regarded her father as an exemplary visionary, an energetic man who dreamed dreams that he realized and others emulated, to the lasting benefit of his community. As she explained to her Chronicle, he dreamed of rails, warehouses, clean water, libraries, churches, and armouries; and his dreams "one by one" came true, "and we are thankful for his dreams and energy."[17] She also had dreams. Like her father, she sought certainty and identity in history, genealogy, and community leadership, and she was resolved to maintain his legacy.

For years, too, Elizabeth remembered Gordon, "her darling's birthday," and his "bright legacy" of gentleness and "doing for others."[18] "Without you what would life have been?" Elizabeth pondered in her Chronicle's thinly disguised, third-person self-examination entitled "In Praise of Life and Love." Before, Elizabeth's autobiographical paean continued, "she seemed to see her life as half-night, half-day, half-alive." Gordon taught her to "listen to the rush of spring life, the sweet sight of wind in the maples, the breath of new mown grass."[19] To honour her "darling's" memory Elizabeth sought to understand and emulate his life, and to dedicate herself to his scientific and social mission to improve and refine the social, civic, and cultural life of her community.

An inveterate anglophile, Elizabeth descanted frequently on the superiority of British goods and the necessity of resisting American intrusions. After an exhilarating day on her farm, nothing pleased her more than to revel in an evening by a hardwood fire reading the English weeklies: *Illustrated London News*, *The Tatler*, *Public Opinion*, and the *Manchester Guardian*.[20] She washed her hair with English shampoo powder, and bought British products, confident that "British goods [were] always satisfactory."[21] She raged against the substitution of American for British trade, especially now "that we are as a nation more sensitively British minded than ever before." Why, she interrogated her long-suffering Chronicle, "can't we rage outwardly, form a procession, wave flags, and beat drums and denounce this thing [the appointment of a customs official with American business ties, suspected of favouring the importation of American products] that the government has done to us?"[22]

Elizabeth cast herself as a Canadian country "squire." Her community's life emanated from her "manor house," Borden Place. Her estate provided employment for regular, seasonal, and casual farm and household workers. Services and suppliers benefited from the estate's patronage. The community looked to her for leadership; and those who did not received it anyway. She participated in its associational life, determined to promote its physical, cultural, and moral welfare. During municipal, provincial, and federal elections her regular and occasional field and household workers were transported to the polls. Opponents and sceptics who resisted her initiatives were reduced to silence or obfuscation.

An apostle of contemporary Canadian women's journals' advocacy of useful female wage employment,[23] Elizabeth's community endeavours were invariably didactic and designed to be uplifting; she was convinced that she was working for "unselfish ends."[24] She was a pillar of her church and her community's Women's Institute,[25] Literary Society, and Temperance Society, all charged with active, reforming agendas. On one "beautiful night" in 1926, members of Canning's Literary Society heard a lecture on Shakespeare and Ruskin, then listened to a cello, violin, and piano trio (presumably Elizabeth was the pianist), after which they were treated to healthy Northern Spy apples (probably from her orchard). On another occasion members heard her friend Colonel Byng Hall, a British Great War veteran, lecture on his experiences of life in a Chinese village.[26] Another evening, members heard Harry Britton, the husband of Lady Borden's friend and artist, Henriette Britton, speak on art and farming, a topic that kindled Elizabeth's fond memories of Gordon.[27]

Elizabeth, like Gordon and her father, sought practical solutions to problems. Her local Women's Institute encouraged women to fashion and sell axe handles, baskets, and lampshades, grow and market mushrooms, and become scientific farmers.[28] She led by example, employing teams of seasonal women workers to pick and pack her apples, working ten hours a day, while she worked alongside them.[29] In 1926 she decided to lecture women and men on the benefits of scientific farming (one of Gordon's passions), combining practical advice with moral admonition that mirrored her character and values. All aspiring farmers, she informed her large public audience, must have a precise, well-timed, and well-designed program and a "vision" of their objectives. She then advised them when and how to plough, fertilize, plant, spray, dust, and store apples to avoid waste and shrinkage, warning them to take special care of the trees' bark, since bark "is our bank containing the equivalent of money." Conscious of contemporary time and motion studies and Gordon's fear of indulging "the ease of routine,"[30] she admonished potential farmers to adopt better work habits, avoid indecision, "idle chat and bustle," and remember that "quiet is faster" and neatness is necessary for the "best brain work." Timing, she reminded her audience, required careful planning, to avoid cows freshening during pruning, planting, spraying, and harvesting. And although "saving money was the same as making money," she warned farmers never "to economize on rest."[31]

Occasionally Elizabeth had to pull strings to have things done properly, as she did in 1926 to reassure the "gracious" reappointment of Dr. T.W. Hodgson, her and Lady Borden's friend and popular Methodist/United Church minister. Although Elizabeth thought church union "a mistake," she endorsed the new church's abolition of the Methodists' obligatory rotation of its clergy. Contractual renewal still required a congregation's Quarterly Board's consent, and Elizabeth and Lady Borden were determined to make Dr. Hodgson's reappointment unanimous and enthusiastic. That required attendance of all the "right" board members, including Mrs. Charles Eaton.

To assure Mrs. Eaton's attendance Elizabeth and Lady Borden invited her to dine at Borden Place before the meeting. Unfortunately, Mrs. Eaton depended on her daughter's fiancé for transportation to Borden Place, and he had a hockey game in Kentville, a priority that even Elizabeth could not override. Although confident of the Quarterly Board meeting's decision without Mrs. Eaton's attendance, Elizabeth feared it might lack "cheerful enthusiasm." Leaving nothing to chance, she spoke to the board's chairman, instructing him to make his invitation to Dr. Hodgson "really cordial," since normally "we Nova Scotians are so glum and expressionless."[32]

Details and presentation were important to Elizabeth. So, too, were big plans of imperial dimensions, such as the postwar migration of British farmers, labourers, and domestics to Canada.[33] For years imperialists, notably women imperialists,[34] had advocated British female emigration to the colonies to assure the prosperity, security, gender balance and moral character of the British Empire. After the Great War and postwar recession, Canadian social unrest and xenophobia gave imperial emigration a new urgency. Recommended by a 1917 British Royal

Commission and endorsed enthusiastically by the secretary of state for the colonies, Lord Milner, imperial resettlement secured legislation and funding from Britain and Canada to encourage public/private settlement initiatives. This was a big plan tailored to Elizabeth's imaginative economic, social, and political objectives, a tonic to the Valley's lethargic agricultural economy and a welcome reinforcement of its "British" character.

When Colonel Byng Hall became secretary of a Canadian Pacific Railway supported board to promote British immigration to the Valley, Elizabeth became his committed accomplice. The colonel admired Elizabeth's executive energy and British instincts, and regarded her as a person of more than local influence.[35] After an invigorating conference with Elizabeth, Colonel Byng Hall and she decided to call a public afternoon meeting of citizens for 19 February 1926 to consider their ambitious proposal to recruit English agricultural settlers "of his own type," together with experienced, industrious farm labourers, as a stimulus to land prices, labour, and trade.

Elizabeth and her friend, Marion Eaton, listened attentively as Col. Byng Hall promoted their ambitious settlement plan to a small body of local notables gathered around a stove one chilly February afternoon. Col. Byng Hall assured his audience that his settlement plan would attract healthy, experienced migrants, stem regional outmigration, and revitalize the local economy. He explained that his migrants would require land and good homes, with bedrooms and other facilities, and would expect an annual income of between $1,500 and $3,000, which would generate local economic activity. Under their plan a farmer could obtain a $5,000 farm for a down payment of $500 the first year and subsequently invest $1,000 in its improvement. His plan would attract good solid citizens of the "right sort," infuse capital, stimulate the local economy, and populate the community with reliable, enterprising British citizens and promoters.

Elizabeth was baffled by the prolonged silence that greeted the end of Col. Byng Hall`s rousing address, as the small "expressionless" audience edged closer to the stove, "scratched their heads, shuffled their feet and gazed at one another," until one or two broke the silence with some carefully weighed, noncommittal observations, after which another proposed a committee of three consisting of Mr. Meek and Mr. Pazant (and presumably Colonel Byng Hall), to consider the matter. Disappointed by the stalemate, Elizabeth confided her discouragement to her daily Chronicle. In retrospect she mused, "I should have said I would take my father's place": her father, the dreamer, doer, and public benefactor whose imagination and industry had called into existence rails, warehouses, libraries, water, and sanitary facilities.[36] Alas, she concluded, visionaries and activists were woefully absent in Canning; instead, the community seemed "stale, flat and unprofitable."[37]

Elizabeth, however, was more than a forthright, practical farmer and crusading anglophile engaged in local development projects. She was the subject of Frank Hector Thompkins's painting "Lady in the Pink Shawl" a sensitive, appreciative connoisseur of music, literature, theatre, art, and opera, a welcoming hostess, lively conversationalist, congenial housemate, and travelling companion. Elizabeth could also laugh at herself. She was especially amused by her recently hired housemaid Hazel, a "good looking strong strapping girl" who arrived for her interview "with sleeveless dress and silk stockings," clearly impressed by the social standing of her perspective employer but puzzled by the amount of time Elizabeth spent "receiving and talking to rough clad workers."[38]

Elizabeth professed to believe in a benevolent meritocracy, a community composed of honest, industrious citizens with "superior minds," public servants with social commitment and community leaders "giving out their best" for the common good, a world she contrasted with the idle "society people" and superficially "cultured ones."[39] But for all of Elizabeth's strictures she had no difficulty mixing appreciatively with the "cultured ones" or employing her talents to build, reform, and refine society. Elizabeth also aspired to the role of a literary activist, a writer of vigorous, "clean, wholesome," chivalric, patriotic, uplifting literature, in the vein of the Reverend Ralph Connor (1860–1937), the popular contemporary United Church minister and novelist.

In 1928 Elizabeth enrolled in a ten-assignment short story writing course with the Home Correspondence School in Springfield, Massachusetts, assignments for which she earned grades in the 90s. In her application to the Home Correspondence School, she cited "common sense, right values and acute observation" as a writer's most useful qualities, and association with the "best literature" and "superior minds" as a writer's most instructive educators. She noted her own sound grounding in English literature, her regular reading of the *Atlantic Monthly*, and her desire to write about ordinary people, the honest farmer, toiling fishermen, noble firemen "risking their lives," and "mothers going without to give their daughters better clothing," and about boxing apples and raising cows and pigs.[40] Although her rustic, romantic subjects resemble those of the contemporary "song fishermen of Nova Scotia,"[41] her records contain no reference to their writings or her associations with their authors.

Elizabeth's papers provide only one complete example of her literary endeavours, a story entitled "Speculative Investment," promoting vision, determination, family, and patriotism. Its hero, George Young, is a decisive young student athlete from Toronto, interested "not in the stock market but the market of ideas," who finds Canada "too fumbling, cautious and individual as a nation" and decides to lead by example. During a dutiful visit to his ill mother, George, who held ten silver cups for swimming competitions, decided to enter a distance swimming contest in California as a tribute to his mother and Canada. Although without money to finance his expensive journey, he "plunged forward as in a snowstorm." His mother and supportive friends listen in on a crackling radio to the subsequent tense, breathless report of his closely contested international competition, rewarded by George's predictable Canadian victory, his exemplary speculative "investment" a stinging rebuke to timid, selfish individualism a triumph of will and daring, his venture an affirmation of the collective values of family and nation. Elizabeth's Britannic nationalism, respect for history and tradition, and her sense of duty, public service, and commitment to nation-building were familiar themes among women of her time, place, and class,[42] as well as the themes of inspiring Methodist sermons of the time. Elizabeth loved good sermons and preachers, and often attended morning and evening services and took notes for discussion at Sunday dinner and evening fireside conversation.

But was Elizabeth a feminist? Her papers' silence on gender rights and discrimination, and her failure to claim a pioneering role as a "lady farmer," may be misleading.[43] Her reading of biographies of, and admiration for, bold, daring women, and her gender-neutral signature, "E.B. Hewitt, farmer," together with her ambiguous literary interests, cited in her application to the Home Correspondence School , suggest that she feared gender bias in the school's admission and subsequent evaluation of her writing.[44] If so, her knowledge of English literature and of contemporary women "who dared" might well have reinforced her apprehensions. But as Julia Bush has reminded us, contemporary feminism lacked a singular definition or expression.[45]

Whatever Elizabeth thought or felt, she lived a feminism that reflected her experience, values, and objectives: a "prudent," pragmatic, intra-gender lifestyle, validated by her family, church, and community, who accepted it as a prerogative of class or character. Elizabeth came from a succession of active, able, and versatile women, including her stepmother and maternal grandmother. Her family's commitment to higher education for women, her Methodist Church's increasing dependence on women to implement its social gospel and governance, her father's support of women's historical societies, officers' ranks for female nurses, and female rifle clubs and participation in the Strathcona Trust program of physical training,[46] suggest an elasticity and contingency of gender norms within her world. Then there was her marriage, based on respect and companionship, their shared love of travel, music, art, and nature, causes she pursued after her husband's death, with the publishing of his final manuscript and her chairing of the National Council of Women's Committee on Conservation.

A practising more than a professing feminist, Elizabeth's feminism was an ethic, defined by need and purpose, rather than an ideological straitjacket. She was interested in business, and upon her father's death, came to the family's council's post mortem with a complete list of her father's assets, ready and able to discuss the estate's settlement. She decided to become a scientific farmer and make farming a profitable endeavour. Despite postwar rear-guard institutional efforts to reaffirm gender roles, to "teach women to be women,"[47] Elizabeth rejected gender constraints. Meanwhile she remained free to enjoy music, art, literature, and travel, to make her own choices, and follow her own path, for which she possessed the will and material means.

Chapter Twenty-Five

Intersecting Lives

Lady Borden and Elizabeth's cohabitation provided companionship, complicity, and solidarity. Neither was disabled, destitute, or dependent. Both had personal resources, friends, and interests. Cohabitation, however, required accommodation and adjustments, sharing physical and social space, and balancing autonomy with interdependence. Occasionally different personal habits, "tedious" friends, dress, and personal opinions called for restraint and perspective. But generally, Lady Borden and Elizabeth lived supportive, intersecting lives, and were congenial travelling companions and partners in family, church, and community activities.

Lady Borden never expected Elizabeth or Maude to fill the void left by Sir Frederick's death. She had material and personal resources, her own friends, and broad interests. She read, corresponded, attended concerts and theatre (and later cinema). She entertained and travelled. An assiduous correspondent, she penned some fifty-five letters during three months of her five-month 1930–1 European tour to relatives, friends, and neighbours. Many of her correspondents were accomplished women such as Professor Edna Virginia Moffett,[1] Henrietta Britton,[2] Edith Brown,[3] Esther Brown,[4] Dr. Annie Carmelle Rondinella,[5] Kim Goodwin,[6] and Dr. Helen MacMurchy,[7] women with whom she discussed family, health, politics, religion, books, music, cinema, and travel, and whom she visited and entertained at Borden Place.

None of Lady Borden's correspondents was more prolific than Sir Frederick's cousin Mary Gertrude Grew, nee Brown (1863–1940), the widowed matron of Ottawa's influential Brown clan. Born in Wolfville, Mary was the daughter of Sir Frederick's maternal Uncle John Lothrop Brown. Upon her father's death and the failure of their large family farm, Mary, her recently married husband, Herbert Lincoln Grew, and her mother joined other family members in Boston in 1894. Upon

Herbert's death from tuberculosis on 30 December 1902, Mary, her three children, her sister Agnes, and their mother moved to Ottawa, where they rented a house, first at 648 Rideau Street, and then purchased one on Mann Street in Sandy Hill, not far from Stadacona Hall.[8] Mary and Lady Borden became close friends and when they were not both in Ottawa they corresponded. They wrote of health, family, politics, books, and music. Both were loyal supporters of Sir Wilfrid Laurier rather than "Rob," even during the divisive conscription crisis.[9]

In the late spring, summer, and early fall Lady Borden entertained local and out-of-town guests at Borden Place, often lunching at her large wicker table in her meticulously manicured garden. In the late autumn and early winter, she visited Ottawa, residing at her house at 15 Blackburn Avenue with her cook and two servants.[10] In Ottawa she dined with family and friends, including Mackenzie King, who invariably invited her to lunch, occasionally at his 231-hectare Kingsmere estate, where they discussed books, friends, and politics.[11] From time to time she sought King's advice or favour. He invited her to the August 1927 unveiling of the statue of Sir Wilfrid Laurier, and insisted she receive the 1935 George V Silver Jubilee Medal and the 1937 George VI Coronation Medal. At times, King even dreamed of Lady and Sir Frederick Borden, "Canada's best minister of Defence."[12] In Montreal she visited Isabel May Megarry, the widow of Jeffrey Hale Burland,[13] an entrepreneur, scientist, militia officer, and former friend of Sir Frederick, and the Roberts in Montreal or Beauharnois.

During the winter Lady Borden spent weeks in Atlantic City and/or Baltimore with fellow snowbirds, family, and friends. In the late 1920s she preferred Bermuda, Barbados, Jamaica, Saint Lucia, and Trinidad, accessible from Halifax since 1928 thanks to the Canadian National's RMS *Lady Hawkins* and *Lady Rodney*, fortnightly postal, passenger, and produce vessels. While she valued her independence, she often felt lonely and vulnerable, and welcomed Elizabeth's return to Canning to share and care for Borden Place. During the court case Lady Borden and Elizabeth apparently had decided to cohabit and develop their properties, an agreement that seemed to entail Elizabeth's oversight of her mother's Blomidon farm and Lady Borden's transfer of Borden Pace to Elizabeth, though the transfer did not occur until 17 October, 1932.[14] Lady Borden marked Elizabeth's return to Borden Place in 1926 by purchasing a new motor car: Elizabeth enjoyed driving, and Lady Borden enjoyed having a chauffeur.[15]

Cohabitation required adjustments, however, delineating physical and personal space and responsibilities. Lady Borden had scarcely repatriated her Ottawa possessions from 15 Blackburn when she had to find room in Borden Place for Elizabeth's furniture, books, pictures, and mementos. Borden Place's library had already reached its capacity, and shelves had to be installed on the second floor for Elizabeth's collection. (It was at this time that Lady Borden attempted to purge family papers.) Equally important was the assignment of supervisory responsibilities for household staff and outside workers. Borden Place summers rarely lacked guests, both family and friends. Some they shared, others they endured, and a few regulars who stayed for weeks.

Elizabeth appreciated Lady Borden's sense of decorum, her warmth and generosity, her gracious reception of relatives, friends, and acquaintances, and her formal public bearing. She understood her mother's introspective, fatalistic nature, her "addiction" to books, her affection for costume and fashion, her passion for culture and travel. She also recognized her mother's restlessness, her allergy to boredom, and her impulsive desire to break free on short notice to reserve a hotel room in Halifax, shop and see friends, or arrange a brief Caribbean vacation.

Lady Borden reciprocated Elizabeth's understanding. Together they hosted garden parties, dinners, church meetings, and volunteer societies. They shared friends, causes, and values, though sometimes Lady Borden found Elizabeth's friends "quite a bore," to be endured only because "Aunta" was "so anxious" that they visit. It was a small price to pay for their cohabitation.[16] Lady Borden respected, even if she did not always share, Elizabeth's forthright opinions, commitments, and engagements. More difficult to disguise was Lady Borden's disapproval of Elizabeth's dress and habits, an irritation that predated their cohabitation and grew over time and in close quarters. She appreciated Elizabeth's organizational and executive abilities, however, and her assistance in transforming her property into a lucrative asset that funded their extended travels. Lady Borden loved to travel, but age made her dependent on Elizabeth for her European ventures.

Although educational and recreational tourism were not mutually exclusive, Lady Borden and Elizabeth regarded travel to the American seaboard and the Caribbean as a commodity and social ritual, a pleasant, relatively sedentary winter or early spring opportunity to visit family and friends. European travel, however, was serious entertainment: informative, affirmative, and instrumental, a continuation of the "grand tour." It "stimulated thinking," and replenished social capital. It confirmed, refined, and challenged ethno-cultural identity, shaped social aspirations, and provided an opportunity to explore the quaint and exotic. Lady Borden and Elizabeth were especially committed to cultural tourism, a passion inspired by their books, well-worn atlas, religion, and empire.[17] Quite apart from exemplifying the virtues of co-habitation, Lady Borden and Elizabeth's travels reflect their character, perception, and interests, their sketchy diary providing voice to their experience.

Elizabeth had often visited Europe with her parents, and had joined them for two coronations, her anglophilia sustained by her happy marriage and English friends. But the Great War, the flu epidemic, and the family's unsettled estate had effectively prohibited transatlantic tourism, a seven-year drought that enhanced her Anglophilia. Elizabeth had managed to translate her 1921 English rescue mission into a vacation in Switzerland and Italy. Although Lady Borden had visited the American eastern seaboard alone or accompanied for years and would continue to do so, transatlantic travel was complex and daunting, and she had never undertaken it alone. Once the estate had been settled and she and Elizabeth had a sense of their finances, she lost little time embarking on a four-month European tour that entailed education, entertainment, and duty. Their itinerary included visits with Gordon's family in Macclesfield and with Maude and Rosamond in Paris.

It was snowing heavily on 5 January 1924 when Lady Borden and Elizabeth closed Borden Place to begin their circuitous journey to board the SS *Montcalm* in Saint John for Liverpool. They spent their first day with their Wolfville dressmaker, their first night in Kentville's comfortable Cornwallis Inn, and the next three nights at Halifax's Queen's Hotel before proceeding by rail to Digby and the ferry to Saint John where they boarded the *Montcalm*. It was still snowing, and the ship was covered with sleet as they left Saint John and headed into the Bay of Fundy's heavy swells. Lady Borden and Elizabeth were both ill for the next three days. Once they recovered and their ship entered calmer water, they found the Montcalm to be an attractive, steady vessel, with some interesting passengers aboard. Not least was Canada's 1924 Winter Olympic hockey team, the Toronto Granites, managed by William Abraham Hewitt (1875–1966), whose surname intrigued Elizabeth.

Europe had changed since Lady Borden's last visit in June 1912. Change was particularly noticeable in Britain, her principal reference. There, few of her well-placed British friends and acquaintances still occupied public offices. Nor had she claim to official hospitality or recognition. Nevertheless, expatriots and old London friends welcomed her, now as a private citizen and tourist, dependent on Elizabeth's agenda and interests, which generally she shared.

A poor sailor and chronically sensitive to cold, Lady Borden found January travel to England daunting. Before they left home, she and Elizabeth had decided to keep a joint travel diary which they maintained sporadically for this and subsequent European journeys. Since only one page of their 1924 travel diary has survived, information on their travel is confined largely to scattered alternate sources. Macclesfield was their first destination after disembarking in Liverpool. Gordon's niece's cordial reception and the sight of an attractive flower market along the route compensated for their damp, cold rail journey from the port.[18] Their next stop was London, which Lady Borden later described as "the most wonderful and satisfying city in the World." Booked at the Mead Hotel, she and Elizabeth undoubtedly spent their five-week sojourn in London shopping, visiting museums and friends, attending theatre and concerts, and dining at good restaurants, as they usually did in London. After London they spent three weeks in Paris with Maude (and Rosamond on weekends), dining together once or twice a day, sightseeing, and visiting Maude's favourite tailor shop. From Paris they travelled by rail to Rome and Pompeii. Their subsequent itinerary is unclear, but Lady Borden rarely went to Italy without visiting Florence. Returning to Britain via Paris in time to board the *Montcalm* at Liverpool, Lady Borden and Elizabeth arrived in Quebec on 23 May 1924.

The survival of a larger segment of Lady Borden and Elizabeth's joint travel diary provides voice and detail to their next four-month European expedition. Maude's persistent entreaties had finally prevailed, and Lady Borden and Elizabeth joined them in Paris in March 1928, after a chilly month in Britain. Unable to leave her farm during the summer or fall, Elizabeth and her mother and their nine pieces of luggage had boarded the SS *Arabia* in Halifax on 29 January 1928, again in sub-zero temperatures and blowing snow. On both occasions their vessel was "completely covered" with ice and snow. Originating in New York, the *Arabia* was bound for Plymouth, Southampton, Antwerp, and Cherbourg. Coincidentally, their vessel again carried Canada's Olympic team under William Hewitt's supervision. A large noisy dockside crowd, including many "bellowing varsity boys," cheered the Olympic team as it left the Halifax pier.

Aboard the vessel's messy, disorganized, overheated quarters things were less cheerful. Lady Borden and Elizabeth's discomfort was compounded by its New York staff's mistaken assignment of their cabin to a "demented woman," being deported from the United States, who refused to move until security agents escorted her ashore at Southampton. And it was not until the ship's Halifax departure at 5 pm that they were reassignmed to a large, overheated cabin with two windows. Things improved as the vessel found calmer waters, and "balmier" weather. While Lady Borden nursed her usual initial headaches and nausea, Elizabeth explored the ship and met many of its passengers.

Among her finds was Margaret O'Bannon Vandercook (1877–1958), an American woman her own age and author of patriotic girl guide, campfire, and ranch stories, a literary fiction that Elizabeth appreciated, and a Mr. Rogers, a PEI silver fox farmer who knew her father.

After an otherwise uneventful voyage, Lady Borden and Elizabeth disembarked at Plymouth very early Sunday morning on 29 January, plodded sleepily through the port's official reception before securing a taxi to their chilly bedrooms in the well-appointed Duke of Cornwall Hotel. While Lady Borden recovered in her frigid room, Elizabeth climbed the winding footpath to the cliffs of Plymouth Hoe, which reminded her of Quebec City's terrace, to view the ships moored in the city's impressive harbour. Still curious, she stopped by the fifteenth-century St. Andrew's Church, where she was kept awake by the minister's Ezekiel-inspired sermon on "deception."

The next day a restored Lady Borden retraced Elizabeth's steps to Plymouth Hoe, walking and resting in the wind shelters, enjoying the sunny weather, the birds, trees, flowering shrubs, "delicious air," and splendid view of the harbour, full of vessels, including warships that she identified by name. Enchanted by Plymouth, they decided to stay for a week or more if they could find warmer, cheaper accommodations. Upon the advice of a lady at the Marigold Tea Shop Elizabeth found a tiny third-floor sitting room with a fireplace and two adjacent bedrooms, which became their Plymouth headquarter for two weeks. While their new quarters permitted them to "poke their own fire," their beds were so "awful" and the rooms so "frigid" that Lady Borden moved to a first-floor bedroom with an electric heater, leaving Elizabeth to the cold mercies of the third floor. "Funny," Lady Borden mused in their journal, "when the English know so much, they do not know how to make a room comfortable."[19]

During their next two weeks Lady Borden and Elizabeth organized day trips to several Devon and Cornish towns, Dartmoor, Tavistock, Looe, Polperro, and Torquay, all within a 20–45 kilometre distance from Plymouth and accessible by train or bus, and full of historical, literary, cultural, and topographical attractions. They associated Dartmoor with Conan Doyle's *Hound of the Baskervilles*, Tavistock with Sir Francis Drake (whose statute they had admired on Plymouth Hoe), Polperro with the Knights Templar, and Torquay with the Interlaken, one of their favourite Swiss resorts – a veritable "Riviera without the Alps." All rewarded their search for the ancient, quaint, and scenic ivy-covered stone walls, the romantic ruins, the narrow winding streets and tiny houses. So enchanted were they that Lady Borden urged Elizabeth to write a travel book on Cornwall and Devon's charms. They were no less enthralled by the Plymouth repertoire theatre's productions of *A Man of No Importance, The Unfair Sex,* and *Madya,* whose "actors were artists," and whose productions possessed "hardly a weak spot." It was all so enjoyable that Lady Borden would have remained longer except for her fear of the cold.

Lady Borden and Elizabeth's month in London confirmed the benefits of travelling together. Lady Borden's previous official London visits had been guided by staff and ordered by public business, its hosts' agendas, and social obligations. In those days she had tried to reserve time for personal interests. As a private citizen, she was now free to explore London's world of theatre, concerts, restaurants, and historical sites, a rich but confusing menu. Fortunately, Elizabeth could negotiate London with confidence. Together they visited historic houses, including those formerly inhabited by Thomas Carlyle (1795–1881), Henry James (1843–1916), and James Whistler (1834–1903), and the treasures of the "splendid" Victoria and Albert Museum. Elizabeth also organized an interesting but exhausting day at the British Industrial Fair.

Although the Mead Hotel provided comfortable beds at "a good price," the hotel's food was "unobjectionable" at best, but that could be remedied. Lady Borden and Elizabeth loved food, especially English food with its beef, fish, meat pies, cheeses, and puddings. Determined to better their hotel's offerings, they dined several times at Simpson's on the Strand, the fashionable restaurant with its Sherlock Holmes association, and Ye Olde Cheshire Cheese, purportedly frequented by Dr. Johnson. While Johnson may never have visited the pub, other literary figures had, notably their family favourite, Charles Dickens. Another favourite restaurant was the Bird in Hand, with its sawdust floors, dark oak panelling, timbered ceilings, old prints, and "fine old-world air" (so old that it admitted women only since 1916); there they enjoyed its renowned "fish ordinaire." Impressed by the Bird in Hand and its staged ritual charm, Elizabeth later hosted a lunch there to thank their dear London friends with a "fish fete," replete with ceremony, speeches, and songs. Altogether Elizabeth proved a "busy conductor" and Lady Borden a willing accomplice, ready to explore "many interesting new places."

Theatre ranked high on their agenda. The *Dancer* was strongly recommended by a London friend, but Lady Borden and Elizabeth found it "clever but not altogether desirable." The Haymarket's production of Eden and Adelaide Phillpotts's *Yellow Sands,* which dealt with matters of inheritance, appealed more to their social liberalism and Methodist conscience. They agreed with the author's contention that turning a "fortune into a common fund" was unrealistic. There was so much else, they reasoned, that was "so sweet and sensible and good we can do individually, in smaller ways," a succinct definition of their pragmatic social philosophy of personal duty and responsibility.

Dependent as Lady Borden was on Elizabeth, she could still manage alone if necessary, and occasionally they went their own way. When Elizabeth accompanied her friends, Mr. and Mrs. Kitty March, to York to visit their son's school, Lady Borden ventured out alone on her first day and boarded a bus to Kensington intending to shop at Liberty's and Dickins & Jones on Regent Street, forgetting that the shops were closed on Saturday, a disappointment that spared her the "temptation to spend & spend & spend." Instead, she wandered about Kensington Park, a sentimental ramble to remind her "of other days." The next day she attended church and visited an ailing friend, shivvering beside a fire that "one could put in a teacup."

Lady Borden and Elizabeth were fascinated by scientific and technological advances and regarded cinema and radio as forms of public education, a means to appreciate contemporary British politics and society. Dedicated monarchists, they could not resist listening in to a radio broadcast of a speech by the Prince of Wales on an unspecified subject. Lady Borden, her royalist sentiments notwithstanding, had lost none of her shrewd, critical powers. Her assessment of the Prince of Wales was as trenchant as it was prescient: he possessed "neither a good voice nor ideas worth thinking of."[20]

Once Lady Borden and Elizabeth's month-long London residence ended, a smooth Channel crossing and rail journey to Paris on 2 March brought an emotional reunion with Maude and Rosamond who escorted them to their comfortable Hotel Cecelia at 11, avenue Mac-Mahon, close to the Arc de Triomphe. Rosamond was now almost twenty-one, an attractive, sophisticated young lady, the affectionate focus of her grandmother and Aunta. Fortuitously, a day before they met for lunch, Rosamond had received her invitation to exhibit at the Société Nationale des Beaux-Arts' May Salon des Tuileries. Her Granny and Aunta's excitement and celebration were difficult to contain. Lady Borden and Elizabeth's remaining three weeks in Paris passed quickly with shopping, dress-fitting, and dining.

Then on 22 March Grace and Allison Borden met Lady Borden and Elizabeth at Monaco's rail station and accompanied them for the next two weeks. Together they basked in Monaco's warmth, gardens, and rockeries, explored by motorcar the area's "snow-capped mountain peaks," fertile valleys, and olive orchards, and visited Arles's Roman amphitheatre, baths, and old churches, and Avignon's famous "Pont," cathedral, and palace of the pope, with its splendid glass and tapestries. Then on Easter Monday, 8 April, they left by rail for Genoa, an evening stopover on their way to Florence, their journey a "perfectly wonderful" panorama of sun, mountains, and "sparkling blue sea." Unfortunately, their next night's expensive Florence hotel offered only one room, which they were obliged to share.

Little, however, could spoil Lady Borden's week in Florence's "dream world" of galleries and churches, where "every crevice was full of interest." To add to their pleasure, Maude and Rosamond joined them for the week, and the four women spent their days in galleries, churches, and restaurants, "trying to realize the past of this old city." Two years later, while preparing for another visit to Italy, Lady Borden recalled that the highlight of their 1928 visit to Florence had been Santa Maria Novella, "too beautiful for words with its cloister behind and gardens."[21] Reluctantly taking their leave of Florence, they visited Rome and Pompeii. In returning to Paris, they stopped for four or five days at Montreux, overlooking the French Alps, where they enjoyed the "most beautiful" scenery "ever seen," In Paris they retrieved their tailor shop purchases before returning to London, where they remained for a month, then boarded the Red Star's SS *Pennland* at Southampton, arriving in Halifax in early June.

Even before Lady Borden and Elizabeth reached Halifax, they began planning their return to Italy. Lady Borden adored London and valued her British heritage, but unlike many English Canadian tourists that heritage was grounded in Western Europe's classical, medieval, and Renaissance art and culture, free from discernable Protestant prejudice.[22] Next time, they resolved to avoid the cold, damp English winter, and begin their tour in Sicily. Inspired by Maude and Rosamond's 1927 Sicilian tour, Lady Borden and Elizabeth knew what they wanted to see, how they wanted to travel, and with whom. Since they had enjoyed their time with Allison and Grace in Monaco in 1928, they agreed to meet them in Palermo in early 1931 and tour Sicily together, coordinating and sharing travel arrangements and expenses.

Lady Borden and Elizabeth's planning continued despite the 1929 stock market crash that heralded the Great Depression. Fortunately, their healthy farm income had cushioned the market's toll on their securities. During the early 1930s Annapolis Valley apple orchards were at peak production. Farm labour was cheap and plentiful, transatlantic freight rates were low, and two successive years of early frosts in Ontario and Quebec gave Annapolis Valley's apple producers unrivalled access to the British market. For the favoured few with personal income, glossy journals, such the *Canadian Homes and Gardens,* advertised cheap, comfortable travel to attractive destinations. Lady Borden and

Elizabeth's 1930–1 itinerary followed a route familiar to the affluent, through Sicily, along the Amalfi coast to Naples, Pompeii, Rome, and Florence,[23] the length of their tour, five and a half months, was comparable to that of other prosperous Canadian tourists.[24]

On 1 December 1930, Lady Borden and Elizabeth were in Boston aboard the SS *Patria*, bound for Marseille. Although the "French food" aboard their transatlantic liner was not to their taste (what they meant by French food is not clear), their quarters were comfortable, the vessel uncrowded, and the passengers pleasant and interesting. Among their number were a well-travelled Miss Mussel and Anne Coleman (Watts) Ladd (1878–1939), an American sculptor and writer, travelling with her two Vassar-educated daughters, with whom Lady Borden and Elizabeth established a lively travel friendship. Observant, curious tourists, Lady Borden and Elizabeth used the *Patria*'s day-long stop at Lisbon for a rapid taxi tour of the "up to date" city, its cathedral, museums, and experimental station, long enough for Lady Borden both to admire the priest's "gorgeous" vestments with a "skirt of priceless lace and coat of brocaded satin" and contrast it with the city's impoverished men, women, and beggars, old and young.

Geopolitics interested Lady Borden. And as the *Patria* entered the Mediterranean, she scanned its shorelines, contrasting the lush, green, gentle coast of Africa with the barren rocky shores of Portugal and Spain. Reminded by her tour book of Horatio Nelson (1758–1805) as they passed Trafalgar, she assessed the strategic importance of Gibraltar, that "great old giant of the sea," commanding the western entrance to the Mediterranean as the Suez Canal did the east. Contemporary politics interested her too, notably the "revolution in Spain," which she worried might spill over into Italy and affect their visit to Italy, obvious concerns from an affluent, sheltered tourist's perspective.

After a fierce two-day thunder and lightning storm and the heaviest sea they had encountered, Lady Borden and Elizabeth disembarked at Palermo on 19 December 1930 and registered at their comfortable hotel. Still shaken by the storm, Lady Borden retired to her room to recover while Elizabeth, Mrs. Ladd, and her daughters examined Monreale's Norman cathedral. By noon Lady Borden had recovered sufficiently to join Miss Mussel for an afternoon visit to the Villa Giulia's adjacent park and gardens.

Lady Borden and Elizabeth wasted little time in Palermo awaiting Allison and Grace. Early the next day she and Elizabeth retraced Elizabeth's steps to the Monreale cathedral, where everything appeared as Lady Borden's guidebook promised: the cathedral "one of the finest I have seen," its architecture, carvings, and mosaics "considered for design and symmetry about as grand examples as there are," and its wall paintings of "biblical stories ... from the creation to the time of Paul." At noon they lunched in the "beautiful garden of the monks," and in the late afternoon visited a few shops. In the evening they crowded into a "horridly little hall," with a "minute stage and hand organ" to view a puppet show they considered "unique, amazing & really artistic." Neither understood the dialogue but guessed that it was a morality tale of a disguised Satan's capture of a woman; their theatre venture was but one example of their curiosity, stamina, sense of adventure, and search for the exotic, and their readiness to stray beyond the tour book's safe recommendations.

Undaunted by the previous day's rigorous demands, Lady Borden, Elizabeth, and Miss Mussel rose early the next morning to visit an unspecified museum and the Byzantine Cappella Palatina, with its Moorish-style ceiling and golden mosaics. Their visit to the chapel of the Norman kings of Sicily was made even more memorable by Sunday mass with "tall priests in their gorgeous vestments." In the afternoon, the three ladies were chauffeured to Santa Maria di Gesù, "perched on the side of one of the many mountainous peeks," about ten kilometres outside Palermo. Although the steep climb to an observatory offered a spectacular view of the surrounding countryside, Lady Borden remained in the safe custody of three boys while a monk guided Elizabeth and Miss Mussel to the next level, Lady Borden's exhaustion understandable for a sixty-six-year-old lady.

Upon Allison and Grace's arrival, Elizabeth and Allison visited Thomas Cook's to arrange travel and accommodations for their four-day motor tour of Sicily. Furnished with a car, driver, and tour book, they drove to Agrigento, Syracuse, and Catania, with day trips to Etna and Taormina, "drinking in the atmosphere of the old world," represented by its ruins, churches, temples, amphitheatres, museums, and gardens. Lady Borden was "transfixed" by the ingenuity, craftsmanship, artistry, and longevity of Sicily's cross-cultural architectural heritage, spectacular natural beauty, "gorgeous sunrises as if Heaven was opening her gates." She was equally fascinated by its village life and the resourcefulness of its people.

Lady Borden retained eight vivid memories of Sicily and its people, viewed through her tour car's window, guidebook, and idyllic perspective. She likened the island's mountainous topography to that of Colorado and marvelled at its soil skilfully tilled up to the top of the hills and mountains, using "ancient methods." She noted the women washing clothes on the banks of the rivers, and drying them "on every hill, wall or boulder." She remarked on the great flocks of sheep on hills or herded along roads by "shepherds in capes and hoods, with fine dogs," the men robed in shawls and gay scarves tied over their ears and long flowing capes and pointed hoods, a reflection of their "Arab ancestry." She admired the men's chair-work and the women's needlework, the artisans seated in front of houses on narrow streets, while droves of goats passed in front of houses in the early morning, pausing briefly as men held the goats while the women milked. Overall, she was impressed by the people's politeness, cheerfulness, and continuous work, the women carrying water on their heads, up steep mountains and the men making, playing, and selling pipes. From Lady Borden's romantic perspective old people were happy, children were beautiful, the women possessed "fine classical" Greek or Roman faces, and the young men and boys were handsome. Although she detected "squalor," she admired the community's ability to live "entirely on their country's products rather than buying outside."[25]

Allison and Grace left Lady Borden and Elizabeth in Catania and travelled to Naples, agreeing to rejoin them in Rome. During Lady Borden and Elizabeth's next two weeks (29 December–14 January) they explored Catania, that "heavenly spot," and adjacent sites, entertained by its small expatriate community, headed by the 5th Duke of Bronte (Alexander Nelson Hood), a British Conservative politician who had inherited Horatio Nelson's Sicilian dukedom. The duke invited Lady Borden and Elizabeth to his refurbished estate in Taormina. Otherwise the community's Church of England "padre" became their tour guide. First he brought them to his church, where he played its seventeenth-century organ, then to the tearoom, where they watched "ordinary people dance" to a "terrifically loud" brass jazz band, then back to his church to hear a children's choir and visit an antique shop. As a courtesy, the next Sunday they attended the padre's "simple" church service. Their hotel, though relatively empty, housed various well-heeled guests (including a Mrs. Steedman, whose daughter had gone to school in Paris with Gwendolyn Borden), who joined Lady Borden and Elizabeth for visits to Catania's tea rooms, restaurants, chapels, cloisters, and gardens.[26]

Unfortunately, Elizabeth became ill on the second day of their Sicilian motor tour, after visiting Agrigento's spectacular Valley of Temples, her illness reversing their roles as Lady Borden monitored Elizabeth's health. Elizabeth had arrived in Catania suffering from a cold, vomiting, and a fever that plagued her for much of her Italian tour. Typically, she soldiered on, not wanting to miss any site or adventure, above all their day trips to Etna, that "cruel looking monster ready to hurl its stone muscles & red-hot land at its adversaries," and Taormina's narrow streets and beautifully situated amphitheatre, commanding the best view of Etna in the world. Equally intrepid, Lady Borden navigated the steep, rocky, path to the Greek Teatro Antico, rewarded by its having met her "every expectation" and "that was saying much."[27]

On 14 January Lady Borden and Elizabeth enjoyed a ceremonious departure from their hotel. The padre, their English friends, and the hotel manager gathered to wish them Godspeed, a safe voyage and return, unlike "in our country," Lady Borden noted, "where we pay the bill to the clerk and slink out as though we were an 'alechee' [alcoholic] being forced out." In contrast to their ceremonial departure, their journey along the rough rail bed to the Strait of Messina proved an ordeal, their tiny sleeper room exposed to toxic fumes as they passed through endless tunnels. At Messina, their train boarded a ferry for Cara, where they were confined to their train until an English gentleman negotiated their release and helped them to rescue their bags at Cara, where they had been thrown off the train "in a heap." Fortunately, their Cook's chauffeur met them with a comfortable car and drove them thirty miles along roads "cut from the side of the mountain overlooking the sea" to Amalfi, the Campagna resort town popular with British aristocracy; there they lodged at the "charming" new San Caterina Hotel and enjoyed excellent food and accommodation.

From their comfortable Amalfi quarters, Lady Borden and Elizabeth admired the turquoise seascape, explored the town's cathedral and gardens, and made short day trips to Naples' Stazione Zoologica and various archeological sites of Greek temples, and where they were scandalized by the contemporary "sacrilege" of removing pillars and artifacts. After three days they exchanged Amalfi's beauty and comfort for Pompeii's rich historical heritage, which they had so enjoyed in 1928. On their way to Pompeii the next day, their Cook's car stopped briefly at Sorrento to visit a wooden box and shawl embroidery factory. They then picnicked by the roadside before reaching the "ancient and once buried city" with its museum, murals, and "extraordinarily clever mythological pictures, sculptures, and tapestries, which elicited "the same thrill" for Lady Borden as she had "felt in 1928."[28]

On 21 January Lady Borden and Elizabeth dressed warmly, prepared to brave Rome's rumoured cold, resolved to return to Amalfi if Rome's weather became unbearable. Allison, Grace, and their niece met them at the Cook's office in Rome and brought them to their dark, cool room in the Hotel Milton; Lady Borden immediately checked the hotel's heating pipes to confirm its promised central heating. Upon Allison, Grace, and their niece's departure a week later, Lady Borden and Elizabeth occupied their brighter, more comfortable rooms with their "superb view of the park and city and seven hills," remaining there for a month.

Elizabeth's "protracted sickness" – better one day and in bed the next – shaped their itinerary.[29] On good days they toured familiar sites, occasionally renting a car and driver but eventually using Rome's "funny little horse buses." Literary, historical, and artistic interests dictated their first days' visits: the Spanish Steps, with its John Keats and Percy Bysshe Shelley associations; the Piazza del Popolo, ancient Rome's northern gateway; and Santa Maria del Popolo, with its Michelangelo Merisi da Caravaggio (c.1571–1610) canvases; ending with an English tea. On other days they visited the Colosseum, the Trevi Fountain, the Terrazza del Pincio, the ruins of the Temple of Vesta, the Quirinal Palace, and the basilicas of St. Peter and St. Paul. Occasionally they simply took "a car ride all around the city." Lady Borden's most sensational Roman memory was the Casino dell' Aurora's *Aurora,* by Guido Remi (1575–1642). While viewing the ceiling painting, she felt as though she were "floating along toward the sun with the beautiful maidens."[30] Although she found Rome "so much cleaner" and its buildings, monuments, and parks more "beautified" than she remembered twenty-five years ago, it still took "imagination to people it as Roman history does."[31] Absent from Lady Borden's account of their visit is any comment on the country's contemporary political context.

On days when Elizabeth felt too ill to tour, Lady Borden took short walks or found other companions. One day she and Miss Mussel, who followed them to Rome, visited the panoramic Janiculum Hill, the reputed site of St Peter's crucifixion. On another day, she and "a nice Miss Ralston" took a horse bus to the rag market, where they found "wonderful things if one came to buy ... selling for half price ... "and not rags by any means." [32] Terrified of the cold, Lady Borden avoided church interiors. Her exception was the old-fashioned Presbyterian church, where she and Elizabeth crowded close to the stove. Its minister, the Reverend Dr. Mackinnon, the brother of Dr. Clarence Daniel Mackinnon, the principal of Pine Hill Divinity College in Halifax, recognized her at once, invited them to tea, and gave them tickets to a lecture on art history.

Increasingly alarmed by Elizabeth's persistently high temperature, Lady Borden decided to act. On Elizabeth's off-days Lady Borden had stayed "pretty close to home," except to "walk to and from the drug store." Lady Borden herself "had developed a cold" for a day or two and had "felt too sick to rise." But she had recovered; Elizabeth had not. Something was wrong, especially after Elizabeth kept to her bed for an entire week. Elizabeth must see an "English doctor." Whatever

Elizabeth's ailment or however efficacious the English doctor's remedy of rest, castor oil, and a liquid diet was, Elizabeth recovered sufficiently to enjoy their last days in Rome before leaving for Florence.[33] The termination of Lady Borden's travel diary in Rome drew a curtain on her and Elizabeth's continuing European itinerary. Perhaps its route and routine were too familiar to record. Given their affection for the Côte d'Azur and the Interlaken, after Florence they are likely to have gone to either, and possibly both, before spending their last month and more in London, and then leaving Southampton on 17 May 1931 for home.

Lady Borden and Elizabeth's five-month Italian tour was Lady Borden's farewell to Europe. Pleasant as it had been, it had been long and strenuous. Elizabeth continued to visit England to check on "dishonest brokers," see friends, visit museums, and attend concerts. But Lady Borden was now sixty-seven, and given her age and location, the Caribbean offered a more convenient escape from cold and boredom, a voyage she could manage without Elizabeth, where she might join friends and acquaintances in the late winter or early spring. In 1937 she went to Bermuda, and in 1938 to Trinidad. By then, Maude and Rosamond's return provided another dimension to her life.

Chapter Twenty-Six

Reconciliation

Improved family finances and marital harmony relieved the worries and tensions that had plagued Maude's years abroad. The family's healthy farm income, land sales, profitable securities, and Leslie's inheritance[1] enabled her and Rosamond to return to a flourishing farm and to enjoy an active, comfortable life in Canning and Ottawa. They were able reoccupy Gables, reactivate their Ottawa social life, employ a maid, and vacation in Europe and the Caribbean. Improved finances even permitted Rosamond to resume her art studies in Europe.[2]

Aging and illness, however, began to take a toll. Maude's deteriorating health, her stomach, back, and leg problems, immobilized her for long periods of time. And Leslie's severe rheumatism, lumbago, lameness, and pain in his right leg and foot, a legacy of his 1911 accident, required medication and periodic hospitalization. Leslie was more relaxed and less driven, however, and more ready to vacation and participate in Canning's and Ottawa's political and social life. And, he had every reason to be content with his success as a "dirt farmer," as he jokingly referred to his thriving apple business.

In 1924 Lady Borden's friends had worried that Leslie's return to his farms would make things unpleasant.[3] And, initially relations were frosty. But Leslie's marketing strategies, material success, and Maude's return softened the resentment and bitterness caused by the trial,[4] though the relationship between Leslie and his in-laws never returned to one of unqualified trust. Leslie continued to address his mother-in-law as Lady Borden, never "dearest mother," as Gordon had done. And Elizabeth remained "Mrs. Hewitt." Leslie treated Lady Borden with deference and Elizabeth with caution. Lady Borden sent Leslie Christmas but not birthday gifts. Elizabeth exchanged Christmas and birthday gifts with Maude and Rosamond, but not with Leslie.

Since Maude's and Leslie's securities and Bell Hill Farm provided the family's principal revenue, Canning became the focus of their lives. Maude marked her return to Canning in 1928 by donating a building and land on the south side of Main Street to the Scotia No. 28 Ancient, Free and Accepted Masons, on the condition that the Women's Institute and the Literary Society continue to meet in their hall, and its premises never be used for political, sectarian, or commercial purposes.[5] The family's farms employed three or four regular farm workers and a fluctuating number of seasonal and day workers, quelling any rumours of the family's disintegration. Maude, Leslie, and Rosamond's re-engagement in the town's economic and associational life confirmed their return to their roots, without renouncing their national standing and aspirations.

Gables reaffirmed their national standing. There they spent the late autumn and winter, or as occasion required, in its larger residence, where they could participate in Ottawa's more active social season.[6] Family finances enabled Leslie and Maude to retrieve their furniture and books from storage, and repair, redecorate, and landscape Gables, working closely with Sir Robert Borden on their adjoining properties.[7] Improved family finances also funded their renewed social life of teas, dinners, dances, and recreational and civic activities. Leslie conducted business from his Ottawa residence, confined largely to old clients, relatives, and friends. Robert Borden purchased insurance from Leslie, and faithful corporate clients such as the Railway Passenger Assurance Company and the Furness-Withy Shipping Company retained his agency.[8] Leslie's languid Ottawa business left him more time for civic activities, especially the vice-regally patronized Horticultural Society's annual garden competition, whose reports often mentioned his lawns and gardens.

Once Gables' restorations were complete, in March 1930 Maude and Leslie announced their Ottawa return with a "smart house dance" in honour of Rosamond and Miss Betty Behan's visit from New York, an event widely reported in the *Ottawa Evening Journal*.[9] In Ottawa Rosamond resumed her friendship with Roma Vals Gilmour, Sue Houston, Lucy Crowdy, Norah (Rosamond) Hughes, and Gwen (Borden) Blair.[10] She attended films[11]theatre,[12]concerts, bridge parties, and dinner dances. She skied with Vals Gilmour at the newly opened Lac Lucerne ski resort, as interested in its male skiers as its slopes.[13] When her parents were not in residence, she stayed next door with Sir Robert Borden.[14] Encouraged by her cousin Gwen (Borden) Blair, Rosamond joined the Twentieth Century Liberal Women's Association's Council, an organization designed to draw women into politics, an association promoted by Mackenzie King and populated by daughters and granddaughters of serving and past senators and cabinet ministers. Although Rosamond did not abandon her art, she does not appear to have corresponded with contemporary Canadian sculptors; nor is there evidence that she joined the Women's Art Association in Ottawa or the newly (1928) founded, Toronto-based, Sculptor's Society of Canada or participated in its controversies and exhibitions in Montreal or Ottawa, her apparent non-involvement, attributable, perhaps, to her unsettled residence, active social life, and longing to return to Europe.

Rosamond had left Paris with a heavy heart, uncertain when she might return. But scarcely a year after her return she was back in Europe with her parents on an apple-marketing trip to the United Kingdom, registered at London's comfortable Cumberland Hotel, enjoying the city's cultural offerings, reconnecting with her London friends, and visiting her Irish relatives in Belfast. She even persuaded her parents to include a side trip to Paris and return to Canada via Cherbourg. During the winters she joined her parents' annual pilgrimages to the Caribbean, principally Bermuda and Jamaica. Pleasant as the Caribbean might be, it was not Europe.

During her 1929 London visit, Rosamond looked up her school friend Betsy Greenhill, and invited her to Bell Hill Farm the next summer, a three-week venture the distinguished artist recalled as a memorable occasion. The highlight of Betsy's 1930s late summer Canning visit was Rosamond's family's "large orchard" at harvest time, where she joined "teams of women ... picking and packing apples ... working ten hours a day." And much to Greenhill's delight and surprise, after two weeks of exhausting labour, Rosamond's father handed her and Rosamond "a substantial cheque," a windfall they put to good use during a ten-day trip to New York prior to Betsy's departure, where they looked up friends, "saw about six plays," and dined at a speakeasy, because it served "the best food in the city."[15]

Betsy's visit fired Rosamond's desire to continue her artistic studies in Europe. And in 1936 family finances permitted Rosamond's return for a six-month practicum in Brussels. In December 1936, notwithstanding his car's malfunctioning defrosting mechanism, Leslie drove Rosamond to Halifax, where she and Sheila Poulis boarded the *Westernland*, a German passenger ship, owned by the Red Star Bernstein line, destined for Antwerp. In 1930 the Red Star had converted from freight to passenger service, offering its clients reasonably priced tourist-class fares. Originating in New York, the *Westernland* boarded passengers in Boston before sailing to Halifax. Among its passengers was "a large consignment of 'German-Jews" who had found work in the United States and were returning home "to fetch their wives and children." Although the ship was plagued by cockroaches and unkept bathrooms, its drinks were cheap and once Rosamond recovered from a two-day cold and sore throat, she and Sheila had a wonderful time. Each day they awoke near noon, dressed for dinner, and danced well into the night, the unaccompanied Germans being fond of music and "good dancers." Rosamond had such a wonderful time that she reported speaking "broken English" at the end of the voyage.[16]

During their transatlantic crossing Rosamond became the centre of a curious intrigue after she found an anti-Jewish pamphlet in the centre of a cardboard toilet roll, addressed to the ship's crew and staff. She hid the pamphlet in her cabin until she could speak to a "nice Jewish doctor" who had given a delightful concert the previous afternoon. The doctor shared her concern and swore her to secrecy until he could call a meeting in Sheila's cabin of "all the Jews" and a "nice Englishman." There the doctor translated the pamphlet "in very bad English." Apart from the pamphlet's "funny illustrations" and "lurid looking figures" Rosamond found little of interest in the pamphlet except mention of their vessel. Rosamond later learned that several months prior the captain had found similar pamphlets in his ship and had all the cabins searched and the pamphlets burned, dismissing them as "French toilet paper." Rosamond speculated that the captain had the *Westernland* searched before they boarded and had all the offensive material burned, except for the pamphlet she had found and had somehow escaped discovery,[17] an ominous incident that foreshadowed her European venture. [18]

Rosamond was now twenty-nine. Although she had lived a sheltered life, she was capable of managing her resources and negotiating her needs and objectives. She was organized and well-prepared and knew and liked Brussels. She knew where she wanted to live and the artists with whom she might work. She and Sheila would board at Mlle Givern's familiar guest house on 96, rue Souveraine (previously located on 54, rue de la Longue Haie), a residence that housed some twenty female temporary and long-term guests who formed a curious, eccentric community who respected each other's privacy, traded information, enjoyed tea parties, and played bridge.[19]

Choosing a mentor required skilful negotiation. Rosamond and Sheila considered three possibilities: Mrs. W. Beekmann, Egide Rombaux (1865–1942), and Marnix D'Havelosse (1885–1973). Since Mrs. Beekmann was too expensive, and they disliked Rombaux's symbolist work, their preference was D'Haveloose, the professor and director of the Brussels Art Academy. A sculptor and painter, D'Haveloose had spent his war years in Britain, where he retained many admirers. His studio was in his home on 210, rue du Trone, a short walk from Mlle Givern's guest house, and his posted fees were half those of Mrs. W. Beekmann.

As soon as Rosamond and Sheila secured bank accounts, police photos, and identity cards, they went "shaking" in their shoes to request admission to D'Havelosse's studio. A warm, talkative artist, D'Havelosse welcomed them to his studio, packed with his own work, which he praised for over half an hour before "talking business." He warned them that he permitted only ten to twelve "good students" to his studio and would require photos of their work before admitting them. Rosamond and Sheila returned promptly the next day with photos to await his decision.

After examining their photos D'Havelosse agreed to their admission, announced his fees, their workplace, and schedule. Rosamond and Sheila were delighted with his acceptance but regretted their inability to pay his fees and the necessity of finding another mentor. Their tactic worked, and after much humming and hawing D'Haveloose, accustomed to titled English matrons and "rich old American women,"[20] reduced his monthly fee from 500 to 400 francs, on the condition they tell none of his other students. Fresh from that victory, Rosamond and Sheila secured a comparable "confidential" fee reduction from their studio model, 15 rather than 17 francs per month, shared among four students.

Rosamond liked D'Haveloose's work. His style was less classical than that of Émile-Antoine Bourdelle and "not so strong." She shared D'Haveloose's fascination with movement, inspired by the acclaimed dancer, Isadora Duncan (1877–1927), though Rosamond feared she might have difficulty adapting to his smoother, fluid lines when she began "cutting into clay a la Bourdelle."[21] While D'Haveloose boasted of his insistence that students "work out things for themselves," he urged Rosamond to erase Bourdelle's classical influences, and with some success. Overall, she found D'Haveloose a "good sort" with a "marvellous disposition," who talked and joked unceasingly and complimented her on her very "good construction."[22]

Impressed by D'Haveloose's insistence on the interplay of sculpture, dance, music, and film, Rosamond and Shelia assembled an impressive cultural agenda. Soon after their arrival they procured tickets for a performance of a ballet by Kurt Jooss (1901–1979). Jooss had gained some notoriety for his clash with the Nazi authorities, resulting in his flight to England.[23] They also acquired tickets for performances of the Ballets Russes,[24] the Polish pianist Ignacy Jan Paderewski (1860–1941), the Austrian-American violinist Fritz Kreisler (1875–1962), Richard Wagner's *Tannhauser* (sung in French), La Scala's version of Giacomo Puccini's *La Boheme*, and Giuseppe Verdi's *La Traviata*. Sheila's limited French excluded theatre, except for an English travelling company's production of *Romeo and Juliet*. Both, however, enjoyed contemporary French silent films such as *La Rosière des Halles* (which Maude had seen in Hull/Gatineau) and *Les Demi-Vierges*. In recommending *Les Demi-Vierges* to her mother and Granny, Rosamond regretted that the film was not as exciting as it sounded, simply "lots of drinking and kissing and dresses falling off shoulders."[25] They saw the American films *My Man Godfrey* and *The Garden of Allah* (accessible in English) , and *Ninth Symphony*, an Austrian silent film. The Cathedral of St. Michael and St. Gudula's Easter high mass offered "marvellous music and singing," and "smart hats,"as well, and the economy of evading tickets and payment "by a little skillful manoeuvring."[26]

Europe gave Rosamond an opportunity to remake her image, restyle her hair, and refurbish her wardrobe.[27] In her search for reasonably priced haute couture she attended fashion shows, and consulted books and magazines such as the *Femina* and *Marie Claire*, and was fascinated by contemporary "modists" such as Nina Ricci.[28] Rosamond had arrived in Brussels with an allowance and "thoughtful" cheques from her father, Granny, and Aunta, funds that she managed very carefully. She and Sheila travelled third class, washed and ironed their own laundry, and bet on horse races. Rosamond insisted upon competitive prices for quality silk stockings, scarves, hats, gloves, belts, and material to take to Mme Benoît, her dressmaker, for their "grand sessions," fashioning and refashioning dresses, tunics, coats, and jackets. Given her sensitivity to presentation and her slight disability, her shoemaker's fashionable, reasonably priced, kid leather summer shoes were irresistible.[29] No less enjoyable was reporting her acquisitions to her mother, Granny, and Aunta: her stylish shell-pink quilted dressing jacket, pyjamas, tweeds, and wool coat with detachable collar, thanks to their generous cheques.[30]

Preoccupied as Rosamond was with fashion and Brussels' cultural life, she retained a keen interest in politics. She noted the flags and ceremony accompanying the visit of Gustaf V (who she remembered from the Côte d' Azur) to Leopold III following the tragic death of Leopold III's wife, Astrid of Sweden. Nor had her interest in contemporary politics waned. She monitored American pro-German sentiment and anti-English remarks and speculated on the outcome of Belgian elections.

Except for day trips to Ghent and Bruges, Rosamond's art studio grounded her in Brussels, while Rosmond jealously reserved four weeks to visit London. Mesmerized by the psychodrama surrounding Edward VIII's renunciation of his throne on 10 December 1936, Rosamond reported to her curious mother, father, and grandmother European reactions to the tawdry British spectacle, often expressed in limericks and aimed at Mrs. Simpson and not "fit to print."[31] Raised on stories of royal occasions, Rosamond could not resist visiting London for the rapidly staged 12 May 1937 coronation of George VI, if it could be done economically and include a brief trip to Paris.

Once Rosamond and Shelia had booked their third-class tickets, *aller-retour*, two-day Parisian stopovers and inexpensive accommodation at the Hôtel Pas de Calais, on 27 April 1937 they left Brussels, each with a trunk and valise, for London via Dieppe-New Haven. In London Elizabeth (Betsy) Greenhill had resolved their search for reasonably priced accommodation in the overcrowded, overpriced city. While visiting Rosamond in Brussels, Betsy had offered to shelter Rosamond and Sheila during their coronation venture. Rosamond then wrote to Ruth Grierson (Cundill), her Ottawa friend who was serving as secretary to Vincent Massey, Canada's high commissioner to the United Kingdom, asking her to reserve places on the stands outside Canada House and a buffet lunch inside, and tickets to the review of the fleet on 20 May.[32] Once settled at Betsy's Roland Gardens home, they attended shows, shopped, and revisited the British Museum, the Tate Gallery, and the Victoria and Albert Museum.[33]

Upon their return to Paris, Rosamond and Sheila confronted more serious political issues at the Exposition internationale des arts et techniques dans la vie moderne. There the Soviet Union and Nazi Germany vied for visitors' attention. At the Spanish pavilion, Pablo Picasso's *Guernica* and Joan Miró's *Reaper/The Catalan Peasants' Revolt* (lost or destroyed the following year) reminded Rosamond and Sheila of the "gathering storm" in Europe, which they had first sensed aboard the *Westernland*. Scarcely a week after their return to Brussels on 29 May 1937, Rosamond and Shelia collected their belongings, refurbished wardrobes, and family gifts, and said goodbye to their friends and curious guesthouse residents, and left for Antwerp, where they had shipped their trunks, and boarded the Bernstein line's *Pennland*, scheduled to reach New York on 7 June.[34]

Rosamond's departure was not her final farewell to prewar Europe. Eighteen months later she was back in Britain with her father and mother on a four-month sales trip / vacation, a visit that included a visit with her Aunt Nora in Dublin. The trip began in Halifax aboard the Manchester Lines' *Manchester Progress* and ended with the Furness Withy's SS *Newfoundland*'s return to Halifax in April 1939. Registered at London's elegant Cumberland Hotel in Marble Arch, Rosamond, Maude, and Leslie occupied ringside seats as Europe slipped slowly into a war that neither they nor their country would escape unscathed.

Chapter Twenty-Seven

War

Dressed very smartly in bright colours and very regal, Lady Borden hosted an elegant dinner party in May 1939 (a month after Maude, Leslie, and Rosamond's return) to celebrate the seventh Annapolis Valley Apple Blossom Festival. It was the only occasion on which one family member recalled seeing her dressed in any colour but black.[1] Lady Borden loved apple blossom time and had much to celebrate. Her family's reunification and harmony, and apple-induced prosperity, had carried them comfortably through the Great Depression and restored their family's standing. Less happy was the state of European politics. Try as she may, Lady Borden could not suppress her nagging fears, as she watched British prime minister Neville Chamberlain's promise of "peace in our time" crumble. She knew from personal experience the personal and material costs of war.

No member of Lady Borden's family was more deeply affected by the war than Rosamond. An only child, born at the pinnacle of her extended family's influence, Rosamond enjoyed their protection, care, and affection. She lived in a world shaped by their values, material comfort, and social and public standing. She was proud of her family's history and wished to maintain its standing. With no warning or preparation, war, marriage, and motherhood dismantled that comfortable dependency, leaving her with a failing marriage, an arrested artistic career, the care of her Granny, and a fragile family economy.

For some time, the Kentville-based Canadian *Danish Herald* had warned its readers of the "lies" and "brutality" of Germany's Nazi government, its antisemitic and anti-Roma rhetoric, and its threat to neighbouring states.[2] Founded by the Danish Canadian Society's mutual aid society, the *Danish Herald* (*Danske Herald*) was co-owned and edited by Odin Beril Peter Kuntze (1884–1939)[3] and his stepson, Edmund Charles St. Jean Green (1909–1980),[4] who assumed full editorial responsibilities during his ailing stepfather's final years. Edmund's mother, Margaret Agnes Hornby, was born on 31 January 1884 in Cheshire, England. She had married a Scottish timber salesman, St. Jean Green (1880–1917) on 2 September 1908, and they had two sons, Edmund and Hugh.[5] A 2nd lieutenant in the Royal Inniskilling Fusiliers, St. Jean Green had been killed on 6 December 1917, and on 3 October 1921, Margaret married Odin Kuntze and moved to Elsinore, Denmark (the setting of Shakespeare's *Hamlet*) with her two sons, where they completed their education at a "Danish high school" before joining their stepfather's printing and "major newspaper" business in Copenhagen.[6]

In 1930 the family moved to Nova Scotia, purchased a farm in Lakeville, Kings County, and in 1934 Odin Kuntze began editing the weekly *Danish Herald* until his untimely death on 7 December 1939. On 4 March 1939, six months before the outbreak of war in Europe, Odin's elder son, Edmund, joined Canada's naval forces as a temporary lieutenant. On 4 September 1940 he transferred to active service as a lieutenant-commander.[7] Given his maturity, writing ability, anti-Nazi credentials, and mastery of English, his "near fluency" in Danish, Swedish, and Norwegian, a "working knowledge" of German, "a certain knowledge of French,"[8] and his British manners, Edmund was an obvious candidate for naval intelligence and liaison with the British military authorities.[9] After passing the requisite tests, he joined the Naval Boarding Service, charged with the internal security of, and liaison with, merchant ships, arrest of deserters, oversight and welfare of crews, resolution of "crew troubles," and "disciplinary action under the Merchant Seamans Orders."[10]

Where, when, and how Rosamond and Edmund met is unclear. Most of Rosamond's friends had married during the previous decade.[11] By 1941 Rosamond and Edmund were older than the national average age at marriage.[12] Rosamond may have found Edmund an attractive companion: a five feet nine and a half inch tall, blue-eyed, good-looking, athletic, smartly dressed, well-mannered naval officer serving his country in war. He was also convivial, and an amusing conversationalist, and had a European background, an eye for well-dressed women, and well-placed friends. And Edmund could scarcely have been indifferent to the attractive, fashionably dressed, sophisticated only daughter of the county's leading family, a family of national and imperial standing whose activities were noted in the national press and whose association promised a measure of status and influence.[13] Rosamond and Edmund were both dog lovers; they enjoyed riding, fishing, camping, hiking, and swimming, and though her friends found Edmund a bit fussy and "stuck-up" and "dismissive of those he disliked,"[14] Rosamond's social credentials immunized her against all that. Assigned to active home service, Edmund's Halifax posting and travels to Saint John, Montreal, and Ottawa facilitated their meeting, even during wartime.

Rosamond and Edmund were married on 2 August 1941 in a quiet afternoon ceremony at Montreal's St James the Apostle Anglican Church,[15] witnessed by her father, Edmund's good friend and best man Lieutenant-Commander Frederick Henry Davies and bridesmaid Mary Adelaide L. Beardmore.[16] Unfortunately, severe back and leg pain had "inhibited Maude's locomotion" since January and prevented her attendance. Elizabeth substituted for Maude's absence. Out of respect for wartime rationing, Rosamond wore a simple "pale green and white printed crepe frock," and a small white straw hat with a green veil, and carried a bouquet of gardenias. And a slightly balding Edmund wore his white dress naval uniform. The church was decorated with roses and wildflowers. Following the ceremony Adelaide Beardmore's parents held a reception for some twenty guests at their large house on 1570 Pine Avenue. Their guests included Dorothy and Elsie Cotton and their niece, Rosamond's school friend Norah (Rosamond) Hughes, and her husband; Gwendolyn (née Borden) and her husband Douglas Blair; and Edmund's naval colleagues. A photo of the smiling couple appeared in the *Montreal Herald* and the *Ottawa Evening Citizen*.[17] Their honeymoon consisted of a brief fishing trip in the Laurentians.[18]

Rosamond's mother and father continued Rosamond's allowance.[19] Her Aunta sent practical household items and her Granny provided art books and generous cheques, money sometimes used to refurbish Edmund's uniforms. Although Rosamond's family could do little to secure better housing in crowded wartime Halifax, Bell Hill Farm and Borden Place offered a convenient escape as time and occasion permitted. Finding housing in their second posting, Montreal, in March 1942 required a sustained search before they located flat 8 on 495, rue Prince Arthur, only marginally better than their Halifax quarters, and frequently overpopulated by visiting relatives and live-in help.

In December 1941, four months after their marriage, Rosamond and Edmund were still stationed in Halifax when Maude and Leslie arrived in the city to await transport to Barbados, where they sought rest and sunshine to relieve their various ailments. Scheduled to sail on the Canadian National's 7,988-ton SS *Lady Hawkins* sometime in early January, friends tried to dissuade them from sailing since the Americans' final entry into the war against Germany had removed their cordon sanitaire protecting the Atlantic coastline from German torpedoes. But Leslie and Maude had made their reservations and took the risk.[20]

On 17 January Leslie and Maude left Canning for the "great wicked city of Halifax" and stayed at the Lord Nelson Hotel while awaiting a place at Hillside Hall.[21] Earlier that month Leslie had undergone an operation in the Kentville hospital on his right ankle and foot (injured during his coronation rehearsal) and had scheduled a series of electrical treatments for his rheumatism and lumbago at Halifax's Victoria General Hospital before they sailed. Rosamond, who was recovering from an unspecified surgery, accompanied her parents to Halifax. But when the *Lady Hawkins*'s departure was delayed a week, Rosamond returned to Borden Place to be with her Granny and Aunta and attend to family business.[22]

Once installed at Hillside Hall on South Street, Leslie wrote Rosamond amusing letters of his medical encounters, and thanked her for her Christmas present of two books, *Wide Is the River* and *Botany Bay*. He also wrote Edmund, seeking privileged information on the sailing of the *Lady Hawkins* and telling him where to find a bottle of Gordon's gin at Bell Hill Farm for the New Year's party at the Cornwallis Inn. He penned a more formal note to "My dear Lady Borden," thanking her for the cardigan she had given him for Christmas, promising to keep her in touch during their journey.[23] Finally aboard the *Lady Hawkins*, Maude was in a light mood as they waited to "slide out unexpectedly" into the night. Conscious that her mail might be censored, she amused Rosamond, a fellow people-watcher, with descriptions of the thirty or so "cinderellas" aboard, "not very young and no real beauties," and at least "one exotic type."[24] This was wartime Halifax, and as Maude noted earlier there were "20 men to one woman instead of vice versa," as it had been before the war.[25]

Maude's letter was Rosamond's last communication from her mother. Some hours after the *Lady Hawkins* "slid into the night," it stopped at Boston to pick up 51 American construction workers, then sailed unescorted toward Bermuda and its other Caribbean destinations. About 2 am on 19 January the *Lady Hawkins* was about 300 kilometres east of Cape Hatteras, zigzagging its way toward Bermuda to avoid detection, when a torpedo fired by a U-66, commanded by Richard Zapp, severed the vessel's' stern, followed by a second torpedo that destroyed five of the steamer's six lifeboats.[26] The ship sank within 30 minutes. Only the remaining overcrowded lifeboat (built for 43 persons) with its 71 passengers survived, and then only after a torturous five-day ordeal. The rest of the 251 passengers perished, including Maude and Leslie.

Since wartime press censorship was then more rigorous in Canada than in the United States, rumours of the *Lady Hawkins's* fate reached Lady Borden, Rosamond, and Elizabeth well before official confirmation of Maude and Leslie's death.[27] While officials completed their futile search for survivors, Lady Borden, Elizabeth, and Rosamond waited, their agony magnified by United States' press reports, describing the 71 survivors' brutal ordeal, and the cries and efforts of the drowning victims to board the single overcrowded lifeboat, captained by Chief Officer Percy O. Kelly, a "38 year old sandy haired weather beaten Nova Scotian."

Two weeks after the torpedo attack, Rosamond, Lady Borden, and Elizabeth received official notification that Maude and Leslie's recovery was "unlikely."[28] The qualified confirmation, the absence of bodies, and funeral ritual prolonged their agony, feeding their desperate hopes that Maude and Leslie might yet be found. Friends, family, and acquaintances sent letters of hope and later condolences.[29] Still Lady Borden and Elizabeth maintained their futile vigil. They knew the *Lady Hawkins* well and its Caribbean route and pondered how the "German U-boats got at our continent." Everything seemed so familiar, reviving their memories of Harold's death, an earlier war casualty. Life "seems full of very hard places," Lady Borden mused stoically, "but I expect it is for our good – to make us care less for it."[30]

Lady Borden and Elizabeth's first concern was for Rosamond, aware of how closely her life had been intertwined with her parents, and she so recently married and now obliged to settle and manage her family's estate. In the following months Lady Borden and Elizabeth wrote Rosamond almost every week, sharing their grief and offering their support. "I miss your mother so much – so much," Lady Borden wrote in May 1942; "I think the past week has been quite bad, about the worst yet." A month later things had improved little as Lady Borden sat by her window penning a letter to Rosamond: "You have been in my mind so much today – In fact I have not been able to get you out of my mind & I do hope you are both pretty well & that you had a really good fishing trip & I hope without the company of the mosquitos."

Fortunately, Maude and Leslie had avoided Sir Frederick's folly and had revised their wills before they left Canning. Leslie had mandated Montreal's Royal Trust to be his executor, and named his wife his sole legatee, followed by his daughter, and in the event of her death and the absence of a grandchild his assets were to be shared among his Irish siblings. The nature and extent of Leslie's assets are unclear. Apart from his Irish inheritance, and whatever securities he had retained from his unsteady brokerage business, Gables appeared to have been his major asset, its worth estimated at $35,000 plus $2,500 with furniture, minus a $1,500 mortgage, when Rosamond sought to sell it in 1944, though she was ready to accept $25,000, without the furniture.[31]

Maude's assets were comparable. Her executor, the Eastern Trust Company in Halifax, took more than a year and half to settle her will. According to the trust company's calculations, Maude's estate's gross value was $36,992 (approximately $513,000 in current purchasing power). Once expenses, commissions, debts, fees, and charges were paid and cash disbursed for living expenses, Rosamond received some $25,046 from her mother's estate.[32] Her most valuable assets were Bell Hill Farm ($4,500), equity in the Borden Fruit Company (unstated value), Imperial Trust securities ($11,205), outstanding income from the wartime Nova Scotia Apple Marketing Board ($6,438), and miscellaneous, livestock, farm implements, and household furniture ($2,050).

Inheritance entailed decisions and responsibilities. Rosamond and Edmund had to decide what to do with Rosamond's two principal income streams, Gables and Bell Hill Farm. Should they occupy, rent, or sell Gables? They decided to sell, but until they had a purchaser, they needed tenants. Bell Hill Farm was different. It functioned as a *pied-à-terre*; it was close to their families and an asset, well-managed by Wilfrid Bishop. Besides, Mrs. Kuntze might occupy and care for Bell Hill Farm in their absence. Suddenly, too, Rosamond became the effective custodian of her beloved, increasingly dependent Granny and Aunta, a responsibility made more difficult by Edmund's war postings in Halifax, Montreal, and Saint John.

The war is "changing everything," Lady Borden lamented to a friend, even before Maude and Leslie's tragic deaths. It had even cut into her annual Christmas shipment of barrels of apples to relatives and friends. More difficult was maintaining Borden Place. Boys who had worked for 15 cents an hour now refused to work for 30 cents. Fallen plaster remained unrepaired, peeling paint was unattended, gardens were neglected. Gasoline shortages limited Lady Borden and Elizabeth's travel, especially inconvenient during apple blossom time.[33] Keeping their large, drafty residence warm during the winter seemed a losing battle, until Rosamond later persuaded Lady Borden to spend winter in a boarding lodge or in Kentville's recently reconstructed Cornwallis Inn.

The arrival of spring brought additional problems. "Shortly we shall have no help outside," Lady Borden lamented as she paced Borden Place from window to window, admiring the chestnut tree's "candle-like blooms," the purple and white lilacs, the roses, irises, primula, bleeding-heart, and caragana, anticipating their impending neglect. Her only solution was to try to "to get up" her own "muscles for lifting and lugging." To make matters worse Amy Minard, Lady Borden's sixty-one-year-old, widowed live-in "companion," had been hospitalized indefinitely in Wolfville, costing Lady Borden $2 a day (approximately $27 in current purchasing power), an expense she feared she might not be able to sustain.[34]

In addition to Maude and Leslie's tragic deaths, old age and wartime constrained Lady Borden's movements, fed her anxiety, and brought endless news of deaths and casualties. Her aging friends wrote gloomily of death, illness, ailments, and scarcity.[35] She and Elizabeth did "all in their power" to support the war effort. They joined the Red Cross, "knitted away," and later sent "bundles to Britain."[36] At times it all seemed too much. Occasionally she booked a hotel room in crowded wartime Halifax, to see friends and shop. But she tired easily, was apprehensive, and prayed for the Allied invasion to begin, the war to end, and her world to be restored.

Elizabeth's health and behaviour were also a worry. Elizabeth's failing eyesight limited her reading and plans to write a family "book of their lives," tracing the family's genealogical origins (a continuation of her father's project) and her father's time at Harvard and his public life. She was often ill, erratic, and irritable, and Lady Borden found her more and more difficult to manage, her dress an embarrassment, and her friends a burden.[37] Some days Elizabeth spent the day on her horse, riding about her farm. In June 1944 Lady Borden confided her frustrations to Rosamond:

> It is dark this morning, dark and cold. And Elizabeth is flying about the house dressed most desperately bad. I cannot get her to banish her old black and white skirt. I am hoping for a change for the better. Nessie [the maid] complains to me about her going downstairs so early – often at 7:30 & the fire just started. She flies around for an hour then goes up stairs & gets her bath etc. Her room is in an awful condition & I do not know how long it will have to go on.[38]

Elizabeth faced her own professional and personal trials. Spring frosts and late summer storms were the bane of apple growers. But nothing prepared Annapolis Valley apple growers for the war's disruption of the lucrative English apple market. The virtual absence of wartime transatlantic commercial transportation, together with the costs and shortage of farm labour, sapped Elizabeth's farm income. Try as she did to compensate for the English market's loss by cultivating Kentville and Halifax's military markets, Elizabeth fought a rearguard battle. Fortunately, the federal government's Nova Scotia Apple Marketing Board guaranteed a market for three-quarters of her farm's production. But a guaranteed market was not the same as a competitive market the vindication of scientific farming, organization and diligence.

Elizabeth, too, felt constricted, bored, and restless. An intrepid traveller within Canada and abroad, Elizabeth had enjoyed her annual London "check on dishonest English marketers" and visit with friends. The war had ended all that. From time to time she visited Halifax, Saint John, Montreal, or Ottawa to see Rosamond and Edmund or visit and assist friends "in need," but she found wartime cities crowded, noisy, dirty, and "greatly changed," less interesting than formerly and no substitute for London.[39] During the depression years Elizabeth, absorbed in the management of her farm, spent less time on community projects, content to lead by example and to travel. She continued to support her church, especially its Women's Missionary Society, which she and Lady Borden often hosted at Borden Place.[40] But her health was beginning to fail and in the late summer of 1944 she underwent surgery in the Kentville hospital, followed by a three-month convalesce.

War strained Rosamond's marriage as well. She and Edmund had been mature adults, accustomed to their own routines. They had come from different backgrounds and had lived different lives. Edmund's wartime travels between Halifax, Saint John, Montreal, and Ottawa, a brief tour of duty in the United Kingdom in 1943–4, his irregular hours, and the confidentiality surrounding his intelligence activities left little time for the couple to share interests and adjust to marriage. Edmund relished the covert, ambiguous nature of his work and sought his superiors' approval. He was often "out in the evening" and "required" to sleep over, and Rosamond who liked to talk, missed having "someone to talk to."[41] During Edmund's travels he wrote Rosamond about dog shows, clothes, and manicures; he shared gossipy accounts of friends and acquaintances, and told tales of binges, "polishing off a bottle of Rye," and party pranks such as ladies losing their "unmentionables."[42]

Edmund complained of various health problems, apart from seasonal contagions. His work was stressful, and he often lived "on his nerves." He suffered from recurring strep throat, "chronic" tonsillitis, migraine headaches, depression, "nervous tension," fatigue, and irritability. He put on weight, developed high blood pressure, and smoked "two packs of cigarettes a day to keep his weight down."[43] He was "on and off" the wagon, and when he dieted "his disposition wasn't good."[44] Six months after his marriage he went on sick leave for two weeks, suffering from what the doctors diagnosed variously as "psychoneurosis," "neuro-muscular hypertension," and "hysteria," caused by "increased responsibility in his home" and work-related conflict, namely "his inability to adjust himself to a position of lesser importance than the head of his unit."[45] When Edmund and Rosamond were together she accommodated his friends and preferences for mess activities, parties, dances, and formal dinners. While they enjoyed cinema,[46] animals, and outdoor recreation, Edmund had little time for theatre, found opera tedious, and was dismissive of art.[47]

Although war, marriage, and motherhood derailed Rosamond's art, she was no wallflower.[48] She had friends, interests, and activities, especially in Montreal, and could manage on her own. Her helpful family friends, Dorothy and Elsie Cotton, now lived and worked in Montreal, as did Adelaide Beardmore and Ruth (Grierson) Cundill, her old Ottawa friend.[49] Mrs. Kuntze, Elizabeth, and Rosamond's Ottawa friends visited often and shared their limited quarters. Rosamond and her friends shopped at Morgan's, attended the cinema, chatted, lunched, or had tea at the Ritz or the Mount Royal Hotel. Proud of her family's military history and public service, Rosamond enlisted in the Women's Volunteer Services (WVS), a civilian organization that offered daycare; its members sewed, knitted, canvassed for funds and supplies, distributed information, and monitored regulations. By February 1944, Rosamond had clocked close to 200 hours of service, twice the number of hours required for a uniform and a WVS badge.[50]

Parenthood altered Rosamond and Edmund's relationship as well. Ten months after their marriage, and six months after her parents' deaths, Rosamond suspected that she was pregnant. Once the doctor confirmed her suspicions and certified her good health, she broke the news to her delighted Granny and Aunta. They began knitting and crocheting bootees, jackets, hats, and blankets, as did Rosamond. Apart from an early bout of morning sickness and anemia, Rosamond had a relatively easy pregnancy. She was cared for by Dr. Henry, who recommended a nourishing diet of milk, cheese, meat, vegetables, fruit, and vitamin tablets.[51] Rosamond "never missed a meal" during her pregnancy. Her waist expanded from 24 to 28 inches and she gained 13 pounds. She slept well, and had "an easy delivery," surrounded by doctors and nurses.

Rosamond "enjoyed" her stay in the hospital (as she usually did), except for "the medical staff's love of waking people at ungodly hours to take temperatures etc."[52] During her ten-day hospitalization she received a stream of visitors, bearing gifts and flowers. She announced the baby's name and planned her baptism. She and Edmund had decided that if the baby were a girl, they would name her Julia Leslie and if a boy, Julian Leslie, to honour Rosamond's deceased parents. For godparents they chose Edmund's brother Hugh and Adelaide (Beardmore) and Bubbles (Gwendolyn Blair), two godmothers!

Leaving the hospital's protective precincts was a shock. Although Rosamond had a live-in nurse and the assistance of Edmund's mother, who shopped, cooked, and did household chores, Rosamond found motherhood's relentless imperatives overwhelming. She was fascinated nonetheless by her daughter's vulnerability, determined character, and occasional "mulish expression" as she "clamped her jaws together" and refused to feed, a tactic she later deployed on tapioca.[53] Edmund assessed his daughter's behaviour with a certain amount of pride, especially her forceful dispatch of unwanted playmates.[54] "She is going to be very strong willed," Rosamond warned her Granny.[55]

Granny and Aunta were familiar with strong personalities.[56] They greeted Leslie's (Julia's) birth as providential, a replacement of their loss. Her birth gave their family a future. Granny and Aunta became an insatiable audience for Rosamond's reports on Leslie's health, physical and social development, and "sayings and doings," and were grateful recipients of photographs, which Granny kept on her bedside table. Granny and Aunta sent cheques (with which Rosamond bought war stamps), clothes, dolls, and toys, including crayons and scissors, gifts well beyond Leslie's age but betrayed their aspirations for her. Extensive preparations preceded Rosamond, Edmund, and Leslie's visits to Borden Place, assembling a crib, high chair, playpen, pram, and "toidy." The warmest bedroom was reserved for Leslie and her nurse.[57] With every visit Leslie appeared "more wonderful than ever."[58]

Rosamond adapted slowly to their transfer to Saint John in February 1944, with its limited housing, shopping, recreational facilities, and constant sound of foghorns. Despite her preoccupation with Leslie's care, Rosamond found time for a small flower garden on 184 Princess Street.[59] She participated in officers' wives' activities, dined with the city's notables, and, pressed by her Granny, she enrolled in a drawing class.[60] The classes provided an opportunity to talk to the teacher, students, and models, conversations she lacked at home. A devoted Liberal, she voted in the August 1944 provincial election, sent her nurse to the polls, and celebrated the party's impressive victory. Above all Saint John offered easier access to Bell Hill Farm and Borden Place to visit her Granny and Aunta, increasingly in need of attention.

Conscious of life's fragility and her own vulnerability, Lady Borden welcomed Rosamond and Edmund's posting to Saint John. Their proximity, the sale of Gables, and the Allied invasions in Western Europe in June 1944 seemed an answer to her prayers for peace and the return of her prewar world. The arrival of Gables' furnishings, and trunks of books, many familiar items vying for diminishing space in Borden Place, stirred memories of authors, donors, and occasions of their gifts or purchases. All were welcome instalments on Lady Borden's anticipated postwar family restoration.[61] And that could not come soon enough, for in the autumn, winter, and spring of 1944–5 Lady Borden needed all the support she could muster.

The weather had been unsettling even before the "Great Atlantic Hurricane" battered sections of the Atlantic seaboard in September 1944. An unusually dry spring had parched the earth and slowed gardens. Nothing, however, prepared Canning farmers for the sudden destructive storm that struck Nova Scotia on 15 September during apple harvesting time, wreaking havoc on their farms, damaging orchards and bridges, destroying dykes and aboiteaux, and turning hundreds of acres of farmland into salt marsh, the Borden properties a prime target of the hurricane's wrath.

Meanwhile Elizabeth became seriously ill but was unable to secure immediate hospitalization owing to a scarcity of beds. Rosamond rushed from Saint John to Canning to assist her Granny and remained there for several months during Elizabeth's eventual hospitalization.[62] Elizabeth's subsequent surgery, lengthy convalescences and future care worried Rosamond and Lady Borden. Could Lady Borden accommodate Elizabeth's return to Borden Place, especially with the wartime scarcity of domestic labour? And if not, what was to be done? Then in the spring of 1945, before farmers had replaced or repaired their dykes and aboiteaux, a spring thaw and heavy rains reflooded the farmland, carrying away bridges and temporarily cutting Canning's direct access to the provincial highway.

The storms heralded the region's difficult postwar economic adjustment and accelerated the family's economic decline. Contrary to Lady Borden's fondest hopes and prayers, peace failed to restore the Annapolis Valley fruit growers' prewar prosperity.[63] The wartime growth of apple orchards in England and postwar overseas competition effectively erased the Annapolis Valley's sales to the English market. Between 1939 and 1951 Kings and Annapolis counties' orchard acreage declined by nearly half. Roughly "one fifth of the Annapolis Valley's commercial farms went out of business."[64] And, unlike post–World War I, the Valley's English apple market never recovered, and the Canadian government paid apple growers to uproot their orchards.

Although apple growers had their "backs to the wall,"[65] their industry was far from finished. The Nova Scotia Fruit Growers Association lobbied vocally and vigorously for assistance and adaptation. The federal Department of Agriculture advised better practices and published a guide, *Orchard Soil Management and Apple Nutrition*.[66] Local and other public officials advocated improved cold storage facilities and packaging, replacing their unrooted trees with varieties more appropriate to the domestic market, such as Cortland and Pippins, and producing derivatives such as juice, pie, sauce, and butter.[67] Many apple growers diversified and supplemented their orchards with livestock, poultry, vegetables, tobacco, and apiculture.[68] Even those in the Valley's more prosperous fruit belt of Northville, Berwick, Port William, and Canning reduced their apple acreage and sought alternative products and markets.[69]

In 1945 Rosamond and Edmund confronted additional problems. Not only had war disrupted their farm's principal market but the country's massive postwar military demobilization left Edmund without a salary income.[70] Aware of Rosamond and Edmund's anxieties, Lady Borden wrote to William Lyon Mackenzie King, on 10 August 1945, congratulating him on his recent re-election, and seeking his aid in finding Edmund postwar employment. The prime minister responded immediately, apologizing for his dictated, typewritten letter, necessitated by the pressure of work, but managed to pen several lines at the end of the letter. King regretted his inability to meet Lady Borden's "wishes on so small a matter," pleading his reluctance to interfere in departmental appointments "on personal grounds" and his fear of public criticism. He promised nonetheless to "have a personal word in confidence with the Minister of National Defence for Naval Affairs" (Douglas Charles Abbott had replaced Angus L. Macdonald on 17 April 1945 as minister) on Edmund's behalf.[71] Meanwhile, he urged Edmund to apply to the Civil Service Commission and provided Lady Borden with the name of the commission's chairman. Lady Borden conveyed King's suggestion to Rosamond, advice that Edmund disregarded, and on 24 October 1945 he was placed on the active service list with the rank of lieutenant-commander.[72]

Edmund, Rosamond, and Leslie returned to Bell Hill Farm, and for the next three years, according to Edmund's testimony, he administered his wife's "inherited properties ... including real estate in Ottawa, orchards, and a fruit company."[73] But he had sold Gables during the closing months of the war, careful to secure Rosamond's consent to its price and the disposal of its furnishings. That reduced "his management" to Bell Hill Farm, the Borden Fruit Company, and Rosamond's investments. Even so, Wilfrid Archibald Bishop, the family's able farm manager, supervised Bell Hill Farm, and the Eastern Trust Company managed Rosamond's investments.

The loss of Edmund's military salary left the family dependent on its farm's fragile income and Rosamond's investments. The family responded to the postwar farm crisis, as did other farmers and fruit growers, by reducing costs and diversifying production and marketing. They mechanized, expanded their potato production, increased their livestock (profiting from the outbreak of hoof and mouth disease on the Canadian prairies in the early 1950s), added apiculture to their income stream, and marketed their produce regionally to food producers, benefiting from the region's improved highways to distribute their produce. They also sold small portions of land from time to time.

The sole heir of her family's material and reputational heritage, Rosamond tried to sustain its social standing. She entertained friends and notables, her culinary hospitality inspired by her copy of the *Boston Cooking-School Cookbook*. She participated in the community's civic and religious life, worshipped at All Saints' Anglican Church, joined its Ladies Guild, and served as its president.[74] She searched the family's papers, identified photographs, and wrote a brief account of her father's early life. She even attempted to supplement her family's income by freelance journalism.[75] But as her Aunta's health declined and her Granny became more dependent, she became increasingly preoccupied with their care.

Chapter Twenty-Eight

Great Granny

Rosamond, Edmund, and Julia's return to Bell Hill Farm was an answer to Lady Borden's prayers. Their proximity gave Lady Borden a greater sense of security, someone to consult, assist, and substitute for Elizabeth, whose declining eyesight, tenuous health, care, and erratic behaviour had become a worry.[1] The war's end however was replaced shortly by a "Cold War" that offered the family no immunity from the effects of international politics.

On 5 September 1945, three days after World War II ended, the USSR's Ottawa cipher clerk, Igor Gouzenko (1919–1982), defected from his embassy, carrying documents exposing an extensive soviet spy network in Canada and abroad. His exposures ended Allied cooperation with "Uncle Joe" Stalin's Soviet Union, and marked the beginning of an escalating Cold War. The European Recovery Program (1948), also known as the Marshall Plan, the installation of a communist government in Czechoslovakia (1948), the Berlin Blockade (1948–9), the formation of the North Atlantic Treaty Organization (1949), the Korean War (1950–3), and the Warsaw Pact (1955) followed in ominous succession, dividing the world into two armed camps.

Canada's response to the threatening international context was collective security. The country remobilized its military and expanded its Eastern European legations, determined to avoid the errors of the "low, dishonest decade" that preceded World War II.[2] Preparations did not stop at the doors of Bell Hill Farm. And, iIn September 1947, the RCN's flag officer Atlantic coast asked Edmund to return to the Royal Canadian Navy for special active service. In recommending his appointment, the flag officer cited Edmund's war experience, knowledge of the Atlantic coast, and linguistic abilities (for which the flag officer later provided compensation).[3] The next month Edmund joined the staff of the flag officer's naval intelligence and worked with them for the next fifteen months.

Edmund's appointment refuelled Lady Borden's apprehension and sense of isolation. Then, in May 1948, just before the sixteenth annual Apple Blossom Festival, Elizabeth had a heart attack and was carried from Borden Place on a stretcher and transported to the Eastern Kings Memorial Hospital in Wolfville, where she died on 11 May 1948.[4] Trinity United Church's minister, the Reverend William D. Van Zoost, and the Reverend T.W. Hodgson conducted her well-attended funeral service. Hodgson, Elizabeth's friend, now resident in Digby, spoke of Elizabeth's commitment and "spirit of service" to her home, community, and the world. A full choir and congregation's rendition of "Unto the Hills" and "Peace, Perfect Peace" underlined Elizabeth's faith and assurance.[5]

Elizabeth's death taxed Lady Borden's stoicism. She had lived with Elizabeth longer than with any other family member. Occasionally they had irritated one another. More often they had assisted, respected, and complemented one another. They had participated in extraordinary events, dined with kings and queens, and visited fascinating places. They had shared hardships and tragedies, defended their interests, and pooled their resources. Resolved to honour Elizabeth's public service, Lady Borden donated electric chimes to their church, dedicated during a special service in December 1948, their minister describing the chimes as a monument to Elizabeth's life, a call to worship, belief, and devotion.[6] Elizabeth had also directed her executors to fund a Mount Allison scholarship in memory of Harold and Maude.

Upon Elizabeth's death and Edmund's naval posting in Halifax, Rosamond, and Leslie moved into Borden Place with "Great Granny." Then, in January 1950, Edmund was transferred to the Canadian naval headquarters' tri-forces intelligence branch in Ottawa with top secret clearance. Rosamond and Leslie joined him in their rented Ottawa residence at 582 Lisgar Street. Lady Borden tried to see the posting as a temporary, seasonal separation, and was consoled by Rosamond and Leslie's summer return to Canning.[7] But a year later Edmund's appointment as Canadian naval attaché to Stockholm, with responsibility for Sweden, Norway, and Finland, erased that fragile consolation, deepening Lady Borden's anxiety and isolation.

Political influence may account for Edmund's 1948 appointment, but his war service and linguistic competence were sufficient justification for the authorities' choice. Nonetheless, social diplomacy was an important, time-honoured instrument of diplomacy and intelligence gathering, an assignment enhanced by "diplomatic wives," and Rosamond's family was well-regarded in Ottawa.[8] As Edmund later explained to a prospective employer, his Stockholm appointment entailed being "seconded from time to time to visiting dignitaries and officials from foreign countries" and being honoured to have as his "guests many high-ranking government officials including amongst these His Royal Highness the Duke of Edinburgh."[9] A cultivated, charming person who spoke both English and French fluently and had a conversational command of Italian, Rosamond understood the importance of dress, deportment, and protocol, and the genial effects of hospitality, good food, and wine. While she accepted her unremunerated, gendered social responsibilities and enjoyed some of its benefits, the role exacted a heavy personal price.

Rosamond welcomed her return to Western Europe, an opportunity to enjoy its cultural life and travel, renew friendships, and meet interesting people. She saw the posting as public service, in keeping with her formation and family's standing. It also alleviated her family's financial dependence on its farm and securities. In anticipation of her social responsibilities, she shipped her silver, plate, glass, household linens, and her *Boston Cooking-School Cookbook*, ready to play her part.[10] More difficult was leaving her beloved Granny, just when her Granny needed her most.

Lady Borden supressed her anxieties, determined to do everything to assist Rosamond play a role comparable to what she had once envisaged for herself. Rosamond appreciated her Granny's support. She also detected her Granny's unspoken apprehensions and made every effort to ensure her physical and social welfare during their absence. Fortunately, she could count on two dependable seasonal "companions," Mrs. Amy Minard (from Halifax) and Mrs. Daisy Emms. Both respected her Granny's standing and autonomy. Lady Borden could reside at the Cornwallis Hotel in the winter and in the late spring her companions could rejoin her at Borden Place.

Rosamond saw her "great" Granny as more than a ward. She understood her social, intellectual, and cultural needs. Conscious of her Granny's dependence upon books and magazines, especially given her limited access to theatre, concerts, cinema, and travel, Rosamond instructed her "companions" to never leave her Granny without books and magazines. During Rosamond's absence abroad she sent her Granny books, magazines, and clothing. She wrote to her every week or ten days, aware of her Granny's joy in reading and rereading her letters, vicariously living in Rosamond's world. Edmund and Julia (in Stockholm Leslie assumed her first name) also wrote "great Granny" from time to time.

Rosamond penned informative, amusing reports on family activities, household management, entertainment, travel, and special events, all tailored to her Granny's interests and amusement. She described their large five-bedroom residence on 67, Gronviksvagan, Bromma, its furnishings, some resembling those at Borden Place, and her trials finding, training, and retaining her cook, housekeeper, and nanny.[11] She wrote of Julia's health, education,[12] development, and friends, her "bon mots"; her mastery of Swedish; her pets (fish, birds, and mice); her riding, swimming, weaving, and sewing; and her participation in Christmas concerts at embassy and legation children's parties.[13] She recounted Edmund's audience with King Gustaf VI Adolf (1882–1973), the son of Gustaf V, whom she had seen in 1926 and 1937. She wrote, too, of Edmund's travels to England, Norway, Denmark, and Finland, his hosting dinner parties for colleagues and stag parties for his friends, his growing fascination with dog breeding and dog shows. She paid special attention to formal dinners,[14] her own and those of others, the guests, the menu, and protocol. Predictably, too, she informed her Granny on fashions, her purchases, and planned purchases, to which her Granny often responded with a generous cheque.

Aware of her Granny's sense of humour and appreciation of the contingent, Rosamond related stories of restraints and mishaps. She grumbled about Gustaf V's (1858–1950) death in October 1950, restricting official entertainment for a year and a half, obliging women "to go around looking like old crows."[15] She knew, too, that her Granny would enjoy the story of her short-staffed, "hectic" first official luncheon. Things began poorly when her "idiot" serving maid presented her guests with undiluted tin soup, having failed to read the Swedish label's instructions. Then, just as Rosamond was finishing her pudding, she felt her hat being lifted off her head and, and looking up, saw it impaled on her inexperienced maid's serving fork, which Rosamond retrieved without drawing undue attention. To add to the luncheon's chaos "Pavot," their dog, gave birth to two puppies (one of which died), which required Rosamond's assistance between courses.[16]

Given her Granny's broad interests and curiosity, Rosamond described Stockholm's weather, winter sports, its flora, birds (waxwings, finches, magpies, woodpeckers), fruit harvests, and poor rural roads, likening them to Nova Scotia's. She noted the Swedes' curious flag day celebrations, their chronic punctuality, and trademark lines of washing. She recounted her and Julia's visit to Drottningholm Palace, its furniture and paintings, and Julia's distaste for pictures of dead horses. She provided a travelogue of her 1952 motor trip from Stockholm to Copenhagen, Frankfurt, Heidelberg, and Paris with the Canadian military attaché, Major William Strachan, his wife, and ten-year old son, once nearly ending up in the Soviet zone. She described the remains of destroyed villages, ghost towns, pockmarked buildings, broken doorways, reconstructed highways, well-dressed but sullen people, and the noisy "badly behaved" American occupying forces. She reported the arrival of special visitors, such as Vincent Massey's son, and amused her Granny with accounts of East European diplomats rapaciously "munching apples and sucking oranges" at official Western receptions.

Rosamond knew that her Granny would appreciate a full account of two special events, the 1952 Olympics in Helsinki and the 1953 coronation in London. Lady Borden had twice crossed the Atlantic with Canada's Olympic team, enjoyed recreational sports, and relished Rosamond's account of the XV Olympiad in Helsinki, with its 5,000 athletes from 69 countries, including Germany, Japan, and the Soviet Union for the first time since World War II. What interested her even more was Rosamond's meeting "the two dukes," the Duke of Edinburgh, and the Duke of Kent.

In mid-July, 1952, Rosamond and Edmund had left Stockholm for Helsinki with Thomas Archibald Stone (1900–1965), Canada's envoy extraordinary and minister plenipotentiary, to Finland and Sweden (1949–52), and his wife, with whom they shared a house outside Helsinki. The day after their arrival, Thomas Stone and Edmund, in full dress and sword, were presented to the dukes. Subsequently Stone and Edmund attended the Duke of Edinburgh's unveiling of a plaque, in the presence of the University of Toronto's eight-man Olympic rowing team, commemorating Nicholas Ignatieff, the former warden of Hart House, who had initiated a work-study exchange between the University of Toronto and Helsinki's Polytechnic Institute.[17] Of even greater interest to Lady Borden was a formal dinner, where the "etiquette" was "simply terrific," followed by a large house dance where Rosamond (though recovering from minor surgery on one of her feet) was photographed dancing with the thirty-one-year-old Duke of Edinburgh, a photograph that received wide coverage in the Swedish press.[18]

Lady Borden was no less interested in Rosamond, Edmund, and Julia's account of London's celebration of Queen Elizabeth II's coronation, a spectacle they and Betsy Greenhill viewed from London street stands,[19] as Rosamond and Betsy had done in 1937. In her full account of the pageant, Rosamond explained to her Granny that Julia seemed more interested in the horses than the royal carriage's occupants. Rosamond also sent her Granny coronation programs and fashion magazines and a black, silk-lined woollen dress and jacket. Rosamond, Edmund, and Julia lodged at Roland Gardens in South Kensington with

Betsy's family, who were still struggling with postwar British rationing of sugar and meat. Lady Borden responded typically to the Greenhill's limited supplies by shipping a "much appreciated" ham.[20]

Rosamond and Betsy had become very close friends. As soon as Rosamond had arrived in Stockholm in 1950, Betsy had visited Rosamond for three weeks to help her settle in. Two years later, when Rosamond came to Paris with the Strachans, Betsy had joined her there and together they had toured museums and galleries, a routine they had repeated in London during the 1953 coronation, as they had done in 1937. After the coronation Julia spent a rainy week on her paternal cousin's farm north of London,[21] while Rosamond visited her Aunt Norma in Belfast; Leslie's sister had an affection for Rosamond and subsequently remembered Rosamond in her will.

Contrary to Rosamond's reports in her entertaining letters to her Granny, her domestic life was often tense and stressful. Anxious to maintain appearances and meet expectations, Rosamond tried to serve as mother, wife, hostess, and custodian of her Granny, and still retain some personal space. She found it difficult at times to reconcile appearances with reality. Sometimes she was distracted, distant, cold, nervous, and torn by her life's conflicting demands. And like her father, she "could explode under pressure." During their first years in Stockholm, she fretted about Julia's possible exposure to polio, that recurring contempory "middle class" disease that left thousands of children paralysed. Consigned to her governess's care and isolated from other children, Julia often felt abandoned.[22] Rosamond worried about Edmund's dependence on alcohol,[23] his preoccupation with dog breeding, and his indifference to her interest in art and music. She appreciated his taste in women's clothing and sought his approval during Paris or London shopping excursions. Otherwise, their relationship had become nominal and instrumental, a failed or failing marriage.

Rosamond worried, too, about the maintenance of Borden Place and Bell Hill Farm, about falling plaster, September storms, and uncertain markets.[24] Most of all she worried about her Granny's care, declining health, weak and unsteady knees, and failing eyesight, so evident in her large, shaky handwriting. Lady Borden would begin a letter, become "discouraged," and have Mrs. Minard or Mrs. Emms finish it. By 1953 she could barely identify Rosamond's signature. Her companions read Rosamond's letters to her, to which Rosamond often appended instructions for her companions' eyes only, asking them to write no more Christmas cheques on Lady Borden's behalf to Edmund's father, who had been dead since 1917, or to his stepfather, who had been dead since 1939. Lady Borden remained well physically and retained an interest in public affairs, especially elections, though her memory often failed, and she longed for Rosamond's return.[25]

In September 1952 Rosamond returned to Canning for several weeks to monitor her Granny's health and revise her Granny's will. Elizabeth had willed Borden Place to Lady Borden, but Lady Borden had failed to revise her own will following Elizabeth's death. Lady Borden's revised will named Edmund as her executor, the Royal Trust as her trustee, and Rosamond as the sole proprietor of Borden Place, its lands, buildings, furnishings, all her personal effects including her jewelry, and $6,000. It mandated two trusts to administer the residue of her securities. The first trust was to distribute annually the sum of $200 to her United Church (Trinity) for its needs and for the maintenance of the Hillaton Cemetery; an annual $100 to the Blanch Fraser Memorial Hospital, which had cared for Elizabeth; and an unspecific amount to Mount Allison's Harold Lothrop Borden Scholarship Fund. The second trust provided $10 a month for Julia's education until she reached 25 years old, much as her father had for his grandchildren.

Little more than a year after Rosamond returned to Stockholm from Canning, and a few months after her coronation venture, she began preparing for their return to Canada. In November 1953 Edmund received notice of his transfer to Halifax, to work with "the staff officer, Atlantic Coast." Rosamond accompanied Edmund on a round of farewell receptions in Stockholm, Oslo, and Helsinki. She and Julia then left Stockholm for London a few weeks before Edmund, to shop and visit friends, before boarding the Cunard Line's old passenger vessel, the RMS *Ascania*, in Liverpool for Halifax, where they arrived at the end of March 1954. In the autumn, Julia enrolled at Edgehill School for Girls, an elite boarding school located in Windsor, Nova Scotia.

Lady Borden was now quite immobile, confined largely to her second-floor bed-sitting room. She still welcomed her family and friends and retained an interest in current events, despite her short-term memory. To her community she remained a village icon, a relic of a former era, respected and honoured by friends and associations. In August 1954 Mount Allison invited her to their Ladies' College's centennial dinner, one of their seven oldest living students. Although unable to attend, she sent her congratulations, greetings, and a photograph, which appeared in the *Mount Allison Record*.[26] Less than a month before her death on 28 February 1956, the Kings County Liberal Women's Association, meeting in Kentville, re-elected her their honorary president.[27]

Six days short of her ninety-third birthday "the Queen," as Lady Borden was known locally, died at Borden Place of heart failure. She had surpassed the average mortality age of contemporary Canadian women by almost two decades. The prime minister, Louis St-Laurent, wrote to "Mrs. Green," extending his condolences. Hughes Lapointe, the minister of veteran affairs (1950–7), sent a more personal note to "Dear Rosamond."[28] The presence of the lieutenant-governor, Alistair Fraser, and the recently chosen premier, Henry Hicks, and his wife (Pauline Banks) among the congregation at the Saturday afternoon funeral service on 3 March 1956 at Trinity United Church testified to Lady Borden's public stature.[29]

Once the chief mourners were seated, six black-clad pallbearers, accompanied by honorary pallbearers, placed Lady Borden's casket at the front of the church. While the church's minister, Reverend J.W. Barbour officiated, Lady Borden's former pastor, Dr. T.W. Hodgson, gave the eulogy, reminding the crowded church of Lady Borden's "Christian character" and her "life of service to the church and the community." With Mrs. L.S. Burbidge "presiding" at the piano and Mrs. Scott Blenkhorn "presiding" at the organ, the church's full choir and congregation sang "The Lord Is my Shepherd" and "The Sands of Time Are Sinking."[30] It was during the post-funeral reception at Borden Place that the Nova Scotia premier and his wife spotted boxes of Sir Frederick's papers and later "rescued" them for the Public Archives of Nova Scotia.

The Queen Is Dead

"The Queen is dead," is how Esther Clark Wright began her description of mid-twentieth-century Canning in her book *Blomidon Rose,* published a year after Lady Borden's death. Wright wrote that the elderly, titled, and regal Lady Borden had lived "in the brown mansion above the Habitant," from which she ruled "in stately fashion her little kingdom."[1] Wright knew Lady Borden, her life and style, her local, national, and imperial reputation. She knew Canning and its surrounding area, its people's pride and curiosity in their community's titled resident, ensconced at Borden Place, close to the monument to her son.

For Lady Borden's sole great-granddaughter, Julia Green MacKay, Lady Borden's death was the end of an era. Her great-grandmother had outlived her siblings, her husband, her stepchildren, and their spouses. She had survived the other Lady Borden, the wife of Sir Robert Borden, by sixteen years. At the time of Lady Bessie Borden's death, few people knew her precise age since on birthdays she reputedly subtracted a year from her age, and those who knew deferred to her affirmation, for though physically feeble and often confused, she remained regal to the end. Fewer still could recall the details of her long, eventful life and how it mirrored her region's demography, political economy, and layered, gendered society.

Lady Borden's death was indeed the end of an era, a story of the slow rise and decline of an affluent Nova Scotia family in which its men became marginal, though never marginalized.[2] Born before Confederation into a prominent merchant family at the height of the region's "golden age of sail," Lady Borden witnessed its economic transition to a lucrative land-based economy that redrew its economic and political boundaries, and redirected "'Her' Majesty's Yankees" Atlantic seaboard focus to an imperial transatlantic world that blended into a liberal international community. For the better part of a century Lady

Borden's family managed and benefited from these transitions. And during that time, Lady Borden was an active, affluential agent.

Upon Sir Frederick's death, genetics, war, and disease left Lady Borden in command of her elite family. For thirty-nine years her reign was prolonged by health, fortune, and her suppression of its sole internal challenge. Content to reign, Lady Borden could rule, as she demonstrated during her extended quarrel with her son-in-law, Leslie Macoun, over Sir Frederick's estate. The untimely death of her other son-in-law, Gordon Hewitt, though an unlikely challenger, left her in undisputed control, a responsibility she shared later with her stepdaughter Elizabeth, a joint tenancy subject to her consent and influence.

From birth until death, family defined Lady Borden's world, a world in which she was a beneficiary, partner, and custodian. An active agent in establishing her family's economic and social hegemony, she and Sir Frederick maintained their dominance by cultivating the complicities of family, business, and politics. Far from a stereotypical "mismanaging widow,"[3] Lady Borden proved a vigilant custodian of her family's socio-economic standing, a generous matriarch, responsive to her family's material, social, and cultural needs. A concomitant instrument of her ascendancy was her "invisible and institutional power," her cultivation and transmission of patrician values and aspirations,[4] through education, language, dress, and decorum, reinforced by religion and public service that bonded, branded, and extended her family's cross-generational socio-economic power.

A disciple of John Ruskin, Lady Borden believed in the social refinement of knowledge, art, and culture. She funded and patronized churches, colleges, libraries, and symphonies. She upheld elite customs and rituals. Within her "little kingdom" she exercised her social hegemony by hosting the executives of voluntary associations, offering social space to its leaders, with teas and receptions. Her residence, title, hospitality, and travel reaffirmed her social authority. The sight of her chauffeur-driven Cadillac or Packard emerging from the spacious, ordered grounds of Borden Place, or passing the village's monument to her son, turned the private into the public.[5] Her presence reminded Canning's residents of her family's status; it evoked their respect, sense of "moral continuity,"[6] and envy,[7] an example of the power and place of material culture, display, and hierarchy in rural Nova Scotia.[8]

In Lady Borden's rural Nova Scotia, economic and social power were personal, reciprocal, and qualified. Lady and Sir Frederick Borden understood the complicity of family, business, and politics, and their community's subsistent, seasonal economy, and generally managed it to their advantage.[9] Impervious and inequitable as the family's economic and social power might appear, it was constrained occasionally by their uncritical confidence in their associates' ethics, or challenged by competing political and material interests, best exemplified by Sir Frederick's electoral defeats in 1882 and 1911, and the "Burgess mess." Their social power was no less qualified, as Elizabeth and her mother acknowledged during their successful reappointment of their favourite Methodist minister, and Elizabeth and Colonel Byng Hall's abortive British migration scheme.

A study of the Borden family suggests how public service enhanced personal economic and social power. It demonstrates how a family, though lacking great wealth, translated local political and social power into national and imperial standing, permitting them to make claim to the most prestigious appointment within the Canadian government. It also suggests the resilience and durability of social power, its power to command public respect and consideration long after the erosion of its economic and political base.

Lady Borden's family's story confirms Suzanne Morton and Janet Guilford's contention that late nineteenth-, early twentieth-century Atlantic Canadian women lived "remarkably varied" lives, moving "freely between the so-called public sphere of the market, religion and politics, and the private sphere of the home,"[10] their mobility facilitated by the "ambiguities and contradictions inherent in" their "separate spheres."[11] Far from inhabiting cloistered separate spheres, Bessie Borden clerked in her family's store, stoked her furnace, tended her gardens and poultry, and contributed to her family's economic, religious, and civic life.[12] She managed household accounts and her children's inheritance; she watched capital markets, held equity in her own name, and executed her mother's will; she monitored her resources and exacted accountability from her children, estate manager, and husband's executor; and she defended her family's interests in the courts.

All four women were educated, articulate, well travelled, curious, and autonomous. All managed money and property, and engaged in public service. And all but Lizzie managed difficult marriages. All were practical, proficient, and forthright, ready to test class and gender borders, though not always ready to speak and live their lives "regardless of what the world or society might think."[13] Lady Borden and Elizabeth employed a female real estate agent. Maude hired a domestic cleaning man. When wartime labour shortages threatened Lady Borden's gardens, she was prepared to engage in manual work. Maude taught herself typing and stenography to hasten Leslie's settlement of her father's estate. Elizabeth became a farmer, working alongside her male and female apple pickers, graders, and shippers. Nor was family an ideological straitjacket. Lady Borden, Harold, and Elizabeth's strong religious faith and practice contrasted with Sir Frederick, Maude, and Rosamond's more instrumental, pragmatic approach. Their attitudes toward Britain were no less personal, generational, and opportunistic.

Class, however, still accorded and circumscribed elite women's gender expression and opportunities. Educated and talented, Elizabeth's limited initial career opportunities contrasted sharply with those available to Harold. Similarly, Bessie Borden did things that "Lady" Borden did not or might not do, or might do differently. Class and gender, however, were chameleon, malleable, and evolving, more flexible at the micro than the macro levels, and moulded by character and circumstance.[14]

Each woman responded to class and gender in her own way and time. An accomplice and friend of Lady Aberdeen and "organized womanhood,"[15] and a member of the National Federation of Liberal Women, Lady Borden resisted public advocacy. Although Elizabeth incited her mother to speak in public and not fear "putting Lady Aberdeen in the shade,"[16] Lady Borden disliked public speaking. Content to lead by example, to influence, encourage, and advise, she worked through her husband, son, and daughters, and lobbied friends such as Makenzie King. Although not an obvious example of "the new woman," she was interested in the status of women in Japan, admired her professional friends, Dr. Helen MacMurchy and Professor Edna Virginia Moffett, and supported Elizabeth's various public interventions.

Assertive, decisive, and didactic, Elizabeth was a woman who dared. Married to a man ten years her junior, she had no children, and spent all but a decade of her life as a single woman, refusing to restrict herself to stereotypical class or gendered categories.[17] An educated, accomplished pianist, apprentice author, amateur naturalist, and community worker, at forty-eight she became a successful commercial farmer. Although the Great War accelerated the silent revolution of class and gender, pressing women into wage employment what distinguished Elizabeth's postwar farming career was her economic power. She owned the means of production.[18] Dressed in her riding breeches, she hired, fired, and worked alongside male and female employees, a management style that mixed the traditional and personal with scientific organization.

Maude dared as well, in her reasoned, tenacious way. She managed a fraught marriage and the size of her family and supervised her daughter's education abroad for six years on limited resources.[19] Pragmatic and conciliatory she, like her father, could be pushed, but only so far. A gregarious person who enjoyed the company of the "well born," she crossed class and gender lines, matched needs to means, and like her sister, monitored land prices and marketing opportunities, and instructed farm labourers on the care and fertilization of trees with authority and knowledge.

Born and raised in an affluent family at the height of its social and economic power, Rosamond presided over her family's decline. An only child in an extended caring family, who attended to her education, health, and welfare Rosamond demonstrated stamina, resilience, and agency in dealing with the tragic death of her parents, her blocked artistic career, and a failing marriage. Like her grandmother, mother, and aunt she could manage money as she demonstrated during her Belgian practicum, travels, and the sale of Gables. And she, like they, endeavoured to maintained her family's standing through public service at home and abroad.[20]

All four women enjoyed a measure of economic autonomy.[21] Together, their stories suggest the range and variety of lives available to affluent nineteenth- and early twentieth-century Nova Scotia women living within the changing, commodious bounds of family, class, and gender.

Appendix A

In his self-promoting memoirs, Major-General E.T.H. Hutton, the disgruntled former general officer commanding the Canadian militia (1898–1900), insinuated that Lieutenant-Colonel James Domville possessed incriminating information linking Frederick Borden to "a criminal act" in his early life,[1] and used that information to secure Borden's support in the colonel's quarrel with the major-general.[2] Hutton's claim may have been based on a nebulous contemporary rumour circulating in Ottawa concerning Borden's involvement in an insurance claim that threatened his political career.

In July 1896, just before Borden entered Wilfrid Laurier's cabinet, Douglas Woodworth (1841–1900), Borden's erstwhile political rival, convinced William West and his brother John to sign affidavits stating that they, at Borden's "initiative," had conspired "to defraud the Mutual Benefit Life Company of Hartford Connecticut"[3] on an insurance policy Borden and the West brothers held on the life of an elderly widow, Sarah Alice Brown of Delhaven, Lower Pereaux, Kings County. Woodworth, having heard rumours of the "fraud," met first with William, then John, to warn them of the gravity of their "fraud" and "conspiracy," and to suggest how they might escape punishment by signing an affidavit casting the blame entirely on Frederick Borden, who was better placed to protect himself than they. Woodworth warned the West brothers that should they refuse his proposal "nothing could save them from the penitentiary," The affidavits, notarized by Charles Pineo, Woodworth's cousin, declared that neither brother had "the slightest idea of the fraud," since they had no "understanding" of insurance "before or since."[4]

According to the affidavits Woodworth prepared for John and Will West's signatures, on 9 February 1882 Borden and John and Will West had purchased a $3,000 policy from the Mutual Benefit Life Company on Sarah Brown's life against "some outstanding debt," and four years later (October 1886) Borden, having tired of paying the premiums, had persuaded the West brothers to claim that Sarah Brown had died and to collect the insurance, even though they were all "aware that she was still alive." On 24 December 1886, after several meetings, the conspirators agreed that William should represent himself as the undertaker, secure the signatures of Dr. James S. Miller, testifying to Brown's death, and the Congregational minister Joseph Cox, claiming to have performed the burial ceremonies, and have their signatures sworn before D.M. Dickie, notary public, or anyone else. Will West further testified that he had secured Dr. Miller's and Joseph Cox's signatures but had failed to have them witnessed by D.M. Dickie, and "at the suggestion and dictate of the said Frederick Borden,"[5] he (William) had written out answers to questions on printed insurance forms, testifying to Sarah Brown's death and burial. And, on 11 March 1887, the Mutual Benefit Life had remitted their claim.

How Frederick Borden could have been unaware of this "fraud" is difficult to understand, given Sarah Brown's residence at Lower Pereaux, and Borden's legendary knowledge of Kings County. Moreover, at the time of Brown's alleged death, Borden had written to the insurance company's agent that he had "just returned after a short absence over Christmas to … learn of the death of Mrs. Sarah A. Brown for which I am also the beneficiary." He was, he explained, "not altogether unprepared for this having heard of an attack of paralysis which the old lady [81 years old] had last summer though I had begun to look upon her as an exceptional case." Borden also asked the insurance agent to send John West "all necessary papers and instructions" including "blanks for making up the proofs."[6] Furthermore, when, on 5 January 1887, Borden learned that John West had failed to have the signatures notarized, he had them "signed and sworn by David M. Dickie," notary public, and "witnessed" by his cousin and former bank clerk, A.M. Borden.

People, goods, and rumours circulated freely within the Eastern Seaboard's fluid borders. In 1894 the Mutual Benefit Life Insurance Company, heavily invested in real estate, was placed in receivership of the Hyde, Gross & Hyde law firm. During Hyde's examination of Mutual Benefit's records, three men developed an unhealthy interest in the Sarah Brown dossier. The first man, George Griswold Sill (1829–1907), was a graduate of Yale University, an attorney, former lieutenant-governor of Connecticut, and a director of the Mutual Benefit Life Insurance Company, who worked at its head office; the second, Abbott, was a "Boston lawyer" who travelled between Ottawa and Boston; the third, Charles E. Starr, was a peripatetic Nova Scotian residing in Pittsburgh, and a partner in a Boston "foreign fruits, nuts and confectionary supplies" company, who retained a farm in the Canning area.[7] Their relationships and interest in the Brown file is unclear. According to William West's subsequent affirmation, the three simply sought to trade the documents for a "lift" (slang for theft). Their relationship to a fourth man, Douglas Woodworth, is even more obscure. Woodworth, however, had his own interests in the West brothers' incriminating affidavits.

Borden learned of the smoldering rumours regarding the fallacious insurance claim in the summer of 1894, and immediately placed the matter in the hands of Theodore Tyndale, his Boston legal counsel. In doing so he represented himself as the victim of a fraud, anxious to reimburse the Mutual Benefit Insurance Company, with interest. Tyndale spoke at once to William Hyde (1854–1915), the senior partner in Hyde, Gross & Hyde. A "high minded, honourable man," Hyde had his own reasons to cooperate, embarrassed as he was by the Brown documents' apparent "escape" from his legal offices.

Meanwhile, on 27 December 1894, Charles Starr wrote Hyde that he had come to Hyde's Hartford office the previous day, during Hyde's absence in New York, to inquire about an insurance claim on the life of a Mrs. James Brown. He assured Hyde that the information he sought would prove "no injury" to Hyde's company, as he was acting only "on the square for a friend."[8] Over a month later Starr renewed his unrequited request, explaining that all he needed were the names of parties to whom money had been paid, dates of payments, and proof of Brown's death.[9] On 2 February 1895 Starr wrote Hyde that he no longer needed the information, presumably having secured it elsewhere.[10] Five days later George Sill explained to Hyde that he had given "his client," Abbott, the original "proofs" of Sarah Brown's "death" in order to prosecute Borden in Boston, supposedly on behalf of the receiver general.[11]

Upon learning of Sill's action and Abbott's intentions, Hyde assured Tyndale, Borden's lawyer, that George Sill had "not an atom of authority to act for the Receiver-general," nor was Abbott likely to secure leave to prosecute Borden in Boston or would the receiver-general "ever get a cent." While Hyde did not feel free to tell Tyndale all he knew about Sill, what Hyde knew persuaded him that Sill was "an accomplice to an intended swindle": a "private plan" by Sill and Abbott "formulated to get what money they could."[12] Very shortly Abbott confirmed Tyndale's suspicions. Having been refused permission to prosecute Borden in Boston, Abbott contacted Tyndale and Borden directly, "on behalf of his partners," offering to sell his incriminating papers for an initial sum of $1,000.[13] Tyndale cautioned Borden neither to meet nor communicate with Abbott but to leave things entirely to him since "if we pay it will be to the right person."[14]

Tyndale had no difficulty persuading Hyde that Borden had been the victim of a fraud. For not only did Hyde agree to Borden's repayment of his and the West brothers' false insurance claim, plus 6 per cent interest, but thanked Borden profusely for his "honourable conduct in promptly and voluntarily calling attention to this matter ... never having had the faintest suspicion that there was any claim against you." "Your action," he effused, was "high and above reproach," with no intention of availing yourself "of any advantage derived through another's evil actions ... Your behaviour has been a most gratifying surprise and I beg you to accept my thanks."[15]

Hyde, however, refused to exonerate the West brothers,[16] despite Borden's plea that they had repaid their share of the illicit claim. Although Hyde assured Borden that he had no intention of pursuing the West brothers, his refusal left John and William dangerously exposed, since the incriminating documents were still at large.[17] In January 1896 John West, upon learning of Starr's brief return to his Canning farm, attempted to "frighten" him into surrendering the incriminating documents, reminding Starr that Hyde was after the stolen papers and "he pitied the man that had the papers." Starr denied possession of the documents but admitted that Abbott had purchased the them from Sill for "a fee" and promised West to procure them from Abbott upon Starr's return to Boston.[18]

Starr's failure to secure the documents from Abbott made the West brothers more than receptive to Woodworth's offer of assistance, especially as Borden became preoccupied with the 1896 federal election. A few days after John West had signed the Woodworth-dictated affidavit he had second thoughts and revisited Woodworth to retrieve or amend his affidavit, claiming that some of its statements were untrue. Woodworth, however, refused to surrender or amend the affidavit, and left Canning shortly for his California residence. (Woodworth was a very elusive man, and after his 1887 electoral defeat he had moved to Nevada, then to Oakland, California, leaving his wife in Suffolk, Massachusetts, where she died in 1902.)

Borden, upon learning of John's "folly," was more than anxious to help him relieve his "conscience." He suggested that John speak to W.E Roscoe, Borden's political ally and legal counsel,[19] and on 7 August 1897 John West signed an affidavit before E.D. Cogswell, notary public, repudiating his 1896 affidavit, conscious that he had done Frederick Borden a grave injustice. According to John West's renunciation, Borden had no reason to know that Sarah Brown was still alive since she lived in a remote area of the county. On 1 July 1898 John's brother, Will, signed an even more contrite confession, assuming full responsibility for the fraud, admitting that he, not Borden, had "found the premiums well nigh impossible to keep up," and that he had taken care to see that "Brown should not be seen by any who might speak" to Borden. Moreover, he did "not wish that [he] should obtain relief from any acts of mine by connecting them to Frederick Borden as I was told" by Woodworth.[20]

Woodworth, however, had not played his last card. In August 1899, as Borden was deeply immersed in the acrimonious debate over Canada's possible participation in the impending South African War, Woodworth wrote Borden from the Commercial Hotel in Vancouver, asking to meet at Ottawa's Russell House the following week to show Borden the West affidavits he had in his possession. As Woodworth explained in his threatening letter: "implacable and unfair though you have been, yet I will give you every doubt possible in the Sarah Alice Brown story before proceeding further." Woodworth's forbearance, however, had a price. Borden must use his "influence with the Minister of the Interior," employing any means "you can devise," to "set aside" Archibald Beaton's gold mining claim on Dominion Creek near Dawson, and have it transferred to "someone's name you can trust but really for me." In Woodworth's estimate, Beaton's Klondyke claim was worth a "small fortune". Borden was also to verify the soundness of the Klondyke claim and put up the deposit "which the tenders call for," and for which Woodworth promised to reimburse Borden when they met in Ottawa. "This must be done," Woodworth ordered, "and you can do it in the name of all that is fair and just."[21]

Almost two weeks later, Woodworth wrote Borden from Oakland, California, to reschedule their failed Ottawa meeting for the next week. Three days later he dispatched a telegram, demanding that his request be carried out immediately, employing counsel if necessary. Four days later, still detained in Oakland, Woodworth telegraphed Borden, demanding confirmation that Borden had done what Woodworth had instructed, to which Borden replied that the matter was before the minister, to be decided "on its merits."[22] On 2 January 1900 Woodworth died in Oakland, California.

Notwithstanding Woodworth's death, the insurance saga resurfaced before the 1904 federal election. W. John Kidd, an Ottawa "lawyer" working closely with a John L. Gemmill, wrote to Genevieve L. Pineo, seeking information and documents on the location of the "West boys," making clear that he was really "after a man by the name of Borden."[23] Woodworth had cohabited with Genevieve and had left her the West brothers' original affidavits. (Genevieve subsequently married Charles H. Pineo, Woodworth's cousin, the man who had notarized West's original affidavit.) In response to Kidd's request, Genevieve sent Kidd "copies" of the West brothers' affidavits, for which Kidd paid $15 and promised her "more if he could use them."[24] To use them successfully Kidd needed contemporary confirmation that the West brothers would stand by their original affidavits. (He was seemingly oblivious to their subsequent renunciations.) While Pineo disclaimed any interest in money, she went to some lengths to locate the West brothers, carelessly writing to George Murray, the Liberal premier of Nova Scotia, and friend of Sir Frederick Borden!

Alerted to Kidd's interest in the insurance fiasco, Sir Frederick sent a private detective, H.H. Norwood, to San Francesco, in December 1904, to investigate. Norwood, representing himself as A.G. West and a relative of the West brothers, wrote to Genevieve Pineo, seeking a meeting, which she failed to keep initially, though she was sufficiently interested to reschedule. In reporting their rescheduled meeting Norwood informed Sir Frederick that Pineo "appeared rather nervous and lied like hell." She claimed she possessed the original affidavits and promised Norwood copies the next day. After postponing that meeting for two days, on 8 January 2005 Pineo (a typist) arrived with freshly typed copies of the affidavits, explaining that Kidd retained the originals but that she would request their return. According to Norwood's information, Pineo had tried to sell the documents just before the November 1904 election, but Kidd had refused her offer unless she secured the West brothers' confirmation, which she failed to do. Should she produce the originals, Norwood assured Sir Frederick, he could "get them for a song." Meanwhile, Norwood advised Sir Frederick that had "W. [Woodworth] anything that he dared to spring on you, he would have done so when he was hard up."[25] With that, the "scandal" seemed to have died, except for references to it in rumours and in the documentary shards in the Black Box.

Appendix B

BORDEN FAMILY

Perry Borden (1773–1862)………………………Lavina Fuller (1785–1825)

|

(a) Dr. Jonathan Borden (1809–1875)
(b) Andrew Borden (1816–1900)

Dr. Jonathan Borden……………Maria Frances Brown (1814–1862)

|

(a) Sir Frederick William Borden (1847–1917)

Sir Frederick William Borden……(1) Julia Maude Clarke (1850–1880)
(2) Elizabeth Blanche Clarke (1863–1956)

|

(a) Elizabeth Borden (1874–1948)…………Gordon Hewitt (1885–1920)
(b) Harold Borden (1876–1900)
(c) Julia Maude Borden (1879–1942)

Julia Maude Borden…………………………..Leslie Macoun (1874–1942)

|

(a) Elizabeth Rosamond Macoun (1907–1986)……Edmund Green (1909–1980)

|

(a) Julia Leslie Green MacKay

TUPPER FAMILY

Charles Tupper (1748–1821)……………….Elizabeth West (1753–1839)

|

(a) Agustus Tupper (1792–1850) (b) Reverend Charles Tupper (1794–1881)

| |

(a) Elizabeth Mary Tupper (1829–1919) (b) Sir Charles Tupper (1821–1915)

CLARKE FAMILY

John Hopson Clarke (1810–1888)……Elizabeth Mary Tupper (1829–1919)

|

(a) Agustus Tupper Clarke (1848–1924)
(b) Julia Maude Clarke (1850–1880)
(c) Elizabeth Blanche Clarke (1863–1956)

Notes

Preface: The Black Box

1 Robert Craig Brown, *Robert Laird Borden: A Biography 1854–1914* (Toronto: Macmillan of Canada, 1975), 2:74; Carol McLeod, *Wives of the Canadian Prime Ministers* (Hantsport: Lancelot Press, 1985), 83, 87. John English described Robert and Laura Borden at the time of their marriage as "rather old newlyweds" in *Borden, His Life and World* (Toronto: McGraw-Hill Ryerson Limited, 1977), 49. See, too, P.B. Waite's excellent review of Brown's Borden biography, "The Mind and Character of Robert Borden," *Acadiensis* 6, no. 1 (Autumn 1976): 129–34.

2 Alice Miller, R.B. Bennett's secretary, purged his papers of what she considered to be "Unhistorical." P.B. Waite, *In Search of R.B. Bennett* (Montreal and Kingston: McGill-Queen's University Press, 2012), xiii.

3 Private Borden Papers, hereafter, PBP. A handwritten note, from Mrs. St. John Green, on a scrap of paper, 7 August 1970, signed by C. Bruce Ferguson, provincial archivist, described the transferred material as "a collection of letters and papers related to Dr. Jonathan Borden, Sir Frederick Borden and Harold Borden on loan."

4 Important business, personal, and estate papers, however, remained in the archive's extensive F.W. Borden fond.

5 PBP Elizabeth Hewitt, Chronicle, 27 February 1926

6 Ibid.

7 PBP, Bessie to Rosamond Green, May 1944.

8 Cecilia Morgan, *Happy Holidays: English Canadians and Transatlantic Tourism, 1870–1930* (Toronto: University of Toronto Press, 2008). Mary Elizabeth Kirkland, "Mothering Citizens: Elite women in Montreal, 1890–1914," PhD thesis, McGill University, 2002, ch. 5.

9 Herbert Butterfield, *The Whig Interpretation of History* (New York: Norton & Company, 1965.

10 Thomas Mann, *Budenbrooks: The Decline of a Family* (London: Martin Secker, 1930).

11 P.L. Payne, *British Entrepreneurship in the Nineteenth Century* (London: Macmillan, 1974), 25.

12 Jose Harris has reminded us that nineteenth- and early twentieth-century British "families remained surprisingly strong," even if historians "disagree profoundly on the structure, function, and affective nature of the family. Jose Harris, *Private Lives, Public Spirit: A Social History of Britain, 1870–1914* (Oxford: Oxford University Press, 1993), 61–2, 92.

13 Harris, Private Lives, 66, 77–9. See, too, Peter Baskerville, *A Silent Revolution? Gender and Wealth in English Canada, 1860–1930* (Montreal: McGill-Queen's University Press, 2008), 3–9.

14 Janet Guildford and Suzanne Morton, eds., *Separate Spheres: Women's Worlds in the 19th-Century Maritimes* (Fredericton: Acadiensis Press, 1994), 9. Peter Baskerville agrees that the role of "separate spheres" provides "limited utility" in understanding the role of women and wealth; see Baskerville, *A Silent Revolution*, 240. See, too, Harris, *Private Lives*, 92, and Veronica Strong-Boag, *The New Day Recalled: Lives of Girls and Women in English Canada, 1919–1939* (Markham, ON: Penguin Books, 1988), 9.

15 Joan Sangster, *Demanding Equality: One Hundred Years of Canadian Feminism* (Vancouver: UBC Press, 2021). Guilford and Morton, *Separate Spheres*, 20.

16 Anne-Marie Adams, "Female Regulation of the Healthy Home," in James Opp and John C. Walsh (eds.), *Home, Work and Play* (Toronto: Oxford University Press, 2006), 3–17; Baskerville, *A Silent Revolution?*, 9.

1. Bessie

1 Rev. B.C. Borden, quoted in John G. Reid, *Mount Allison: A History, to 1963* (Toronto: University of Toronto, Press, 1984), 1: 225.

2 Thomas Raddall, *His Majesty's Yankees* (Toronto: Harlequin, 1952).

3 Kirkland, "Mothering Citizens," 191. Unlike Montreal's elite anglophone women, Bessie's ancestors were pre-Loyalist Planters, proud of their New England heritage.

4 See Debra McNabb, "Land and Families in Horton Township, 1760–1830," MA thesis, University of British Columbia, 1986; Rusty Bittermann, "The Hierarchy of the Soil: Land and Labour in a 19th Century Cape Breton Community," *Acadiensis* 18, no. 1 (Autumn 1988): 33–55.

5 Between "Calvinist" and "Free Will" Baptists.

6 Philip Buckner, "Sir Charles Tupper," *Dictionary of Canadian Biography* (Toronto: University of Toronto Press), 14:1014; Barry Moody, "Rev.

Charles Tupper," *Dictionary of Canadian Biography* (Toronto: University of Toronto Press), 11:895–6.

7 Brian Cuthbertson, *Johnny Bluenose at the Polls: Epic Nova Scotia Election Battles, 1757–1848* (Halifax: Formac Publishing, 1994), 104.

8 Founded as Queen's College in 1838 to honour Queen Victoria, its name was changed to Acadia College in 1841 owing to its failure to receive royal approval.

9 Cuthbertson, *Johnny Bluenose*, 107; George Rose, ed., *A Cyclopedia of Canadian Biography* (Toronto: Rose Publishing Company, 1886–8), 318.

10 Jose Harris, *Private Lives Public Spirit: A Social History of Britain, 1870–1914* (Oxford: Oxford University Press, 1993), 195.

11 P.B. Waite, *In Search of R.B. Bennett* (Montreal and Kingston: McGill-Queen's University Press, 2012), 6–7.

12 Marguerite Van Die, "The Marks of a Genuine Revival: Religion, Social Change, Gender and Community in Mid-Victorian Branford Ontario," *Canadian Historical Review* 79, no. 3 (September 1998): 524–63.

13 Hannah M. Lane, "Wife, Mother, Sister, Friend Methodist Women in St Stephen, New Brunswick, 1861–1881," in *Separate Spheres: Women's Worlds in the 19th-Century Maritimes* ed. Janet Guildford and Suzanne Morton (Fredericton: Acadiensis Press, 1994), 113–14.

14 They also advocated for women in business. Peter Baskerville, *A Silent Revolution? Gender and Wealth in English Canada, 1860–1930* (Montreal: McGill-Queen's University Press, 2008), 33–4.

15 William H. Magney, "The Methodist Church and the National Gospel, 1884–1914," *United Church Bulletin* (1968): 20.

16 In 1874 the Eastern British North America Wesleyan Methodist Conference, the Primitive Methodist, the New Connection Methodists, and the Bible Christian Churches united with the Wesleyan Methodist Church of Canada. Ten years later they were joined by the Methodist Episcopal Church.

17 Magney, "The Methodist Church and the National Gospel," 20.

18 PBP, Mother to Harold, Sunday, 21st, n.d.

19 PBP, Mother to Elizabeth, Home, Sunday night [1893–4].

20 Thomas Mann, *Buddenbrooks the Decline of a Family* (London: Martin Secker, 1930), 255.

21 PBP, Henrietta Britten to Lady Borden, 3 January 1941. Mary Elizabeth Kirkland noted religion's role in shaping elite women's values: "Mothering Citizens," 12.

22 Alison Prentice, *The School Promoters: Education and Social Class in Mid-Nineteenth Century Upper Canada* (Toronto: University of Toronto Press, 1977), 21. Bruce Curtis, *Ruling by Schooling Quebec* (Toronto: University of Toronto Press, 2012); E.A. Heaman, *A Short History of the State* (Toronto: University of Toronto Press, 2015), 102.

23 Unlike the Baptists' Horton Academy in Wolfville or the Church of England's King's College in Windsor, Acacia Villa was not a "denominational school"; its founder, Joseph Hea, however, was a strict Methodist who came from the Wesleyan Academy in Sackville, as did Arthur McNutt Patterson, who owned and ran the school for years. See M.V. Marshall, *A Short History of Acacia Villa School* (Wolfville: Acadia University Institute, 1963), 11; Reid, *Mount Allison University: A History*, 1:31, 1:69.
24 *Kentville Advertiser*, 24 July 1947.
25 PBP, Elizabeth Hewett, Chronicle, 22 February 1926.
26 PBP, Mother to my dear Elizabeth, Home, Sunday Night [1893–4].
27 Henry James Morgan, *Types of Canadian Women* (Toronto: William Briggs, 1903), 1:vi. See, too, Robert Lanning, "Henry James Morgan," *Dictionary of Canadian Biography* (Toronto: University of Toronto Press, 1998), 14:768–9.

2. Julia

1 John Reid, *Mount Allison University: A History to 1963* (Toronto: University of Toronto Press, 1984), 1:116. See, too, John Reid, "The Education of Women at Mount Allison, 1854–1914," *Acadiensis* 12, no. 2 (Spring 1983): 3–33.
2 Reid, *Mount Allison*, vol. 1, table 15, 86–8, 371.
3 Reid, *Mount Allison*, vol. 1, table 7, 360.
4 John Reid, "Mary Mellish," *Dictionary of Canadian Biography* (Toronto, University of Toronto Press, 1994), 13:697–8.
5 Reid, *Mount Allison*, 1:120.
6 Reid, *Mount Allison*, 1:60, 1:61, 1:122.
7 Quoted in Reid, *Mount Allison*, 1:61.
8 Reid, *Mount Allison*, 1:56.
9 Leverett De Veber Chipman had "inherited" his seat from his father, the late William Henry Chipman, the county's anti-Confederation MP. The capricious, self-serving behaviour of the forty-three-year-old patronage-hungry incumbent, at times voting with the Liberal/Reform Party, and at times with the Conservative government, as personal interest dictated, had so angered the Liberal/Reform Party's leadership that it refused to endorse his candidacy in the general election of 1872. Upon the Liberal/Reformers' assumption of power following the Pacific Scandal, Levertt De Veber sought to "re-join" the government benches!
10 Canada, Sessional Paper 60 (1873), 99.
11 Carman Miller, *A Knight in Politics* (Montreal and Kingston: McGill-Queen's University Press, 2010), 43–5.
12 In 1872 John A. Macdonald's Conservative government promised a charter to a syndicate to build a railway to the Pacific coast in exchange for a $360,000 election contribution.

13 Dr. Edward Lothrop Brown represented Horton Township 1847–59, Kings County's South Division 1863–7, and Kings County 1867–71 in the Nova Scotia Assembly; his brother John Lothrop Brown, a merchant and farmer, represented Kings County's South Division 1859–63 in the Nova Scotia Assembly.
14 Named Lothrop after Frances Brown's maternal grandfather.
15 Canada, Census 1881.
16 Reid, *Mount Allison*, vol. 1, table 15, 371.
17 Reid, *Mount Allison*, 1:223.
18 PBP, Harry Brown, Memoir, 1.
19 Reid, *Mount Allison*, vol. 1, table 11, 364.
20 Reid, *Mount Allison*, 1:171–2.
21 Reid, *Mount Allison*, 1:243.
22 Maria Tippett, *By A Lady: Three Centuries of Art by Canadian Women* (Toronto: Viking Press, 1993).
23 Nancy Vogan, "Music Education in the Maritimes between the Wars: A Period of Transition," in *Myth and Milieu" Atlantic Literature and Culture 1918–1939*, ed. Gwendolyn Davies (Fredericton: Acadiensis Press, 1993), 77–86.
24 Reid, *Mount Alison University*, 1:176.

3. Mrs. Borden

1 Landers vs. Woodworth, (1878) 2 SCR 158.
2 Sandra Gwyn, *The Private Capital: Ambition and Love in the Age of Macdonald and Laurier* (Toronto: McClelland & Stewart, 1984), 350.
3 Unidentified newspaper clipping: "Wives of Cabinet Ministers."
4 PBP, Harold to Dear Father, 10 August 1899.
5 Canada, House of Commons, Debates, 27 February, and 4 March 1880.
6 Michael Lawrence Smith, "Desire Girouard," *Dictionary of Canadian Biography* (Toronto: University of Toronto Press, 1998), 14:411.
7 PBP, Fred to Bessie, 19 October 1911.
8 PBP, Registrar General of Nova Scotia, Certificate of Marriage Certificate, 14 February 1952 [12 June 1884]. The NS certification Bessie obtained to obtain Old Age Security.
9 Jose Harris, *Private Lives, Public Spirit: A Social History of Britain, 1870–1914* (Toronto: Oxford University Press, 1993), 89.
10 P.B. Waite, *The Man from Halifax: Sir John Thompson, Prime Minister* (Toronto: University of Toronto Press, 1985), 20–33.
11 Unlike the gendered private space of the very rich. Mary Elizabeth Kirkland, "Mothering Citizens: Elite Women in Montreal, 1890–1914," PhD thesis, McGill University, 2012, 70–4.

12 PBP, Elizabeth Hewitt, Chronicle, 16 February 1926; account of sales at auction on 29 January 1875 of certain articles belonging to the estate of the late Jonathan Borden.
13 PBP, FWB to my dear wife, 26 December 1897.
14 See Richard Florida, *The Rise of the Creative Class* (New York: Basic Books, 2002).
15 PBP, Elizabeth's nostalgic "Notes, My first visit to England, Scotland, Belgium and France," April 1899.
16 Quoted in Kirkland, "Mothering Citizens," 1.
17 See Kim K.P. Johnson and Sharon J. Lennon, eds., *Appearance and Power* (New York: Berg, 1999).
18 Jacqueline Beaudoin-Ross, *Formes et Modes: Le Costume à Montréal au XIXe siècle* (Montreal: McCord Museum, 1992), 14.
19 Julia Leslie Green MacKay to Carman Miller, 13 January 2010.
20 PBP, Hewitt Chronicle, 4 May 1926.
21 PBP, Fred to Dear Bessie, 14 September [1908]; Fred to my dear wife, Saturday a.m. [August 1905].
22 PBP, Your loving husband to My dear Bessie, 8 March 1893
23 PBP, letter fragment from Your loving husband, at New Hotel Bellevue, no date.
24 PBP, Fred to My dear Bessie, 8 March 1893, including a blanketed pink flannel nightgown.
25 PBP, Your loving husband to My darling wife, 20 April [1893]; FWB to my dear Bessie, 27 January 1898.
26 PBP, Fred to my dear Bessie, 28 December 1897.
27 The Berwick *Register*, 26 January 1898.
28 PBP, H.L. Borden Diary, 11 and 21 June 1898.
29 PBP, Fred to dearest Bessie, Sunday, 19 [October 1911].
30 PBP, Fred to My dear wife, Saturday a.m. [August 1905]. During Sir Frederick's 1905 western tour with his two daughters and Percy Lake to promote his military reforms, he regretted "dreadfully" Lady Borden's absence owing to health: "I wanted those Western people to see you for believe me dearest I love you & am very proud of you."
31 PBP, Lady Borden's Travel Diary (Colorado) 12 June 1921.
32 E.A. Heaman, *A Short History of the State in Canada* (Toronto: University of Toronto Press, 2015), 109.

4. Business Partner

1 Peter Baskerville, *A Silent Revolution? Gender and Wealth in English Canada, 1860–1930* (Montreal and Kingston: McGill-Queen's University Press, 2008), 53, 242.

2 Carman Miller, *A Knight in Politics* (Montreal and Kingston: McGill-Queen's University Press, 2010), 58–60, 30–8. Borden owned shares in the *Golden Light*, the *Habitant*, the *Recovery*, the *Blomidon*, and the *Harold Borden*.

3 Although a property qualification for Senate membership remains, the Dominion Election Act (1874) abolished a property qualification for election to the House of Commons.

4 PBP, Probate Court Transcript, 12.

5 Robert Alexander MacKinnon, "The Historical Geography of Agriculture in Nova Scotia, 1851–1951," PhD thesis, University of British Columbia, 1991, 195.

6 Miller, *A Knight in Politics*, 39–41.

7 PBP, Harry Brown, Memoir, 2. Aubrey Melbourne Brown, Fred's Uncle John's twenty-year-old son (November 1885–May 1886); Harry Brown, Aubrey's brother (1887–9); Frederick Alexis Brown (August 1889–May 1891), and John William Borden, his Uncle Andrew Borden's son (May 1891–6).

8 FWB was agent for the Bank of Nova Scotia (September 1882–May 1891), then agent of the Halifax Banking Company (1891–96).

9 See Appendix A.

10 Only in 1884 did women have the right to hold property in Nova Scotia, and only in 1898 did they have the right to dispose of property. Baskerville, *A Silent Revolution?*, 7.

11 Kings County Registry, John H. Clarke, Will, Item B 168, Probate Court, 10 February 1917.

12 Legal documents detailing "ownership" of bonds, mortgages, and property of the F.W. Borden Company and its successors continued to name "Sir Frederick and Bessie B. Borden his wife," See PBP, Transcript, 25. Bessie's management of Mr. Clarke's educational legacy seemed to have been rooted in custom rather than legal obligation. See Philip Girard and Rebecca Veinott, "Married Women's Property Law in Nova Scotia, 1850–1910" in *Separate Spheres: Women's Worlds in the 19th Century Maritimes*, ed. Janet Guildford and Suzanne Morton (Fredericton: Acadiensis Press, 1994), 73.

13 PBP, Montreal Tram and Power, Affidavit, Property Value, Elizabeth Clarke, 12 November 1919.

14 PBP, Elizabeth Tupper Clarke, Last Will, 21 October 1903.

15 PBP, Elizabeth Clark's Will, 21 October 1903.

16 PBP, Fred to My dear Wife, Saturday, a.m. [August 1905].

17 PBP, Bessie to Dearest Fred, 28 April [1907]; Your Bessie" to Dear Fred, 10 p.m., Thursday, 11 [April 1907]; Fred to My dear Wife, Saturday, a.m. [Fall 1905].

18 Frederick Borden and Robert Borden were both interested in creating the Blomidon national park. See Gwendolyn Davies, "John Frederick Herbin," *Dictionary of Canadian Biography* (Toronto: University of Toronto Press, 2005), 15:473.

19 Julia Bush, *Edwardian Ladies and Imperial Power* (Leicester: Leicester University Press, 1999), 30.

20 PBP, Your loving Fred to My dear Bessie, 11 February 1893.

21 Lisa Stefanik, "Botanical Gleanings: Susan Fenimore Cooper, Catherine Parr Trail and the Representation of flora," in *Susan Fenimore Cooper: New Essays on Rural Hours and Other Works,* ed. Rochelle Johnson and Daniel Patterson (Athens: University of Georgia Press, 2001), 240. See also Ann Shteir, *Flora's Fieldworkers: Women and Botany in Nineteenth Century Canada* (Montreal and Kingston: McGill-Queen's University Press, 2022).

22 E.A. Heaman, *A Short History of the State in Canada* (Toronto: University of Toronto Press, 2015), 53, 126.

23 PBP, watercolour of Annapolis River at Wilmot, signed B.B.

24 PBP, Mother to dear Elizabeth, Home, Sunday night [1893–4].

5. Dearest Mother

1 The Ottawa Beechwood Cemetery, Register 1873–1990, reported the death of "Baby Borden," parents Frederick and Bessie Borden, 1901.

2 Loren Lerner, "Youth and Sunlight: Reflections of Childhood," in *Canada and Impressionism,* ed. Katerina Atanassova (Ottawa: National Gallery of Canada, n.d.), 83–93.

3 Jose Harris, *Private Lives, Public Spirit: A Social History of Britain, 1870–1914* (Oxford: Oxford University Press, 1993), 86–8.

4 PBP, Fred to Bessie, 20 April [1893]. Fred commented on Harold's criticism of his father's failure to visit him at school on one occasion, saying he "would have had to screw my courage up a good deal to have addressed" his father as Harold had done, but "I am sure the dear boy meant no harm and I am glad he is not afraid of me, at least."

5 Harris, *Private Lives,* 54–5. Bessie was particularly attached to Fanny Farmer's *Boston Cooking-School Cook Book* (Little, Brown & Company, 1896), which advocated cooking based on "scientific knowledge."

6 PBP, Mother to [Harold], Sunday 21st, n.d.

7 PBP, Mother to Harold, n.d. [1897].

8 PBP, Elizabeth's Chronicle, 4 May 1926.

9 PBP, Mother to Frederick, 4 September, n.d. [1859].

10 PBP, Elizabeth's Chronicle, 24 March 1926.

11 PBP, Harold to Elizabeth, 10 December 1899; F.W. Borden to Elizabeth, 16 May 1894.

12 PBP, your aff[ectionate] Guirly to father, n.d.
13 PBP, your loving husband to dear wife, Ottawa, Sunday, 20 April [1889].
14 PBP, Charlie [Hewitt] to my dear mother, Sunday 27 April [1913?]. His parents called him Charlie; in Canada he used the name Gordon.
15 Rev. Charles Tupper died at the age of 86; Sir Charles Tupper died at the age of 94; Elizabeth (Tupper) Clarke died at the age of 93; Bessie Borden died six days short of her 93rd year.
16 PBP, Elizabeth to Mama, 8 June, n.d.; Maude to dear Papa, 22 March, n.d.
17 PBP, Fred to Bessie, November 1911.
18 Frederick followed Harvard and Kings alumni news; he contributed to alumni and special funds to Mount Allison University, University of New Brunswick, and Acadia University, and had his investment in Butte Central Copper Syndicate succeeded he planned to fund a chair in mining engineering at UNB.
19 Reid, *Mount Allison*, 1:175–6.
20 The son of George Newton Borden, Byron Crane Borden (1850–1929) graduated from Mount Allison with a BA in 1878; he began pastoral work in Bermuda, where he married. His brother, Robert Allison Borden, graduated from Mount Allison in 1866. Fred's second cousin, the Rev. Arthur Cummings Borden, earned his BA (1885), B.D. (1891), and MA (1895) from Mount Allison, and became a distinguished Methodist missionary to Japan.
21 Reid, *Mount Allison*, 1:175.
22 Jane Tisdale, "John Hammond, 1843–1939," *Dictionary of Canadian Biography*, vol. 16 (online).
23 Reid, *Mount Allison*, 1:212.
24 Reid, *Mount Allison*, 1:213.
25 PBP, Maude to My dear Mother, 20 March 1897.
26 Reid, *Mount Allison*, 1:210, 221.
27 PPB, Elizabeth's Chronicle, 13 February 1926.
28 PBP, F.W. Borden to Elizabeth, 16 May 1895; Your loving husband to my dear wife, Sunday [April 1895]; Elizabeth's "Notes, My first visit to England, Scotland, Belgium and France," April 1899.
29 PBP, Elizabeth's "Notes."
30 PBP, Your loving husband to My loving wife, Sunday, [April 1895].
31 PBP, Elizabeth's Chronicle, 13 February 1926; Elizabeth's nostalgic "Notes."
32 PBP, Father to Elizabeth, 9 June 1894.
33 PBP, Your loving Fred to My dear Bessie, 5 March 1893.
34 PBP, Harold to Papa, 23 March 1889.
35 *Halifax Morning Chronicle*, 30 January 1900.
36 Robert Borden, quoted by Roy McLaren in "Harold Borden," *Dictionary of Canadian Biography* (Toronto, University of Toronto Press, 1990), 12:114–15. See also PBP, Harold to Dear Mother, 22 June 1893.

37 PBP, Harold to Elizabeth, 28 January 1894.
38 Ibid.
39 G. Rice, "The First Break in 97," *The Argosy* 37, no. 1 (October 1900): 6–8; PBP, Harold to Mother, 22 June 1893.
40 PPB, Maude to My dear Mama, 20 March 1897.
41 PPB, Maude to My dear Mother, 20 March 1897; Maude to My dear Mother, 21 February 1897.
42 PBP, Harold to Mother, 22 June 1893; Maude to My dear Mama, 20 March 1897.
43 PBP, Harold to Mother, 22 June 1893.

6. Political Spouse

1 Suzanne Morton, *Wisdom, Justice, and Charity: Canadian Social Welfare through the Life of Jane B. Wisdom, 1884–1975* (Toronto: University of Toronto Press, 2014), 185.
2 Carman Miller, "Family, Business and Politics in Kings County, N.S.: The Case of Sir Frederick Borden, 1874–1896," *Acadiensis* 8 (Spring 1987): 60–75.
3 Ibid.
4 PBP, Elizabeth's Chronicle, 17 and 18 February 1926.
5 According to the *Western Chronicle*, 19 February 1887, Fred joined Canning's branch of the Templars in February 1874, and once or twice was in arrears and refused to pay, "saying he was no longer a member"; he later paid rather than being expelled, and then resigned until October 1886, when he renewed his membership.
6 Carman Miller, *A Knight in Politics* (Montreal and Kingston: McGill-Queen's University Press, 2015), 60.
7 *Western Chronicle*, 12 and 19 February 1887.
8 During a 1906 banquet honouring Fielding, Sir Frederick acclaimed Fielding as "the acknowledged leader of the Liberal party in the province: *Morning Chronicle*, 2 November 1906.
9 The interventions of prominent party members, patronage, and a promise of a Senate seat. See P.B. Waite, *The Man from Halifax: Sir John Thompson, Prime Minister* (Toronto: University of Toronto Press, 1985), 285.
10 PBP, Your loving Fred to my darling wife, 18 March 1888.
11 Ibid.
12 PBP Fred to Dear Bessie, 27 September 1911.
13 PBP, Bessie to My dear Girlie, Home, Friday a.m.; Your loving Fred to My darling wife, 18 March 1888.
14 PBP, Mum to Lizzie, 18 March [1892].
15 PBP, your loving little Maude to Papa, 19 April [c. 1887]. D.B. Woodworth had defeated Fred in 1882.

16 PBP, Elizabeth to Mama, 8 June, n.d.; Maude to dear Papa, 23 March, n.d.
17 PBP, Fred to my dear wife, 3 March 1892.
18 Mary Elizabeth Kirkland, "Mothering Citizens: Elite Women in Montreal, 1890–1914," PhD thesis, McGill University, 2012, 225.
19 PBP, Bessie to dear Fred, Thursday 11th [May 1907].
20 Salem G. Bland, *James Henderson, D.D.* (Toronto: McClelland & Stewart, 1926), 133, 134. Personal possession, Laurier to Dr. Henderson, 26 December 1910; Laurier to my dear nurse, 26 October 1917.
21 PBP, Your loving husband to My dear Bessie, 8 March 1893.
22 Miller, *A Knight in Politics*, 65.
23 PBP, Your loving Fred to My darling wife, 18 March 1888; Fred to Bessie, 11 February 1893.
24 W. Stewart Wallace, *The Memoirs of the Rt. Hon. Sir George Foster* (Toronto: Macmillan, 1933), 59–60.
25 Frederick Borden had no time for anti-Catholic crusades then or subsequently, a conviction that preceded Alexander Mackenzie's pragmatic political conversion. See James Forbes, "'A Deplorable Speech': The Liberal Party vs. Anti-Catholicism during the Alexander Mackenzie Administration, 1873–1878," *Journal of the CHA* 28, no. 1 (New Series, 2017): 193–216.
26 Marc LaTerreur, "Correspondance Laurier–Mme. Joseph Lavergne, 1891–93", *CHA Report* 43, no. 1 (1964): 37–51. Charles Fischer, ed., *Dearest Emilie: The Love Letters of Sir Wilfrid Laurier to Madame Emilie Lavergne* (Toronto: NC Press, 1989).
27 Carman Miller, "Mowat, Laurier and the Federal Liberal Party, 1887–1997," in *Oliver Mowat's Ontario*, ed. Donald Swainson (Toronto: Macmillan, 1972), 69–92. Borden and Fielding "underwrote" the organizer's salary of $2,000 per year; Borden Papers, Fielding to Borden, 2 December 1899.
28 Canada, House of Commons, Debates, 22 July 1891, 2297.
29 Canada, House of Commons, Debates, 12 June 1894, 4130–42; Alan A. Brookes, "The Golden Age and the Exodus: The Case of Canning, Kings County," *Acadiensis* 10 (Spring 1981): 57–82. Not only did Cartwright commend Fred's exposé of the fraud but printed extracts as Appendix "N" in his Reminiscences (Toronto: William Briggs, 1912), 325–6, 402–5.
30 Speech of Dr. F.W. Borden, M.P., on the budget, Ottawa, Friday 6 April 1894.
31 *Halifax Herald*, 6, 10, 13 July 1896.
32 Miller, *A Knight in Politics*, 297.
33 Harry Whidden Brown was born 1 January 1868. He was educated at Acadia University (BA) and Dalhousie University (LLB), and practised law in Halifax before becoming Fred's private secretary; he later became chief clerk and director of contracts.

34 *Morning Chronicle*, 27 January 1897.

35 PBP, Bessie to Harold, n.d. [1897].

36 PBP, Bessie to Harold, n.d. [1897]; *Halifax Herald*, 24 and 27 May 1897; *Morning Chronicle*, 28 May 1897.

37 *Morning Chronicle*, 20 February 1897.

38 PBP, C.E. Panet to F.W. Borden, 17 February 1897.

39 Jose Harris, *Private Lives, Public Spirit: A Social History of Britain, 1879–1914* (Oxford: University of Oxford Press, 1993), 192.

7. Harold

1 PBP, Mom to Lizzie, 18 March [1892].

2 PBP, Harold to Dear Father, 10 August 1899.

3 *Halifax Chronicle*, n.d. [July 1900].

4 *Berwick Register*, 2 June 1897.

5 PBP, Harold Borden, Diary for 1898, Notes.

6 PBP, Harold to dearest mother, 3 June 1897.

7 *McGill College and University, Session 1897–98* (Montreal: Lovell, 1897), 148.

8 William Edgar Rowley, b. Marysville, NB; BA Mount Allison (1896), MD, CM McGill (1900); on staff of Montreal General Hospital; general superintendent St John General Hospital, 1907–10.

9 PBP, Maude to my dearest Mama, 16 May 1899.

10 One of whom was "Mrs. [Laura] Rob Borden."

11 W.B. Howell, *Francis John Shepherd–Surgeon: His Life and Times, 1851–1929* (Toronto: J.M. Dent and Son, 1934), 29–30.

12 Some of the books listed in his 1898 Diary are Rudyard Kipling's *Captain Courageous* (1897) and *The Jungle Book* (1894), Helen Choate Pratt Prince, *A Transatlantic Chatelaine: A Novel* (1897), Charles Dickens's *David Copperfield* (1850), Thomas Hardy's *Tess of the D'Urbervilles or A Pure Woman Faithfully Presented* (1891), Henry Sienkiewicz's *Quo Vadis* (1895), J.H Shorthouse's *John Inglesant* (1881), Maarten Maartens' *God's Fool* (1892) and *My Lady Nobody* (1895), Margaret Oliphant's *A House in Bloomsbury* (1894), Mrs. Humphry Ward's *Helbeck of Bannisdale* (1896), Maria Edgeworth's *Castle Rack Rent* (1800), William Dean Howells's *Open Eyed Conspiracy: An Idyl of Saratoga* (1897), Keats Louis Tracey's, *The Final War* (1896), Frank Frankfort Moore's *Jessamy Bride* (1897).

13 In September he secured a rare edition of Johnson's *Boswell* for his father.

14 PBP, Diary, 24 and 28 September 1898.

15 For example, *Tess of the D'Ubervilles*, *The Mikado*, and *The Pirates of Penzance*, PBP, Harold's Diary, 18 February 1898, 14 March 1898, 13 and 23 May 1898.

16 PBP, Elizabeth's nostalgic "Notes, My first visit to England, Scotland, Belgium and France," April 1899. In Boston Sir Frederick had heard

Dickens read from his own works during his 1867–8 tour of the United States.

17 Madame Ameneo predicted he would receive a great honour at age 29 and live until he was 75. She described him as sensitive, lacking in self-confidence, kind-hearted, except in the case of old people. She predicted he would probably become a doctor or lawyer, though family members might want him to become a clergyman; she guessed that he was fond of women though changeable in matters of love. She assured him that he would only marry once, and that she would be a lighthearted girl. For her services Madame Ameneo charged $1.20. PBP, Harold's Diary, 19 February 1898.

18 An American "anti-secret fraternity," founded in 1834, became "international" after it admitted McGill to its membership.

19 PBP, Harold's Diary, 19–22 October 1898.

20 Nova Scotia Archives, F.W. Borden Papers, FWB to A.S. Burgess, 13 December 1909.

8. The Grand Tour

1 E.P. Thompson, *The Making of the English Working Class* (New York: Vintage Books, 1963), 43.

2 Dr. William Henry Withrow (1839–1908), editor of the *Canadian Methodist Magazine*, and author of *A Canadian in Europe* (Toronto: Rose-Belford, 1881).

3 See, Cecilia Morgan, *Happy Holiday: English Canadians and Transatlantic Tourism, 1870–1930* (Toronto: University of Toronto Press, 2008).

4 Morgan, *Happy Holiday*, 11.

5 PBP, Elizabeth's nostalgic "Notes, My first visit to England, Scotland, Belgium and France," April 1899.

6 PBP, Maude to My dearest Mama, 16 May 1899.

7 Ibid.

8 Ibid.

9 PBP, Maude to Mama, 17 September 1899.

10 PBP, Harold to Lizzie, 10 December 1899.

11 Arthur James Balfour (1848–1930) was the Scottish Conservative nephew and successor of Lord Robert Salisbury, British prime minister, 1895–1903.

12 Margot Tennant (1864–1945), author and outspoken second wife of H.H. Asquith, British Liberal prime minister 1906–16.

13 In fact, it was based on the life of Ethel Smyth (1858–1944).

14 PBP, Maude to Mama, 29 September 1899.

15 PBP, Lord Strathcona to Dr. Borden, 28 April 1900.

16 PBP, Elizabeth to dearest grandmother 25 January 1900. They also shopped for their mother, and Granny, who was particularly fond of London hair nets though they were not considered fashionable in Paris.

17 PBP, Elizabeth to my dearest mother, no date; Elizabeth to mother dearest, 16 February 1900.
18 Several contemporary Canadian artists enrolled in the Académie Julien who worked closely with Bouguereau.
19 PBP, Elizabeth to Mamma, Hôtel Jean Bart, Paris, n.d.
20 George Herbert (1593–1633), Anglo-Welsh poet, priest, and rector who restored the fourteenth-century church.
21 PBP, Elizabeth to My dear father, 4 May 1900.
22 PBP, Elizabeth to father, May [1900].
23 Ibid.
24 Ibid.
25 PBP, Harold to Lizzie and Maude, 10 December 1899.
26 Ibid.
27 PBP, Elizabeth to mother dearest, 16 February 1900.
28 PBP, Elizabeth to Dearest Grandma, 25 January 1900.
29 R.H. Ryan served in three different units during the South African War, as a sergeant in B Squadron, First Canadian Mounted Rifles (and for a time missing in action), and a lieutenant in the Canadian Scouts.
30 Harold joined the Hussars as a private in 1893, and was promoted to corporal in 1894 and 2nd lieutenant in 1897. That summer (1897) he took a special cavalry course in Toronto, where he received a 1st class, grade A certificate; the following summer he attended Cavalry School and obtained a special certificate, was promoted 1st lieutenant in B Squadron Duke of Connaught's Hussars, attended La Prairie camp and, owing to the illness of the captain, he commanded the squadron with the rank of captain. Then just before the South African War, Harold commanded the Kings Hussars at the Aldershot camp, under Vice-Major J.W. Ryan. See *Morning Chronicle*, 30 January 1900.
31 *Halifax Herald*, 21 December 1899.
32 Nova Scotia Archives, F.W. Borden Papers, Frederick Borden to Dr. A.T. Clarke, 11 January 1900.
33 PBP, Dr. H.O. McLatchy to Dr. Borden, 18 July 1900.
34 *Halifax Herald*, 14 February 1900; Canada, House of Commons, Debates, 13 February 1900, 321.
35 Harold had also helped smuggle aboard William Anderson, a keen but rejected recruit.
36 PBP, F.W. Borden to Minto, 4 May 1901.
37 PBP, Lord Strathcona to Dr. Borden, 28 April 1900.
38 See also Appendix A.
39 For a fuller discussion of Hutton's departure see Carman Miller, *A Knight in Politics*, (Montreal and Kingston: McGill-Queen's University Press, 2010), ch. 7.

40 Andrew had contested the 1847 election in Kings for the Reform Party but lost by only "14 or 15 votes." Nova Scotia Archives, Borden Papers, F.W. Borden to Rev. Byron Borden, 19 January 1906; *The Acadian Recorder*, 7 August 1847.
41 Miller, *A Knight in Politics*, 139–43.
42 Canada, Sessional Paper 35a, 1901, "Report C," 83.
43 The battle also claimed two severely wounded men, Privates A.W. Brown and Lorne W.R. Mulloy, the latter a 24-year-old Ontario schoolteacher whose wounds resulted in blindness, a lifelong reminder of the war's personal cost.
44 PBP, Hutton to Roberts, 17 July 1900.
45 PBP, Dr. A.J. Pretorius to F.W. Borden, 1 November 1923. The grave numbered 383 on a property owned by Dr. A. J. Pretorius. Their bodies were later reinterred at Braamfontein, Johannesburg. The "Canadian" flags were probably red ensigns.
46 PBP, Harry Graham to H.W. Brown, 31 July 1900.
47 *Halifax Chronicle*, n.d.
48 Canada, House of Commons, Debates, 17 July 1900, 10503.
49 PBP, R.L. Borden to A.J. Pretorius, 12 December 1923, and quoted by Roy McLaren in "Harold Borden," *Dictionary of Canadian Biography* (Toronto: University of Toronto Press, 1990), 12:114–15.
50 *Saint John Daily Sun*, 20 July 1900.
51 PBP, Fitz Ponsonby to Dr. F.W. Borden, 28 July 1900.
52 PBP, H.O. McLatchy to Dr. Borden, 18 July 1900; Lord Strathcona to Dr. Borden, 21 July 1900; A. Van Straubenzee to F.W. Borden, 19 July 1900; C V. Anthony to F.W. Borden, 28 July 1900; *Toronto Globe*, n.d.; *Quebec Daily Telegraph*, 18 July 1900.
53 PBP, "Heroes of Canada," a nine-stanza poem, published in the press in August 1900 by an "unknown" author, and a four-stanza poem entitled "Major Harold Borden," by an unknown Canning author, dated 19 July 1900.
54 PBP, H.D. Gordon to F. W. Borden, 8 August 1900; S.H. Snyder to F.W. Borden, 22 July 1900.
55 PBP, William Lane to Dear Friend [Frederick Borden], 22 July 1900.
56 PBP, Extract of Evans's letter to Frederick Borden.
57 PBP, E.B. Biggar to F.W. Borden, 15 August 1900.
58 Ibid.
59 *Halifax Herald*, 28 August 1900.
60 PBP, Granny to Rosamond, 19 February [1945].
61 PBP, Frederick to Bessie, January 1898. During Fred's visit to London in December 1897 Lord Strathcona had invited Fred to his family's Christmas day dinner.
62 PBP, F.W. Borden to Captain Fred Ponsonby, 24 September 1900.

9. Lady Borden

1 PBP, FWB to Judge Robert Linton Weatherbe, 4 January 1900.
2 *Halifax Herald*, 25 October 1900.
3 PBP, Harry Brown to F. Ronan, 17 October 1900.
4 *Halifax Herald*, 31 October 1900.
5 PBP, F.W. Borden to F. Hamilton, 18 November 1900.
6 Robert Craig Brown, *Robert Laird Borden: A Biography* (Toronto: University of Toronto Press, 1975), 1:46.
7 Carman Miller, *A Knight in Politics* (Montreal and Kingston: McGill-Queen's University Press, 2010), ch. 10.
8 "Hon. Frederick William Borden, Minister of Militia," Military Number, *The Canadian Magazine* 14, no. 5 (March 1900): 448–52.
9 J. Castell Hopkins, ed., *Canadian Annual Review of Public Affairs for 1903* (Toronto: Canadian Annual Review Limited, 1903), 403.
10 Henry J. Morgan, *Canadian Men and Women of the Time* (Toronto: William Briggs, 1912), 120.
11 Miller, *A Knight in Politics*, 132–8.
12 Minto Papers, Minto to Garnet Wolseley, 28 May 1900; Minto to St. John Brodrick, 14 May 1901; Minto to Lord Dundonald, 20 March 1902.
13 PBP, Lady Minto to Sir Frederick, Lady and Misses Borden, 27 January, n.d.
14 *The Ottawa Directory for 1901*, 33.
15 PBP, Lady Minto to Sir Frederick and Lady Borden and Misses Borden, 27 January, n.d.
16 Maude was Powell's matron of honour. *Toronto World*, 1 April 1911. See Sandra Gwyn, *The Private Capital* (Toronto: McClelland & Stewart, 1984), 311.
17 *Allison* 1, no. 3, (1903), 20; J. Castell Hopkins, ed., *The Canadian Annual Review of Public Affairs for 1901* (Toronto: Canadian Annual Review Limited, 1902), 257, 321, 351, 354, 397.
18 PBP, FW Borden to Lord Minto, 4 May 1901.
19 PBP, F.W. Borden to Lord Strathcona, 15 October 1901.
20 PBP, FWB to Sir Edward [Ward], 8 February 1903. The restriction was removed in 1902.
21 Minto Papers, Minto to St. John Brodrick, 27 May 1902.
22 Minto Papers, Minto to Roberts, 7 May 1902.
23 Minto Papers, Minto to St. John Brodrick, 14 May 1901; Minto to Joseph Chamberlain, 23 April and 2 September 1901.
24 David Cannadine, *Ornamentalism: How the British Saw the Empire* (Oxford: Oxford University Press, 2010), 10.
25 *Ottawa Citizen*, 16 May 1907; Morgan, *Men and Women*, 120; *First Annual Report of the Soldiers' Wives League*, 1900.
26 Miller, *A Knight in Politics*, 290–1.

27 *The Globe*, 8 January 1917.

28 An assessment shared by Mackenzie King. See Miller, *A Knight in Politics*, 252, 355.

29 *Ottawa Citizen*, 15 January 1908.

30 Christopher McCreery, *The Maple Leaf and the White Cross: A History of the St. John's Ambulance* (Toronto: Dundurn, 2008).

31 PBP, Frederick W. Borden Diary / Agenda, 9 August 1902.

32 PBP, Frederick W. Borden Diary, 10 June 1902.

33 J. Castell Hopkins, ed., *Canadian Annual Review of Public Affairs for 1902* (Toronto: Canadian Annual Review Limited, 1903), 102.

34 E.A. Heaman, *A Short History of the State in Canada* (Toronto: University of Toronto Press, 2015), 51.

35 Julia Bush, *Edwardian Ladies and Imperial Power* (Leicester: Leicester University Press, 1999), 135, 136. During the 1902 coronation celebrations the Victoria League sent out 4,600 invitations.

36 Elizabeth Leigh Child-Villiers, *Fifty-One Years of Victorian Life* (London: John Murray, 1922), 382.

37 PBP, William Burdett-Coutts to Dear Sir Frederick, 24 July 1902. Burdette-Coutts (1851–1921) was the American-born British journalist and author of *The Sick and Wounded in South Africa* (London: Castell, 1900).

38 W.S. Fielding, minister of finance; William Mulock, postmaster-general and minister of labour; William Patterson, minister of customs; all the premiers, except the premier of Quebec, Parent, who was represented by his provincial secretary. Given the broad provincial representation, the premiers used it as an opportunity to hold an interprovincial conference on shared interests.

39 Daniel Hunter McMillan, lieutenant-governor of Manitoba; Hon. Henri Elzear Taschereau, chief justice of the Supreme Court; Hon. Robert Boak, president of Nova Scotia's Legislative Council; Fred White, commissioner of the North-West Mounted Police; Arthur Percy Sherwood, commissioner of the Dominion Police; Robert Harris, portrait artist; Gilbert Parker, novelist.

40 Lord Mount Stephen, Edward Clouston, Henry Pellatt, Hugh Andrew Montague Allan.

41 They included Lady [John A.] Macdonald, Sir Charles and Lady Tupper, Colonel William Otter.

42 Desmond Morton, *The Canadian General Sir William Otter* (Toronto: Hakkert, 1974), 255–6.

43 Castell Hopkins, *The Canadian Annual Review of Public Affairs for 1902*, 102.

44 PBP, Fred to my dear Bessie, 28 December 1897.

45 As a guest of a Miss Chamberlain, Frederick Borden Diary / Agenda, 16 August 1902.

46 Miller, *A Knight in Politics*, ch. 18.
47 PBP, Bessie to Mrs. Clarke, 10 July 1909.
48 PBP, Invitations to Lady Aberdeen's garden party, unspecified functions at Lord and Lady Strathcona's and Leopold Rothchild's residences. Frederick Borden Diary / Agenda, 10 August 1902.
49 PBP, Frederick Borden Diary / Agenda, 29 June 1902.
50 PBP, Sir F.W. Borden to F.W. Borden, 28 August, 22 November, and 12 December 1902.
51 PBP, Borden *Parish Monthly Magazine*, February 1905, 49.
52 Sir Wilfrid and Lady Laurier arrived in Paris from St Malo.
53 PBP, Sir Frederick's Diary / Agenda, Sir Rennell Rodd, Sunday, 1902.
54 In reference to John Ruskin's popular three-volume *Stones of Venice* (1851–3).

10. Borden Place

1 *The Advertiser*, 17 October 1902.
2 *Halifax Chronicle*, 8 October 1902.
3 Julia Bush, *Edwardian Ladies and Imperial Power* (Leicester: Leicester University Press, 1999), 44; Jose Harris, *Private Lives, Public Spirit: A Social History of Britain, 1879–1914* (Oxford: Oxford University Press, 1993), 20–3.
4 Julia Parker Drummond, quoted in Mary Elizabeth Kirkland, "Mothering Citizens: Elite Women in Montreal, 1890–1914," PhD thesis, McGill University, 2012, 1.
5 Stephen Archibald and Sheila Stevenson, *Heritage Houses of Nova Scotia* (Halifax: Formac, 2003), 87.
6 PBP, FWB to A. Clarke, 28 April 1904.
7 In 1968 the Halifax-Dartmouth Real Estate Board advertised the sale of Borden Place for $39,500, an assessed value of $13,000, and a mortgage of $1,500 to be settled by the vendor.
8 Julia Leslie Green MacKay to author, 13 January 2010.
9 A fellow worshipper at Dominion Methodist Church.
10 Both Downey and Langfier were "court photographers," with "Royal Warrants."
11 Robert Alexander Nisbet, *Sociology as an Art Form* (Oxford: Oxford University Press, 1976), 70.
12 George O. Fallis, *A Padre's Pilgrimage* (Toronto: Ryerson Press, 1953), 40.
13 PBP, Bessie B. Borden, Last Will and Testament, 28 October 1952. Lady Borden willed the portrait to King's University College, Sir Frederick's alma mater, where it currently hangs in its library in Halifax.
14 "The Pink Shawl" was signed by Tompkins in 1910 and identified as "Elizabeth Borden Hewitt," though Elizabeth Borden did not become

"Hewitt" until October 1911. The title, perhaps attached later, was a nod to Jean-Baptiste-Corneille Corot's "Pink Shawl." See, too, the "American Gallery Greatest American Painters" website.

15 Julia Green MacKay remembers it at Borden Place in the 1950s.

16 Downey produced a photo of Elizabeth in a white lace trained tea gown, seated on a Victorian settee.

17 See François Rémillard and Brian Merrett, *Belles demeures historiques de l'île de Montréal* (Montreal: Les Éditions de L'Homme, 2016).

18 See Mary Kirkland, "Mothering Citizens," chapter 2, for a description of the houses of Montreal's very rich; see also Rosalind Pepall, "Arts and Crafts Traditions in the Canadian Domestic Interior," in *Artists, Architects, and Artisans: Canadian Art, 1890–1918*, ed. Charles C. Hill (Ottawa: National Gallery of Canada, 1913), 56–88.

19 PBP, List of silver and dinnerware, n.d.

20 Authors included Charles Dickens, Rudyard Kipling, Charlotte and Emily Brontë, John Ruskin, Edmund Spenser, Oliver Goldsmith, Arthur Symons, John Masefield, George Bernard Shaw. PBP, Appendix of books.

21 PBP, Dr. George Ray Johnson to Lady Borden, 30 August 1903.

22 *Morning Chronicle*, 24 September 1903, estimated that 2,000 persons attended.

23 PBP, Notes of Address at the Unveiling of the Monument to Major Harold L. Borden at Canning, N.S., 23 September 1903, 10pp.

24 *Morning Chronicle*, 24 September 1903.

25 V.H. Nelles, *The Art of Nation-Building: Pageantry and Spectacle at Quebec's Tercentenary* (Toronto: University of Toronto Press, 2000), 20.

26 *Morning Chronicle*, 9 November 1904.

27 Nova Scotia Archive, FWB Papers, Borden to B. Nason, 15 November 1904; Barry Cahill, "Edward Mortimer Macdonald," *Dictionary of Canadian Biography*, volume 16. http:www.biographica.ca.

28 Canada, Sessional Paper (1904), No. 37, 277.

29 PBP, Emily Eaton to Rosamond, 2 January 1982.

11. A National Class

1 Nova Scotia Archives, FWB Papers, Borden to Edgar Smith, 10 November 1904.

2 PBP, Bessie to Dearest Fred, 28 April [1907].

3 About $40,300 in current purchasing power.

4 Carman Miller, *A Knight in Politics* (Montreal and Kingston: McGill-Queen's University Press, 2010), 308–9.

5 Robert and Laura Borden, John William Borden, Percy Borden, Harry Whidden Brown, Mary (Brown) Grew.

6 In contrast to elite Anglo Montreal women, Lady Borden (and her husband) identified as being of Planter not Loyalist origin, and (ironically?) sought her roots in the "evil traces of Norman aristocracy" rather than Protestantism. Francophiles, she and her husband valorized their region's romantic Acadian past, visited France, spoke French, and encouraged their children and grandchild to speak French. Sir Frederick founded the Canadian militia in New France, not in post-conquest Canada. Mary Elizabeth Kirkland, "Mothering Citizens: Elite women in Montreal, 1890–1914," PhD thesis, McGill University, 2012, 209; Cecilia Morgan, *A Happy Holiday: English Canadians and Transatlantic Tourism, 1870–1930* (Toronto: University of Toronto Press, 2008), 14, 99; Sir Frederick Borden, "The Canadian Militia-Past, Present and Future," *United Services Magazine*, 1906, 32–4.

7 $1,860,000 in current purchasing power.

8 $104,000 in current purchasing power.

9 "The wives of Cabinet Ministers," unidentified newspaper clipping in the possession of Ken Bezanson.

10 *Ottawa Citizen*, [May 1907].

11 PBP, Lady Borden's Notebook and Travelogue, 1906, ff.

12 Salton was a member of the Ottawa Literary and Scientific Society. Anson A. Card, *The Hub and the Spokes* (Ottawa: Emerson Press, 1904), 107, 111.

13 Sir Frederick and Sir Henry shared interests in the military, the St. John's Ambulance, and the Boy Scouts. Both loved uniforms, and sought titles and recognition. Sir Frederick purchased bonds in Lockport & Buffalo Railroad, which defaulted in 1916. PBP, Transcript of Probate Court, 88.

14 In recommending Pellatt for honours, Sir Frederick informed Lord Strathcona that Pellatt's appointment would be good for business. PBP, Frederick Borden's Diary / Agenda, July 1902; Bill Freeman, *Casa Loma: Canada's Fairy-Tale Castle and Its Owner, Sir Henry Pellatt* (Toronto: Lorimer, 2018), 46.

15 The Bordens introduced Laurier to Henderson before 1911, contrary to Salem Bland's claim that Henderson and Laurier's friendship "lay in the years in which Sir Wilfrid was in opposition." Salem Bland, *The Life of James Henderson, D.D.* (Toronto: McClelland & Stewart, 1926), 228.

16 Sir Robert William Perks (1849–1934), a prominent British Liberal MP and Wesleyan Methodist businessman, was interested in the construction of the Georgian Canal, "with government assistance." *Montreal Gazette*, 5 September 1910. Sir Frederick and Lady Borden dined with Perks in August 1909 during their visit to London. PBP, R.W. Perks to Sir Frederick and Lady Borden, 18 August 1909; Miyoki Shinnizin to Lady Borden, 23 April 1909.

17 *Ottawa Citizen*, 16 May 1907. "Ottawa's upper ten" is borrowed from a British book, compiled by Adam Bisset Thom, entitled *The Upper Ten Thousand: A Biographical Handbook of All the Titled Classes of the Kingdom* (London: Simpkin, Marshall, 1876).

18 *Ottawa Citizen*, 16 May 1907.

19 Sandra Gwyn, *The Private Capital* (Toronto: McClelland & Stewart, 1984), 311.

20 PBP, Rosamond Macoun Green, Record.

21 At Macoun's death in 1942, the *Lady Hawkins*'s ship passenger list gave his age as 70. *Ireland, Births and Baptisms, 1620–1911* records his birth as 31 July 1874 in Castlereagh, County Down. The UK *Outward* passenger list, 1890–1960, estimated his birth year as c. 1874. His marriage certificate records his age in May 1906 as 32.

22 PBP, Rosamond (Macoun) Green, Record.

23 W.A. Waiser, "John Macoun," *Dictionary of Canadian Biography* (Toronto: University of Toronto Press, 1998), 14:731–3.

24 PBP, Rosamond (Macoun) Green, Record.

25 *The Ottawa Directory*, 1896–7, 1897–8, 1898–9, 1901, 305, 319, 329, 346.

26 Ian M. Stewart, "William Saunders," *Dictionary of Canadian Biography* (Toronto: University of Toronto Press, 1998), 14:907–8.

27 PBP, Rosamond (Macoun) Green, Record; Leslie Macoun to Miss Rankin, 27 December 1921.

28 *Ottawa Directory*, 1908, 201. Wurtemburg and Glensmere were demolished in the 1970s.

29 Desmond Morton, "The Cadet Movement in the Moment of Canadian Militarism, 1909–1914," *Journal of Canadian Studies* 13, no. 2 (Summer,1978): 56–68.

30 PBP, Rosamond (Macoun), Record.

31 PBP, Certificate of Marriage, Dominion Methodist Church.

32 Sir Henri-Elzear Taschereau, retired chief justice of the Supreme Court of Canada, and Lady Marie-Louis Taschereau; Mrs. [Mary] Robert Sedgewick, wife of the recently deceased judge of the Supreme Court of Canada.

33 Sir Richard Cartwright, Allan B. Aylesworth, W.S. Fielding, Charles Fitzpatrick, Louis Davies, Andrew Blair, Frank Oliver.

34 Deputy Minister of Militia L.F. Pineault and Madame Marie-Louise Pineault.

35 Professor William Morley Tweedie from Mount Allison gave Maude and Leslie a two-volume copy of Edmund Spenser's *Faerie Queen*. PBP, Granny to Rosamond, 19 February [1945].

36 *Ottawa Citizen*, 22 May 1906.

37 PBP, FW Borden to Leslie Macoun, 8 December 1913.

38 *Ottawa Citizen*, 24 June 1908.

12. Courting London

1 Desmond Morton, "The Cadet Movement in the Moment of Canadian Militarism, 1909–1914," *Journal of Canadian Studies* 13, no. 2 (Summer 1978): 56–68.

2 Oscar Douglas Skelton, *Life and Letters of Sir Wilfrid Laurier* (Toronto: McClelland & Stewart, 1965), 2:114; *Toronto Globe*, 8 January 1917.

3 Gregory P. Marchildon, *Profits and Politics: Beaverbrook and the Gilded Age of Canadian Finance* (Toronto: University of Toronto Press, 1996), 63.

4 Carman Miller, *A Knight in Politics* (Montreal and Kingston: McGill-Queen's University Press, 2010), 307–20; See also Carman Miller, "Sir Frederick Goes to London: Money, Militia and Gentlemanly Capitalists," in *Imperial Canada, 1867–1917*, ed Colin M. Coates (Edinburgh: University of Edinburgh Press, 1997), 155–65.

5 Julia Bush, *Edwardian Ladies and Imperial Power* (London: Cassell, 2000), 5, 16–17.

6 Bush, *Edwardian Ladies*, 8.

7 Bush, *Edwardian Ladies*, 18.

8 Bush, *Edwardian Ladies*, 19, 34.

9 Bush, *Edwardian Ladies*, 20.

10 Bush, *Edwardian Ladies*, 86.

11 Donna McDonald, *Lord Strathcona: A Biography of Donald Alexander Smith* (Toronto: Dundurn, 2002), 446.

12 PBP, Lord Strathcona to F.W. Borden, 28 April 1900.

13 Sir Frederick held 500 preferred shares in the Strathcona Coal Company, a property and coal mine located in River Herbert, Cumberland Co., Nova Scotia.

14 McDonald, *Lord Strathcona*, Appendix 2, 527ff.

15 Miller, *A Knight in Politics*, 206–7.

16 For example, (Lt.-Col.) Arthur Morton and Lady Victoria Sybil Mary (Grey) Grenfell, the 4th Earl Grey's daughter.

17 For example, Sir Gilbert Parker (1862–1932), Canada's popular historical novelist. PBP, Sir Gilbert Parker to Lady Borden, 4 August, n.d.

18 Sir W.J. Gascoigne (1844–1926) served as general officer commanding the Canadian militia, 1895–8.

19 Richard O'Grady-Haly, general officer commanding the Canadian militia 1900–2. His father, William, had been officer commanding of the British forces in North America (Halifax, 1873–8) and sometime vice-regal "administrator."

20 Sir Frederick shared Sir Trevor's interest in aeronautics and broadcasting, and befriended Vickers's representatives, such as A.S. Davison, their British sales representative, and F.O. Lewis, their Canadian representative,

with whom Sir Frederick had other business dealings. Miller, *A Knight in Politics*, 215, 217.

21 Susan Mann, "Gossip in History," *Journal of the Canadian Historical Association* 20, no. 1 (1985): 1–10.

22 PBP, Edith Perks to Lady Borden, 18 August 1909.

23 PBP, M.E. Jersey to Lady Borden, 19 June 1911.

24 PBP, Lady Harcourt to Lady Borden, 20 May, 23 May; 30 June 1911.

25 Madeleine emulated her mother, a twice-married London hostess, knighted in 1925 for her war service.

26 PBP, Duchess of Marlborough to Lady Borden, 23 June [1911].

27 PBP, Mary Harcourt to Lady Borden, 6 May 1912.

28 PBP, Maude Verney to Lady Borden, 9 August [1909].

29 PBP, Mary Harcourt to Lady Borden, 6 May 1912.

30 Mary Ethel Harcourt, the daughter of an Anglo-American banker, W.H. Burns, and Mary Lyman (Morgan), was knighted for her war service in 1918; so, too, was Ethel Perrott, the first lady superintendent of the St. John's Ambulance Brigade. Another of Lady Borden's friends was Rosamond (Guest) Ridley, married to Matthew White, 2nd Viscount Ridley (1874–1916) and daughter of 1st Baron Wimborne and Lady Cornelia Henrietta Marie Spencer-Churchill (1849–1927), a first cousin of Winston Churchill. She, too, was knighted in 1918 for her war service, organizing a hospital for wounded servicemen. Lady Borden corresponded frequently with Maude Sarah (Williams) Verney (1847–1937), the daughter of Sir John Hay-Williams, 2nd Baron of Boddelwydden, Wales, and wife of Frederick William Verney (1846–1913), a Liberal politician and stepsister of Florence Nightingale. Lady Borden shared an interest in music with the 9th Duchess of Marlborough (Consuelo Vanderbilt), the wealthy American who bought her way into the highest level of British society. Prominent British imperial ladies sought out "colonials" and Anglo-Americans, conscious that they were "especially sensitive to these personal considerations." See PBP, Mary Harcourt to Lady Borden, 6 May 1912; Maude Verney to Lady Borden, 9 August [1909]; Duchess of Marlborough to Lady Borden, 23 May 1911; Leigh Child-Villiers, *Fifty-One Years of Victorian Life* (London: John Murray, 1922), 382.

31 *Osterley Park* (London: Victoria and Albert Museum, 1972), 61 pp.

32 J. Castel Hopkins, ed., *The Canadian Annual Review of Public Affairs for 1903* (Toronto: Canadian Annual Review Publisher, 1904), 476.

33 Miller, *A Knight in Politics*, 161–75.

34 Nova Scotia Archives, F.W. Borden Papers, Borden to Alfred Lyttelton, 1 March 1904; NA (UK), Colonial Office 42 (896), Minute. Lyttelton, 12 January 1904.

35 PBP, Louis Harcourt to FWB, n.d., 1911.

36 Max Beloff, *Imperial Sunset* (London: Methuen, 1971), 1:83; Franklyn Arthur Johnson, *Defence by Committee: The British Committee of Imperial Defence, 1885–1959* (London: Oxford University Press, 1960), 58.
37 PBP, Strathcona to Borden, 11 June 1898; Miller, *A Knight in Politics*, chs. 17 and 18.
38 Donald C. Gordon, *The Dominion Partnership in Imperial Defence, 1870–1914* (Baltimore: Johns Hopkins University Press, 1965), 168; Richard Preston, *Canada and "Imperial" Defence* (Durham, NC: Duke University Press, 1967), 406.
39 PBP, Lady Borden's Travel Diary, 14 September 1906.
40 Ibid.
41 Ibid.
42 Ibid.
43 Ibid.
44 Lord Grey's assessment, quoted in John Hilliker, *Canada's Department of External Affairs* (Montreal and Kingston: McGill-Queen's University Press, 1990), 1:33.

13. Our Lady of the Snows

1 See, Lisa Gaudet, "The Empire Is Women's Sphere: Organized Female Imperialism in Canada, 1880s–1920s," PhD thesis, Carleton University, 2001; Mary Elizabeth Kirkland, "Mothering Citizens: Elite Women in Montreal, 1890–1914," PhD thesis, McGill University, 2012, ch. 4; Suzanne Morton, *Wisdom, Justice, and Charity: Canadian Social Welfare through the Life of Jane B. Wisdom, 1884–1975* (Toronto: University of Toronto Press, 2014), 185.
2 Mary Elizabeth Kirkland's "Mothering Citizens" documents elite Montreal women's political success, well before their enfranchisement. Similarly, Julia Bush and Jose Harris explain how the nature of British women's political engagement depended upon personal experience and opportunity. Julia Bush, *Edwardian Ladies and Imperial Power* (Leicester: Leicester University Press, 1999), 24, 178, 181. Jose Harris, *Private Lives, Public Spirit: A Social History of Britain, 1870–1914* (Oxford: Oxford University Press, 1993).
3 Anne-Marie Kinahan, "Transcendent Citizenship: Suffrage, the National Council of Women of Canada and the Politics of Organized Womanhood," *Journal of Canadian Studies* 43, no. 3 (2008): 5–27. See also Bush, *Edwardian Ladies*, 63.
4 Bush, *Edwardian Ladies*, 181.
5 According to Bush, the line dividing elite women on the franchise was a "false dichotomy between equality and deference feminism," since both

were committed to participation in public affairs: Bush, *Edwardian Ladies*, 173.

6 Salem Goldworth Bland, *James Henderson, D.D.* (Toronto: McClelland & Stewart, 1926), 134.

7 Nancy Christie, "Young Men and the Creation of Civic Christianity in Urban Methodist Churches, 1880–1914," *Journal of the CHA*, New Series, 17, no. 1 (2006). PBP, Charles [Gordon Hewitt] to Father, 2 June 1912; Charles [Gordon Hewitt] to Mother, 27 April 1913.

8 *Ottawa Citizen*, 16 May 1907.

9 PBP, Lady Borden to Mijoko Shinnizn, 23 April 1909.

10 Bush, *Edwardian Ladies*, 80.

11 Ibid., 181.

12 See, Carl Berger, *The Sense of Power: Studies in the Ideas of Canadian Imperialism, 1867–1914* (Toronto, University of Toronto Press, 1970), ch. 1; Lisa Gaudet, *The Empire Is Women's Sphere*.

13 Bush, *Edwardian Ladies*, 68–70..

14 Bush, *Edwardian Ladies*, 84, 85, 100; see also Katie Pickles, *Female Imperialism and National Identity: Imperial Order Daughters of the Empire* (Manchester: Manchester University Press, 2002), 17–18.

15 Lady Borden's approach to "British imperialism" resembled Boston Brahmins's sense of cultural affinity but with political independence.

16 Lady Borden's "national identity" resembled that of their Ottawa neighbour, Sir Joseph Pope. See Carman Miller, "Sir Joseph Pope: A Pragmatic Tory," in *Architects and Innovators*, ed. Greg Donaghy and Kim Richard Nossal (Montreal and Kingston: McGill-Queen's University Press, 2008), 12–13.

17 Rudyard Kipling's 1897 poem "Our Lady of the Snows."

18 Jocelyn Letourneau, *A History for the Future: Rewriting Memory and Identity in Quebec* (Montreal and Kingston: McGill-Queen's University Press, 2004).

19 Kirkland, "Mothering Citizens," ch. 5, "Hearth to the Ends of the Earth."

20 Pickles, *Female Imperialism*.

21 Bush, *Edwardian Ladies*, 80; P.T. Rooke and R.T Schnell, *No Bleeding Heart: Charlotte Whitten, a Feminist on the Right* (Vancouver: University of British Columbia Press, 1987), 211.

22 Marguerite Thibaudeau Lamothe (1853–1939), the daughter of Senator Joseph-Rosaire Thibaudeau (a close friend of Sir Wilfrid Laurier), was married to Gustave Lamothe, chief justice of the Court of King's Bench. She was president of Notre Dame Hospital, a member of the women's branch of the Societé Saint Jean-Baptiste, the National Council of Women, the Women`s Historical Society, the Parks and Playground Association and the Ladies' Board of the Numismatic and Antiquarian Society. See also Kirkland, "Mothering Citizens."

23 O.D. Skelton, *Life and Letter of Sir Wilfrid Laurier* (Toronto: McClelland and Stewart, 1965), 2:213.

24 Laurier shrewdly detected and exploited British interdepartmental disagreements and rivalries to block or paralyse imperial schemes. Carman Miller, *A Knight in Politics* (Montreal and Kingston: McGill-Queen's University Press, 2010), 244–9.

25 Phillips Payson O'Brien, "The Titan Refreshed: Imperial Overstretch and the British Navy before World War I," *Past & Present*, August 2001, 150, 159.

26 PBP, Lily McConnell to Lady Borden, 2 April [1926]. Not only was it "the King's constitutional understanding" but that of John Anderson, chief clerk in the Colonial Office, National Archives (UK), Colonial Office 42 (875), Minute John Anderson, 7 April 1900.

27 PBP, In Elizabeth's "Notes, My first visit to England, Scotland, Belgium and France," April 1899 she writes that the Boer War "may not have been" necessary, an opinion that Lady Borden may have shared or have come to share, too.

28 Skelton, *Life and Letters*, 2:114.

29 PBP, Bessie to dearest Fred, Saturday, 28 April [1907].

30 The recently knighted Sir Frederick informed the *Halifax Chronicle*, 9 October 1902: "Imperialism is a good word, a high-sounding word, it is euphonious, a word to which I have no objection, but it conveys little meaning, or rather any meaning you like to give it. I often ask my friends what they mean by it. Imperialism can be left alone because it will work itself out all right. Our great business is to work out the interests of Canada. Out policy should be 'Canada first,' 'Canada for Canadians,' a policy of Canadian patriotism, that is the true policy."

31 Kirkland, "Mothering Citizens," 158. Montreal's elite ladies lobbied municipal, provincial, and federal politicians for social causes and personal favours, and sometimes through their wives, such as J.M. Dandurand's lobbying Laurier and Lady Aberdeen for a senate seat for her husband.

14. Scandal

1 Under the English Matrimonial Causes Act, 1857, adultery was cause for divorce if committed by a woman, but not by a man, unless his adultery was accompanied by desertion or cruelty.

2 James Snell, "Martial Cruelty, Women and the Nova Scotia Divorce Court, 1900–1939," *Acadiensis* 18 (Autumn 1988): 3–33.

3 E.A Heaman, *A Short History of the State in Canada* (Toronto: University of Toronto Press, 2015), 109.

4 Nova Scotia Archives, F.W. Borden Papers, Frederick Borden to Justice Francis Gordon Forbes, 22 October 1909. In 1894 Fred had also to deal with the Sarah Brown insurance claim. See Appendix A.
5 Carman Miller, *A Knight in Politics* (Montreal and Kingston: McGill-Queen's University Press, 2010), ch. 22.
6 Nova Scotia Archives, F.W. Borden Papers, Frederick to Robert Borden, 30 December 1899.
7 Grant MacEwan, *Eye-Opener Bob: The Story of Bob Edwards* (Calgary: Brindle & Glass, 2011), 96–7; Hugh Dempsey, "Robert Chambers Edwards," *Dictionary of Canadian Biography* (Toronto: University of Toronto Press, 2005), 15:326–8.
8 While sympathetic toward Conservatives, he attacked Lord Strathcona for corruption, infuriated R.B. Bennett, and accused Robert Borden of fathering a child out of wedlock. See MacEwan, *Eye-Opener Bob*, 96ff.
9 Nova Scotia Archives, F.W. Borden Papers, Borden to Charles Russell, 26 October 1907.
10 H. Hamilton Fyfe, "The 'Pure Politics' Campaign in Canada," *Nineteenth Century and After*, no. 368 (1907): 665.
11 Nova Scotia Archives, F.W. Borden Papers, Borden to Charles Russell, 26 October 1907.
12 *Nineteenth Century and After*, no. 370 (1907), 1030. Sir Frederick initially blamed "low level politicians" for the attack on his reputation. Later, he believed their real target was his cousin, Robert Borden, at least in the case of the *Toronto World*. Nova Scotia Archives, F.W. Borden Papers, Borden to J.S. Willison, 5 December 1907.
13 Sam Hughes, Sir Frederick's Conservative friend, intervened on Sir Frederick's behalf (or perhaps Robert's). During internal party leadership intrigues Hughes remained staunchly loyal to Robert Borden. See, Robert Craig Brown, *Robert Laird Borden, A Biography* (Toronto: Macmillan of Canada, 1975), 1:164–9.
14 *Ottawa Citizen*, 24 June 1908.
15 Brown, *Robert Laird Borden*, 123.
16 *Ottawa Citizen*, 24 June 1908.
17 J. Castell Hopkins, ed., *Canadian Annual Review for 1908* (Toronto: Annual Review Publishing, 1909), 244.
18 See, H.V. Nelles, *The Art of Nation-Building: Pageantry and Spectacle at Quebec's Tercentenary* (Toronto: University of Toronto Press, 1999).
19 J.M. Beck, *Pendulum of Power* (Scarborough: Prentice Hall of Canada, 1968), 107.
20 Nova Scotia Archives, F.W. Borden Papers, Borden to D.A. Armstrong, 13 November 1908. Sir Frederick believed that about half of the county's 60–70 clergy opposed the United Reform Party; he also believed the party

overplayed its hand, and had the campaign lasted another week he would have doubled his number of votes.

21 Miller, *A Knight in Politics*, ch. 22, "Political Purity."
22 Established in February 1909, the Sir Frederick Borden Scholarship was valued at $75 (about $500 in today's purchasing power), financed by a 6 per cent "perpetual" mortgage on Borden Place. The award, open to a Kings County resident who had spent his or her last year at Canning's public school and obtained the highest average in provincial examinations, could be applied to any Nova Scotia college or Mount Allison University. In 1923 the probate court allotted the sum of $1,250 to Lady Borden to maintain the scholarship.
23 *Morning Chronicle*, 14 October 1909.
24 PBP, Lady Borden's Notebook and Travelogue, loose leaves, 8, 9, 16 December [1908].
25 Castell Hopkins, *The Canadian Annual Review of Public Affairs for 1908*, 600.
26 PBP, Lady Borden's Notebook and Travelogue, loose leaves, 6 January [1909].
27 In 1910 Pope Pius X refused an audience with former American president Theodore Roosevelt and his former vice-president, Charles Fairbanks, the pope's reason being their attendance at a Methodist Congress.
28 Edward P. Kohn, "Pride and Prejudice: Theodore Roosevelt`s Boyhood Contact with Europe," *America's Transatlantic Turn*, ed. Hans Krabbendam and John M. Thompson (New York: Palgrave Macmillan, 2012), 15–30.
29 Stephen Harris, *Canadian Brass, The Making of a Professional Army, 1860–1939* (Toronto: University of Toronto Press, 1988), 71.
30 C.P. Stacey, *Canada and the Age of Conflict: A History of Canadian External Policies* (Toronto: University of Toronto Press, 1981), 1:82.
31 Ibid., 1:75.
32 *Halifax Herald*, 14 June 1909.
33 *Halifax Herald*, 29 June 1909.
34 Réal Bélanger, *Wilfrid Laurier quand la politique devient passion*, (Quebec City: Les presses de L'Université Laval, 1986), 352.
35 In 1896, Fred brought John William Borden, Robert's brother, to Ottawa to manage his department's accounts and contracts, and subsequently appointed him financial member of the Militia Council, and then paymaster-general.
36 Charles Panet replaced Harry Brown as Sir Frederick's private secretary and sometime business partner.
37 See W.A.B. Douglas, "Kingswell, Sir Charles Edmund," *Dictionary of Canadian Biography* (Toronto: University of Toronto Press / Universite Laval, 2003). https: / / www.biographi.ca / en / bio / 16E.html.
38 PBP, Bessie to my dear mother, 6 July 1909.

39 Ibid.
40 PBP, Lady Pentland to Lady Borden, 20 August 1909; Madelene Middleton to Lady Borden, 1 August 1909; M. Harrowby to Lady Borden, 11 August 1909; Lulu Dawson to Lady Borden, 17 July 1909; Emily Synge to Lady Borden, 8 August 1909; Louise Vickers to Lady Borden, 18 August 1909.
41 Phillips Payson O'Brien, "'The Titan Refreshed': Imperial Overreach and the British Navy before the first World War," *Past and Present* 172 (August 2001): 160.
42 H. Blair Neatby, *Laurier and a Liberal Quebec* (Toronto: McClelland and Stewart, 1973), 185.
43 Miller, *A Knight in Politics*, 363–9.
44 *Morning Chronicle*, 14 October 1909.
45 *Morning Chronicle*, 15 October 1909.
46 *Morning Chronicle*, 18 October 1909.
47 Nova Scotia Archives, F.W. Borden Papers, William Cotton to F. W. Borden, 6 December 1910.
48 PBP, Bessie to Dearest Fred, 28 April [1907].
49 Thorstein Veblen, *The Portable Veblen* (New York: Viking, 1950), 270; Miller, *A Knight in Politics*, ch. 19.

15. Their Imperial Sunset

1 *Toronto World*, 1 April 1911.
2 In addition to Covent Garden's *Louise*, Gustave Charpentier's Bohemian opera; the Haymarket's romantic comedy *Pomander Walk*, by Louis Parker; Graham Moffat's experimental film *Till the Bells Ring*; Beryl Faber and Cosmos Hamilton's *A Sense of Humour*; and the Playhouse's comedy *Cousin Kate*, by Hubert Henry Davis.
3 Designated as the Royal Canadian Navy following the coronation.
4 J. Castell Hopkins, ed., *Canadian Annual Review of Public Affairs for 1911* (Toronto: Annual Review Publishing, 1912), 613.
5 Julia Bush, *Edwardian Ladies and Imperial Power* (London: Cassells, 2000), 136.
6 D.S. Ryan, "Staging the Imperial City: The Pageant of London," *in Landscape, Display and Identity*, ed. F. Driver and D. Gilbert (Manchester University Press, 1999), 117–35. See also John MacKenzie, *Propaganda and Empire: The Manipulation of British Public Opinion, 1880–1960* (Manchester: Manchester University Press).
7 Sophie C. Lomas, *Festival of Empire Souvenir of the Pageant of London* (London: Bemrose & Sons, 1911).
8 Some 125 Canadian Boy Scouts and 11 scout masters under the command of Lt.-Col. F. Minden Cole attended Baden-Powell's post-coronation 30,000-strong scout rally. See Patricia Dirks, "Part of the British Empire

Too: French Canada and Colonization Propaganda," in *Canada and the British World: Culture, Migration and Identity*, ed. Philip Buckner and R. Douglas Frances (Vancouver: University of British Columbia Press, 2006), 118.

9 *The Spectator*, 20 May 1911.

10 Hopkins, *The Canadian Annual Review of Public Affaires for 1911*, 616.

11 *Ottawa Citizen*, 26 June 1911.

12 PBP, Rosamond's Record.

13 Sir Montague Allan of Montreal had eyed the post and had deep pockets. Hopkins, *Canadian Annual Review of Public Affairs for 1908*, 597.

14 Hopkins, *Canadian Annual Review of Public Affairs for 1911*, 628.

15 Ibid., 631.

16 *Winnipeg Free Press*, 21 July 1911.

17 PBP, Frederick Borden to wife, 1911, n.d.

18 PBP, Lady Harcourt to Lady Borden, 30 June 1911.

16. Lady Alone

1 Richard Clippindale, *The Power of the Pen: The Politics of Nationalism and the Influence of Sir John Willison* (Toronto: Dundurn Press, 2012).

2 J. Castell Hopkins, ed., *Canadian Annual Review of Public Affairs for 1911* (Toronto: Annual Review Publishing, 1912), 264–5.

3 Carman Miller, *A Knight in Politics* (Montreal and Kingston: McGill-Queen's University Press, 2010), 344–9.

4 *The Broad Arrow*, December 1901.

5 Ronald Haycock, *Sam Hughes* (Waterloo, ON: Wilfrid Laurier University Press, 1986), 130.

6 PBP, Fred to dearest Bessie, 19 October 1911.

7 PBP, Fred to Dearest, Sunday [September 1911].

8 Ibid.

9 PBP, Fred to Dear Bessie, 27 September 1911.

10 PBP, Fred to My dear Wife, Saturday, a.m. [September 1905]; Fred to Dear Bessie, 14 September [1905].

11 PBP, Elizabeth to dearest mother, 28 September [1908].

12 In Canada Hewitt answered to the name "Gordon"; to his parents he remained "Charlie."

13 PBP, Macclesfield Grammar School, Hewitt, Report for term ending Christmas 1898, Form IV.

14 Paul W. Riegert, "Charles Gordon Hewitt," *Dictionary of Canadian Biography* (Toronto: University of Toronto Press, 1998), 14:487.

15 PBP, Elizabeth's nostalgic "Notes, "My firstvisit to England, Scotland, Belgium and France," April 1899. "Parks & Gardens," she explained,

"were my delight & country lanes, especially wooded lanes with delightful shrubbery borders tapering off in fungi, ferns and flowers."

16 Paul W. Riegert, "James Fletcher," *Dictionary of Canadian Biography* (Toronto: University of Toronto Press, 1994), 13:348.

17 Anne Drummond, "Sydney Arthur Fisher," *Dictionary of Canadian Biography* (Toronto: University of Toronto Press, 2005), 15:351–4.

18 PBP, George Maheux [Quebec provincial entomologist] eulogy: "Gordon Hewitt," in C. Gordon Hewitt, *The Conservation of the Wildlife of Canada* (New York: C. Scribner's Sons, 1921).

19 PBP, Gordon Hewitt to Elizabeth, Vancouver, 15 October 1910.

20 Ibid.

21 Hewitt had been twice engaged. See Laura Jean Cameron, *Friend Beloved: Marie Stopes, Gordon Hewitt, and an Ecology and the Intimacy of Letters* (Montreal and Kingston: McGill-Queen's University Press, 2021).

22 PBP, Hewitt to Elizabeth 15 October 1910. I assume the reference is to Jacques Offenbach's Barcarolle.

23 PBP, Gordon Hewitt to Elizabeth, 15 October 1910.

24 PBP, Charlie [Gordon] to my dear Father, 2 June 1912; Charlie [Gordon] to dear Mother, 27 April 1913.

25 *Morning Leader*, 12 October 1912.

26 PBP, Charlie [Gordon] to Mother, 14 October 1911.

27 Ibid.

28 Ibid.

29 Ibid.

30 Riegert, "Charles Gordon Hewitt," 487.

31 Published in instalments in the *Quarterly Journal of Microscopical Science* (1907–8), and subsequently by the University of Manchester Press (1914), republished (2012) and reprinted in paper (2015).

32 *Pall Mall Gazette*, 21 November 1912. Reprinted in paperback in 2012.

33 See Daniel F. Brunton, "Origins and History of the Ottawa Field-Naturalists' Club," *The Canadian Field-Naturalist* 118, no. 1 (January–March 2004); and the *Ottawa Naturalist* 22, no. 6 (December 1918).

34 Second International Conference of Entomology, *Proceedings*, vol. I, (London: Hazell, Watson & Viney, 1914).

35 Riegert, "Charles Gordon Hewitt," 487.

36 The farm's location in Sir Frederick's constituency predates Gordon's elevation.

37 Valued in 1923 at $15,000 with goods and furniture, PBP, Transcript, 50.

38 PBP, Charlie [Gordon] Hewitt to Father 2 June 1912.

39 PBP, Leslie Macoun to FWB, 8 December 1913.

40 PBP, FWB to Leslie Macoun, 12 December 1913.

41 Castell Hopkins, *Canadian Annual Review of Public Affairs for 1911*, 264–5. Miller, *A Knight in Politics*, 4–5.

42 LAC, Robert Borden Papers, Robert Borden to F.W. Borden, 15 September 1915.
43 D.J. Hall, *Clifford Sifton, The Young Napoleon* (Vancouver: University of British Columbia Press, 1981), 214.
44 PBP, Chairman National Committee (New York) to Sir Frederick Borden, 16 January 1912.
45 Castell Hopkins, *Canadian Annual Review of Public Affairs for 1912* (Toronto: Annual Review Publishing, 1913), 255.
46 Miller, *A Knight in Politics*, 313–20.
47 Nova Scotia Archives, FWB Papers, Borden to Freeman Davison, 23 November 1910.
48 LAC, WLM King Papers, Diary, 31 December 1914.
49 Miller, *A Knight in Politics*, 302–3.
50 Procured for $6,000 from Clinton Bigelow, secured by a mortgage (later traded to Mrs. Annie Campbell) and a promissory note signed by Sir Frederick, the mortgage to be paid off from farm profits. PBP, Probate Court Transcript, 18, 65.
51 Miller, *A Knight in Politics*, 308–13
52 *Morning Chronicle*, 8 January 1917.
53 PBP, Probate Court Transcript, 10 May 1922, 152.
54 *Toronto Globe*, 8 January 1917, *Halifax Herald*, 9 January 1917, *Saint John Standard*, 8 January 1917, *Manchester Guardian*, 8 January 1917; *The Graphic Daily*, 9 January 1917; *The Observer*, 7 January 1917; *Liverpool Post*, 8 January, 1917; *Boston Transcript*, 6 January 1917.
55 *Halifax Morning Chronicle*, 10 January 1917.
56 *Halifax Herald*, 9 January 1917.
57 "Handsome floral tributes" from Lady Borden, Mr. and Mrs. Leslie Macoun, Dr. and Mrs. Gordon Hewitt, Sir Robert and Lady Borden, Sir Wilfrid and Lady Laurier, Hon and Mrs. W.S. Fielding, Mrs. Jeffrey Burland (Montreal), Mr. and Mrs. E.A. Robert (Montreal), Hon. and Mrs. A.K. Maclean (Halifax), the Halifax Tramway Company, the Government and Legislature of Nova Scotia, etc., PBP, Funeral Service, 3 pp.
58 *Halifax Morning Chronicle*, 10 January 1917.
59 *Toronto Globe*, 8 January 1917.
60 LAC, W.L. M. King Papers, Diary, 12 January 1917.
61 PBP, William Mulock to my Dear Lady Borden, 22 January 1917.
62 *Halifax Morning Chronicle*, 10 January 1917.
63 PBP, Probate Court, Typescript (Sir Frederick's estate), 152.
64 Veronica Strong-Boag, *The New Day Recalled* (Toronto: Copp Clark Pitman, 1987), 183–4.
65 PBP, Mary Grew to dearest Bessie, 31 March 1918.

17. Administrator

1 Carman Miller, *A Knight in Politics* (Montreal and Kingston: McGill-Queen's University Press, 2010), 308–15.
2 PBP, Transcript, 3.
3 PBP, Transcript, 10 May 1922, 150–3; PBP, L. Macoun to J.L. Ilsley, 5 January 1923.
4 PBP, Transcript, 132.
5 PBP, Transcript, 17, item 203.
6 PBP, Connor to Lady Borden, 11 September 1918.
7 PBP, Lady Borden to Connor, 12 September 1918; Leslie Macoun to Shaftner, Outhit & Ilsley, 15 February 1919.
8 PBP, Connor to Lady Borden, 24 September 1918.
9 PBP, Lady Borden to Connor, 2 October 1918.
10 PBP, Macoun to Shaftner, Outhit & Ilsley, 15 February 1919.
11 PBP, Shaftner, Outhit & Ilsley to Macoun, 5 October 1918.
12 1918 Supreme Court of Nova Scotia, 4296, Victor F. Connor and Leslie S Macoun, 21 December 1918.
13 PBP, Macoun to Shaftner, Outhit & Ilsley, 1 and 27 May 1919.
14 PBP, Dr. Max C. Klotz, certificate, 2 June 1919.
15 PBP, Macoun to Shaffner, Outhit & Ilsley, 15 February 1919.
16 Ibid.
17 PBP, Macoun to Shaffner Outhit & Ilsley, 29 April 1919.
18 PBP, Macoun to Lady Borden, 20 August 1920.
19 PBP, Macoun to Lady Borden, 14 June 1920.
20 PBP, Macoun to Lady Borden, 20 August 1920.
21 PBP, Macoun to Lady Borden, 19 July 1921.
22 PBP, Macoun to Lady Borden, 14 June 1920.
23 PBP, Macoun to Lady Borden, 20 August 1920.
24 PBP, Macoun to Lady Borden, 14 June 1920.
25 PBP, Macoun to Lady Borden, 14 June 1920; 23 October 1920.
26 PBP, Macoun to Lady Borden 20 August 1920; 23 October 1922.

18. Executor

1 PBP, Bessie B. Borden to Probate Court, 31 January 1917. Most of the family's 5,177 acres of land had been traded to the Supply Company for a $100,000 bond at 6 per cent.
2 PBP, Probate Court Transcript, 6–7. Note that the figures given do not seem to square precisely; what may have been added or subtracted is unclear.
3 PBP, Transcript, 68–9.

4 Carman Miller, *A Knight in Politics* (Montreal and Kingston: McGill-Queen's University Press, 2010), 304–3. By 1922 Davison was bankrupt, unable to repay a $9,000 loan from Sir Frederick, secured by 200 shares in the Eastern Oregon Light & Power in the name of Philip Farley. PBP, Macoun to J.L. Ilsley, 13 October 1922. Sir Frederick had also endorsed a $4,500 note for Davison that carried an overdue interest charge of $1,600. Leslie had a very low opinion of Davison: "I don't suppose that there are many who know better than I do what a thorough blackguard he is. Sir Frederick did not toward the end entertain a high opinion of him, nor did he entrust any important matter to him. Davison I believe pretended so as to impress Sir Frederick to his own advantage that he had political ambitions in the direction of Hants County where he was born." And, during the 1911 election: "Davison and another thug from Boston" came to Hants County and "raised a large sum of money on a note made by them, and endorsed by certain men in Hants County, put the money in their pockets and returned to Boston leaving [the Conservative Hadley Brown] at the head of the poll and Dr. Black and others to foot the bill." PBP, Leslie to Shaftner, Outhit & Ilsley, 7 March 1919.

5 For example, Sir Frederick secured an 8 per cent mortgage from Chaudiere Heights Reality, a company in which he was a shareholder and director. PBP, Transcript, 74.

6 PBP, L.S. Macoun to Sir Frederick Borden, 11 July 1912.

7 Nova Scotia Archives, FWB Papers, Borden to W.T. White, 23 November 1901.

8 Sir Frederick's Toronto political / business friends Henry Pellatt, Robert Jeffrey (Republic Mines Company), George Ross, and George Cox.

9 The loss of his sailing vessel *Harold Borden* and the destruction by fire of his large Pereau livestock barn. *Halifax Herald*, 22 November 1900, 6.

10 Loans backed by mortgages on the company's property.

11 Alfred Potter took $1,500, and Captain W.R. Potter $2,000; Boak transferred his $500 to the new company (Borden held an equal sum in Boak's company), the Manufacturers Life ($10,000), Bessie Borden ($5,000), and Sir Frederick ($85,000).

12 Miller, *Knight in Politics*, 297–302.

13 PBP, Transcript, 12.

14 PBP, Transcript, 168.

15 PBP, Transcript, 25.

16 Scottish-born president of the Nova Scotia Legislative Council Robert Boak (1822–1904) was a prominent West Indian merchant, president of the Halifax Banking Company, and recipient of lucrative militia contracts.

17 PBP, Transcript, 38. This security was encumbered by $23,000 worth of mortgages, $9,771 of which was held by the family, a sum comparable to Mrs. Clarke's mortgage holdings in the Supply Company.

18 The Supply Company's management excluded the Blomidon, Woodside, and Habitant farms and the Kingsport lumber mill. PBP, Leslie Macoun to Sir F.W. Borden, 1 April 1913.
19 PBP, Transcript, 18.
20 PBP, Transcript, 12.
21 PBP, Transcript, 167.
22 PBP, Macoun to Lady Borden, 22 March 1922.
23 The $95,000 consisted of $87,500 to the National Trust, $5,000 to Manufacturers Life, and $2,500 to the Boak estate. PBP, Transcript, 12.
24 PBP, Macoun to Ilsley, 19 August 1921, 10 December 1921.
25 PBP, Transcript, 18–24.
26 Miller, *A Knight in Politics*, 313–20.
27 John H. Dales, *Hydroelectricity and Industrial Development in Quebec, 1898–1940* (Cambridge, MA: Harvard University Press, 1957), 111–12; William Fong, *J.W. McConnell: Financier, Philanthropist, Patriot* (Montreal and Kingston: McGill-Queen's University Press, 2008), 155–6.
28 William H. Atherton, *The History of Montreal from 1535 to 1914* (Montreal: S.J. Clark, 1915), 2:634.
29 Miller, *A Knight in Politics*, 314–20.
30 PBP, Transcript, 33, 51.
31 Dales, *Hydroelectricity*, 113.
32 PBP, Transcript, 26, 114–16.
33 Robert assisted Macoun in negotiating the fourth (17 October 1917) instalment of $7,000 by persuading Imperial Trust to grant the estate a loan of $4,000 at 6 per cent, backed by their shares in Nova Scotia Tram. PBP, Transcript, 143.
34 PBP, Transcript, 27, 133, 136.
35 PBP, Transcript, 148.
36 PBP, A.S. Burgess to L.S. Macoun, 6 January 1913. Burgess invested in Sir Frederick's stillborn Blomidon Railway Company. Province of Nova Scotia, Statutes, I George V, Chapter III, 31 March 1911, 395.
37 *Monetary Times*, 3 May 1913.
38 PBP, Macoun to Shafner Outhit & Ilsley, 26 May 1920.
39 Claire Dutkewych, Matthew Marner, and David Duke, "The University Farm, Past and Present: A Timeline," http://history.acadiau.ca.
40 PBP, Shaftner Outhit & Ilsley to Macoun, 22 April 1920.
41 PBP, Macoun to Shaftner Outhit & Ilsley, 6 March, 17 March, and 5 April 1920.
42 PBP, Shaftner Outhit & Ilsley to Macoun, 22 April 1920.
43 PBP, Macoun to Shaftner Othit & Ilsley, 16 March 1920. Leslie counselled Sir Frederick against several unethical or illegal practices. Miller, *A Knight in Politics*, 330.
44 PBP, L.S. Macoun to A.S. Burgess, 7 January 1913; L.S. Macoun to A.S. Burgess, 8 January 1913. Burgess had proposed that the Cornwallis

Trading Company's liabilities be covered (disguised?) by the Supply Company purchasing $13,750 unsubscribed stock in the Cornwallis Trading Company, during a fictional director's meeting in Ottawa, though it was not legal to hold Director meetings outside of the provincially chartered company.

45 PBP, Macoun to Shaftner Outhit & Ilsley, 6 March 1920.
46 PBP, Macoun to Burgess, 26 January 1917.
47 PBP, Macoun to Ilsley, 9 August 1920.
48 PBP, Macoun to Shaftner Outhit & Ilsley, 25 May 1920. Supreme Court of Nova Scotia, 1920 A No 3401, *Macoun v. Burgess*, 8 May 1920.
49 PBP, Macoun to Shaftner Outhit Ilsley, 26 May 1920.
50 PBP, Macoun to Shaftner Outhit & Ilsley, 19 April 1920; Shaftner Outhit & Ilsley to Macoun, 13 May 1920.
51 PBP, Macoun to Ilsley, 9 August 1920, 10 December 1920.
52 PBP, Ilsley to Macoun, 16 August 1920.
53 PBP, Macoun to Shaftner Outhit & Ilsley, 6 March 1920.
54 PBP, Macoun to Shaftner Outhit & Ilsley, 27 March 1920.
55 PBP, Macoun to Ilsley, 23 June 1920.
56 PBP, Macoun to Lady Borden, 14 June 1920.
57 PBP, Ilsley to Macoun, 2 July 1920.
58 PBP, Macoun to Ilsley, 23 June 1920.
59 PBP, Macoun to George Holt, 26 July 1920.
60 It included an 88-acre lot, mortgaged at 6 per cent to Williard Ilsley as late as 4 June 1920.
61 PBP, Macoun to Lady Borden, 23 October 1922.
62 PBP, Ilsley to Macoun, 9 August 1920.
63 PBP, Ilsley to Roscoe, 23 October 1920; Macoun to Lady Borden, 20 August 1920.
64 PBP, Isley to Macoun, 9 August 1920, and 21 and 25 October 1920.
65 PBP, Macoun to Lady Borden, 23 October 1920.
66 PBP, Ilsley to Macoun, 16 December 1920. Macoun to Ilsley, 10 December 1920.
67 PBP, Macoun to Lady Borden, 23 October 1920.
68 On 19 July 1921 Leslie wrote to Lady Borden that "their friend" Arthur Burgess, suffered from paralysis and had become "speechless and half of him being paralysed," adding sarcastically that "he has been mentally and morally paralysed for many years."
69 PBP, Macoun to Lady Borden, 19 July 1921.

19. Deaths and Delays

1 PBP, Transcript, 147.
2 PBP, Transcript, 3–7.

3 PBP, Macoun to Lady Borden, 20 August 1920.
4 PBP, Transcript, 168.
5 PBP, Transcript, 15, 22.
6 PBP, Transcript, 147.
7 PBP, Transcript, 12.
8 PBP, Transcript, 50. Lady Borden's and Mrs. Clarke's investments confirm Baskerville's finding that women "did not invest differently from the majority of men." Peter Baskerville, *A Silent Revolution? Gender and Wealth in English Canada, 1860–1930* (Montreal and Kingston: McGill-Queen's University Press, 2008), 46.
9 PBP, Transaction, 136.
10 Henry Percy Borden (1872–1922), born at Port la Tour, educated at Mount Allison and McGill (BSc), had resided in Ottawa since 1916, worked for the CPR as a civil engineer, and served on the Canadian government's Board of Engineers; he later established a private consulting firm. *Ottawa Citizen*, 22 October 1922.
11 PBP, Mary Grew to Bessie, 23 February 1919.
12 PBP, Last Will, Elizabeth M. Clarke, 21 October 1903. Although Mrs. Clarke's will named Gus and Lady Borden her executors, Gus left the task entirely to his sister.
13 Ibid. Mrs. Clarke possessed $2,000 in Supply Company Bonds and $3,000 in Montreal Tram bonds.
14 PBP, Elizabeth's Chronicle, 20–3 February [1926].
15 Jean-Marie Perron, "Georges Maheux," *Antennac* (Spring 2006), 14–18.
16 Gordon Hewitt, *The Conservation of the Wildlife of Canada* (New York: C. Scribner's Sons, 1921).
17 Ibid.
18 Janet Foster, *Working for Wildlife: The Beginning of Preservation in Canada* (Toronto: University of Toronto Press, 1998), 217.
19 J. Castell Hopkins, ed., *The Canadian National Review of Public Affairs for 1923* (Toronto: Annual Review Publishing, 1924), 494.
20 *Ottawa Directory* for 1923.
21 During a six-year period Leslie distributed $24,471 (probably $340,000 in current value) to each heir.
22 Elizabeth entered hospital in 1914, 1925, and 1944. In 1913 she suffered from "neuralgia." PBP, Gordon Hewitt to dear mother, 27 April 1913. In 1914 she sought osteopathic treatment in Boston for a back aliment; in 1925 she was hospitalized in Ottawa for unspecified reasons; and in 1944 she had surgery and a three-month convalescence in a Kentville hospital. But as Annemarie Adams has written, between 1893 and 1943 hospitals changed from institutions designed largely "for the poor" to big, safe, homey convalescent facilities for middle-class, paying guests, where patients remained so long as they could afford. See Annemarie Adams,

Medicine by Design: The Architect and the Modern Hospital, 1893–1943 (Minneapolis: University of Minnesota Press, 2008), ch. 3, "The Patient."

23 For example, Mary Brown (1886–1968), the wealthy US-born English resident, outspoken, "rebellious" novelist, and advocate for women's rights.

24 PBP, Transcript, 160; Macoun to Shaftner Outhit & Ilsley, 12 May 1921.

25 PBP, Charles [Gordon] to father, 2 June 1912.

26 Sir Frederick was president and "heavily invested" in the Stadacona Oil and Improvement Company of Colorado, of which Gus was manager, and when their oil well failed, they turned to farm and land improvement, a joint enterprise entitled the Colorado Land Title Company. PBP, Gus to My dear Fred, 1 June 1916.

27 PBP, Transcript, 157.

28 Leslie complained that Mrs. Hewitt removed some of Sir Frederick's personal items without Leslie's consent. Lady Borden believed that the Victrola she had given Sir Frederick for Christmas 1909 should revert to her rather than be valued as part of the estate. They disagreed, too, on the value assigned to Sir Frederick's uniforms, which Leslie believed to be worth $2,000. PBP, Transcript, 79–80.

29 PBP, Transcript, 158.

30 PBP, Transcript, 159.

31 PBP, Transcript, 91.

32 PBP, Transcript, 122–3; Leslie to Lady Borden, 22 May 1919.

33 PBP, Transcript, 157.

34 PBP, Transcript, 18.

35 PBP, Transcript, 166, 168.

36 PBP, Transcript, 160, 7.

37 PBP, Transcript, 160–1.

38 PBP, Macoun to Shaftner Outhit & Ilsley, 22 May 1920.

39 PBP, Macoun to A.G. Parker (MacLean, Burchell & Ralston, Chronicle Building, Halifax), 20 January 1923.

40 Alexander Kenneth Maclean (1869–1942), Nova Scotia MLA (1901–4, 1909–11), MP (1904–9, 1911–23). He served as Nova Scotia attorney general and with Crown Lands, as a Canadian minister without portfolio (1917–20), and president of the Exchequer Court of Canada, 1923–42. Charles Burchell became counsel for the SS *Imo* during the litigation over responsibility for the Halifax Explosion.

41 PBP, Macoun to Ilsley, 5 January 1923.

20. Lady in Court

1 The composition of small law firms changed frequently. In 1923 J.L. Ilsley was in partnership with H.M. Chase. In 1920 he had been a partner of W.P Shaftner and J. Frank Outhit, Sir Frederick's political friend.

2 PBP, Macoun to Miss Brankin, 27 December 1921. Leslie claimed that his estate duties had cost him a $2,000 annual potash contract, in addition to a rubber company contract; with little to fall back upon he was obliged to "depend upon his wife for financial assistance."
3 PBP, Transcript, 7.
4 PBP, Stuart to Ilsley, 12 January 1923; Macoun to Ilsley, 5 January 1923.
5 PBP, Ilsley to Macoun, 8 January 1923.
6 $5, 217.05 ($1,675.95 for travel) for the six years, PBP, Transcript, 60.
7 PBP, Transcript, 132, 153.
8 PBP, Transcript, 166.
9 PBP, Transcript, 151.
10 PBP, Transcript, 177.
11 PBP, Transcript, 47.
12 PBP, Transcript, 5. Governor Allen of Montana $21,688.74, A.S. Burgess $1,266.17, Noiseless Typewriter $21,328.63, Federal Trust (First National: Davidson) $15,000.00.
13 PBP, Transcript, 179.
14 PBP, Transcript, 132.
15 PBP, Transcript, 179–80, 166.
16 PBP, Transcript, 133, 136, 140–1.
17 PBP, Transcript, 170.
18 PBP, Transcript, 147.
19 These included the Noiseless Typewriter ($19,027), Howe Sound Mining Company ($8,337), Eastern Oregon Light and Power Company (200 shares pressed upon Sir Frederick by the "Boston thug"), Boston and Montana Consolidated Copper and Silver Mining Company ($20,500, a project promoted by Montana's lieutenant governor William R. Allen (1879–1953).
20 PBP, Decree, Province of Nova Scotia, County of Kings, Court of Probate, Barclay Webster, "In the Estate of Sir Frederick Borden, Deceased," 17 May 1923, 9 June 1923.
21 PBP, Webster, "In the Estate of Sir Frederick Borden. Deceased," 17 May 1923, 2.
22 Costs included Leslie's six years of executor's commission ($16,423), legal counsel ($2,505), repayment of a loan from Maude ($1,521), court costs, and miscellaneous expenses. PBP, Webster, "In the Estate of Sir Frederick W. Borden," 9 June 1923.
23 PBP, Ilsley to Macoun 18 June 1923.
24 Leslie had already distributed $24,471 to each of the heirs-at-law.
25 PBP, Petition, Lady Borden and Elizabeth Borden Hewitt, 18 June 1923. In fact, Leslie had received $5,332 from the Tram transaction: PBP, Webster, "In the Estate of Sir Frederick Borden, Deceased," 17 May 1923.
26 PBP, Ilsley to Leslie, 11 July 1923; 24 August 1923.
27 PBP, Ilsley to Leslie, 20 June 1923. This would mean a maximum of $8,923.

28 PBP, Ilsley to Leslie, 20 June 1923.
29 PBP, Ilsley to Macoun, 23 August 1923.
30 PBP, Maude to dearest mother, 25 July 1925.
31 PBP, Maude to dearest mother, 10 March 1925, mentions the possibility of a contract with the Eddy Match Company.
32 Leslie estimated his agency's average net income to have been $2,210 during the years 1917–1922 (and $1,000 in 1922). PBP, Transcript, 10 May 1923, 41, 43.
33 PBP, Ilsley to Leslie, 24 August 1923.
34 Leslie self-identified in passenger lists variously as a broker, fruit grower, and farmer.

21. Maude

1 PBP, Maude to dearest mother 1926. Senator Henri-Severin Beland had described Maude as a "true and worthy daughter of my old friend Sir Frederick ... Her speech and her manners reminded me of that illustrious son of Nova Scotia." "Very nice of him," Maude modestly wrote her mother, "I only wish the first part were true; the second maybe a little bit."
2 PBP, Province of Nova Scotia, County of Kings, Court of Probate. Decree, Barclay Webster, "In the Estate of Sir Frederick Borden, Deceased," 9 June 1923, 4.
3 PBP, Maude to dearest mother, 20 June 1924.
4 PBP, Maude to dearest mother, 1 February 1927.
5 PBP, Norma Cassidy to Lady Borden, 8 December 1942.
6 PBP, Maude to dearest mother, 2 December 1924.
7 PBP, Rosamond to Granny, 23 May 1921.
8 Charles C. Hill, ed., *Artists, Architects and Artisans: Canadian Art, 1890–1918* (Ottawa: National Gallery of Canada, 2013), 23.
9 PBP, Rosamond to Granny, 24 May [1923].
10 While Maude, Leslie, and Rosamond were not an average Canadian family, in 1929 "an average Canadian family" required an annual income of $1,430. Strong-Boag, *The New Day Recalled* (Toronto: Copp Clark Pitman, 1987), 114.
11 PBP, Maude to Elizabeth, May [1925].
12 Maude's income from securities, land sales, and the farm is difficult to determine. She inherited about $37,789 in liquid assets from her father's estate, $2,500 from her grandmother Clarke's will, and her share of Sir Frederick's fixed property. If her liquid securities earned an average annual return during the mid-1920s (years of unusually high returns, on average 15 per cent) she might have earned as much as $6,000 per year. Valley land sales during these years were occasional, and farm income

depended on markets and weather. Without better information on the family's income and expenditures, it is difficult to appreciate her financial restraints. Maude estimated that she and Rosamond managed on £50 a month in Paris and that a divided family "doubled costs." Whatever the numbers, the narrow margin between income and expenditures required careful attention. On one occasion Maude borrowed 1,500 francs from her friend Elsie Cotton. PBP, Maude to dearest mother, 20 June 1924.

13 PBP, Maud to dearest mother 25 October 1924.

14 PBP, Maude, Maude to Elizabeth, 4 June 1925.

15 PBP, Maude to dearest mother, 13 October [1923].

16 PBP, Maude to dearest mother, 6 June 1924.

17 PBP, Maude to Elizabeth, 9 November 1924.

18 PBP, Maude to dearest mother, 9 November 1924.

19 PBP, Shirley [Robert] to Lady Borden, 24 November 1926.

20 PBP, Maude to dearest mother, 6 June 1924.

21 PBP, Maude to dearest mother 12 October 1924.

22 Roy was commissioner-general (1911–28), then envoy extraordinary and minister plenipotentiary (1928–38).

23 PBP, Maude to dearest mother, 19 April [1927].

24 PBP Maude to dearest mother, 23 June 1924.

25 The 4th Duke of Sutherland, a friend of Sir Frederick and Lady Borden's, invested in Canada.

26 PBP, Maude to dearest mother, 14 July 1924.

27 PBP, Maude to dearest mother 27 October [1927].

28 Family visitors included Grace and her husband, Lieutenant-Colonel Allison Hart Borden (1878–1932), who had raised and commanded the 85th (Nova Scotia Highlanders) during the Battle of Vimy Ridge; Gwendolyn and her husband Henry Percy Borden (1872–1922), the brother of Allison Borden, and their daughter Eva; Annie (Smith) and Robert Allison Borden, who was born in Avonport, the son of Newton and Mariam Crane, educated at Acacia Villa and Mount Allison, and a judge in Westmorland County, NB; and Maggie and William Johnson Tupper (1862–1947), a son of Sir Charles Tupper and later lieutenant-governor of Manitoba (1934–40).

29 PBP, Maude to dearest mother, 17 December, n.d.

30 PBP, Maude to dearest mother, 15 November 1927.

31 *The Times*, 30 April 1934.

32 PBP, Maude to dearest mother, 21 May 1925.

33 Elsie and Dorothy Cotton were daughters of Brigadier-General William H. Cotton and Jessie Penner Cotton. Brigadier-General Cotton served as quarter-master general, then inspector-general of the Canadian militia. His eldest son, William Henry, had been killed in South Africa on 30 April 1900, two and a half months before Harold's death; two more of their sons

were killed in the Great War, as was their son-in-law Alexander George Rosamond, and Elsie's fiancé, Gerald Oscar Lees. Dorothy, a graduate of Montreal's Royal Victoria Hospital's nursing program, enlisted on 4 May 1915 in the Canadian Army Medical Corps and served in Europe and Russia. She received two Russian Awards and the Red Cross. Her sister Mary Eleanor married Alex Rosamond (1873–1916).

34 PBP, Elsie to dearest Rosamond, postmarked 7 February 1942.

35 PBP, Maude to dearest mother, 12 October 1924.

36 PBP, Maude to dearest mother, 2 December 1924; Maude to Elisabeth, 17 December 1924.

37 PBP, Maude to dearest mother, 2 July 1924.

38 PBP, Maude to Elizabeth, May [1925].

39 Rachael's brother, James F. Crowdy (1876–1934), was secretary to the Canadian Governor-General; his daughter Lucy was a friend of Rosamond and attended school in Paris.

40 PBP, Maude to dearest mother, 23 June 1924.

41 PBP, Maude to dearest mother, 13 September 1924; Maude to dearest mother, 17 January 1925.

42 PBP, Maude to dearest mother, 24 November 1927.

43 Four shades boxed and shipped cost £225. PBP, Maude to dearest mother, 2 July 1924; Maude to dearest mother, 25 November 1925; Maude to dearest mother, 18 July 1925.

44 Recurring names of friends: Jessie Scarth; Ethel Wyman Fleming and her daughter Margo Fleming; Marg and Eva Lewis (here studying French); Margaret Black; Laura Eaton; Elizabeth (Betsy) Florence Greenhill (1907–2007); Mrs. Charles Cambie (wife of the manager of the Bank of Commerce in London); Lucy Crowdy (Rachael Crowdy's niece); Miss Hendry (Montreal High School); the Duchess of Sutherland, Ethel Fauquier; Marie Louise Dillon; Bunty Peck; Winnifred McConnell (Rockcliffe); Mrs. George Wentworth Hope Johnson; a Mrs. Power and Kitty. "Gwen not as fat but will never be very refined looking, looks too much like Hattie, her aunt, but is cleaner. Eva not happy unless saving money." PBP, Maude to dearest mother, 17 January 1925.

45 PBP, Maude to dearest mother, 4 September 1925.

46 PBP, Maude to Elizabeth, 17 December 1924.

47 PBP, Maude to dearest mother, 10 March 1925, 21 May 1925: comparing their investments in Massey-Harris and Sawyer-Massey.

48 PBP, Maude to dearest mother, 18 July 1925.

49 PBP, Maude to dearest mother, 11 October 1925. Maude thought de Wit a "not a very good representative of our county or any other."

50 PBP, Maude to Elizabeth [May 1925].

51 PBP, Maude to dearest mother, 11 May 1925.

22. Rosamond

1 Eastlake was a cousin of the Cottons.
2 Helene Sicotte, "The Intersecting Paths of Budding Artists," in *1920s Modernism in Montreal the Beaver Hall Group*, ed. Jacques Des Rochers and Brian Foss (Montreal: Montreal Museum of Fine Arts, 2015), 118.
3 PBP, Maude to dearest mother, 19 February 1925.
4 PBP, Maude to dearest mother, 26 May 1926.
5 PBP, Maude to dearest mother, 25 November 1924.
6 PBP, Maude to Elizabeth, May [1925].
7 PBP, Maude to dearest mother, 9 November 1924, 16 March 1925, 30 September [1926].
8 PBP, Rosamond to Grannie, 12 December 1923.
9 PBP, Maude to dearest mother, 21 May 1925.
10 PBP, Maude to dearest mother, 19 February 1925; Maude to Elizabeth [2 May 1925].
11 PBP, Maude to dearest mother, 6 June 1924; 9 November 1924.
12 PBP, Mary Grew to Bessie, 9 November 1925. Mary agreed that it "was very nice to speak French well. It is what we should all do if we were industrious." Later, Norah Rosamond was very active in Ottawa's Little Theatre, playing in Hodge Merton's *The Wind and the Rain* (1936), Maxwell Anderson's *Mary of Scotland* (1937), and Katherine Dayton's *First Lady* (1937).
13 PBP Maude to dearest mother, 20 June 1924.
14 PBP, Maude to dearest mother, 9 November 1924, 17 January 1925.
15 PBP, Rosamond to Granny, 12 December 1923.
16 PBP, Maude to dearest mother, 17 December, n.d. Roma Vals Gilmour (Minnes) was the elder daughter of David Gordon and Roma Pauline Gilmour; she married Dr. Harold Edmund Minnes in Paris on 15 March 1938. *Ottawa Journal*, 16 March 1938.
17 PBP, Maude to dearest mother, 21 May 1925.
18 PBP Maude to dearest mother, 26 May 1926.
19 One month older than Rosamond, Elizabeth (Betsy) Greenhill (1907–2006) was born in Paris to wealthy, francophile British parents. She became the first female president of the British Designer Bookbinders (1975–8). See Elizabeth Greenhill, *Bookbinder: A Catalogue Raissonné* (Pitlochry, Perthshire: Frenich, Foss, K.D. Duval, 1986).
20 PBP, Maude to dearest mother, 15 May [1927]: good manners and no American accent since he had lived on "this side."
21 PBP, Maude to dearest mother, 15 March 1927.
22 PBP, Maude to dearest mother, 30 September 1926. The coat cost $54.
23 PBP, Maude to dearest mother, 19 March 1926.

24 In April 1928 Maude incurred a 1300 franc ($500) bill for her and Rosamond's dental work done in Brussels. PBP, Maude to my dearest mother, n.d. [April 1928]; Maude to dearest mother, 20 June 1924; Maude to dearest Elizabeth, 1 July 1925.
25 PBP, Maude to dearest mother, 14 July 1924.
26 PBP, Maude to dearest mother 14 July 1924; 20 June 1924.
27 PBP, Maude to dearest mother, 17 January 1925.
28 PBP, Maude to dearest mother, 13 September 1924.
29 Margaret Elizabeth married the 4th Viscount Hardinge (1905–1979).
30 PBP, Rosamond to Granny, 20 April 1925.
31 PBP, Maude to dearest mother, 26 April 1925.
32 PBP, Rosamond to dearest Granny, 25 November 1925.
33 PBP, Maude to Elizabeth 1 July 1925. Rosamond's French teacher, Jeannot Browicke, was a doctoral student in law who became a family friend.
34 PBP, Maude to dearest Elizabeth, 1 July 1925.
35 PBP, Maude to dearest mother, 8 July 1925, 18 July 1925.
36 PBP, Maude to dearest mother, Normandie, n.d.
37 PBP, Maude to dearest mother, 8 August 1925; Rosamond to dearest Granny, 12 September 1925.
38 PBP, Maude to dearest mother, 4 December 1925.
39 PBP, Maude to dearest mother, 4 December 1925.
40 PBP, Rosamond to Granny, 5 March 1926.
41 PBP, Maude to dearest mother, 26 December 1925.
42 PBP, Maude to dearest mother, 24 August 1937.
43 R.G. Moyles and Doug Owram, *Imperial Dreams and Colonial Realities* (Toronto: University of Toronto Press, 1988).
44 PBP, Maude to Elizabeth, 30 July [1927].
45 PBP, Maude to Mother, 9 August [1927].

23. Return

1 PBP, Maude to dearest mother, 19 May [1928].
2 PBP, Maude to dearest mother, 17 January 1925.
3 PBP, Maude to dearest mother, 25 November [1926].
4 PBP, Maude to Mother, 26 April 1925.
5 PBP, Maude to dearest mother, 18 January 1926.
6 PBP, Maude to dearest mother, 17 December [1926].
7 PBP, Rosamond to Granny, 8 December [1926].
8 Catalogue, *Le Salon des Tuilleries est au Palais de Bois à la porte Maillot*, Paris 1928, item 1854.
9 Katyerina Atanassova, "Impression of France: Canadians in the Countryside," in *Canada and Impressionism New Horizons* (Ottawa: National Gallery of Canada, n.d.), note 13, p. 71.

10 PBP, Maude to Elizabeth, May [1925].
11 PBP, Rosamond to Granny, 8 December, n.d. [1926].
12 PBP, Rosamond to Granny, 8 December, n.d. [1926].
13 PBP, Maude to dearest mother, 4 February 1927.
14 PBP, Maude to dearest mother, 15 May 1927.
15 PBP Maude to dearest mother 4 February 1927.
16 Charles C. Colby, "The Apple Industry of the Annapolis-Cornwallis Valley," *Economic Geography* 1, no. 3 (October 1925): 337–55. Transatlantic shipping time was cut by half, to about a week.
17 Margaret Conrad, "Apple Blossom Time in the Annapolis Valley 1880–1957," *Acadiensis* 9, no. 2 (Spring 1980): 15.
18 See N.H. Morse, "An Economic History of the Apple Industry of the Annapolis Valley of Nova Scotia," PhD thesis, University of Toronto, 1952.
19 A creation of the War Measures Act, the Nova Scotia Apple Marketing Board guaranteed "farmers a market for three-quarters of their average harvest calculated on a three-year adjustment period." Robert Alexander Mackinnon, "The Historical Geography of Agriculture in Nova Scotia, 1881–1951," PhD thesis, University of British Columbia, 1991, 198–9.
20 Farm expenses included the salary ($960 per year) for Leslie's farm manager, Wilfrid Bishop, and wages for day labourers at $5 a day (three or four as needed for pruning, fertilizing, planting, harvesting, packing, trucking, and shipping. PBP, Macoun Estate, G Schedule, Eastern Trust Inventory of Assets and Liabilities, June 1943.
21 PBP, Maude to dearest mother, 4 February 1927.
22 PBP, Maude to dearest Elizabeth, 1 July 1925; Maude to dearest mother, 4 February 1927.
23 PBP, Maude to dearest mother, 10 March 1925.
24 PBP Rosamond to Granny, 8 May 1927.
25 PBP, Elizabeth and Lady Borden's Travel Diary, 10 March [1928].
26 PBP, Maude to dearest mother, 16 June [1928].

24. Life with Lizzie

1 PBP, Macoun to Ilsley, 5 January 1923.
2 PBP, Ilsley to Macoun, 23 August 1923.
3 Heidi MacDonald, "Maritime Women, the Great Depression, and the Dominion-Provincial Youth Training Programme, 1937–39," in *Making Up the State*, ed. Janet Guildford and Suzanne Morton (Fredericton: Acadiensis Press, 2012), 133.
4 Robert Alexander Mackinnon, "The Historical Geography of Agriculture in Nova Scotia, 1851–1951," PhD thesis, University of British Columbia, 1991, 195.

5 PBP, Quit Claim, Lady Borden, Maude Borden Macoun, and Leslie Macoun to Elizabeth Borden Hewitt, 6 June 1923.
6 PBP, Elizabeth's Chronicle, 1 and 4 March 1926.
7 PBP, Elizabeth's Chronicle, 19, 20, and 24 March 1926.
8 PBP, Elizabeth's Chronicle, 14–16 March 1926.
9 PBP, Lady Borden to Rosamond, June 1942; Elizabeth's Chronicle, 31 March 1926.
10 PBP, Elizabeth's Chronicle, 19 February 1926; 15, 16 March 1926.
11 PBP, Elizabeth's Chronicle, 9 March 1926.
12 PBP, Elizabeth's Chronicle, 24 February 1926. See Mary Borden, *Jane – Our Stranger* (London: William Heinmann, 1923), about a "rebellious" American woman committed to women's rights.
13 PBP, Elizabeth to Dearest Elizabeth, 15 March [1937].
14 The "Borden" label made clear the sisters' property.
15 PBP, Mary Moffit to dear Bessie, 23 January 1935.
16 David Cannadine, *Ornamentalism: How the British Saw Their Empire* (New York: Oxford University Press, 2001), 8–9.
17 PBP, Elizabeth's Chronicle, 18 February 1926.
18 PBP, Elizabeth's Chronicle, 20 and 23 February 1926.
19 PBP, Elizabeth's Chronicle, 23 June 1927.
20 PBP Elizabeth's Chronicle, 1 March 1926.
21 PBP, Elizabeth's Chronicle, 4 March 1926.
22 PBP, Elizabeth's Chronicle, 26 February 1926.
23 Veronica Strong-Boag, *The New Day Recalled* (Toronto: Copp Clark Pitman, 1987), 125–7.
24 PBP, Elizabeth's Chronicle, 6 March 1926.
25 Founded in 1897 by a Canadian, Adelaide Hoodless, to revitalize rural society through education and self-help, more particularly employment for women, women's institutes became popular in the United Kingdom and Canada after the Great War.
26 PBP, Elizabeth's Chronicle, 22 February 1926, 4 March 1926, 9 March 1926.
27 PBP, Elizabeth's Chronicle, 11 March 1926.
28 PBP, Elizabeth's Chronicle, 8 March 1926.
29 Elizabeth Greenhill, Bookbinder A Catalogue Raisonné (Pitlochry, Perthshire: French, Foss, K.D. Duval, 1986), 16.
30 PBP, Elizabeth's Chronicle, 15 February 1926. According to Elizabeth, Gordon pasted on his dressing mirror a version of the Jewish fathers' admonition "The work is great; the day is short; it is not incumbent on thou to complete the work, but thou must not therefore cease from it."
31 PBP, "Notes," Elizabeth's Chronicle [1926].
32 PBP, Elizabeth's Chronicle, 3 March 1926.

33 John A. Schutz, "Leaven for the Lump: Canada and Empire Settlement, 1918–1939," in *British Settlement in the Dominions between the Wars*, ed. Stephen Constantine (Manchester: University of Manchester Press, 1998). See also "Colonization," *Bulletin of the Canadian League/Le Bulletin de La Ligue Canadienne*, no. 2 (May 1926): 28–35.
34 The Society for Overseas Settlement of British Women, the Girls' Friendly Society, the British Women's Emigration Association. See Julia Bush, *Edwardian Ladies and Imperial Power* (Leicester: Leicester University Press, 1999), 146.
35 Hall asked Elizabeth to recommend him for "head of the RCMP." PBP, Elizabeth's Chronicle, 4 March 1926.
36 PBP, Elizabeth's Chronicle, 19 February 1926.
37 PBP, Elizabeth's Chronicle, 26 February 1926.
38 PBP, Elizabeth's Chronicle, 28 February, 10 March 1926.
39 PBP, Application to Home Correspondence School, 1928.
40 PBP, Elizabeth's Chronicle, 24 March 1926: She began, "reading Dickens as a child & followed … by Thackeray, Scott, Hawthorne, George Elliott, Hugo; and later, Meredith, Henry James, Stevenson, Kipling, Arnold Bennett, Hutchinson; some contemporary fiction and French and English plays."
41 Ian McKay, *The Quest of the Folk* (Montreal and Kingston: McGill-Queen's University Press, 1994); Carole Gerson, "The Literary Culture of Atlantic Women between the Wars, in *Myth and Milieu Atlantic Literature and Culture, 1918–1939*, ed. Gwendolyn Davies (Fredericton: Acadiensis Press, 1993), 62–70.
42 Lisa Gaudet, "The Empire is Women's Sphere: Organized Female Imperialism in Canada, 1880–1920," PhD thesis, Carleton University, 2001.
43 Elizabeth fits somewhere between the first ("access to education, the professions and the franchise") and the second wave of feminists ("gendered roles began to be challenged"), though silent or ambiguous on the franchise. Both she and Lady Borden were members of the National Council of Women after it endorsed women's franchise, as well as the Liberal Party's women's organization. Margaret Conrad, "Remembering Firsts: Female Politicians in the Atlantic Provinces in the 20th Century," in *Making Up the State*, ed. Janet Guildford and Suzanne Morton (Fredericton: Acadiensis Press, 2010), 70.
44 Elizabeth was not the first educated Atlantic Canadian woman to have an interest in scientific farming. S.M. Risk, "'The Magnitude of My Services': Minnie Bell Adney and the Women of Woodstock," in Guildford and Morton, *Making Up the State*, 39.
45 Bush, *Edwardian Ladies*, 178; Anne-Marie Kinahan, "Transcendent Citizenship: Suffrage, the National Council of Women of Canada and the

Politics of Organized Womanhood," *Journal of Canadian Studies* 45, no. 3 (2008). Janet Guildford emphasizes the regional specificity of gender in her "'Persistence of the Periphery': Advisory Councils on the Status of Women in Atlantic Canada to 2000," in Guildford and Morton, *Making Up the State*, 229.

46 Neil Sutherland, Children in English Canadian Society (Toronto: University of Toronto Press, 1976), 191, and Carman Miller, *A Knight in Politics* (Montreal and Kingston: McGill-Queen's University Press, 2010), 194. Sir Frederick's silence on women's suffrage, an issue federal Liberals relegated to the provincial jurisdiction, may have been to avoid disagreement with H.H. Wickwire, Kings County MLA. Sharon M.H. MacDonald, "A Passionate Voice for Equality, Justice and Peace: Nova Scotia's Mary Russell Chelsey," in Guildford and Morton, *Making Up the State*, 48.

47 Heidi MacDonald, "Maritime Women, the Great Depression, and Dominion-Provincial Youth Training Programme, 1937–39," in Guildford and Morton, *Making Up the State*, 131, 133.

25. Intersecting Lives

1 Edna Virginia Moffett, professor of history at Wellesley College. PBP, Edna Moffett to Dear Lady Borden and Mrs. Hewitt, 19 September 1938.

2 Henrietta Hancock Britton (1873–1963), landscape, seascape, and portrait artist, educator, born in England, came to Canada in 1881, later studied art in England with her artist husband; taught at Bishop Strachan School, Moulton College, and Brandon College; lived in Toronto, Brandon, and in Nova Scotia (1925–36). See Colin S. MacDonald, *A Dictionary of Canadian Artists* (Ottawa: Canadian Paperbacks).

3 Edith Brown (1872–1932) was Sir Frederick's first cousin, an artist who co-founded Boston's Paul Revere School of Ceramics. See Carman Miller, "Edith Brown," Dictionary of Canadian Biography, vol. 16 (forthcoming).

4 Esther Brown, Sir Frederick's first cousin, once removed, completed her MA degree at New York University with a thesis on Henri Matisse. PBP, Esther Brown to Cousin Bessie, 28 December, n.d.

5 Dr. Annie Carmelle Rondinella, MD, Wellesley College.

6 Kim Godwin, college tutor, Harvard University.

7 Dr. Helen MacMurchy (1862–1953), MD, CBE, eugenicist, civil servant, described as "one of the ten leading women physicians in the Western world." See *Canadian Medical Journal*, March 1934, 305; Dianne Dodd, "'Advice to Parents': The Blue Books, Helen MacMurchy, M.D. and the Department of Health, 1920–34," *Canadian Bulletin of Medical History* 8 (1991): 203–30. Dr. MacMurchy was a close friend of the Brown family. PBP, Mary [Grew] to dearest Bessie, 9 November 1925.

8 Mary's brother, Harry Brown, Sir Frederick's private secretary, boarded with Mary, later joined by their brothers, Ralph and Walter.

9 References to reading *Short Stories*, by Henry James (1843–1916), and *Babbitt*, by Sinclair Lewis (1885–1951); classical music included a J.S. Bach concert at Saint Andrew's Church, Ottawa, given by Dr. James Healey Willan (1880–1968). PBP, Mary [Grew] to dearest Bessie, 9 November 1924.

10 The Blackburn house had a 7 per cent mortgage held by P.D. Ross. PBP, Macoun to Lady Borden, 14 June 1920.

11 King facilitated the family's $1,494 expropriation claim ("property damages"). Canada, House of Commons, Debates, 8 April 1926.

12 LAC, WLM King Papers, Diary, 27 January 1935, 12 August 1938, 5 December 1940, 8 December 1941.

13 Peter Keating, "Jeffery Hale Burland," *Dictionary of Canadian Biography* (Toronto: University of Toronto Press), 14:158–9.

14 PBP, Court of Probate, 6 June 1923; Registry of Deeds, Kentville, 17 October 1932, Book 133, p. 339. Borden Place was conveyed to Lady Borden by deed on 6 June 1923 and transferred (indentured) to Elizabeth, 17 October 1932, for $1.

15 PBP, Lady Borden to Maude, May 1926.

16 PBP, Lady Borden to Rosamond, June 1942.

17 Mary Elizabeth Kirkland, "Mothering Citizens: Elite wWmen in Montreal, 1890–1914," PhD thesis, McGill University, 2012, ch. 5.

18 PBP, Loose page of Travel Diary, undated.

19 PBP, Travel Diary, 1928.

20 PBP, Travel Diary, 2 March [1928].

21 PBP, Travel Diary, 10 March [1928], December 1930.

22 Cecilia Morgan, *A Happy Holiday: English Canadians and Transatlantic Tourism, 1879–1930* (Toronto: University of Toronto Press, 2008), 11–12, 14.

23 See Peter Haring Judd, ed., *Affection: Ninety Years of Family Letters, 1850–1930* (New York: Lulu, 2007), 2:282–8.

24 Morgan, *A Happy Holiday*, 26.

25 PBP, Travel Diary, January 1931.

26 PBP, Travel Diary, January 1931.

27 PBP, Travel Diary, January 1931.

28 PBP, Travel Diary, 21 January 1931.

29 Travel Diary, 22 January 1931.

30 Travel Diary, 13 February 1931.

31 Travel Diary, 23 January 1931.

32 Travel Diary, 23 January 1931.

33 Travel Diary, 23 February 1931.

26. Reconciliation

1 In 1937 their Imperial Trust securities paid 6 per cent. PBP Maude to dearest mother, 1937.

2 Jamaica, Barbados, and Martinique (December 1932), SS *Colborne*; Puerto Rico (December 1933); Bahamas (April 1934), SS *Lady Hawkins;* British West Indies (April 1935), SS *Lady Hawkins*; Demerara Guyana (April 1938). SS *Lady Nelson*.

3 PBP, Mary Grew to Dearest Bessie, 22 June 1924.

4 David A. Reisman, *The Social Economics of Thorstein Veblen* (Cheltenham: Edward Elgar Publishing Limited, 2012), 384.

5 PBP, Agreement, Maude Borden Macoun and Arthur Wood, trustee, 22 November 1928.

6 *Montreal Gazette*, 19 May 1936; *Ottawa Citizen*, 26 April 1935.

7 PBP, Robert Laird Borden to Dear Mac[oun], 27 August 1935.

8 They corresponded, worked together, and shared costs on their adjacent properties, Robert on the assumption that his property benefited, and during absences they watched each other's houses. PBP, R.L. Borden to My dear Mac, 11 August, 21 August 1931, 3 September 1931, and 27 August 1935.

9 *Ottawa Evening Journal*, 14 March 1930, 10.

10 Roma Vals Gilmour (Ninnes), Sue Houston, Dorothy Peck, Lucy Crowdy (Mrs. Kenneth Weir), Gwendolyn Borden (Mrs. Douglas Blair), Mrs. Edward Fauquier, Sylvia Smellie. Marjorie Borden and Alice Peck studying art in New York.

11 *Top Hat* featured Fred Astaire (1899–1987) and Ginger Rogers (1911–1995); *Rose of Rancho* featured Gladys Swarthout (1900–1969).

12 Although Rosamond attended the Ottawa Little Theatre's production of Susan Tweedsmuir's dramatization of her father's *The Path of the King*, and Bernard Shaw's *Saint Joan* (1936), unlike her friends, Vals Gilmour, Norah Rosamond (Hughes), and Gwendolyn Borden (Blair), Rosamond did not work with Ottawa's Little Theatre.

13 A friend of prominent Canadian skiers Bill Burnett, Alistair Graham, and Brian Meredith, Rosamond was fascinated by the presence of Prince Colonna, "A marvelous looking person, black flashing eyes, black hair and moustached, slim, dicey looking character; great relief to see a prince that looked like a prince, since most look like a gardener's dressy brother." PBP, Rosamond to dearest Granny, Monday, n.d.

14 PBP, R.L. Borden to dear Mac[oun], 17 May 1935.

15 Elizabeth Greenhill, *Bookbinder: A Catalogue Raisonné* (Pitlochry, Perthshire: Frenich, Foss, K. Duval 1986), 16.

16 PBP, Rosamond to Mom and Dad, Monday, [December] 1936.

17 PBP, Rosamond to dearest Mom and Dad, Monday, [December 1936].
18 The ship's German owner, Arnold Bernstein (1888–1971), was imprisoned for "currency fraud" by Nazi authorities but released before the outbreak of World War II and fled to the United States.
19 PBP, Rosamond to dearest Mum, 20 December [1936]: An elderly Miss Craig who "took to her room a year ago and hasn't been down since, too lazy to get dressed, looking at old newspapers and arranging things in little parcels." Rosamond once encountered Miss Craig on her way to the bathroom: "She had on a trailing rose coloured dressing gown – a heavy brown shawl over her shoulders and an enormous turban on her head – She really gave me quite a fright, as the hall was dark"; in reference to another guest house inhabitant, "Miss Oak has been here for several years."
20 PBP, Rosamond to dearest Mum, 9 January [1937].
21 PBP, Rosamond to dearest Mum, 16 January [1937].
22 PBP Rosamond to dearest Mum, 20 December, [1936], 9 January [1937].
23 PBP, Rosamond, to Dad, 1 February [1937].
24 PBP, Rosamond to Mum, 20 December [1936] Uncertain of the principal dancer's name, she suggested it might be "Shakaroff" (Alexander Sakharoff (1886–1963?).
25 PBP, Rosamond to dearest Mum, 16 January [1937].
26 PBP, Rosamond to Mum and Dad, 29 March [1937].
27 PBP, Rosamond to dearest Mum, 9 January [1937].
28 PBP, Rosamond to dearest Mum, 22 March [1937].
29 PBP, Rosamond to Mum and Dad, 29 March [1937].
30 PBP, Rosamond to dearest Mum, 9 January [1937].
31 Such as, "Hark the herald angels sing, Mrs. Simpson pinched our King"; "The difference between Mrs. Simpson and Mae West is that Mae West would do it for half a crown." PBP, Rosamond to Mum and Dad, December [1936].
32 PBP, Rosamond to Mum and Dad, December [1936].
33 PBP, Rosamond to Granny, 11 May 1937.
34 PBP, Rosamond to Mum and Dad, 29 March [1937].

27. War

1 Interview with Joan Murray, Toronto, 23 June 1999.
2 *Secret Intelligence Report Bulletin*, 13 May 1940, Weekly Summary, RCMP Headquarters, Ottawa, 243.
3 According to family lore, Odin's mother was either "Jewish" or a "Gypsy."
4 Edmund Charles St. Jean Green died of cancer, 10 August 1980 at the Western Kings Memorial Hospital. PBP, unidentified news clipping.

5 Certified copy of his birth, General Register Office, London, England [BXA 267524], 11 February 1977. Hugh Green served in Sicily in the Canadian forces during World War II, and later worked for the Imperial Tobacco Company, Delhi, Ontario.
6 LAC, Department of National Defence, Draft résumé, Edmund Green, [November 1956].
7 *Naval Forces of the Dominion of Canada*, p. 1907; *Royal Canadian Naval Volunteer Reserve*, List A 1945; *Naval Forces of the Commonwealth (Canada)*, p. 1108; *Naval Forces of the Dominion of Canada Royal Canadian Naval Volunteers*, List A, p. 826.
8 LAC, Edmund's handwritten draft letter and résumé for a future employer, November 1956.
9 Leslie visited England once during the war, "assisted" by a British officer. PBP, Rosamond to dearest Granny, 31 January, n.d.; Rosamond to dearest Granny n.d. [1943].
10 LAC, Department of National Defence, Edmund Green, draft résumé [November 1956].
11 For example, Vals Gilmour (Harold Edmund Minnes), Lucy Crowdy (Hope Johnson), Gwendolyn Borden (Douglas Blair), and Nora Rosamond (William M. Hughes).
12 In 1941 Edmund was 33 and Rosamond 34. The Canadian average age at marriage for males was 28.9 and for females 25.1. M.C. Urquhart and K.A. Buckley, Historical Statistics of Canada (Toronto: Macmillan, 1965), 42.
13 *Ottawa Citizen*, 17 November 1942.
14 Interview with Julia Green MacKay, 6 August 2017.
15 Their marriage certificate refers incorrectly to St. John the Apostle Church, conflating Saint James the Apostle with St. John the Evangelist. PBP, Marriage Certificate, 1 August 1941; See also *Ottawa Citizen*, 2 August 1941.
16 LAC, Pension Form, 23 July 1941, Edmund names L.-Com. Davies (friend) as his Next of Kin.
17 *Ottawa Evening Citizen*, 2 August 1941.
18 *Montreal Herald*, 1 August 1941.
19 Rosamond received $75 a month and $200 semi-annually. PBP, Estate of Maude Borden Macoun, Eastern Trust Company, Statement of Assets and Liabilities, Schedule G.
20 PBP Gwen [Borden] to Rosamond, Friday [1942].
21 PBP, Dad to dearest Dickie, 1 January 1942.
22 PBP, Maude to dearest mother, Monday evening [December 1941].
23 PBP, Leslie to my dear Lady Borden, 6 January 1942.
24 PBP, Mum to dearest Rosamond, 14 January 1942.
25 PBP, Maude to dearest mother, Monday evening [December 1941].
26 One source claimed the torpedo struck at 7 am.

27 The *New York Times* was still naming victims and locations of vessels sunk by German U-boats.

28 PBP, Manager, Passenger Traffic, CNR Steamships, 4 February 1942.

29 PBP, George Truman to Lady Borden, 20 February 1942; Sheila to Rosamond, postmarked 30 January 1942; Gwen [Borden] to Rosamond, Friday [1942]; Elsie [Cotton] to dearest Rosamond, postmarked 7 February 1942.

30 PBP, Lady Borden to Rosamond, 4 May 1942.

31 PBP, Edmund to Darling [Rosamond, 1944].

32 Maude's assets amounted to $5,050 real property, $11,508 personal property, $6,438 cash, $2050 miscellaneous. PBP, Estate of Maude Borden Macoun, Eastern Trust Company, 1 October 1943.

33 PBP, Lady Borden to darling Rosamond, May 1944.

34 PBP, Lady Borden to Rosamond, 1 June 1944.

35 Mary (Brown) Grew died in 1940 (predeceased by her sister Agnes in 1938 and her brother in 1936). PBP, Harry Brown to Dear Bessie, 15 December 1944. Laura Borden died on 7 September 1940 (Robert had died 10 June 1937); Allison Borden had died suddenly in March 1932, scarcely a year after their Italian tour. PBP, Rosamond to Dearest Elizabeth, 17 July 1932.

36 PBP, Henrietta Britton to Lady Borden, 3 January 1941.

37 In 1944 Lady Borden wrote to Rosamond: "Daisy is coming this week. I know she will be quite a bore and I know she will be here until October! I dread her awfully, but Aunta was so anxious she should come. Tomorrow Amy [Minard] is coming. I hope to have a couple of people for dinner. Then Mrs. Philips comes next Tuesday night for a month. I hope she will be better than I fear."

38 PBP, Lady Borden to Rosamond, 4 June 1944.

39 PBP, Elizabeth to mother, 22 March 1944. She remained in Montreal from December 1943 to March 1944, assisting Greta Finlay (residing at the Chateau) and relieving Mrs. Julia's nurse from time to time.

40 *Kentville Advertiser*, 12 June 1947.

41 PBP, Rosamond to dearest Granny, 30 December 1943. Edmund rounded up "deserters from ships" and "leaves at an unusual hour in the morning, comes back at 2, sleeps 2 hours, then out, back again for an hour for dinner, then not back until 12:30 or 1." Rosamond to dearest Granny, n.d. [March 1944].

42 PBP Edmund to Darling [Rosamond], 6 October 1944; Edmund to Darling, 12 September 1944; he later suffered from "floating kidneys" (rephroptosie), and stomach ulcers: Edmund to Lady Borden, 16 December 1953.

43 LAC, Clinical Notes, Case Sheet Special Report, Edmund Green, RCNH, Stadacona, 1 October 1945.

44 PBP, Rosamond to dearest Granny, 18 May 1944; Edmund to Darling, 12 September 1944.
45 LAC, Lieutenant (Dr.) K. Wellman to Staff Medical Officer, 28 March 1942: "Medical History of an Invalid: 'Edmund Green.'" Edmund complained "for the past five months" of episodes of short duration characterized by a sensation of constriction of the throat, gagging, at times vomiting.
46 *Mrs. Miniver* (1942), *National Velvet* (1944).
47 PBP, Rosamond to dear Aunta, n.d. [Autumn 1943]. Edmund never "got over" a production of *Aida* and only accepted "under protest" the Beardmores' invitation to *Tosca* featuring Grace Moore (1898–1947).
48 "To marry often signalled the death knell of women's art career": Devon Smither, "No Nudes, Please, We're Canadian," *Literary Review of Canada*, May 2017, 14.
49 Robert Borden was Ruth Grierson's godfather. See Christopher Risso-Gill, *Routines and Orgies: The Life of Peter Cundill* (Montreal and Kingston: McGill-Queen's University Press, 2014), 16ff.
50 PBP, Rosamond to dearest Granny, 18 May 1944.
51 PBP, Rosamond to dear Aunta, Wednesday [Autumn 1943].
52 PBP, Rosamond to dear Aunta, [c. 9 March 1943].
53 PBP, Rosamond to dearest Granny, Tuesday, n.d. [Montreal 1943].
54 PBP, Rosamond to dearest Granny, 18 May 1944.
55 PBP, Rosamond to dearest Granny, 31 January, n.d. [1944].
56 PBP, Rosamond to dearest Granny, Thursday [1944].
57 PBP, Rosamond to dear Aunta, 11 May 1944.
58 PBP, Elizabeth to Mother, 22 March 1944.
59 They lived on 213 Lancaster Avenue, Saint John West, during the first months.
60 PBP, Rosamond to dearest Granny, n.d. [May 1944], dinner with Captain and Mrs. Oland in Rothesay; Rosamond to Aunta, 14 June (1944).
61 PBP, Granny to Rosamond, 19 February [1945].
62 PBP, Edmund to darling, 12 September 1944.
63 Margaret Conrad, *George Nowlan, Maritime Conservative in National Politics* (Toronto: University of Toronto Press, 1986), 92–3.
64 Before 1940 three-quarters of Nova Scotia apple production was marketed in Britain; after the war Britain absorbed only 4 per cent of the province's production. Robert Alexander Mackinnon, "The Historical Geography of Agriculture in Nova Scotia, 1851–1951," PhD thesis, University of British Columbia, 1991, 134, 199.
65 *Kentville Advertiser*, 8 April 1948.
66 M.B. Davis and H. Hill, *Orchard Soil Management and Apple Nutrition* (Ottawa: Department of Agriculture, 1948).
67 *Kentville Advertiser*, 19 January 1956.

68 *Kentville Advertiser*, 2 January 1947; 22 April 1948. A packaging plant was established in Coldbrook; in 1936 Scotian Gold, a division of the United Fruit Companies of Nova Scotia in Middleton, began producing applesauce, apple flakes, and apple honey to complement their juice industry.
69 Mackinnon, "The Historical Geography of Agriculture in Nova Scotia," 202.
70 Between 1945 and 1949 the number of naval personnel fell from some 93,000 to 8,800.
71 PBP, William L. Mackenzie King to Lady Borden, 18 August 1945.
72 PBP, Lady Borden to Darling Rosamond, 20 August 1945.
73 LAC, Edmund Green résumé, November 1956.
74 *Kentville Advertiser*, 9 February 1956.
75 PBP, Rosamond to Granny, n.d. I found no published reference to "Xmas in the West Indies."

28. Great Granny

1 Rosamond's ability to drive Lady Borden's large Packard freed Lady Borden from her dependence on Elizabeth. Julia remembers one occasion when her distracted mother's failure to park the car properly obliged Lady Borden to crawl out of the car on her knees. Interview with Julia Green MacKay, 1 September 2014.
2 John Hilliker and Donald Barry, *Canada's Department of External Affairs* (Montreal and Kingston: McGill-Queen's University Press, 1995), 2:12.
3 LAC, Edmund Green file, Naval Secretary to Edmund Green, 22 March 1949.
4 Interview with Julia Green MacKay, 16 August 2013.
5 *Kentville Advertiser*, 27 May 1948.
6 *Kentville Advertiser*, 23 December 1948.
7 PBP, Granny to Leslie, 10 July 1950.
8 See Cynthia Enloe, *Bananas, Beaches and Bases: Making Feminist Sense of International Relations* (Berkeley: University of California Press, 1990).
9 LAC, Lieutenant-Commander St. John Green, RCN, 0-29110, Résumé [1956].
10 PBP, Rosamond to dearest Granny, 31 April [1951]; LAC, Green to HMS Dockyard Halifax, 12 July 1954.
11 PBP, Rosamond to dearest Granny, 22 March [1951].
12 The Department of National Defence paid Julia's tuition and she followed the Nova Scotia Department of Education's curriculum.
13 PBP, Rosamond to dearest Granny, 2 November 1951; Rosamond to dearest Granny, 22 March [1951].
14 PBP, Rosamond to Dearest Granny, 1 April [1952].
15 George VI's death in February 1953, followed the next month by Queen Mary's death. PBP, Rosamond to Dearest Granny, 9 May [postmarked in Canning, 14 May 1952].

16 PBP, Rosamond to Dearest Granny, 2 November 1951.
17 *Toronto Star*, 23 April 2014.
18 PBP Rosamond to Dearest Granny, 26 July [1952].
19 PBP, Rosamond to Dearest Granny, 30 July 1953.
20 PBP, Rosamond to Dearest Granny, 7 June [1953].
21 Joan and Tom Robinson and their daughter Belinda: email correspondence, Julia Green MacKay to Carman Miller, 20 August 2018.
22 Interview with Julia Green MacKay, 6 August 2017.
23 He suffered from external hemorrhoids and thrombophlebitis, for which he later had surgery.
24 PBP, Rosamond to dearest Granny, postmarked 19 September 1953.
25 PBP Lady Borden to Rosamond, 29 August 1953. She hoped the 19 August 1953 federal election might hasten Rosamond's return.
26 *Mount Allison Record*, Fall, 1954, 77–8, 103.
27 *Kentville Advertiser*, 3 February 1956.
28 PBP, Louis St. Laurent, to Mrs. Green, 1 March 1956; Hughes Lapointe to Dear Rosamond, 1 March 1956.
29 The lieutenant-governor and premier were in Wolfville to attend the "world premier" of the "Mod at Grand Pre," the light opera written by Watson Kirkconnell and E.A. Collins, Acadia University's contribution to the "commemoration" of the Grand Dérangement of 1755! *Kentville Advertiser*, 23 February 1956.
30 *Kentville Advertiser*, 8 March 1956.

The Queen Is Dead

1 Esther Clark Wright, *Blomidon Rose* (Toronto: Ryerson Press, 1957), 54.
2 In "Borden's of Nova Scotia" *Maclean's Magazine*, November 1913. W.A. Craick noted that neither Robert Borden, Frederick Borden, John William Borden, nor R.A. Borden left a male heir.
3 Peter Baskerville, *A Silent Revolution? Gender and Wealth in English Canada, 1870–1930* (Montreal and Kingston: McGill-Queen's University Press, 2008), 31.
4 Anthony Giddens, *Sociology* (Cambridge: Cambridge University Press, 1997), 583, underlines the power of shared ideas and beliefs in reinforcing dominance.
5 E.A. Heaman, *A Short History of the State in Canada* (Toronto: University of Toronto Press), 96.
6 Kerwin Lee Klein, "Finding Meaning in Memory: A Methodological Critique of Collective Memory Studies," *History and Theory*, May 2002, 181.
7 Pierre Bourdieu, *A Social Critique of the Judgment of Taste* (Cambridge, MA: Harvard University Press, 1984).

8 Rusty Bittermann, "The Hierarchy of the Soil: Land and Labour in the 19th Century Cape Breton Community," *Acadiensis* 18, no. 1 (Autumn 1988): 33–55.
9 Carman Miller, "Family Business and Politics in Kings County, N.S: The case of F.W. Borden, 1874–1896," *Acadiensis* 6 (1987): 60–75.
10 Janet Guildford and Suzanne Morton, eds., Separate Spheres: Women's Worlds in the 19th-Century Maritimes (Fredericton: Acadiensis Press, 1994), 9. See also Baskerville, *A Silent Revolution?*, 240–3.
11 Janet Guildford, "Separate Spheres the Feminization of Public-School Teaching in Nova Scotia, 1838–1880," in *Separate Spheres*, 119.
12 Veronica Strong-Boag suggests that working-class societies and rural communities "may have been less intimidated by" gendered stereotypes. Veronica Strong-Boag, *The New Day Recalled Lives of Girls and Women in English Canada, 1919–1939* (Toronto: Copp Clark Pitman, 1987), 31.
13 PBP, Fred to Dearest Bessie, Sunday 19 [October] 1911.
14 Baskerville, *A Silent Revolution?*, 245.
15 Anne-Marie Kenahan, "Transcendent Citizenship: Suffrage, the National Council of Women of Canada and the Politics of Organized Womanhood," *Journal of Canadian Studies* 43, no. 3 (2008): 5–27.
16 PBP, Lizzie to My dear father, 4 May 1899.
17 A study of contemporary marital discrepant-age difference suggests that only 1 per cent of wives were ten years older than husbands. See, Monica Boyd and Anne Li, "Canadians in Age-Discrepant Relationships," *Canadian Social Trends*, Statistics Canada, Autumn 2003.
18 Strong-Boag, *The New Day*, ch. 2.
19 Family oral evidence suggests Maude limited her family by birth control (including abortion), in the 1920s considered "the particular preserve of the left," though practice and justification was not restricted to ideologues. Strong-Boag, *The New Day*, 89–90. Gordon Hewitt was a friend and correspondent of Marie Stopes (1880–1958), the popular birth control advocate and British paleobotanist. Email, Laura Cameron to Carman Miller, 1 June 2018.
20 For a discussion of the economic challenges to marriage, see Strong-Boag, *The New Day*, ch. 3.
21 Baskerville, *A Silent Revolution?*, 29–31.

Appendix A

1 British Library, E.T.H. Hutton Papers, "Memoir," 146.
2 See, Carman Miller, *A Knight in Politics* (Montreal and Kingston: McGill-Queen's University Press, 2010), 103–7.
3 The *Insurance Times*, March 1882, 168, described the Mutual Benefit Life Company, established in 1846, as "one of the largest and best."

4 PBP, Affidavit, William West, farmer, Medford, declared before Charles Pineo, Notary Public, n.d., [1 July 1896]; Affidavit, Will West of Medford, Kings County, signed in Kentville, 1 July 1898, before E.D. Cogswell, Notary Public and Commissioner for Supreme Court of Kings County.
5 PBP, Affidavit, William West, farmer, Medford, declared before Charles Pineo, Notary Public, n.d. [1 July 1896].
6 PBP, F.W. Borden to DeWitt J. Peck, 27 December,1886. Their relationship to one another and their interest in the Brown file is unclear.
7 PBP, Theodore Tyndale to Frederick Borden, 4 September 1895; Affidavit, John West, No. 2, Charles Pineo, Canning.
8 PBP, Charles Starr to William Hyde, 27 December 1894.
9 PBP, Charles Starr to William Hyde, 31 January 1895.
10 PBP, Charles Starr to William Hyde, 2 February 1895.
11 PBP, Sill to Hyde, 7 February 1895.
12 PBP, Tyndale to Frederick Borden, 11 October 1895.
13 PBP, Tyndale to Borden, 16 August 1895; Tyndale to Borden, 11 October 1895.
14 PBP, Tyndale to Borden, 11 October 1895.
15 PBP, Hyde to Borden, 6 November 1895.
16 PBP, Tyndale to Borden, 4 September 1895.
17 PBP, Tyndale to Frederick Borden, 4 September 1895.
18 PBP, John West to dear brother, 21 January 1896; John West to Borden, 29 February 1896.
19 PBP, W.E. Roscoe to Borden, 7 August 1897.
20 PBP, William West of Medford, farmer, signed at Kentville, 1 July 1898, before E.D. Cogswell, Notary Public.
21 PBP, Woodworth to Borden, 16 August 1899.
22 PBP, Woodworth to Borden, 29 August 1899; telegrams, Woodworth to Borden, 31 August, 4 September 1899.
23 PBP, H.H. Norwood to Sir Frederick Borden, 3 January 1905.
24 PBP, H.H. Norwood to Sir Frederick Borden, 4 January 1905.
25 PBP, G.L. Pineo to Mr. West, 4 January 1905; H.H. Norwood to Sir Frederick Borden, 6 January 1905.

Index